INTERMEDIATE FINANCIAL THEORY

Jean-Pierre Danthine

University of Lausanne, CEPR and FAME

John B. Donaldson

Graduate School of Business
Columbia University

Prentice
Hall

UPPER SADDLE RIVER, NJ 07458

Library of Congress Cataloging-in-Publication Data

Danthine, Jean-Pierre
    Intermediate financial theory / Jean-Pierre Danthine, John B. Donaldson.
       p.   cm.
    Includes bibliographical references and index.
    ISBN 0-13-017446-7
    1. Finance. I. Donaldson, John B. II. Title.
  HG173 .D283 2001
  332—dc21   2001018561

Acquisitions Editor: Mickey Cox
Editor-in-Chief: P. J. Boardman
Assistant Editor: Cheryl Clayton
Editorial Assistant: Melanie Olsen
Media Project Manager: Bill Minick
Marketing Manager: Joshua McClary
Marketing Assistant: Christopher Bath
Production Manager: Gail Steier de Acevedo
Production Coordinator: Kelly Warsak
Permissions Coordinator: Suzanne Grappi
Associate Director, Manufacturing: Vincent Scelta
Manufacturing Buyer: Natacha St. Hill Moore
Cover Designer: Renée-Paule Danthine
Composition: BookMasters, Inc.
Full-Service Project Management: BookMasters, Inc.
Printer/Binder: RRD/Harrisonburg
Cover Printer: Phoenix Color Corp.

10 9 8 7 6 5 4 3 2 1
ISBN 0-13-017446-7

LIST OF FREQUENTLY USED SYMBOLS AND NOTATION

A text such as this is, by nature, relatively notation intensive. We have adopted a strategy to minimize the notational burden within each individual chapter at the cost of being, at times, inconsistent in our use of symbols across chapters. We list here a set of symbols regularly used with their specific meaning. At times, however, we have found it more practical to use some of the listed symbols to represent a different concept. In other instances, clarity required making the symbolic representation more precise (e.g., by being more specific as to the time dimension of an interest rate).

ROMAN ALPHABET

a	Amount invested in the risky asset
A^T	Transpose of the matrix (or vector) A
c	Consumption
c_θ^k	Consumption of agent k in state of nature θ
CE	Certainty equivalent
d	Dividend rate or amount
E	Generally used to denote the expectations operator; in select chapters also used to denote the strike or exercise price of an option
e_θ^k	Endowment of agent k in the state of nature θ
f, g	Probability density function
f	Futures position (Chapter 14)
F, G	Cumulative distribution function
$K(\tilde{x})$	Kurtosis of the random variable $\tilde{x}$
L	A lottery
$\mathcal{L}$	Lagrangian
m	Pricing kernal
M	The market portfolio
MU_θ^k	Marginal utility of agent k if state θ is realized
p	Price of an arbitrary asset
p^f	Price of a futures contract (Chapter 14)
P	Prudence coefficient (Chapter 4)
q	Arrow-Debreu price
q^b	Price of a risk-free discount bond, occasionally denoted p^{r_f}

q^e	Price of equity
r_f	Rate of return on a risk-free asset
R_f	Gross rate of return on a risk-free asset
$\tilde{r}$	Rate of return on a risky asset
$\tilde{R}$	Gross rate of return on a risky asset
R_A	Absolute risk aversion coefficient
R_R	Relative risk aversion coefficient
s	Usually denotes the amount saved
S	In the context of discussion options, used to denote the price of the underlying stock
$S(\tilde{x})$	Skewness of the random variable $\tilde{x}$
T	Transition matrix
U	Utility function
$\mathcal{u}$	von Neuman-Morgenstern utility function
V	Usually denotes variance-covariance matrix of asset returns; occasionally is used as another utility function symbol; may also signify value, V_p, as in the value of portfolio P or V_F, as in the value of the firm
w_i	Portfolio weight of asset i in a given portfolio
Y_0	Initial wealth (sometimes denoted as W_0 as well)

GREEK ALPHABET

α	Intercept coefficient in the market model (alpha)
β	The slope coefficient in the market model (beta)
δ	Time discount factor
η	Elasticity
λ	Lagrange multiplier
μ	Mean
π_θ	State probability of state θ
π^{RN}	Risk-neutral probability
Π	Risk premium
$\rho(\tilde{x}, \tilde{y})$	Correlation of random variables $\tilde{x}$ and $\tilde{y}$
σ	Standard deviation
σ_{ij}	Covariance between random variables i and j
θ	Index for state of nature
Ω	Rate of depreciation of physical capital
ψ	Compensating precautionary premium

NUMERALS AND OTHER TERMS

$\mathbf{1}$	Vector of ones
$>$	Is strictly preferred to
$\geq$	Is preferred to (non strictly, that is allowing for indifference)
GBM	Geometric Brownian Motion stochastic process
FSD	First-order stochastic dominance
SSD	Second-order stochastic dominance

INTERMEDIATE FINANCIAL THEORY

PRENTICE HALL FINANCE SERIES

Personal Finance

Keown, *Personal Finance: Turning Money into Wealth, Second Edition*

Trivoli, *Personal Portfolio Management: Fundamentals & Strategies*

Winger/Frasca, *Personal Finance: An Integrated Planning Approach, Fifth Edition*

Investments/Portfolio Management

Alexander/Sharpe/Bailey, *Fundamentals of Investments, Third Edition*

Fabozzi, *Investment Management, Second Edition*

Fischer/Jordan, *Security Analysis and Portfolio Management, Sixth Edition*

Francis/Ibbotson, *Investments: A Global Perspective*

Haugen, *Modern Investment Theory, Fifth Edition*

Haugen, *The New Finance*

Haugen, *The Beast on Wall Street*

Haugen, *The Inefficient Stock Market, Second Edition*

Holden, *Spreadsheet Modeling: A Book and CD-ROM Series* (Available in Graduate and Undergraduate Versions)

Sharpe/Alexander/Bailey, *Investments, Sixth Edition*

Taggart, *Quantitative Analysis for Investment Management*

Winger/Frasca, *Investments, Third Edition*

Options/Futures/Derivatives

Hull, *Fundamentals of Futures and Options Markets, Fourth Edition*

Hull, *Options, Futures, and Other Derivatives, Fourth Edition*

Risk Management/Financial Engineering

Mason/Merton/Perold/Tufano, *Cases in Financial Engineering*

Fixed Income Securities

Handa, *FinCoach: Fixed Income* (software)

Bond Markets

Fabozzi, *Bond Markets, Analysis and Strategies, Fourth Edition*

Corporate Finance/Survey of Finance/Financial Economics

Bodie/Merton, *Finance*

Emery/Finnerty/Stowe, *Principles of Financial Management*

Emery/Finnerty, *Corporate Financial Management*

Gallagher/Andrew, *Financial Management: Principles and Practices, Second Edition*

Keown/Martin/Petty/Scott, *Financial Management, Ninth Edition*

Keown/Martin/Petty/Scott, *Foundations of Finance: The Logic and Practice of Financial Management, Third Edition*

Mathis, *Corporate Finance Live: A Web-based Math Tutorial*

Shapiro/Balbirer, *Modern Corporate Finance: A Multidisciplinary Approach to Value Creation*

Van Horne, *Financial Management and Policy, Twelfth Edition*

Van Horne/Wachowicz, *Fundamentals of Financial Management, Eleventh Edition*

International Finance

Baker, *International Finance: Management, Markets, and Institutions*

Click/Coval, *The Theory and Practice of International Financial Management*

Grabbe, *International Financial Markets, Third Edition*

Rivera-Batiz/Rivera-Batiz, *International Finance and Open Economy Macroeconomics, Second Edition*

Capital Budgeting

Aggarwal, *Capital Budgeting Under Uncertainty*

Bierman/Smidt, *The Capital Budgeting Decision, Eighth Edition*

Mergers/Acquisitions/Takeovers

Weston/Siu/Johnson, *Takeovers, Restructuring, and Corporate Governance, Third Edition*

Short-Term Finance

Hill/Sartoris, *Short Term Financial Management, Third Edition*

Taxes

Scholes/Wolfson, *Taxes and Business Strategy: A Global Planning Approach, Second Edition*

Insurance

Black/Skipper, *Life and Health Insurance, Thirteenth Edition*

Dorfman, *Introduction to Risk Management and Insurance, Seventh Edition*

Rejda, *Social Insurance and Economic Security, Sixth Edition*

Financial Markets and Institutions/Capital Markets

Arshadi/Karels, *Modern Financial Intermediaries and Markets*

Dietrich, *Financial Services and Financial Institutions*

Fabozzi/Modigliani, *Capital Markets: Institutions and Instruments, Second Edition*

Fabozzi/Modigliani/Ferri/Jones, *Foundations of Financial Markets and Institutions, Second Edition*

Kaufman, *The U.S. Financial Systems*

Van Horne, *Financial Market Rates and Flows, Sixth Edition*

Commercial Banking

Sinkey, *Commercial Bank Financial Management, Fifth Edition*

Entrepreneurial Finance

Adelman/Marks, *Entrepreneurial Finance*

Vaughn, *Financial Planning for the Entrepreneur*

Cases in Finance

May/May/Andrew, *Effective Writing: A Handbook for Finance People*

Weston, *Cases in Dynamic Finance: Mergers and Restructuring*

Financial Statement Analysis

Fraser/Ormiston, *Understanding Financial Statements, Fourth Edition*

Behavioral Finance

Nofsinger, *Behavioral Finance*

Financial Theory

Danthine/Donaldson, *Intermediate Financial Theory*

Finance Center

For downloadable supplements and much more . . . visit us at *www.prenhall.com*

Please select Finance in the Discipline Finder

N'estime l'argent ni plus ni moins qu'il ne vaut:
c'est un bon serviteur et un mauvais maître
(*Value money neither more nor less than it is worth:*
It is a good servant and a bad master.)
Alexandre Dumas, fils, *La Dame aux Camélias* (Préface)

CONTENTS

PREFACE

The market for financial textbooks is crowded at both the introductory and doctoral levels, but much less so at the intermediate level. Teaching opportunities at this level, however, are multiplying rapidly with the advent of masters of science programs in finance (master in computational finance, in mathematical finance, and the like) and the strengthening demand for higher-level courses in MBA programs.

The Masters in Banking and Finance Program at the University of Lausanne admitted its first class in the fall of 1993. One of the first such programs of its kind in Europe, its objective was to provide advanced training to finance specialists in the context of a one-year theory-based degree program. In designing the curriculum, it was felt that students should be exposed to an integrated course that would introduce a wide breadth of topics in financial economics, similar to what is found at the doctoral level. Such exposure could, however, ignore the particulars and detailed proofs and arguments and concentrate on the larger set of issues and concepts to which any advanced practitioner should be exposed.

Our ambition in this text is, accordingly, first to review rigorously and concisely the main themes of financial economics (those that students should have encountered in prior courses) and, second, to introduce a number of *frontier* ideas of importance for the evolution of the discipline and of relevance from a practitioner's perspective. We want our readers to be at ease with the main concepts of standard finance (MPT, CAPM, etc.) while also being aware of the principal new ideas that have marked the recent evolution of our discipline. Contrary to introductory texts, we aim at depth and rigor; contrary to higher-level texts, we do not emphasize generality. Whenever an idea can be conveyed through an example, this is the approach we chose. We have, similarly, ignored proofs and detailed technical matters unless a reasonable understanding of the related concept mandated their inclusion. Throughout the book the emphasis is on the notion of competitive financial equilibrium—what it means and how it is characterized in a variety of contexts ranging from the Arrow-Debreu model to the consumption capital asset pricing model. These concepts are presented as a platform for an in-depth understanding of the newer arbitrage pricing approaches.

Intermediate Financial Theory is intended primarily for masters level students with a professional orientation, a good quantitative background, and a preliminary education in business and finance. As such, the book is targeted for masters students in finance, but it is also appropriate for an advanced MBA class in financial economics, one with the objective of introducing students to the precise modeling of many of the concepts discussed in their capital markets and corporate finance classes. In addition, we believe the book will be a useful reference for entering doctoral candidates in finance whose lack of prior background might prevent them from drawing the full benefits of the abstract material typically covered at that level. Finally, it is a useful refresher for well-trained practitioners.

As far as prerequisites go, we take the view that our readers will have completed at least one introductory course in finance (or read the corresponding text) and will not be intimidated by mathematical formalism. Although the mathematical requirements of the book are not large, some confidence in the use of calculus as well as matrix algebra is helpful.

Over the years, we have benefited from numerous discussions with colleagues over issues related to the material included in this book. We are especially grateful to Paolo Siconolfi and Jeremy Staum, both of Columbia University. We are also indebted to several generations of teaching assistants—François Christen, Philippe Gilliard, Tomas Hricko, Aydin Akgun, Paul Ehling—and of MBF students at the University of Lausanne who have participated in the shaping of this material. Their questions, corrections, and comments have lead to a continuous questioning of the approach we have adopted and have dramatically increased the usefulness of this text. In addition to these, we would like to acknowledge our reviewers, John Primus of California State University–Hayward and Victor Abraham of Pasadena City College. Finally, we would like to thank the Fondation du 450ème of the University of Lausanne for providing "seed financing" for this project.

Jean-Pierre Danthine,
Lausanne, Switzerland

John B. Donaldson,
New York City

CHAPTER 1

ON THE ROLE OF FINANCIAL MARKETS AND INSTITUTIONS

1.1 FINANCE: THE TIME DIMENSION

Why do we need financial markets and institutions? We have chosen to address this question as our introduction to this text on financial theory. In doing so we touch on some of the most difficult issues in finance and introduce concepts that will eventually require extensive developments. Our purpose here is to phrase this question as an appropriate background for the study of the more technical issues that will occupy us at length. We also want to introduce some important elements of the necessary terminology. We ask the reader's patience as most of the sometimes-difficult material introduced here will be taken up in more detail in the following chapters.

A financial system is a set of institutions and markets permitting the exchange of contracts and the provision of services for the purpose of allowing the income and consumption streams of economic agents to be desynchronized—that is, made less similar. It can, in fact, be argued that indeed the *primary* function of the financial system is to permit such desynchronization. There are two dimensions to this function: the time dimension and the risk dimension. Let us start with time. Why is it useful to dissociate consumption and income across time? Two reasons come immediately to mind. First, and somewhat trivially, income is typically received at discrete dates, say monthly, while it is customary to wish to consume continuously (i.e., every day).

Second, and more importantly, consumption spending defines a *standard of living* and most individuals find it difficult to alter their standard of living from month to month or even from year to year. There is a general, if not universal, desire for a *smooth* consumption stream. Because it deeply affects everyone, the most important manifestation of this desire is the need to save (consumption smaller than income) for retirement so as to permit a consumption stream in excess of income (dissaving) after retirement begins. The *lifecycle* patterns of income generation and consumption spending are not identical, and the latter must be created from the former. The same considerations apply to shorter horizons. Seasonal patterns of consumption and income, for example, need not be identical. Certain individuals (car salespersons, department store salespersons) may experience variations in income arising from seasonal events (e.g., most new cars are purchased in the spring and summer), which they do not like to see transmitted to their ability to consume. There is also the problem created by temporary layoffs due to business cycle fluctuations. While temporarily laid off and without substantial income, workers do not want their family's consumption to be severely reduced.

Furthermore, and quite crucial for the growth process, some people—entrepreneurs, in particular—are willing to accept a relatively small income (but not consumption!) for a period of time in exchange for the prospect of high returns (and presumably high in-

---

BOX 1-1

Representing Preference for Smoothness

The preference for a smooth consumption stream has a natural counterpart in the form of the utility function, $U(\ )$, typically used to represent the relative benefit a consumer receives from a specific consumption bundle. Suppose the representative individual consumes a single consumption good (or a basket of goods) in each of two periods, now and tomorrow. Let c_1 denote today's consumption level and c_2 tomorrow's, and let $U(c_1) + U(c_2)$ represent the level of utility (benefit) obtained from a given consumption stream (c_1, c_2).

Therefore, preference for consumption smoothness must mean, for instance, that the consumption stream $(c_1, c_2) = (4, 4)$ is preferred to the alternative $(c_1, c_2) = (3, 5)$, or

$$U(4) + U(4) > U(3) + U(5),$$

Dividing both sides of the inequality by 2, this implies

$$U(4) > \tfrac{1}{2}U(3) + \tfrac{1}{2}U(5).$$

As shown in Figure 1-1, when generalized to all possible alternative consumption pairs, this property implies that the function $U(.)$ has the rounded shape that we associate with "strict concavity."

FIGURE 1-1 A Strictly Concave Utility Representation

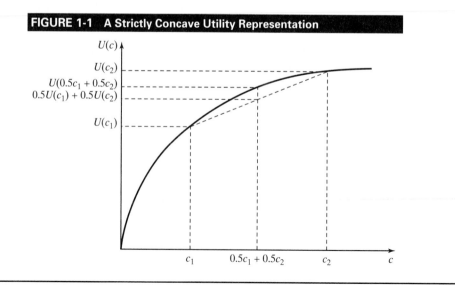

come) in the future. They are operating a sort of "arbitrage" over time. This does not disprove their desire for smooth consumption; rather they see opportunities that lead them to accept what is formally a low income level initially, against the prospect of a relatively high income level later (followed by a zero income level when they retire). They are investors who, typically, do not have enough liquid assets to finance their projects, hence the need to raise capital by borrowing or selling shares.

Therefore, the first key element in finance is **time.** In a timeless world, there would be no assets, no financial transactions (although money would be used, it would have only a transaction function), and no financial markets or institutions. The very notion of a (financial) contract implies a time dimension.

Asset holding permits the desynchronization of consumption and income streams. The peasant putting aside seeds, the miser burying his gold, or the grandmother putting a few hundred dollar bills under her mattress are all desynchronizing their consumption and income, and in doing so, presumably provide a higher level of well-being for themselves. A fully developed financial system should also have the property of fulfilling this same function *efficiently.* By that we mean that the financial system should provide versatile and diverse instruments to accommodate the widely differing needs of savers and borrowers in so far as size (many small lenders, a few big borrowers), timing and maturity of loans (how to finance long-term projects with short-term money), and the liquidity characteristics of instruments (precautionary saving cannot be tied up permanently). In other words, the elements composing the financial system should aim at *matching* as perfectly as possible the diverse financing needs of different economic agents.

1.2   DESYNCHRONIZATION: THE RISK DIMENSION

We argued above that time is of the essence in finance. When we talk of the importance of time in economic decisions, we think in particular of the relevance of choices involving the present versus the future. But the future is, by essence, uncertain: Financial decisions with implications (payouts) in the future are necessarily risky. Time and risk are inseparable. This is why **risk** is the second key word in finance.

For the moment let us compress the time dimension into the setting of a "Now and Then" (present vs. future) economy. The typical individual is motivated by the desire to smooth consumption between "Now" and "Then." This implies a desire to identify consumption opportunities that are as smooth as possible among the different possibilities that may arise "Then." In other words, *ceteris paribus*—most individuals would like to guarantee their family the same standard of living whatever events transpire tomorrow: whether they are sick or healthy; unemployed or working; confronted with bright or poor investment opportunities; fortunate or hit by unfavorable accidental events. This characteristic of preferences is generally described as "aversion to risk."

A productive way to start thinking about this issue is to introduce the notion of *states of nature.* A state of nature is a complete description of a possible scenario for the future across all the dimensions relevant for the problem at hand. In a "Now and Then" economy, all possible future events can be represented by an exhaustive list of states of nature or *states of the world.* We can thus extend our former argument for smoothing consumption across time by noting that the typical individual would also like to experience similar consumption levels across all future states of nature, whether good or bad.

An efficient financial system offers ways for savers to reduce or eliminate, at a fair price, the risks they are not willing to bear (risk shifting). Fire insurance contracts eliminate the financial risk of fire, and put contracts can prevent the loss in wealth associated with a stock's price declining below a predetermined level, to mention two examples. The financial system also makes it possible to obtain relatively safe aggregate returns from a large number of small, relatively risky investments. This is the process of diversification. By permitting economic agents to *diversify,* to *insure,* and to *hedge,* an efficient financial system fulfills the function of redistributing purchasing power not only over time, but also across states of nature.

1.3   THE SCREENING AND MONITORING FUNCTIONS OF THE FINANCIAL SYSTEM

The business of desynchronizing consumption from income streams across time and states of nature is often more complex than our initial description may suggest. If time implies uncertainty, uncertainty may imply not only risk, but often *asymmetric information* as well. By this term, we mean situations where the individuals involved have different information, with some being potentially better informed than others. How can a saver find a borrower with a good ability to repay or an investor with a good project, yielding the most attractive return for him and hopefully for society as well? What do "good" and "most attractive" mean? Do these terms refer to the highest potential return? What about risk? What if the return is itself affected by the actions of investors (a phenomenon labeled "moral hazard")? How does one share the risks of a project in such a way that both investors and savers are willing to proceed, taking actions acceptable to both? An efficient financial system not only assists in these information and monitoring tasks, but also provides a range of instruments (contractual arrangements) suitable for the largest number of savers and borrowers, thereby contributing to the channeling of savings toward the most efficient projects.

In the terms of the preeminent economist, Joseph Schumpeter (1961), "Bankers are the gatekeepers of capitalist economic development. Their strategic function is to screen potential innovators and advance the necessary purchasing power to the most

---

BOX 1-2

Representing Risk Aversion

Let us reinterpret the two-date consumption stream (c_1, c_2) of Box 1-1 as the consumption levels attained "Then" or "Tomorrow" in two alternative, equally likely, states of the world. The desire for a smooth consumption stream across the two states, which we associate with risk aversion, is obviously represented by the same inequality

$$U(4) > \tfrac{1}{2}U(3) + \tfrac{1}{2}U(5)$$

This implies the same general shape for the utility function. In other words, assuming plausibly that decision makers are **risk averse,** an assumption in conformity with most of financial theory, implies that the utility functions used to represent agents' preferences are **strictly concave.**

promising." For highly risky projects, such as the creation of a new firm exploiting a new technology, venture capitalists provide a similar function today.

1.4   THE FINANCIAL SYSTEM AND ECONOMIC GROWTH

The performance of the financial system matters at several levels. We shall argue that it matters for growth, that it impacts the characteristics of the business cycle, and most importantly, that it is a significant determinant of economic welfare. We tackle growth first. Channeling funds from savers to investors efficiently is obviously important. Whenever more efficient ways are found to perform this task, society can achieve a greater increase in tomorrow's consumption for a given sacrifice in current consumption.

Intuitively, more savings should lead to greater investment and thus greater future wealth. Figure 1-2 indeed suggests that, for 90 developing countries over the period 1971 to 1992, there was a strong positive association between saving rates and growth rates. When looked at more carefully, however, the evidence is usually not as strong.[1] One important reason may be that the hypothesized link is, of course, dependent on a ceteris

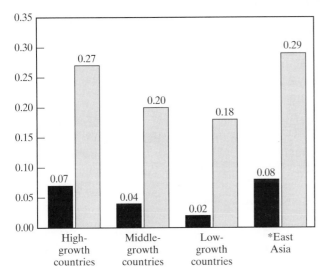

■ Real GDP growth (% increase)

☐ Total savings (% GDP)

*Hong Kong, Singapore, Taiwan, S. Korea, Indonesia, Malaysia, Thailand

FIGURE 1-2   Savings and Growth in 90 Developing Countries

Source: IMF World Economic Outlook, May 1993 (Annual data, 1971–1992).

---

[1] In a straightforward regression in which the dependent variable is the growth rate in real per capita GNP, the coefficient on the average fraction of real GNP represented by investment (I/Y) over the prior five years is positive but insignificant. Together with other results, this is interpreted as suggesting a reverse causation from real per capita GNP growth to investment spending. See Barro and Sala-i-Martin (1995), Chapter 12, for a full discussion. There is also a theoretically important distinction between the effects of increasing investment (savings) (as a proportion of national income) on an economy's level of wealth and its growth rate. Countries that save more will *ceteris paribus* be wealthier. They need not grow more rapidly. The classic growth model of Solow (1956) illustrates this distinction.

paribus or "everything else maintained equal" clause: It applies only to the extent savings are invested in appropriate ways. The economic performance of the former Union of Soviet Socialist Republics reminds us that it is not enough only to save; it is also important to invest judiciously. Historically, the investment/GDP (Gross Domestic Product) ratio in the Soviet Union was very high in international comparisons, suggesting the potential for very high growth rates. After 1989, however, experts realized that the value of the existing stock of capital was not consistent with the former levels of investment. A great deal of the investment must have been effectively wasted, in other words, allocated to poor or even worthless projects. Equal savings rates can thus lead to investments of widely differing degrees of usefulness from the viewpoint of future growth. However, in line with the earlier quote from Schumpeter, there are reasons to believe that the financial system has some role to play here as well.

The following excerpt from *Economic Focus* (UBS Economic Research, 1993) is part of a discussion motivated by the observation that, even for high-saving countries of Southeast Asia, the correlation between savings and growth has not been uniform.

> The paradox of raising saving without commensurate growth performance may be closely linked to the inadequate development of the financial system in a number of Asian economies. Holding back financial development ('financial repression') was a deliberate policy of many governments in Asia and elsewhere who wished to maintain control over the flow of savings. (. . .) Typical measures of financial repression still include interest rate regulation, selective credit allocation, capital controls, and restricted entry into and competition within the banking sector.

These comments take on special significance in light of the recent Asian crisis, which provides another, dramatic, illustration of the growth-finance nexus. Economists do not fully agree on what causes financial crises. There is, however, a consensus that in the case of several East-Asian countries, the weaknesses of the financial and banking sectors, such as those described as "financial repression," have to take at least part of the blame for the collapse and the ensuing economic regression that have marked the end of the 1990s in Southern Asia.

Let us try to go further than these general statements in the analysis of the savings and growth nexus and of the role of the financial system. Following Barro and Sala-i-Martin (1995), one can view the process of transferring funds from savers to investors in the following way.[2] The least efficient system would be one in which all investments are made by the savers themselves. This is certainly inefficient because it requires a sort of "double coincidence" of intentions: Good investment ideas occurring in the mind of someone lacking past savings will not be realized. Funds that a non-entrepreneur would like to save would not be put to productive use. Yet, this unfortunate situation is a clear possibility if the necessary confidence in the financial system is lacking with the consequence that savers do not entrust the system with their savings. One can thus think of circumstances where savings never enter the financial system, or where only a small fraction does. When it does, it will typically enter via some sort of depository institution. In an international setting, a similar problem arises if national savings are primarily in-

---

[2]For a broader perspective and a more systematic connection with the relevant literature on this topic, see Levine (1997).

vested abroad, a situation that may reach alarming proportions in the case of less developed countries.[3] Let *FS/S* represent, then, the fraction of aggregate savings (*S*) being
entrusted to the financial system (*FS*).

At a second level, the functioning of the financial system may be more or less costly.
While funds transferred from a saver to a borrower via a direct loan are immediately
and fully made available to the end user, the different functions of the financial system
previously discussed are often best fulfilled, or sometimes can only be fulfilled, through
some form of intermediation, which typically involves some cost. Let us think of these
costs as administrative costs, on the one hand, and costs linked to the reserve requirements of banks, on the other. Different systems will have different operating costs in
this large sense, and as a consequence, the amount of resources transferred to investors
will also vary. Let us think of *BOR/FS* as the ratio of funds transferred from the financial system to borrowers and entrepreneurs.

Borrowers themselves may make diverse use of the funds borrowed. Some, for example, may have pure liquidity needs (analogous to the reserve needs of depository institutions), and if the borrower is the government, it may well be borrowing for
consumption! For the savings and growth nexus, the issue is how much of the borrowed
funds actually result in productive investments. Let *I/BOR* represent the fraction of borrowed funds actually invested. Note that *BOR* stands for borrowed funds whether private or public. In the latter case a key issue is what fraction of the borrowed funds are
used to finance public investment as opposed to public consumption.

Finally let *EFF* denote the efficiency of the investment projects undertaken in society at a given time, with *EFF* normalized at unity; in other words, the average investment project has *EFF* = 1, the below-average project has *EFF* < 1, and conversely for
the above average project—a project consisting of building a bridge leading nowhere—
would have an *EFF* = 0; *K* is the aggregate capital stock, *Y* aggregate income, and Ω the
depreciation rate. Then we may write

$$\dot{K} = EFF \cdot I - \Omega K \tag{1.1}$$

or, multiplying and dividing *I* with each of the newly defined variables

$$\dot{K} = EFF \cdot (I/BOR) \cdot (BOR/FS) \cdot (FS/S) \cdot (S/Y) \cdot Y - \Omega K \tag{1.2}$$

where our notation is meant to emphasize that the growth of the capital stock at a
given savings rate might be influenced by the levels of the various ratios introduced
above.[4] Let us now review how this might be the case.

One can see that a financial system performing its matching function efficiently will
positively affect the savings rate (*S/Y*) and the fraction of savings entrusted to financial
institutions (*FS/S*). This reflects the fact that savers can find the right savings instruments for their needs. In terms of overall services net of inconvenience, this acts like an

---

[3]The problem is slightly different here. Although capital flight is a problem from the viewpoint of building
up a country's home capital stock, the acquisition of foreign assets may be a perfectly efficient way of
building a national capital stock. The effect on growth may be negative when measured in terms of GDP
(Gross Domestic Product), not necessarily so in terms of national income or GNP (Gross National Product). Switzerland is the example of a rich country investing heavily abroad and deriving a substantial income flow from it. It can be argued that the growth rate of the Swiss Gross National Product (but probably
not GDP) has been enhanced rather than decreased by this fact.
[4]$\dot{K} = dK/dt$, that is, the change in *K* as a function of time.

increase in the return to the fraction of savings finding its way into the financial system. The matching function is also relevant for the *I/BOR* ratio. With the appropriate instruments (like flexible overnight loan facilities) firm's cash needs are reduced and a larger fraction of borrowed money can actually be used for investment.

By offering a large and diverse set of possibilities for spreading risks (insurance and hedging), an efficient financial system will also positively influence the savings ratio (*S/Y*) and the *FS/S* ratio. Essentially this works through improved return/risk opportunities, corresponding to an improved trade-off between future and present consumption (for savings intermediated through the financial system). Furthermore, in permitting entrepreneurs with risky projects to eliminate unnecessary risks by using appropriate instruments, an efficient financial system provides, somewhat paradoxically, a better platform for undertaking riskier projects. If, on average, riskier projects are also the ones with the highest returns, as most of financial theory reviewed later in this book leads us to believe, one would expect that the more efficiently this function is performed, the higher (ceteris paribus), the value of *EFF*; in other words, the higher, on average, the efficiency of the investment undertaken with the funds made available by savers.

Finally, a more efficient system may be expected to more effectively screen alternative investment projects and to better and more cost efficiently monitor the conduct of the investments (efforts of investors). The direct impact is to increase *EFF*. Indirectly this also means that, on average, the return/risk characteristics of the various instruments offered savers will be improved and one may expect, as a result, an increase in both *S/Y* and *FS/S* ratios.

The previous discussion thus tends to support the idea that the financial system plays an important role in permitting and promoting the growth of economies. Yet growth is not an objective in itself. There is such a thing as excessive capital accumulation. Jappelli and Pagano (1994) suggest that borrowing constraints,[5] in general a source of inefficiency and the mark of a less than perfect financial system, may have led to more savings (in part unwanted) and higher growth. While their work is tentative, it underscores the necessity of adopting a broader and more satisfactory viewpoint and of more generally studying the impact of the financial system on social welfare. This is best done in the context of the theory of general equilibrium, a subject to which we shall turn in Section 1.6.

1.5 FINANCIAL INTERMEDIATION AND THE BUSINESS CYCLE

Business cycles are the mark of all developed economies. According to much of current research, they are in part the result of external shocks with which these economies are repeatedly confronted. The depth and amplitude of these fluctuations, however, may well be affected by some characteristics of the financial system. This is at least the im-

---

[5]By "borrowing constraints" we mean the limitations that the average individual may experience in his or her ability to borrow, at current market rates, from financial institutions.

port of the recent literature on the financial accelerator. The mechanisms at work here are numerous, and we limit ourselves to giving the reader a flavor of the discussion.

The financial accelerator is manifest most straightforwardly in the context of monetary policy implementation. Suppose the monetary authority wishes to reduce the level of economic activity (inflation is feared) by raising real interest rates. By increasing firms' costs of capital, investment spending will be reduced as marginal projects are eliminated from consideration.

According to financial accelerator theory, however, there may be further, substantial, secondary effects as well. In particular, the interest rate rise will reduce the value of firms' collateralizable assets. For some firms, this reduction may significantly diminish their access to credit, making them credit constrained. As a result, they are less able to acquire inputs to their production process, or less able to finance an adequate level of finished goods inventories. Either way, a credit-constrained firm's output tends to be further reduced and the economic downturn made correspondingly more severe. By this same mechanism, any economy-wide reduction in asset values may have the effect of reducing economic activity under the financial accelerator.

Which firms are most likely to be credit constrained? We would expect that small firms, those for which lenders have relatively little information about long-term prospects, would be principally affected. These are the firms from which lenders demand high levels of collateral. Bernanke et al. (1996) provide empirical support for this assertion using U.S. data from small manufacturing firms.

The financial accelerator has the power to make an economic downturn, of whatever origin, more severe. If the screening and monitoring functions of the financial system can be tailored more closely to individual firm needs, lenders will need to rely to a lesser extent on collateralized loan contracts. This would diminish the adverse consequences of the financial accelerator and perhaps the severity of business cycle downturns.

1.6   FINANCIAL MARKETS AND SOCIAL WELFARE

Let us now consider the role of financial markets in the allocation of resources and, consequently, their effects on social welfare. This perspective provides insight on the engine behind the process of financial innovation in the context of the theory of general economic equilibrium and the central concepts are closely associated with the Ecole de Lausanne, and the names of Léon Walras, and Vilfredo Pareto.

Our starting point is the first theorem of welfare economics that defines the conditions under which the allocation of resources implied by the general equilibrium of a decentralized competitive economy is efficient or optimal in the Pareto sense.

First, let us define the terms involved. Assume a timeless economy where a large number of economic agents interact. There is an arbitrary number of goods and services, n. Consumers are endowed with a certain quantity (possibly zero) of each of these n goods (in particular, they have the ability to work a certain number of hours per period). They can sell some of these goods and buy others at prices quoted in markets. There are a large number of firms, each represented by a production function—that is, a given ability (constrained by what is technologically feasible) to transform some of the available goods or services (inputs) into others (outputs); for instance, combining labor and capital to produce consumption goods. Agents in this economy act selfishly: Individuals maximize their well-being (utility) and firms maximize their profits. General equilibrium theory tells us that, thanks to the action of the price system, order will emerge out of this uncoordinated chaos, provided certain conditions are satisfied. In the main, these hypotheses (conditions) are as follows:

H1: *Complete markets.* There exists a market on which a price is established for each of the n goods valued by consumers.

H2: *Perfect competition.* The number of consumers and firms (i.e., demanders and suppliers of each of the n goods in each of the n markets) is large enough so that no agent is in a position to influence (manipulate) market prices; that is, all agents take prices as given.

H3: Consumers' preferences are convex.

H4: Firms' production sets are convex as well.

H3 and H4 are technical conditions with economic implications. Somewhat paradoxically, the convexity hypothesis for consumers' preferences approximately translates into strictly concave utility functions. In particular, H3 is satisfied (in substance) if consumers display risk aversion, an assumption crucial for understanding financial markets, and one that will be made throughout this text. As already noted (Box 1-2), risk aversion translates into strictly concave utility functions (See Chapter 2 for details). H4 imposes requirements on the production technology. It specifically rules out increasing returns to scale in production. While important, this assumption is not at the heart of things in financial economics.[6]

A **general competitive equilibrium** is a price vector p^* and an allocation of resources, resulting from the independent decisions of consumers and producers to buy or sell each of the n goods in each of the n markets, such that, at the equilibrium price vector p^*, supply equals demand in all markets simultaneously and the action of each agent is the most favorable to him or her among all those he or she could afford (technologically or in terms of their budget computed at equilibrium prices).

A **Pareto optimum** is an allocation of resources, however determined, where it is impossible to redistribute resources (i.e., to go ahead with further exchanges), without reducing the welfare of at least one agent. In a Pareto efficient allocation of resources, it is thus not possible to make someone better off without making someone else worse off. Such a situation may not be just or fair, but it is certainly efficient in the sense of avoiding waste.

Omitting some purely technical conditions, the main results of general equilibrium theory can be summarized as follows:

1. *The existence of a competitive equilibrium:* Under H1 through H4, a competitive equilibrium is guaranteed to exist. This means that there indeed exists a price vector and an allocation of resources satisfying the definition of a competitive equilibrium as stated above.

2. *1st welfare theorem:* Under H1 and H2, a competitive equilibrium, if it exists, is a Pareto optimum.

---

[6]Since for the most part we will abstract from the production side of the economy.

3. *2nd welfare theorem:* Under H1 through H4, any Pareto-efficient allocation can be decentralized as a competitive equilibrium. In other words, there is a price vector and a set of initial endowments such that an arbitrary Pareto-efficient allocation can be achieved as a result of the free interaction of maximizing consumers and producers interacting in competitive markets. Typically, to achieve a specific Pareto-optimal allocation, some redistribution mechanism will be needed to reshuffle initial resources. The availability of such a mechanism functioning without distortion (and thus waste) is, however, very much in question. Hence the dilemma between equity and efficiency that faces all governments.

The necessity of H1 and H2 for the optimality of a competitive equilibrium provides a rationale for government intervention when these hypotheses are not naturally satisfied. The case for antitrust and other "pro-competition" policies is implicit in H2; the case for intervention in the presence of externalities or in the provision of public goods follows from H1, because these two situations are instances of missing markets.[7]

Note that so far there does not seem to be any role for financial markets in promoting an efficient allocation of resources. To restore that role, we must abandon the fiction of a timeless world, underscoring, once again, the fact that time is of the essence in finance! Introducing the time dimension does not alter the usefulness of the general equilibrium apparatus presented above, provided the definition of a good is properly adjusted to take into account not only its intrinsic characteristics, but also the time period in which it is available. A cup of coffee available at date t is different from a cup of coffee available at date $t + 1$ and, accordingly, it is traded on a different market and it commands a different price. Thus, if there are two dates, the number of goods in the economy goes from n to $2n$.

It is easy to show, however, that not all commodities need be traded for future as well as current delivery. The existence of a spot and forward market for one good only (taken as a numeraire) is sufficient to implement all the desirable allocations, and, in particular, restore, under H1 and H2, the optimality of the competitive equilibrium. This result is contained in Arrow (1964). It provides a powerful economic rationale for the existence of credit markets, markets where money is traded for future delivery.

Now let us go one step further and introduce uncertainty, which we will represent conceptually as a partition of all the relevant future scenarios into separate "states of nature." To review, a state of nature is an exhaustive description of one possible relevant configuration of future events. Using this concept, the applicability of the welfare theorems can be extended in a fashion similar to that used with time above, by defining goods not only according to the date but also to the state of nature at which they are (might be) available. This is the notion of contingent commodities. Under

---

[7] Our model of equilibrium presumes that agents affect one another only through prices. If this is not the case, an economic externality is said to be present. These may involve either production or consumption. For example, there have been substantial negative externalities for fishermen associated with the construction of dams in the western United States: The catch of salmon has declined dramatically as these dams have reduced the ability of the fish to return to their spawning habitats. If the externality affects all consumers simultaneously, it is said to be a public good. The classic example is national defense. If any citizen is to consume a given level of national security, all citizens must be equally secure (and thus consume this public good at the same level). Both are instances of missing markets. Neither is there a market for national defense, nor for rights to disturb salmon habitats.

this construct, we imagine the market for ice cream decomposed into a series of markets: for ice cream today, ice cream tomorrow if it rains and the Dow Jones is at 7,000; if it rains and . . . , etc. Formally, this is a straightforward extension of the basic context: There are more goods, but this in itself is not restrictive[8] [Arrow (1964) and Debreu (1959)].

The hypothesis that there exists a market for each and every good valued by consumers becomes, however, much more questionable with this extended definition of a typical good, as the prior example suggests. On the one hand, the number of states of nature is, in principle, arbitrarily large and, on the other, one simply does not observe markets where commodities can routinely be traded contingent on the realization of individual states of nature. One can thus state that *if* markets are complete in the above sense, a competitive equilibrium is efficient, but the issue of completeness (H1) then takes center stage. Can Pareto optimality be obtained in a less formidable setup than one where there are complete contingent commodity markets? What does it mean to make markets "more complete?"

It was Arrow (1964), again, who took the first step toward answering these queries. Arrow generalized the result alluded to earlier and showed that it would be enough, in order to effect all desirable allocations, to have the opportunity to trade one good only, across all states of nature. Such a good would again serve as the numeraire. The primitive security could thus be a claim promising $1.00 (i.e., one unit of the numeraire) at a future date, contingent on the realization of a particular state, and zero under all other circumstances. We shall have a lot to say about such *Arrow-Debreu securities* (A-D securities from now on), which are also called *contingent claims*. Arrow asserted that if there is one such contingent claim corresponding to each and every one of the relevant future date/state configurations, hypothesis H1 could be considered satisfied, markets could be considered complete, and the theorems of welfare would apply. Arrow's result implies a substantial decrease in the number of required markets.[9] However, for a complete contingent claim structure to be fully equivalent to a setup where agents could trade a complete set of contingent commodities, it must be the case that agents are assumed to know all future spot prices, contingent on the realization of all individual states of the world. Indeed, it is at these prices that they will be able to exchange the proceeds from their A-D securities for consumption goods. This hypothesis is akin to the hypothesis of rational expectations.[10]

A-D securities are a powerful conceptual tool and are studied in depth in Chapter 7. They are not, however, the instruments we observe being traded in actual markets. Why is this the case, and in what sense is what we do observe an adequate substitute? To answer these questions, we first allude to a result (derived later on) that states that there is no single way to make markets complete. In fact there is potentially a large number of alternative financial structures achieving the same goal, and the complete A-D

---

[8]Since n can be as large as one needs without restriction.
[9]Example: 2 dates, 3 basic goods, 4 states of nature: complete commodity markets require 12 contingent commodity markets + 3 spot markets versus 4 contingent claims and 2×3 spot markets in the Arrow setup.
[10]For an elaboration on this topic, see Drèze (1971).

securities structure is only one of them. For instance, we shall describe, in Chapter 8, a context in which one might think of achieving an essentially complete market structure with options or derivative securities. We shall make use of this fact for pricing alternative instruments using arbitrage techniques. Thus, the failure to observe anything close to A-D securities being traded is not evidence against the possibility that markets are indeed complete.

In an attempt to match this discussion on the role played by financial markets with the type of markets we see in the real world, one can identify the different needs met by trading A-D securities in a complete markets world. In so doing, we shall conclude that, in reality, different types of needs are met through trading alternative specialized financial instruments (which, as we shall later prove, will all appear as portfolios of A-D securities).

As we have already observed, the time dimension is crucial for finance and, correspondingly, the need to exchange purchasing power across time is essential. It is met in reality through a variety of specific noncontingent instruments, which are promised future payments independent of specific states of nature, except those in which the issuer is unable to meet his obligations (bankruptcies). Personal loans, bank loans, money market and capital market instruments, social security and pension claims are all assets fulfilling this basic need for redistributing purchasing power in the time dimension. In a complete market setup implemented through A-D securities, the needs met by these instruments would be satisfied by a certain configuration of positions in A-D securities. In reality, the specialized instruments mentioned above fulfill the demand for exchanging income through time.

One reason for the formidable nature of the complete markets requirement is that a state of nature, which is a complete description of the relevant future for a particular agent, includes some purely personal aspects of almost unlimited complexity. Certainly the future is different for you, in a relevant way, if you lose your job or if your house burns, without these contingencies playing a very significant role for the population at large. In a pure A-D world, the description of the states of nature should take account of these *individual contingencies* viewed from the perspective of each and every market participant! In the real world, insurance contracts are the specific instruments that deal with the need for exchanging income across purely personal or individual events or states. The markets for these contracts are part and parcel of the notion of complete financial markets. While such a specialization makes sense, it is recognized as unlikely that the need to trade across individual contingencies will be fully met through insurance markets because of specific difficulties linked with the hidden quality of these contingencies (i.e., the inherent asymmetry in the information possessed by suppliers and demanders participating in these markets). The presence of these asymmetries strengthens our perception of the impracticality of relying exclusively on pure A-D securities to deal with personal contingencies.

Beyond time issues and personal contingencies, most other financial instruments not only imply the exchange of purchasing power through time, but are also more specifically contingent on the realization of particular events. The relevant events here, however, are defined on a collective basis rather than being based on individual contingencies; they are contingent on the realization of events affecting groups of individuals and observable by everyone. An example of this is the situation where a certain level of profits for a firm implies the payment of a certain dividend against the ownership of that firm's stock, or the payment of a certain sum of money associated with the ownership of an option or a financial futures. In the later cases, the contingencies (sets of states of nature) are dependent on the value of the underlying asset itself.

1.7 CONCLUSIONS

To conclude this introductory chapter, we propose a vision of the evolution of financial systems progressively tending to a complete market situation, starting with the most obviously missing markets and slowly, as technological innovation decreases transaction costs and allows the design of more sophisticated contracts, completing the market structure. Have we arrived at a complete market structure? Have we come significantly closer? There are opposing views on this issue. While more optimistic views are proposed by Merton (1990) and Allen and Gale (1994), we choose to close this chapter on two healthily skeptical notes. Tobin (1984, p. 10), for one, provides an unambiguous answer to the above question:

> New financial markets and instruments have proliferated over the last decade, and it might be thought that the enlarged menu now spans more states of nature and moves us closer to the Arrow-Debreu ideal. Not much closer, I am afraid. The new options and futures contracts do not stretch very far into the future. They serve mainly to allow greater leverage to short-term speculators and arbitrageurs, and to limit losses in one direction or the other. Collectively they contain considerable redundancy. Every financial market absorbs private resources to operate, and government resources to police. The country cannot afford all the markets the enthusiasts may dream up. In deciding whether to approve proposed contracts for trading, the authorities should consider whether they really fill gaps in the menu and enlarge the opportunities for Arrow-Debreu insurance, not just opportunities for speculation and financial arbitrage.

Shiller (1993, pp. 2–3) is even more specific with respect to missing markets:

> It is odd that there appear to have been no practical proposals for establishing a set of markets to hedge the biggest risks to standards of living. . . . Individuals and organizations could hedge or insure themselves against risks to their standards of living if an array of risk markets—let us call them macro markets—could be established. These would be large international markets, securities, futures, options, swaps or analogous markets, for claims on major components of incomes (including service flows) shared by many people or organizations. The settlements in these markets could be based on income aggregates, such as national income or components thereof, such as occupational incomes, or prices that value income flows, such as real estate prices, which are prices of claims on real estate service flows.

Complementary Readings

As a complement to this introductory chapter, the reader will be interested in the historical review of financial markets and institutions by Allen and Gale (1994) in their first chapter. Bernstein (1992) is a lively account of the birth of the major ideas making up modern financial theory including personal portraits of their authors.

References

Allen, F., and D. Gale, *Financial Innovation and Risk Sharing*, Cambridge, Mass.: MIT Press, 1994.

Arrow, K. J., "The Role of Securities in the Allocation of Risk," *Review of Economic Studies*, 31 (1964): 91–96.

Barro, R. J., and X. Sala-i-Martin, *Economic Growth*, New York: McGraw-Hill, 1995.

Bernanke, B., M. Gertler, and S. Gilchrist, "The Financial Accelerator and the Flight to Quality," *The Review of Economics and Statistics,* 78 (1996): 1–15.

Bernstein, P. L., *Capital Ideas. The Improbable Origins of Modern Wall Street*, New York: The Free Press, 1992.

Debreu, G., *Theory of Value: An Axiomatic Analysis of Economic Equilibrium*, New York: Wiley, 1959.

Drèze, Jacques H., "Market Allocation Under Uncertainty," *European Economic Review*, 2 (1971): 133–165.

Jappelli, T., and M. Pagano, "Savings, Growth, and Liquidity Constraints," *Quarterly Journal of Economics,* 109 (1994): 83–109.

Levine, R., "Financial Development and Economic Growth: Views and Agenda," *Journal of Economic Literature,* 35 (1997): 688–726.

Merton, R.C., "The Financial System and Economic Performance," *Journal of Financial Services,* 4 (1990): 263–300.

Schumpeter, Joseph, *The Theory of Economic Development,* Leipzig: Duncker & Humblot. Trans. R. Opie, Cambridge, Mass.: Harvard University Press, 1934. Reprinted, New York: Oxford University Press, 1961.

Shiller, Robert J., *Macro Markets—Creating Institutions for Managing Society's Largest Economic Risks*, Oxford: Clarendon Press, 1993.

Solow, R. M., "A Contribution to the Theory of Economic Growth," *Quarterly Journal of Economics,* 32 (1956): 65–94.

Tobin, J., "On the Efficiency of the Financial System," *Lloyds Bank Review* (1984): 1–15.

UBS Economic Research, *Economic Focus*, Union Bank of Switzerland, no. 9, August 1993.

A P P E N D I X

Introduction to General Equilibrium Theory

The goal of this appendix is to provide an introduction to the essentials of General Equilibrium Theory thereby permitting a complete understanding of Section 1.6 of the present chapter and facilitating the discussion of subsequent chapters (from Chapter 7 on). To make this presentation as simple as possible we'll take the case of a hypothetical exchange economy (that is, one with no production) with two goods and two agents. This permits using a very useful pedagogical tool known as the Edgeworth-Bowley box.

Let us analyze the problem of allocating efficiently a given economy-wide endowment of 10 units of good 1 and 6 units of good 2 among two agents, A and B. In Figure A1-1, we measure good 2 on the vertical axis and good 1 on the horizontal axis. Consider the choice problem from the origin of the axes for Mr. A, and upside down (that is, placing the origin in the upper right corner), for Ms. B. An allocation is then represented as a point in a rectangle of size 6×10. Point E is an allocation at which Mr. A receives 4 units of

good 1 and 2 units of good 2. Ms. B gets the rest, that is, 2 units of good 1 and 8 units of good 2. All other points in the box represent feasible allocations, that is, alternative ways of allocating the resources available in this economy.

PARETO OPTIMAL ALLOCATIONS

In order to discuss the notion of Pareto optimal or efficient allocations, we need to introduce agents' preferences. They are fully summarized, in the graphical context of the Edgeworth-Bowley box, by indifference curves (IC) or utility level curves. Thus, starting from the allocation E represented in Figure A1-1, we can record all feasible allocations that provide the same utility to Mr. A. Exactly how such a level curve looks is person specific, but we can be sure that it slopes downward. If we take away some units of good 2, we have to compensate him with some extra units of good 1 if we are to

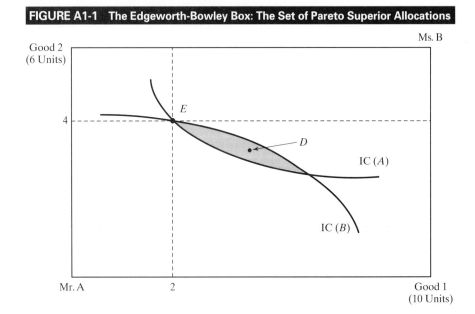

FIGURE A1-1   The Edgeworth-Bowley Box: The Set of Pareto Superior Allocations

leave his utility level unchanged. It is easy to see as well that the ICs of a consistent person do not cross, a property associated with the notion of transitivity (and with rationality) in our next chapter. And we have seen in Boxes 1-1 and 1-2 that the preference for smoothness translates into convex-to-the-origin level curves as drawn in Figure A1-1. The same properties apply to the IC of Ms. B, of course viewed upside down with the upper right corner as the origin.

With this simple apparatus we are in a position to discuss further the concept of Pareto optimality. Arbitrarily tracing the level curves of Mr. A and Ms. B as they pass through allocation E (but in conformity with the properties derived in the previous paragraph), only two possibilities may arise: they cross each other at E or they are tangent to one another at point E. The first possibility is illustrated in Figure A1-1, the second in Figure A1-2. In the first case, allocation E cannot be a Pareto optimal allocation. As the picture illustrates clearly, by the very definition of level curves, if the ICs of our two agents cross at point E there is a set of allocations (corresponding to the shaded area in Figure A1-1) that are simultaneously preferred to E by both Mr. A and Ms. B. These allocations are Pareto superior to E, and, in that situation, it would indeed be socially inefficient or wasteful to distribute the available resources as in-

dicated by E. Allocation D, for instance, is feasible and preferred to E by both individuals.

To the contrary, if the ICs are tangent to one another at point E' as in Figure A1-2, no redistribution of the given resources exists that would be approved by both agents. Inevitably, moving away from E' decreases the utility level of one of the two agents if it favors the other. In this case, E' is a Pareto optimal allocation. Figure A1-2 illustrates that it is not generally unique, however. If we connect all the points where the various ICs of our two agents are tangent to each other, we draw the line, labeled the contract curve, representing the infinity of Pareto optimal allocations in this simple economy.

An indifference curve for Mr. A is defined as the set of allocations that provide the same utility to Mr. A as some specific allocation; for example, allocation E:

$$\{(c_1^A, c_2^A) : U(c_1^A, c_2^A) = U(E)\}.$$

This definition implies that the slope of the IC can be derived by taking the total differential of $U(c_1^A, c_2^A)$ and equating it to zero (no change in utility along the IC), which gives:

$$\frac{\partial U(c_1^A, c_2^A)}{\partial c_1^A} dc_1^A + \frac{\partial U(c_1^A, c_2^A)}{\partial c_2^A} dc_2^A = 0, \quad \textbf{(A1.1)}$$

and thus,

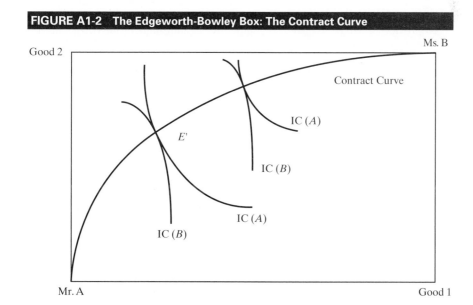

FIGURE A1-2   The Edgeworth-Bowley Box: The Contract Curve

Good 2

Ms. B

Contract Curve

IC (A)

E'

IC (B)

IC (A)

IC (B)

Mr. A

Good 1

$$\frac{dc_2^A}{dc_1^A} = -\frac{\dfrac{\partial U(c_1^A, c_2^A)}{\partial c_1^A}}{\dfrac{\partial U(c_1^A, c_2^A)}{\partial c_2^A}} \equiv -MRS_{1,2}^A. \qquad \textbf{(A1.2)}$$

That is, the negative (or the absolute value) of the slope of the IC is the ratio of the marginal utility of good 1 to the marginal utility of good 2, specific to Mr. A and to the allocation (c_1^A, c_2^A) at which the derivatives are taken, which defines Mr. A's Marginal Rate of Substitution (MRS) between the two goods.

Equation (A1.2) permits a formal characterization of a Pareto optimal allocation. Our former discussion has equated Pareto optimality with the tangency of the ICs of Mr. A and Ms. B. Tangency, in turn, means that the slopes of the respective ICs are identical. Allocation E, associated with the consumption vector $(c_1^A, c_2^A)^E$ for Mr. A and $(c_1^A, c_2^A)^E$ for Ms. B, is thus Pareto optimal if and only if

$$MRS_{1,2}^A = \frac{\dfrac{\partial U(c_1^A, c_2^A)^E}{\partial c_1^A}}{\dfrac{\partial U(c_1^A, c_2^A)^E}{\partial c_2^A}}$$

$$= \frac{\dfrac{\partial U(c_1^B, c_2^B)^E}{\partial c_1^B}}{\dfrac{\partial U(c_1^B, c_2^B)^E}{\partial c_2^B}} \equiv MRS_{1,2}^B. \qquad \textbf{(A1.3)}$$

Equation (A1.3) provides a complete characterization of a Pareto optimal allocation in an exchange economy except in the case of a corner allocation, that is, an allocation at the frontier of the box where one of the agents receives the entire endowment of one good and the other agent receives none. In that situation it may well be that the equality could not be satisfied except, hypothetically, by moving to the outside of the box, that is, to allocations that are not feasible since they require giving a negative amount of one good to one of the two agents.

So far we have not touched on the issue of how the discussed allocations may be determined. This is the viewpoint of Pareto optimality analysis exclusively concerned with deriving efficiency properties of given allocations, irrespective of how they were achieved. Let us now turn to the concept of competitive equilibrium.

COMPETITIVE EQUILIBRIUM

Associated with the notion of competitive equilibrium is the notion of markets and prices. One price vector one price for each of our two goods, or simply a relative price taking good 1 as the numeraire, and setting $p_1 = 1$, is represented in the Edgeworth-Bowley box by a downward sloping line. From the viewpoint of either agent, such a line has all the properties of the budget line. It also represents the frontier of their opportunity set. Let us assume that the initial allocation, before any trade, is represented by point I in Figure A1-3. Any line sloping downward from I does represent the set of allocations that Mr. A, endowed with I, can obtain by going to the market and exchanging (competitively, taking prices as given) good 1 for 2 or vice versa. He will maximize his utility subject to this budget constraint by attempting to climb to the highest IC making contact with his budget set. This will lead him to select the allocation corresponding to the tangency point between one of his ICs and the price line. Because the same prices are valid for both agents, an identical procedure, viewed upside down from the upper right-hand corner of the box, will lead Ms. B to a tangency point between one of her ICs and the price line. At this stage, only two possibilities may arise: Mr. A and Ms. B have converged to the same allocation (the two markets, for goods 1 and 2, clear—supply and demand for the two goods are equal and we are at a competitive equilibrium); or the two agents' separate optimizing procedures have lead them to select two different allocations. Total demand does not equal total supply and an equilibrium is not achieved. The two situations are described, respectively, in Figures A1-3 and A1-4.

In the disequilibrium case of Figure A1-4, prices will have to adjust until an equilibrium is found. Specifically, with Mr. A at point A and Ms. B at point B, there is an excess demand of good 2 but insufficient demand for good 1. One would expect the price of 2 to increase relative to the price of good 1 with the likely result that both agents will decrease their net demand for 2 and increase their net demand for 1. Graphically, this is depicted by the price curve tilting with point I as the axis and looking less steep (indicating, for instance, that if both agents wanted to buy good 1 only, they could now afford more of it). With regu-

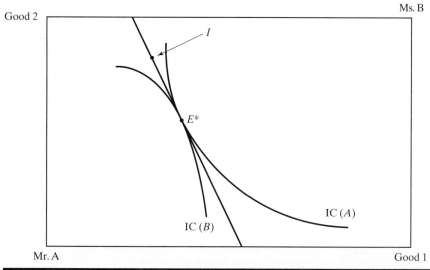

Good 2

Ms. B

I

E^*

IC (A)

IC (B)

Mr. A

Good 1

FIGURE A1-3   The Edgeworth-Bowley Box: Equilibrium Achieved at E^*

lar ICs, the respective points of tangencies will converge until an equilibrium similar to the one described in Figure A1-3 is reached.

We will not say anything here about the conditions guaranteeing that such a process will converge. Let us rather insist on one crucial necessary precondition: that an equilibrium exists. In the text we have mentioned that assumptions H1 to H4 are needed to guarantee the existence of an equilibrium. Of course H4 does not apply here. H1 states the necessity of the existence of a price for each good, which is akin to specifying the existence of a price line. H2 defines one of the characteristics of a competitive equilibrium: that prices are taken as given by the various agents and the price line describes their perceived

FIGURE A1-4   The Edgeworth-Bowley Box: Disequilibrium, Excess Demand for Good 2, Excess Supply for Good 1

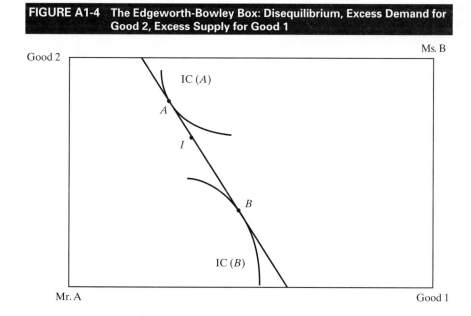

Good 2

Ms. B

IC (A)

A

I

B

IC (B)

Mr. A

Good 1

opportunity sets. Our discussion here can enlighten the need for H3. Indeed, in order for an equilibrium to have a chance to exist, the geometry of Figure A1-3 makes clear that the shapes of the two agents' ICs are relevant. The price line must be able to separate the "better than" areas of the two agents' ICs passing through a same point—the candidate equilibrium allocation. The better than area is simply the area above a given IC. It represents all the allocations providing higher utility than those on the level curve. This separation by a price line is not generally possible if the ICs are not convex, in which case an equilibrium cannot be guaranteed to exist. The problem is illustrated in Figure A1-5.

Once a competitive equilibrium is observed to exist, which logically could be the case even if the conditions that guarantee existence are not met, the Pareto optimality of the resulting allocation is insured by H1 and H2 only. In substance this is because once the common price line at which markets clear exists, the very fact that agents optimize taking prices as given, leads them to a point of tangency between their highest IC and the common price line. At the resulting allocation, both MRS are equal to the same price line and, consequently, are identical. The conditions for Pareto optimality are thus fulfilled.

FIGURE A1-5   The Edgeworth-Bowley Box: Non-Convex Indifference Curves

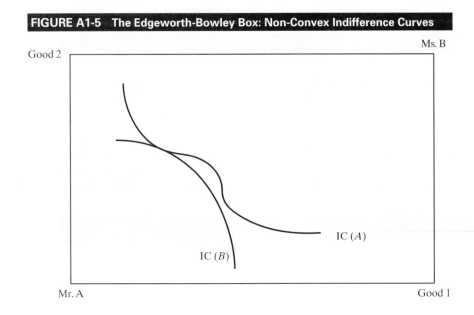

CHAPTER 2

MAKING CHOICES IN
RISKY SITUATIONS

2.1 INTRODUCTION

One of our ultimate objectives is to review and develop alternative theories of asset valuation, and a principal ingredient of such theories must be an understanding of the determinants of the **demand** for securities of various risk classes. Individuals demand securities (in exchange for current purchasing power) in their attempt to redistribute income across time and states of nature. This is a reflection of the consumption-smoothing and risk-reallocation function central to financial markets.

Our endeavor requires an understanding of three building blocks:

1. how financial risk is defined and measured
2. how an investor's attitude toward or tolerance for risk is to be conceptualized and then measured
3. how investors' risk attitudes interact with the subjective uncertainties associated with the available assets to determine an investor's desired portfolio holdings (demands)

In this and the next chapter we give a detailed overview of points 1 and 2; point 3 is treated in succeeding chapters.

2.2 CHOOSING AMONG RISKY PROSPECTS: PRELIMINARIES

When we think of the "risk" of an investment, we are typically thinking of uncertainty in the future cash flow stream to which the investment represents title. Depending on the state of nature that may occur in the future, we may receive different payments and, in particular, much lower payments in some states than others. That is, we model an asset's associated cash flow in any future time period as a **random variable.**

Consider, for example, the investments listed in Table 2-1, each of which pays off next period in either of two equally likely possible states. We index these states by $\theta = 1,2$ with their respective probabilities labelled π_1 and π_2.

First, this comparison serves to introduce the important notion of **dominance.** Investment 3 clearly dominates both investments 1 and 2 in the sense that it pays as much in all states of nature, and strictly more in at least one state. The **state-by-state dominance** illustrated here is the strongest possible form of dominance. Without any qualification, we will assume that all rational individuals would prefer investment 3 to the other two. Basically this means that we are assuming the typical individual to be nonsatiated in consumption: she desires more rather than less of the consumption goods these payoffs allow her to buy.

In the case of dominance the choice problem is trivial and, in some sense, the issue of defining risk is irrelevant. The ranking defined by the concept of dominance is, however, very incomplete. If we compare investments 1 and 2, one sees that neither dominates the other. Although it performs better in state 2, investment 2 performs much worse in state 1. There is no ranking possible on the basis of the dominance criterion. Therefore, one productive direction is to begin characterizing the different prospects from a variety of angles. Here the concept of risk enters necessarily.

On this score, we would probably all agree that investments 2 and 3 are comparatively riskier than investment 1. Of course for investment 3, the dominance property means that the only risk is an upside risk. Yet, in line with the preference for smooth consumption discussed in Chapter 1, the large variation in date 2 payoffs associated with investment 3 is to be viewed as undesirable in itself. When comparing investments 1 and 2, the qualifier "riskier" undoubtedly applies to the latter. In the worst state, the payoff associated with 2 is worse; in the best state it is better.

These comparisons can alternatively, and often more conveniently, be represented if we describe investments in terms of their performance on a per dollar basis. We do this by computing the state contingent rates of return (ROR) that we will typically associate with the symbol r. In the case of the previous investments, we obtain the results in Table 2-2.

One sees clearly that all rational individuals should prefer investment 3 to the other two and that this same dominance cannot be expressed when comparing 1 and 2.

The fact that investment 2 is riskier, however, does not mean that all rational individuals would necessarily prefer 1. Risk is not the only consideration and the ranking between the two projects is, in principle, preference dependent. This is more often the case than not; dominance usually provides a very incomplete way of ranking prospects. This is why we have to turn to a description of preferences, the main object of this chapter.

The most well-known approach at this point consists of summarizing such investment return distributions (that is, the random variables representing returns) by their mean (Er_i) and variance (σ_i^2), $i = 1.2$. The variance (or its square root, the standard de-

TABLE 2-1 Asset Payoffs ($)			
	$t = 0$	$t = 1$	
	Cost at $t = 0$	Value at $t = 1$ $\pi_1 = \pi_2 = \frac{1}{2}$	
		$\theta = 1$	$\theta = 2$
Investment 1	−1,000	1,050	1,200
Investment 2	−1,000	500	1,600
Investment 3	−1,000	1,050	1,600

TABLE 2-2 State Contingent ROR (r)

	$\theta = 1$	$\theta = 2$
Investment 1	5%	20%
Investment 2	−50%	60%
Investment 3	5%	60%

viation) of the rate of return is then naturally used as the measure of "risk" of the project (or the asset). For the three investments just listed, we have:

$Er_1 = 12.5\%; \quad \sigma_1^2 = \frac{1}{2}(5 - 12.5)^2 + \frac{1}{2}(20 - 12.5)^2 = (7.5)^2, \text{ or } \sigma_1 = 7.5\%$
$Er_2 = 5\% \qquad \sigma_2 = 55\% \quad \text{(similar calculation)}$
$Er_3 = 32.5\% \quad \sigma_3 = 27.5\%$

If we decided to summarize these return distributions by their means and variances only, investment 1 would clearly appear more attractive than investment 2: It has both a higher mean return and a lower variance. In terms of the mean-variance criterion, investment 1 dominates investment 2; 1 is said to *mean-variance dominate* 2. Our previous discussion makes it clear that **mean-variance dominance** is neither as strong, nor as general a concept as state-by-state dominance. Investment 3 mean-variance dominates 2 but not 1, although it dominates them both on a state-by-state basis! This is surprising and should lead us to be cautious when using any mean-variance return criterion. We will, later on, detail circumstances where it is fully reliable. At this point let us anticipate that it will not be generally so, and that restrictions will have to be imposed to legitimize its use.

The notion of mean-variance dominance can be expressed in the form of a criterion for selecting investments of equal magnitude, which plays a prominent role in modern portfolio theory:

1. For investments of the same Er, choose the one with the lowest σ.
2. For investments of the same σ, choose the one with the greatest Er.

In the framework of modern portfolio theory, one could not understand a rational agent choosing investment 2 rather than investment 1.

We cannot limit our inquiry to this latter concept of dominance, however. Mean-variance dominance provides only an incomplete ranking among uncertain prospects, as Table 2-3 illustrates.

Comparing these two investments, it is not clear which is best; there is no dominance in either state-by-state or mean-variance terms. Investment 5 pays 1.25 times the expected return of investment 4, but, in terms of standard deviation, it is also three times riskier. The choice between 4 and 5, when restricted to mean-variance characterizations, would require specifying the terms at which the decision maker is willing to *substitute* expected return for a given risk reduction. In other words, what decrease in expected return is he willing to accept for a 1% decrease in the standard deviation of returns? Or conversely, does the 1 percentage point additional expected return associated with investment 5 adequately compensate for the (3 times) larger risk? Responses to such questions are preference dependent (i.e., vary from individual to individual).

Suppose, for a particular individual, the terms of the trade-off are well represented by the index E/σ (referred to as the "Sharpe" ratio). Since $(E/\sigma)_4 = 4$ while $(E/\sigma)_5 = 5/3$,

TABLE 2-3 State-Contingent Rates of Return		
	$\theta = 1$	$\theta = 2$
Investment 4	3%	5%
Investment 5	2%	8%

$$\pi_1 = \pi_2 = \tfrac{1}{2}$$

$$Er_4 = 4\%; \sigma_4 = 1\%$$
$$Er_5 = 5\%; \sigma_5 = 3\%$$

investment 4 is better than investment 5 for that individual. Of course another investor may be less risk averse; that is, he may be willing to accept more extra risk for the same expected return. For example, his preferences may be adequately represented by $(E - \tfrac{1}{3}\sigma)$ in which case he would rank investment 5 (with an index value of 4) above investment 4 (with a value of 3⅔).[1]

All these considerations strongly suggest that we have to adopt a more general viewpoint for comparing potential return distributions. This viewpoint is part of utility theory, to which we turn after describing some of the problems associated with the empirical characterization of return distributions in Box 2-1.

BOX 2-1

Computing Means and Variances in Practice

Useful as it may be conceptually, calculations of distribution moments such as the mean and the standard deviation are difficult to implement in practice. This is because we rarely know what the future states of nature are, let alone their probabilities. We also do not know the returns in each state. A frequently used proxy for a future return distribution is its historical return distribution. This amounts to selecting a historical time period and a periodicity, say monthly prices for the past 60 months, and computing the historical returns as follows:

$$r_{s,j+1} = \text{return to stock } s \text{ in month } j + 1$$
$$= ((p_{s,j+1} + d_{s,j})/p_{s,j}) - 1$$

where $p_{s,j}$ is the price of stock s in month j, and $d_{s,j}$ its dividend, if any, that month. We then summarize the past distribution of stock re-

turns by the average historical return and the variance of the historical returns. By doing so we, in effect, assign $\tfrac{1}{60}$ as a probability to each past observation or event.

In principle this is an acceptable way to estimate a return distribution for the future if we think the "mechanism" generating these returns is "stationary": that the future will in some sense closely resemble the past. In practice, this hypothesis is rarely fully verified and, at the minimum, it requires careful checking. Also necessary for such a straightforward, although customary, application is that the return realizations are independent of each other, so that today's realization does not reveal anything materially new about the probabilities of tomorrow's returns (formally, that the conditional and unconditional distributions are identical).

---

[1]Observe that the Sharpe ratio criterion is not immune to the criticism discussed above. With the Sharpe ratio criterion, investment 3 ($E/\sigma = 1.182$) is inferior to investment 1 ($E/\sigma = 1.667$). Yet we know that 3 dominates 1 since it pays a higher return in every state. This problem is pervasive with the mean-variance

2.3   A PREREQUISITE: CHOICE THEORY UNDER CERTAINTY

A good deal of financial economics is concerned with how people make choices. The objective is to understand the systematic part of individual behavior and to be able to predict (at least in a loose way), how an individual will react to a given situation. Economic theory describes individual behavior as the result of a process of optimization under constraints, the objective to be reached being determined by individual preferences, and the constraints being a function of the person's income or wealth level and of market prices. This approach, which defines the *homo economicus* and the notion of **economic rationality,** is justified by the fact that individuals' behavior is predictable only to the extent that it is systematic, which must mean that there is an attempt at achieving a set objective. It is not to be taken literally or normatively.[2]

To develop this sense of rationality systematically, we begin by summarizing the objectives of investors in the most basic way: we postulate the existence of a preference relation, represented by the symbol $\geq$, describing investors' ability to compare various bundles of goods, services, and money. For two bundles a and b, the expression

$$a \geq b$$

is to be read as follows: For the investor in question, bundle a is strictly preferred to bundle b, or he is indifferent with respect to them. Pure indifference is denoted by $a \sim b$, strict preference by $a > b$.

The notion of economic rationality can then be summarized by the following assumptions:

A.1 Every investor possesses such a preference relation and it is *complete,* meaning that he is able to decide whether he prefers a to b, b to a, or both, in which case he is indifferent with respect to the two bundles. That is, for any two bundles a and b, either $a \geq b$ or $b \geq a$ or both. If both hold, we say that the investor is indifferent with respect to the bundles and write $a \sim b$.

A.2 This preference relation satisfies the fundamental property of *transitivity:* For any bundles a, b, and c, if $a \geq b$ and $b \geq c$, then $a \geq c$.

A.3 Investors' preference relations are *relatively* stable over time. We maintain this assumption because preferences are not directly observable. A theory relying systematically on changing preferences would be vacuous in that it could never be falsified or confirmed. A further requirement is also necessary for technical reasons:

A.4 The preference relation $\geq$ is continuous in the following sense: Let $\{x_n\}$ and $\{y_n\}$ be two sequences of consumption bundles such that $x_n \mapsto x$ and $y_n \mapsto y$.[3] If $x_n \geq y_n$ for all n, then the same relationship is preserved in the limit, or $x \geq y$.

---

investment criterion. For any mean-variance choice criterion, whatever the terms of the trade-off between mean and variance or standard deviation, one can produce a paradox such as the one illustrated. This confirms such a criterion is not generally applicable without additional restrictions. The name Sharpe ratio refers to Nobel Prize winner William Sharpe, who first proposed this ratio for this sort of comparison.

[2]By this we mean that economic science does not *prescribe* that individuals maximize, optimize, or simply behave as if they were doing so. It just finds it productive to summarize the systematic behavior of economic agents with such tools.

[3]We use the standard sense of (normed) convergence on R^N.

A key result can now be expressed by the following proposition.

Theorem 2.1:
Assumptions A.1 through A.4 are sufficient to guarantee the existence of a continuous, time-invariant, real-valued utility function[4] u, such that for any two objects of choice (consumption bundles of goods and services; amounts of money, etc.) a and b,

$$a \geq b \text{ if and only if}$$
$$u(a) \geq u(b).$$

Proof:
See, for example, Mas-Colell et al. (1995), Proposition 3.c.1.

This result asserts that the assumption that decision makers are endowed with a utility function (which they are assumed to maximize) is, in reality, no different than assuming their preferences among objects of choice define a relation possessing the (weak) properties summarized in A1 through A4.

Notice that Theorem 2.1 implies that if $u(\ )$ is a valid representation of an individual's preferences, any increasing transformation of $u(\ )$ will do as well since such a transformation by definition will preserve the ordering induced by $u(\ )$. Notice also that the notion of a consumption bundle is, formally, very general. Different elements of a bundle may represent the consumption of the same good or service in different time periods. One element might represent a vacation trip in the Bahamas this year; another may represent exactly the same vacation next year. We can further expand our notion of different goods to include the same good consumed in mutually exclusive states of the world. Our preference for hot soup, for example, may be very different if the day turns out to be warm rather than cold. These thoughts suggest Theorem 2.1 is really quite general, and can, formally at least, be extended to accommodate uncertainty. Under uncertainty, however, ranking bundles of goods (or vectors of monetary payoffs, as we will see later) involves more than pure elements of taste or preferences. In the hot soup example, it is natural to suppose that our preferences for hot soup are affected by the probability we attribute to the day being hot or cold. Disentangling pure preferences from probability assessments is the subject to which we now turn.

2.4 CHOICE THEORY UNDER UNCERTAINTY: AN INTRODUCTION

Under certainty, the choice is among consumption baskets with known characteristics. Under uncertainty, however, our *emphasis* changes. The objects of choice are typically no longer consumption bundles but vectors of state contingent money payoffs (we'll reintroduce consumption in Chapter 5). Such vectors are formally what we mean by an *asset* that we may purchase or an *investment*. When we purchase a share of a stock, for

---

[4]In other words, $u: R^n \to R^+$

example, we know that its sale price in one year will differ depending on what events transpire within the firm and in the world economy. Under financial uncertainty, therefore, the choice is among alternative investments leading to different possible income levels and, hence, ultimately different consumption possibilities. As before, we observe that people do make investment choices, and if we are to make sense of these choices, there must be a stable underlying order of preference defined over different alternative investments. The spirit of Theorem 2.1 will still apply. With appropriate restrictions, these preferences can be represented by a utility index defined on investment possibilities, but obviously something deeper is at work. It is natural to assume that individuals have no intrinsic taste for the assets themselves (IBM stock as opposed to Royal Dutch stock, for example); rather, they are interested in what payoffs these assets will yield and with what likelihood (see Box 2-2, however).

One may further hypothesize that investor preferences are indeed very simple after uncertainty is resolved: They prefer a higher payoff to a lower one or, equivalently, to earn a higher return rather than a lower one. Of course they do not know *ex ante* (that is, before the state of nature is revealed) which asset will yield the higher payoff. They have to choose among prospects, or probability distributions representing these payoffs. And, as we saw in Section 2.2, typically, no one investment prospect will strictly dominate the others. Investors will be able to imagine different possible scenarios, some of which will result in a higher return for one asset, with other scenarios favoring other assets. For instance, let us go back to our favorite situation where there are only two states of nature; in other words, two conceivable scenarios and two assets, as seen in Table 2-4.

There are two key ingredients in the choice between these two alternatives. The first is the probability of the two states. All other things being the same, the more likely is state 1, the more attractive IBM stock will appear to prospective investors. The second is the *ex post* (once the state of nature is known) level of utility provided by the investment. In Table 2-4, IBM yields $100 in state 1 and is thus preferred to Royal Dutch, which yields $90 if this scenario is realized; Royal Dutch, however, provides $160 rather than $150 in state 2. Obviously, with unchanged state probabilities, things would look

---

BOX 2-2

Investing Close to Home

Although the assumption that investors only care for the final payoff of their investment without any trace of romanticism is a standard assumption in financial economics, there is some evidence to the contrary and, in particular, for the assertion that many investors, at the margin at least, prefer to purchase the claims of firms whose products or services are familiar to them. In a recent paper, Huberman (1997) examines the stock ownership records of the seven regional Bell operating companies (RBOCs). He discovered that, with the exception of residents of Montana, Americans are more likely to invest in their local regional Bell operating company than in any other. When they do, their holdings average $14,400. For those who venture farther from home and hold stocks of the RBOC of a region other than their own, the average holding is only $8,246. Considering that every local RBOC cannot be a better investment choice than all of the other six, Huberman interprets his findings as having to do with investors' psychological need to feel comfortable with where they put their money.

TABLE 2-4 Forecasted Price per Share in One Period

	State 1	State 2
IBM	$100	$150
Royal Dutch	$90	$160

Current Price of both assets is $100

different if the difference in payoffs were increased in one state. In Table 2-5, even if state 1 is slightly more likely, the superiority of Royal Dutch in state 2 makes it look more attractive. A more refined perspective is introduced if we go back to our first scenario but now introduce a third contender, Sony, with payoffs of $90 and $150, as seen in Table 2-6.

Sony is dominated by both IBM and Royal Dutch—but the choice between the latter two can now be described in terms of an improvement of $10 over the Sony payoff, either in state 1 or in state 2. Which is better? The relevant feature is that IBM adds $10 when the payoff is low ($90) while Royal Dutch adds the same amount when the payoff is high ($150). Most people would think IBM more desirable, and with equal state probabilities, would prefer IBM. Once again this is an illustration of the preference for smooth consumption (smoother income allows for smoother consumption).[5] In the present context one may equivalently speak of risk aversion or of the well-known microeconomic assumption of decreasing marginal utility.

TABLE 2-5 Forecasted Price per Share in One Period

	State 1	State 2
IBM	$100	$90
Royal Dutch	$150	$200

Current Price of both assets is $100

TABLE 2-6 Forecasted Price per Share in One Period

	State 1	State 2
IBM	$100	$150
Royal Dutch	$90	$160
Sony	$90	$150

Current Price of all assets is $100

[5]Of course, for the sake of our reasoning, one must assume that nothing else important is going on simultaneously in the background, and that other things such as income from other sources, if any, and the prices of the consumption goods to be purchased with the assets' payoffs are not tied to what the payoffs actually are.

The expected utility theorem provides a set of hypotheses under which an investor's preference ranking of investments with uncertain money payoffs may be represented by a utility index combining, in the most elementary way (i.e., linearly), the two ingredients just discussed—the preference ordering on the *ex post* payoffs and the respective probabilities of these payoffs.

We first illustrate this notion in the context of the two assets considered earlier. Let the respective probability distributions on the price per share of IBM and Royal Dutch (RDP) be described, respectively, by $\tilde{p}_{\text{IBM}} = p_{\text{IBM}}(\theta_i)$ and $\tilde{p}_{\text{RDP}} = p_{\text{RDP}}(\theta_i)$ together with the probability π_i that the state of nature θ_i will be realized. In this case the expected utility theorem provides sufficient conditions on an agent's preferences over uncertain asset payoffs, denoted $\succeq$, such that

$$\tilde{p}_{\text{IBM}} \succeq \tilde{p}_{\text{RDP}}$$

if and only if there exists a real valued function U for which

$$EU(\tilde{p}_{\text{IBM}}) = \pi_1 U(p_{\text{IBM}}(\theta_1)) + \pi_2 U(p_{\text{IBM}}(\theta_2)) \geq \pi_1 U(p_{\text{RDP}}(\theta_1)) + \pi_2 U(p_{\text{RDP}}(\theta_2))$$
$$= EU(\tilde{p}_{\text{RDP}})$$

More generally, the utility of any asset A with payoffs $p_A(\theta_1), p_A(\theta_2), \ldots, p_A(\theta_N)$ in the N possible states of nature with probabilities $\pi_1, \pi_2, \ldots, \pi_N$ can be represented by

$$\mathcal{U}(A) = EU(p_A(\theta_i)) = \sum_{i=1}^{N} \pi_i U(p_A(\theta_i))$$

in other words, by the weighted mean of *ex post* utilities with the state probabilities as weights. $\mathcal{U}(A)$ is a real number. Its precise numerical value, however, has no more meaning than if you are told that the temperature is 40 degrees when you do not know if the scale being used is Celsius or Fahrenheit. It is useful, however, for comparison purposes. By analogy, if it is 40° today, but it will be 45° tomorrow, you at least know it will be warmer tomorrow than it is today. Similarly, the expected utility number is useful because it permits attaching a number to a probability distribution and this number is, under appropriate hypotheses, a good representation of the relative ranking of a particular member of a family of probability distributions (assets under consideration).

2.5   THE EXPECTED UTILITY THEOREM

Let us discuss this theorem in the simple context where objects of choice take the form of simple lotteries. The generic lottery is denoted (x, y, π); it offers payoff (consequence) x with probability π and payoff (consequence) y with probability $1 - \pi$. This notion of a lottery is actually very general and encompasses a huge variety of possible payoff structures. For example, x and y may represent specific monetary payoffs,

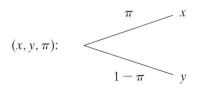

or x may be a payment, y a lottery

$$(x, y, \pi) = (x, (y_1, y_2, \tau_1), \pi):$$

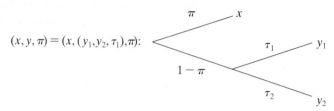

or x and y may both be lotteries,

$$(x, y, \pi) = ((x_1, x_2, \tau_1), (y_1, y_2, \tau_2), \pi):$$

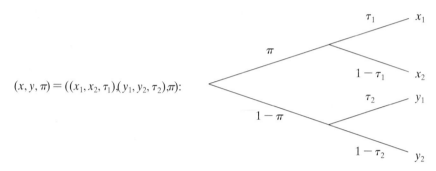

where $\{x_1, x_2, y_1, y_2\}$ are all monetary payoffs. Extending these possibilities, some or all of the x_i's and y_i's may be lotteries, etc. We also extend our choice domain to include individual payments, lotteries where one of the possible monetary payoffs is certain; for instance,

$$(x, y, \pi) = x \text{ if (and only if) } \pi = 1 \text{ (see axiom C.1).}$$

Moreover, the theorem holds as well for assets paying a continuum of possible payoffs, but our restriction makes the necessary assumptions and justifying arguments easily accessible. Our objective is a conceptual transparency rather than absolute generality. All the results extend to much more general settings.

Under these representations, we will adopt the following **axioms and conventions:**

C.1 a. $(x, y, 1) = x$

   b. $(x, y, \pi) = (y, x, 1 - \pi)$

   c. $(x, z, \pi) = (x, y, \pi + (1 - \pi)\tau)$ if $z = (x, y, \tau)$

Note that C.1c informs us that agents are concerned with the net cumulative probability of each outcome. Indirectly, it further accommodates lotteries with multiple outcomes; for example,

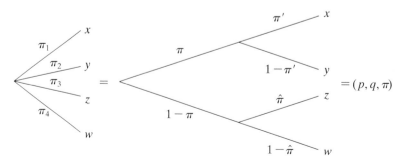

where $p = (x, y, \pi')$, and $q = (z, w, \hat{\pi})$, and $\pi = \pi_1 + \pi_2$, $\pi' = \dfrac{\pi_1}{\pi_1 + \pi_2}$, etc.

C.2 There exists a preference relation $\geq$, defined on lotteries, which is complete and transitive.

C.3 The preference relation is continuous in the sense of A.4 in the earlier section. By C.2 and C.3 alone we know (Theorem 2.1) that there exists a utility function, which we will denote by $\mathcal{U}(\ )$, defined both on lotteries and on specific payments since, by assumption C.1a, a payment may be viewed as a (degenerate) lottery. For any fixed payment x, we will write $U(x) = \mathcal{U}((x, y, 1))$. Our remaining assumptions are thus necessary only to guarantee that this function assumes the expected utility form.

C.4 Independence of irrelevant alternatives. Let (x, y, π) and (x, z, π) be any two lotteries; then, $y \geq z$ if and only if $(x, y, \pi) \geq (x, z, \pi)$.

C.5 For simplicity, we also assume that there exists a best (i.e., most preferred lottery), b, as well as a worst, least desirable, lottery w.

In our argument to follow (which is constructive, i.e., we explicitly define the expected utility function), it is convenient to use relationships that follow directly from these latter two assumptions. In particular, we'll use C.6 and C.7:

C.6 Let x, k, z be consequences or payoffs for which $x > k > z$. Then there exists a π such that $(x, z, \pi) \sim k$.

C.7 Let $x > y$. Then $(x, y, \pi_1) \geq (x, y, \pi_2)$ if and only if $\pi_1 > \pi_2$. This follows directly from C.4.

Theorem 2.2:
If axioms C.1 to C.5 are satisfied, then there exists a function $\mathcal{U}$ defined on the lottery space so that:

$$\mathcal{U}((x, y, \pi)) = \pi U(x) + (1 - \pi)U(y)$$

Proof:
We outline the proof in a number of steps:

1. Without loss of generality, we may normalize $\mathcal{U}(\ )$ so that $\mathcal{U}(b) = 1$, $\mathcal{U}(w) = 0$.
2. For all other lotteries z, define $\mathcal{U}(z) = \pi_z$ where π_z satisfies

$$(b, w, \pi_z) \sim z$$

Constructed in this way $\mathcal{U}(z)$ is well defined since,
   a. by C.6, $\mathcal{U}(z) = \pi_z$ exists, and
   b. by C.7, $\mathcal{U}(z)$ is unique. To see this latter implication, assume, to the contrary, that $\mathcal{U}(z) = \pi_z$ and also $\mathcal{U}(z) = \pi_z'$ where $\pi_z > \pi_z'$. By assumption C.4,

$$z \sim (b, w, \pi_z) > (b, w, \pi_z') \sim z; \text{ a contradiction.}$$

3. It follows also from C.7 that if $m > n$, $\mathcal{U}(m) = \pi_m > \pi_n = \mathcal{U}(n)$. Thus, $\mathcal{U}(\ )$ has the property of a utility function.

(continued)

Theorem 2.2 (*continued*)

4. Lastly, we want to show that $\mathcal{U}(\ )$ has the required property.

Let x, y be monetary payments, π a probability.

By C.1a, $U(x), U(y)$ are well-defined real numbers.

By C.6, $(x, y, \pi) \sim ((b, w, \pi_x), (b, w, \pi_y)), \pi)$

$\sim (b, w, \pi\pi_x + (1 - \pi)\pi_y)$, by C.1c.

Thus, by definition of $\mathcal{U}(\ )$,

$$\mathcal{U}((x, y, \pi)) = \pi\pi_x + (1 - \pi)\pi_y = \pi U(x) + (1 - \pi)U(y)$$

Although we have chosen x, y as monetary payments, the same conclusion holds if they are lotteries.

Before going on to a more careful examination of the assumptions underlying the expected utility theorem, a number of clarifying thoughts are in order. First, the overall Von-Neumann Morgenstern (VNM) utility function $\mathcal{U}(\ )$ defined over lotteries, is so named after the originators of the theory, the justly celebrated mathematicians John von Neumann and Oskar Morgenstern. In the construction of a VNM utility function, it is customary first to specify its restriction to certainty monetary payments, the so-called utility of money function or simply the *utility function*. Note that the VNM utility function and its associated utility of money function are, formally, not the same. The former is defined over uncertain asset payoff structures while the latter is defined over individual monetary payments.

Given the objective specification of probabilities (thus far assumed), it is the utility function that uniquely characterizes an investor. As we will see shortly, different additional assumptions on $U(\ )$ will identify an investor's tolerance for risk. We do, however, impose the maintained requirement that $U(\ )$ be increasing for all candidate utility functions (more money is preferred to less). Second, note also that the expected utility theorem confirms that investors are concerned only with an asset's final payoffs and the cumulative probabilities of achieving them. For expected utility investors the structure of uncertainty resolution is irrelevant (Axiom C.1a).[6]

Third, although the introduction to this chapter concentrates on comparing rates of return distributions, our expected utility theorem in fact gives us a tool for comparing different asset payoff distributions. Without further analysis, it does not make sense to think of the utility function as being defined over a rate of return. This is true for a number of reasons. First, returns are expressed on a per unit (per dollar, Swiss Francs (SF) etc.) basis, and do not identify the magnitude of the initial investment to which these rates are to be applied. We thus have no way to assess the implications of a return distribution for an investor's wealth position. It could, in principle, be anything. Second, the notion of a rate of return implicitly suggests a time interval: The payout is received after the asset is purchased. So far we have only considered the atemporal evaluation of uncertain investment payoffs. In Chapter 4, we generalize the VNM representation to preferences defined over rates of returns.

Finally, as in the case of a general preference ordering over bundles of commodities, the VNM representation is preserved under a certain class of linear transforma-

---

[6]See Section 2.7 for a generalization on this score.

tions. If $\mathcal{U}(.)$ is a Von-Neuman-Morgenstern utility function, then $\mathcal{V}(.) = a\,\mathcal{U}(.) + b$ where $a > 0$, is also such a function. Let (x, y, π) be some uncertain payoff and let $U(\ )$ be the utility of money function associated with $\mathcal{U}$.

$$\mathcal{V}((x, y, \pi)) = a\mathcal{U}((x, y, \pi)) + b$$
$$= a[\pi U(x) + (1 - \pi)U(y)] + b$$
$$= \pi[a\mathcal{U}(x) + b] + (1 - \pi)[a\mathcal{U}(y) + b]$$
$$\equiv \pi\mathcal{V}(x) + (1 - \pi)\mathcal{V}(y)$$

Every linear transformation of an expected utility function is thus also an expected utility function. The utility of money function associated with $\mathcal{V}$ is $[aU(\ ) + b]$; $\mathcal{V}(\ )$ represents the same preference ordering over uncertain payoffs as $\mathcal{U}(\ )$. On the other hand, a nonlinear transformation doesn't always respect the preference ordering. It is in that sense that utility is said to be **cardinal** (see Exercise 2.1 on p. 302).

2.6 HOW RESTRICTIVE IS EXPECTED UTILITY THEORY? THE ALLAIS PARADOX

Although apparently innocuous, the above set of axioms has been hotly contested as representative of rationality. In particular, it is not difficult to find situations in which investor preferences violate the independence axiom. Consider the following four possible asset payoffs (lotteries):

$$L^1 = (10{,}000, 0, 0.1) \quad L^2 = (15{,}000, 0, 0.09)$$
$$L^3 = (10{,}000, 0, 1) \quad\;\; L^4 = (15{,}000, 0, 0.9)$$

When investors are asked to rank these payoffs, the following ranking is frequently observed:

$$L^2 > L^1$$

L^2's positive payoff in the favorable state is much greater than L^1's, and the likelihood of receiving it only slightly less, and,

$$L^3 > L^4$$

the certainty prospect of receiving 10,000 is worth more than the potential of an additional 5,000, at the risk of receiving nothing.

By the structure of compound lotteries it is also easy to see that:

$$L^1 = (L^3, L^0; 0.1)$$
$$L^2 = (L^4, L^0; 0.1) \text{ with } L^0 = (0, 0, 1)$$

By the independence axiom, the ranking between L^1 and L^2 on the one hand, and L^3 and L^4 on the other, should thus be identical.

This is the Allais (1964) Paradox and there are a number of likely reactions to it.

1. Yes, my choices were inconsistent; let me think again and revise them.
2. No, I'll stick to my choices. The following kinds of considerations are missing from the theory of choice expressed solely in terms of asset payoffs:
   • the pleasure of gambling, and/or
   • the notion of regret.

The idea of regret is especially relevant to the Allais paradox, and its application in the prior example would go something like this. L^3 is preferred to L^4 because of the regret involved in receiving nothing if L^4 were chosen and the bad state ensued. We would, at that point, regret not having chosen L^3, the certain payment. The expected regret is high because of the nontrivial probability (.10) of receiving nothing under L^4. On the other hand, the expected regret of choosing L^2 over L^1 is much smaller (the probability of the bad state is only .01 greater under L^2 and in either case the probability of success is small), and insufficient to offset the greater expected payoff. Thus L^2 is preferred to L^1.

The Allais paradox is but the first of many phenomena that appear to be inconsistent with standard preference theory. Another prominent example is the general pervasiveness of *preference reversals,* events that may approximately be described as follows. Individuals, participating in controlled experiments were asked to choose between two lotteries, $(4, 0, .9)$ and $(40, 0, .10)$. More than 70 percent typically chose $(4, 0, .9)$. When asked at what price they would be willing to sell the lotteries if they were to own them, however, a similar percentage demanded the higher price for $(40, 0, .10)$. At first appearances, these choices would seem to violate transitivity. Let x, y be, respectively, the sale prices of $(4, 0, .9)$ and $(40, 0, .10)$. Then this phenomenon implies

$$x \sim (4, 0, .9) > (40, 0, .10) \sim y, \text{ yet } y > x.$$

Alternatively, it may reflect a violation of the assumed principle of procedure invariance, which is the idea that investors' preference for different objects should be in-

---

BOX 2-3

On the Rationality of Collective Decision Making

Although the discussion in the text pertains to the rationality of individual choices, it is a fact that many important decisions are the result of collective decision making. The limitations to the rationality of such a process are important and, in fact, better understood than those arising at the individual level. It is easy to imagine situations in which transitivity is violated once choices result from some sort of aggregation over more basic preferences.

Consider three portfolio managers who decide which stocks to add to the portfolios they manage by majority voting. The stocks currently under consideration are General Electric (GE), Daimler-Chrysler (DC), and Sony (S). Based on his fundamental research and assumptions, each manager has rational (i.e., transitive) preferences over the three possibilities:

Manager 1:   GE $\geq_1$ DC $\geq_1$ S
Manager 2:   S $\geq_2$ GE $\geq_2$ DC
Manager 3:   DC $\geq_3$ S $\geq_3$ GE

If they were to vote all at once, they know each stock would receive one vote (each stock has its advocate). So they decide to vote on pair-wise choices: (GE vs. DB), (DB vs. S), and (S vs. GE). The results of this voting (GE dominates DB, DB dominates S, and S dominates GE) suggest an intransitivity in the aggregate ordering. Although this example illustrates an intransitivity, it is an intransitivity that arises from the operation of a collective choice mechanism (voting) rather than being present in the individual orders of preference of the participating agents. There is a great deal of literature on this subject that is closely identified with Arrow's "Impossibility Theorem." See Arrow (1963) for a more exhaustive discussion.

different to the manner by which their preference is elicited. Surprisingly, more narrowly focused experiments, which were designed to force a subject with expected utility preferences to behave consistently, gave rise to the same reversals. The preference reversal phenomenon could thus, in principle, be due either to preference intransitivity, or to a violation of the independence axiom, or of procedure invariance.

Various researchers who, through a series of carefully constructed experiments, have attempted to assign the blame for preference reversals lay the responsibility largely at the feet of procedure invariance violations. But this is a particularly alarming conclusion as Thaler (1992) notes. It suggests that "the context and procedures involved in making choices or judgements influence the preferences that are implied by the elicited responses. In practical terms this implies that (economic) behavior is likely to vary across situations which economists (would otherwise) consider identical." This is tantamount to the assertion that the notion of a preference ordering is not well defined. While investors may be able to express a consistent (and thus mathematically representable) preference ordering across television sets with different features (e.g., size of the screen, quality of the sound, etc.), this may not be possible with lotteries or consumption baskets containing widely diverse goods.

Grether and Plott (1979) summarize this conflict in the starkest possible terms: "Taken at face value, the data demonstrating preference reversals are simply inconsistent with preference theory and have broad implications about research priorities within economics. The inconsistency is deeper than the mere lack of transitivity or even stochastic transitivity. It suggests that no optimization principles of any sort lie behind the simplest of human choices and that the uniformities in human choice behavior that lie behind market behavior result from principles that are of a completely different sort from those generally accepted."

At this point it is useful to remember, however, that the goal of economics and finance is not to describe individual, but rather market, behavior. There is a real possibility that occurrences of individual irrationality essentially "wash out" when aggregated at the market level. On this score, the proof of the pudding is in the eating and we have little alternative but to see the extent to which the basic theory of choice we are using is able to illuminate financial phenomena of interest. All the while, the discussion above should make us alert to the possibility that unusual phenomena might be the outcome of deviations from the generally accepted preference theory articulated above. While there is, to date, no preference ordering that accommodates preference reversals—and it is not clear there will ever be one—more general constructs than expected utility have been formulated to admit other, seemingly contradictory, phenomena.

2.7 GENERALIZING THE VNM EXPECTED UTILITY REPRESENTATION

Objections to the assumptions underlying the VNM expected utility representation have stimulated the development of a number of alternatives, which we will somewhat crudely aggregate under the title *non-expected utility theory*. Elements of this theory differ with regard to which fundamental postulate of expected utility is relaxed. We consider four. See Machina (1987) for a more systematic survey.

2.7.1 PREFERENCE FOR THE TIMING OF UNCERTAINTY RESOLUTION

To grasp the idea here we must go beyond our current one period setting. Under the VNM expected utility representation, investors are assumed to be concerned only with actual payoffs and the cumulative probabilities of attaining them. In particular, they are assumed to be indifferent to the timing of uncertainty resolution. To get a better idea of what this means, consider the following two investment payoff trees, to be evaluated from the viewpoint of date 0 (today):

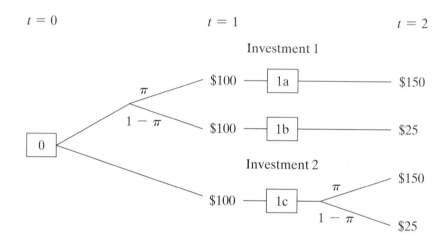

Under the expected utility postulates, these two payoff structures would be valued (in utility terms) identically as

$$EU(\tilde{P}) = U(100) + [\pi U(150) + (1 - \pi)U(25)]$$

This means that a VNM investor would not care if the uncertainty were resolved in period 0 (immediately) or one period later. Yet, people are, in fact, very different in this regard. Some want to know the outcome of an uncertain event as soon as possible; others prefer to postpone it as long as possible.

Kreps and Porteus (1978) were the first to develop a theory that allowed for these distinctions. They showed that if investor preferences over uncertain sequential payoffs were of the form

$$U_0(P_1, P_2(\tilde{\theta})) = W(P_1, E(U_1(P_1, P_2(\tilde{\theta}))))$$

then investors would prefer early (late) resolution of uncertainty according to whether $W(P_1,.)$ is convex (concave) (loosely, whether $W_{22} > 0$ or $W_{22} < 0$). In the above representation P_i is the payoff in period $i = 1, 2$. If $W(P_1,.)$ were concave, for example, the expected utility of investment 1 would be lower than investment 2.

The idea can be easily illustrated in the context of the example above. We assume functional forms similar to those used in an illustration of Kreps and Porteus (1978); in particular, assume $W(P_1, EU) = EU^{1.5}$, and $U_1(P_1, P_2(\tilde{\theta})) = (P_1 + P_2(\tilde{\theta}))^{1/2}$. Let $\pi = .5$, and note that the overall composite function $U_0(\ )$ is concave in all of its arguments. In computing utilities at the decision nodes $\boxed{0}$, $\boxed{1a}$, $\boxed{1b}$, and $\boxed{1c}$ (the latter decisions are trivial ones), we must be especially scrupulous to observe exactly the dates at which the uncertainty is resolved under the two alternatives:

$\boxed{1a}$: $EU_1^{1a}(P_1, P_2(\theta)) = (100 + 150)^{1/2} = 15.811$
$\boxed{1b}$: $EU_1^{1b}(P_1, P_2(\theta)) = (100 + 25)^{1/2} = 11.18$
$\boxed{1c}$: $EU_1^{1c}(P_1, P_2(\theta)) = .5(100 + 150)^{1/2} + .5(100 + 25)^{1/2} = 13.4955$

At $t = 0$, the expected utility on the upper branch is

$$EU_0^{1a,1b}(P_1, P_2(\tilde{\theta})) = EW^{1a,1b}(P_1, P_2(\tilde{\theta}))$$
$$= .5W(100, 15.811) + .5W(100, 11.18)$$
$$= .5(15.811)^{1.5} + .5(11.18)^{1.5}$$
$$= 50.13,$$

while on the lower branch

$$EU_0^{1c}(P_1, P_2(\tilde{\theta})) = W(100, 13.4955) = (13.4955)^{1.5} = 49.57.$$

This investor clearly prefers early resolution of uncertainty which is consistent with the convexity of the $W(\ )$ function. Note that the result of the example is simply an application of Jensen's inequality.[7] If $W(\ )$ were concave the ordering would be reversed.

There have been numerous specializations of this idea, some of which we consider in Chapter 4 (See Weil (1990) and Epstein and Zin (1989)). At the moment it is sufficient to point out that such representations are not consistent with the VNM axioms.

2.7.2 PREFERENCES THAT GUARANTEE TIME-CONSISTENT PLANNING

Our setting is once again intertemporal, where uncertainty is resolved in each future time period. Suppose that at each date $t \in \{0, 1, 2, \ldots, T\}$, an agent has a preference ordering $\geq_t$ defined over all future (state-contingent) consumption bundles, where $\geq_t$ will typically depend on her past consumption history. The notion of *time-consistent planning* is this: if, at each date, the agent could plan against any future contingency, what is the required relationship among the family of orderings $\{\geq_t : t = 0, 1, 2, \ldots, T\}$ that will cause plans which were optimal with respect to preferences $\geq_0$ to remain optimal in all future time periods given all that has happened in the interim (i.e., intermediate consumption experiences and the specific way uncertainty has evolved)? In particular, what utility function representation will guarantee this property?

When considering decision problems over time, such as portfolio investments over a multiperiod horizon, time consistency seems to be a natural property to insist on. In its absence, one would observe portfolio rebalancing not motivated by any outside event or information flow, but simply resulting from the inconsistency of the date t preference ordering of the investor compared with the preferences on which her original

---

[7]Let $a = (100 + 150)^{1/2}$, $b = (100 + 25)^{1/2}$, $g(x) = x^{1.5}$ (convex),

$$EU_0^{1a,1b}(P_1, \tilde{P}_2(\theta)) = Eg(x) > g(Ex) = EU_0^{1c}(P_1, \tilde{P}_2(\theta)) \text{ where } \tilde{x} = \begin{cases} a, \text{ prob} & .5 \\ b, \text{ prob} & .5 \end{cases}.$$

portfolio positions were taken. Asset trades would then be fully motivated by endogenous and unobservable preference issues and would thus be basically unexplainable.

To see what it takes for a utility function to be time consistent, let us consider two periods where at date 1 any one of $s \in S$ possible states of nature may be realized. Let c_0 denote a possible consumption level at date 0, and let $c_1(s)$ denote a possible consumption level in period 1 if state "s" occurs. Johnsen and Donaldson (1985) demonstrate that if initial preferences $\succeq_0$, with utility representation $U(\ )$, are to guarantee time-consistent planning, there must exist continuous and monotone increasing function $f(\ )$ and $\{U_s(.,.) : s \in S\}$ such that:

$$U(c_0, c_1(s) : s \in S) = f(c_0, U_s(c_0, c_1(s) : s \in S), \tag{2.1}$$

where $U_s(.,.)$ is the state s contingent utility function.

This result means the utility function must be of a form such that the utility representations in future states can be recursively nested as individual arguments of the overall utility function. This condition is satisfied by the VNM expected utility form,

$$U(c_0, c_1(s) : s \in S) = U_0(c_0) + \sum_s \pi_s U(c_1(s)),$$

which clearly is of a form satisfying Equation (2.1). The VNM utility representation is thus time consistent, but the latter property can also accommodate more general utility functions. To see this, consider the following special case of Equation (2.1), where there are three possible states at $t = 1$:

$$U(c_0, c_1(1), c_1(2), c_1(3)) =$$
$$\{c_0 + \pi_1 U_1(c_0, c_1(1)) + [\pi_2 U_2(c_0, c_1(2))]^{1/3} \pi_3 U_3(c_0, c_1(3))\}^{1/2} \tag{2.2}$$

where $\quad U_1(c_0, c_1(1)) = \log(c_0, c_1(1)),$
$\qquad U_2(c_0, c_1(2)) = c_0^{1/2}(c_1(2))^{1/2}$, and
$\qquad U_3(c_0, c_1(3)) = c_0 c_1(3).$

In this example, preferences are not linear in the probabilities and thus not of the VNM expected utility type. Nevertheless, Equation (2.2) is of the form of Equation (2.1). It also has the feature that preferences in any future state are independent of irrelevant alternatives, where the irrelevant alternatives are those consumption plans for states that do not occur. As such, agents with these preferences will never experience regret and the Allais Paradox will not be operational.

Consistency of choices seems to make sense and turns out to be important for much financial modeling, but is it borne out empirically? Unfortunately, the answer is: frequently not. A simple illustration of this is a typical pure-time preference experiment from the psychology literature (uncertainty in future states is not even needed). Participants are asked to choose among the following monetary prizes:[8]

Question 1: Would you prefer $100 today or $200 in 2 years?
Question 2: Would you prefer $100 in 6 years or $200 in 8 years?

Respondents often prefer the $100 in question 1 and the $200 in question 2, not realizing that question 2 involves the same choice as question 1 but with a 6-year delay. If these people are true to their answers, they will be time inconsistent. In the case of ques-

---

[8]See Ainslie and Haslan (1992) for details.

tion 2, although they state their preference now for the $200 prize in 8 years, when year 6 arrives they will take the $100 and run!

2.7.3   PREFERENCES DEFINED OVER OUTCOMES OTHER THAN FUNDAMENTAL PAYOFFS

Under the VNM expected utility theory, the utility function is defined over actual payoff outcomes. Tversky and Kahneman (1992) and Kahneman and Tversky (1979) propose formulations whereby preferences are defined, not over actual payoffs, but rather over gains and losses relative to some benchmark, so that losses are given the greater utility weight. The benchmark can be thought of as either a minimally acceptable payment or, under the proper transformations, a cutoff rate of return. It can be changing through time reflecting prior experience. Their development is called *prospect theory*.

A simple illustration of this sort of representation is as follows: Let $\bar{Y}$ denote the benchmark payoff, and define the investor's utility function $U(Y)$ by

$$
U(Y) = \begin{cases} \dfrac{(|Y - \bar{Y}|)^{1-\gamma_1}}{1 - \gamma_1}, \text{if } Y \geq \bar{Y} \\[2ex] \dfrac{-\lambda(|Y - \bar{Y}|)^{1-\gamma_2}}{1 - \gamma_2}, \text{if } Y \leq \bar{Y}. \end{cases}
$$

where $\lambda > 1$ captures the extent of the investor's aversion to "losses" relative to the benchmark, and γ_1 and γ_2 need not coincide. In other words, the curvature of the function may differ for deviations above or below the benchmark. Clearly both features could have a large impact on the relative ranking of uncertain investment payoff. See Figure 2-1 for

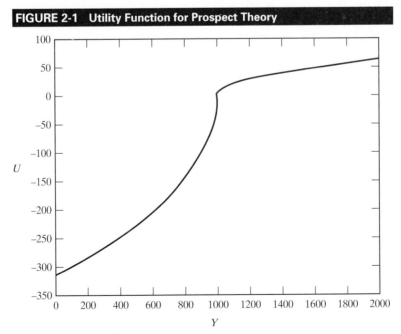

FIGURE 2-1   Utility Function for Prospect Theory

Parameter values: $\bar{Y} = 1000; \gamma_1 = \gamma_2 = 0.5, \lambda = 5$

an illustration. Not all economic transactions (e.g., the normal purchase or sale of commodities), are affected by loss aversion since, in normal circumstances, one does not suffer a loss in trading a good. An investor's willingness to hold stocks, however, may be significantly affected if he has experienced losses in prior periods. We return to the significance of loss aversion in a subsequent chapter.

2.7.4   NONLINEAR PROBABILITY WEIGHTS

Under the VNM representation, the utility outcomes are linear weighted by their respective probability of outcome. Under prospect theory and its close relatives, this need not be the case: outcomes can be weighted using nonlinear functions of the probabilities and may be asymmetric. More general theories of investor psychology replace the objective mathematical expectation operator entirely with a model of subjective expectation. See Barberis et al. (1998) for an illustration.

2.8   CONCLUSIONS

The expected utility theory is the workhorse of choice theory under uncertainty. It will be put to use almost systematically in this book as it is in most of financial theory. We have argued in this chapter that the expected utility construct provides a straightforward, intuitive mechanism for comparing uncertain asset payoff structures. As such, it offers a well-defined procedure for ranking the assets themselves.

Two ingredients are necessary for this process:

1. An estimate of the probability distribution governing the asset's uncertain payments. While is not trivial to estimate this quantity, it must also be estimated for the much simpler and less flexible mean/variance criterion.
2. An estimate of the agent's utility of money function; it is the latter that fully characterizes his preference ordering. How this can be identified is one of the topics of the next chapter.

References

Ainslie, G., and N. Haslan, "Hyperbolic Discounting," in *Choice over Time*, eds. G. Lowenstein and J. Elster, New York: Russell Sage Foundation, 1992.

Allais, M., "Le comportement de l'homme rationnel devant le risque: Critique des postulats de l'école Américaine," *Econometrica*, 21 (1964), 503–546.

Arrow, K. J., *Social Choice and Individual Values*, New Haven, Conn.: Yale University Press, 1963.

Barberis, N., A. Schleifer, and R. Vishny. "A Model of Investor Sentiment," *Journal of Financial Economics*, 49 (1998), 307–343.

Epstein, L., and S. Zin, "Substitution, Risk Aversion, and the Temporal Behavior of Consumption and Asset Returns: A Theoretical Framework," *Econometrica*, 57 (1989): 937–969.

Grether, D., and C. Plott, "Economic Theory of Choice and the Preference Reversal Phenomenon," *American Economic Review*, 75 (1979): 623–638.

Huberman, G., "Familiarity Breeds Investment," Working Paper, Columbia Business School, 1997. Forthcoming, *Review of Financial Studies*.

Johnsen, T., and J. B. Donaldson, "The Structure of Intertemporal Preferences Under Uncertainty and Time Consistent Plans," *Econometrica* 53 (1985): 1451–1458.

Kahneman, D., and A. Tversky, "Prospect Theory: An Analysis of Decision Under Risk," *Econometrica* 47 (1979): 263–291.

Kreps, D., and E. Porteus, "Temporal Resolution of Uncertainty and Dynamic Choice Theory," *Econometrica* 461 (1978): 185–200.

Machina, M., "Choice Under Uncertainty: Problems Solved and Unsolved," *Journal of Economic Perspectives* 1 (1987): 121–154.

Mas-Colell, A., M. D. Whinston, and J. R. Green, *Microeconomic Theory,* Oxford: Oxford University Press, 1995.

Thaler, R. H., *The Winner's Curse*, Princeton, N.J.: Princeton University Press, 1992.

Tversky, A., and D. Kahneman, "Advances in Prospect Theory: Cumulative Representation of Uncertainty," *Journal of Risk and Uncertainty* 5 (1992): 297–323.

Weil, P., "Nonexpected Utility in Macroeconomics," *Quarterly Journal of Economics* 105 (1990): 29–42.

CHAPTER 3

MEASURING RISK AND RISK AVERSION

3.1   INTRODUCTION

We argued in Chapter 1 that the desire of investors to avoid risk, that is variations in the value of their portfolio holdings or to smooth their consumption across states of nature, is one of the primary motivations for financial contracting. But we have not thus far imposed restrictions on the VNM expected utility representation of investor preferences, which necessarily guarantee such behavior. For that to be the case, our representation must be further specialized.

Since the probabilities of the various state payoffs are objectively given, independently of agent preferences, further restrictions must be placed on the utility-of-money function $U(\ )$ if the VNM representation is to capture this notion of risk aversion. We will now define risk aversion and discuss its implications for $U(\ )$.

3.2   MEASURING RISK AVERSION

What does the term risk aversion imply about an agent's utility function? Consider a financial contract where the potential investor either receives an amount h with probability $\frac{1}{2}$, or must pay an amount h with probability $\frac{1}{2}$. Our most basic sense of risk aversion must imply that for any level of personal wealth Y, a risk-averse investor would not wish to own such a security. In utility terms this must mean

$$U(Y) > \tfrac{1}{2}U(Y + h) + \tfrac{1}{2}U(Y - h) = EU,$$

where the expression on the right-hand side of the inequality sign is the VNM expected utility associated with the random wealth levels

$$y + h, \text{probability} = \tfrac{1}{2}$$
$$y - h, \text{probability} = \tfrac{1}{2}.$$

This inequality can only be satisfied for all wealth levels Y if the agent's utility function has the form suggested in Figure 3-1. If this is the case we say the utility function is strictly concave.

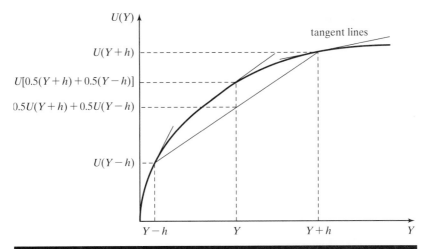

FIGURE 3-1   A Strictly Concave Utility Function

The important characteristics implied by this and similarly shaped utility functions is that the slope of the function decreases as the agent becomes wealthier (as Y increases); that is, the marginal utility (MU), represented by the derivative $d(U(Y))/d(Y) = U'(Y)$, decreases with greater Y. Equivalently, for twice differentiable utility functions, $d^2(U(Y))/d(Y)^2 = U''(Y) < 0$. For this class of functions, the latter is indeed a necessary and sufficient condition for risk aversion.

As the discussion indicates, both consumption smoothing and risk aversion are directly related to the notion of decreasing MU. Whether they are envisaged across time or states, decreasing MU basically implies that income (or consumption) deviations from a fixed average level diminish rather than increase utility. This is because the positive deviations do not help as much as the negative ones hurt.

Risk aversion can also be represented in terms of indifference curves. Figure 3-2 illustrates the case of a simple situation with two states of nature. If consuming c_1 in state 1 and c_2 in state 2 represents a certain level of expected utility EU, then the convex-to-the-origin indifference curve that is the appropriate translation of a strictly concave utility function indeed implies that the utility level generated by the average consumption $(c_1 + c_2)/2$ in both states (in this case a "certain" consumption level) is larger than EU.

We would like to be able to measure the degree of an investor's aversion to risk. This will allow us to compare whether one investor is more risk averse than another and to understand how an investor's risk aversion affects his investment behavior (for example, the composition of his portfolio).

As a first attempt at this goal, and since $U''(\ ) < 0$ implies risk aversion, why not simply say that investor A is more risk averse than investor B, if and only if $|U_A''(Y)| \geq |U_B''(Y)|$, for all income levels Y? Unfortunately, this approach leads to the following inconsistency. Recall that the preference ordering described by a utility function is invariant to linear transformations. In other words, suppose $U_A(\ )$ and $\bar{U}_A(\ )$ are such that $\bar{U}_A(\ ) = a + bU_A(\ )$ with $b > 0$. These utility functions describe the identical ordering, and thus must display identical risk aversion. Yet, if we use the previous measure we have

$$|\bar{U}_A''(Y)| > |U_A''(Y)|, \text{ if, say, } b > 1.$$

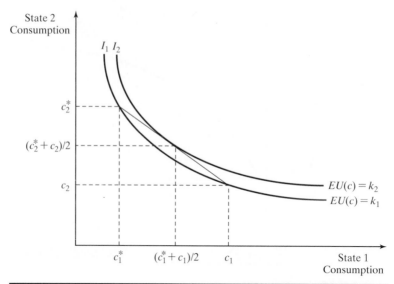

FIGURE 3-2 Indifference Curves

This implies that investor A is more risk averse than he is, himself, which must be a contradiction.

We therefore need a measure of risk aversion that is invariant to linear transformations. Two widely used measures of this sort have been proposed by Pratt (1964) and Arrow (1971):

(i) absolute risk aversion $= -\dfrac{U''(Y)}{U'(Y)} \equiv R_A(Y)$

(ii) relative risk aversion $= -\dfrac{YU''(Y)}{U'(Y)} \equiv R_R(Y)$.

Both of these measures have simple behavioral interpretations. Note that instead of talking of risk aversion, we could use the inverse of the measures just proposed and speak of risk tolerance. This terminology may be preferable on various occasions.

3.3 INTERPRETING THE MEASURES OF RISK AVERSION

3.3.1 ABSOLUTE RISK AVERSION AND THE ODDS OF A BET

Consider an investor with wealth level Y who is offered—at no charge—an investment involving winning or losing an amount h, with probabilities π and $1 - \pi$, respectively. Note that any investor will accept such a bet if π is high enough (especially if $\pi = 1$) and reject it if π is small enough (surely if $\pi = 0$). Presumably, the willingness to accept this "opportunity" will also be related to his level of current wealth, Y. Let $\pi = \pi(Y, h)$ be that probability at which the agent is indifferent between accepting or rejecting the investment. It is shown that

$$\pi(Y, h) \cong \frac{1}{2} + \frac{1}{4}hR_A(Y), \tag{3.1}$$

where $\cong$ denotes "is approximately equal to."

The higher his measure of absolute risk aversion, the more favorable odds he will demand in order to be willing to accept the investment. If $R_A^1(Y) \geq R_A^2(Y)$ respectively, for agents 1 and 2, then investor 1 will always demand more favorable odds than investor 2, and in this sense investor 1 is more risk averse.

It is useful to examine the magnitude of this probability. Consider, for example, the family of VNM utility-of-money functions with the form:

$$U(Y) = -\frac{1}{v}e^{-vY} \text{ where } v \text{ is a parameter.}$$

For this case,

$$\pi(Y, h) \cong \frac{1}{2} + \frac{1}{4}hv,$$

in other words, the odds requested are independent of the level of initial wealth (Y); on the other hand, the more wealth at risk (h), the greater the odds of a favorable outcome demanded. This expression advances the parameter v as the natural measure of the degree of absolute risk aversion appropriate to these preferences.

Let us now derive Equation (3.1). By definition, $\pi(Y, h)$ must satisfy

$$\underbrace{U(Y)}_{\substack{\text{utility if he foregoes} \\ \text{the investment}}} = \underbrace{\pi(Y, h)U(Y + h) + [1 - \pi(Y, h)]U(Y - h)}_{\substack{\text{expected utility if the investment} \\ \text{is accepted}}} \tag{3.2}$$

By an approximation (Taylor's Theorem) we know that:

$$U(Y + h) = U(Y) + hU'(Y) + \frac{h^2}{2}U''(Y) + \underbrace{H_1}_{\substack{\text{remainder terms of} \\ \text{order higher than } h^2}}$$

$$U(Y - h) = U(Y) - hU'(Y) + \frac{h^2}{2}U''(Y) + \underbrace{H_2}_{\substack{\text{remainder terms of} \\ \text{order higher than } h^2}}$$

Substituting these quantities into Equation (3.2) gives

$$U(Y) = \pi(Y, h)\left[U(Y) + hU'(Y) + \frac{h^2}{2}U''(Y) + H_1\right]$$
$$+ (1 - \pi(Y, h))\left[U(Y) - hU'(Y) + \frac{h^2}{2}U''(Y) + H_2\right] \tag{3.3}$$

Collecting terms gives

$$U(Y) = U(Y) + (2\pi(Y, h) - 1)hU'(Y)$$
$$+ \frac{h^2}{2}U''(Y) + \underbrace{\pi(Y, h)H_1 + (1 - \pi(Y, h))H_2}_{=_{\text{def}} H \text{ (small)}}$$

Solving for $\pi(Y, h)$ yields

$$\pi(Y, h) = \frac{1}{2} + \frac{h}{2}\left[\frac{-U''(Y)}{U'(Y)}\right] - \frac{H}{2hU'(Y)}, \tag{3.4}$$

which is the promised expression, since the last remainder term is small—it is a weighted average of terms of order higher than h^2 and is, thus, itself of order higher than h^2—and can be ignored in the approximation.

3.3.2 RELATIVE RISK AVERSION IN RELATION TO THE ODDS OF A BET

Consider now an investment opportunity similar to the one just discussed except that the amount at risk is a proportion of the investor's wealth, in other words, $h = \theta Y$, where θ is the fraction of wealth at risk. By a derivation almost identical to the previous one, it can be shown that

$$\pi(Y, \theta) \cong \tfrac{1}{2} + \tfrac{1}{4}\theta R_R(Y). \tag{3.5}$$

If $R_R^1(Y) \geq R_R^2(Y)$, for investors 1 and 2, then investor 1 will always demand more favorable odds, for any level of wealth, when the fraction θ of his wealth is at risk.

It is also useful to illustrate this measure by an example. A popular family of VNM utility-of-money functions (for reasons to be detailed in the next chapter) has the form:

$$U(Y) = \frac{Y^{1-\gamma}}{1 - \gamma}, \text{ if } \gamma > 1$$

$$U(Y) = \ln Y, \text{ if } \gamma = 1.$$

In the latter case, the probability expression becomes

$$\pi(Y, \theta) \cong \tfrac{1}{2} + \tfrac{1}{4}\theta.$$

In this case, the requested odds of winning are not a function of initial wealth (Y) but depend upon θ, the fraction of wealth that is at risk: The lower the fraction θ, the more investors are willing to consider entering into a fair bet (a risky opportunity where the probabilities of success or failure are both $\tfrac{1}{2}$). In the former, more general, case the analogous expression is

$$\pi(Y, \theta) \cong \tfrac{1}{2} + \tfrac{1}{4}\theta\gamma.$$

Since $\gamma > 1$, these investors demand a higher probability of success. Furthermore, if $\gamma_2 > \gamma_1$, the investor characterized by $\gamma = \gamma_2$ will always demand a higher probability of success than will an agent with $\gamma = \gamma_1$, for the same fraction of wealth at risk. In this sense a higher γ denotes a greater degree of risk aversion for this investor class.

3.3.3 RISK NEUTRAL INVESTORS

One class of investors deserves special mention at this point. They are significant, as we shall later see, for the influence they have on the financial equilibria in which they participate. This is the class of investors who are risk neutral and who are identified with utility functions of a linear form

$$U(Y) = cY + d, \text{ where } c \text{ and } d \text{ are constants and } c > 0.$$

Both of our measures of the degree of risk aversion, when applied to this utility function give the same result:

$$R_A(Y) \equiv 0 \text{ and } R_R(Y) \equiv 0.$$

Whether measured as a proportion of wealth or as an absolute amount of money at risk, such investors do not demand better than even odds when considering risky investments of the type under discussion. They are indifferent to risk, and are concerned only with an asset's expected payoff.

3.4 RISK PREMIUM AND CERTAINTY EQUIVALENCE

The context of our discussion thus far has been somewhat artificial because we were seeking especially convenient probabilistic interpretations for our measures of risk aversion. More generally, a risk-averse agent ($U''(\ ) < 0$) will always value an investment at something less than the expected value of its payoffs. Consider an investor, with current wealth Y, evaluating an uncertain risky payoff $\tilde{Z}$. For any distribution function F_z,

$$U(Y + E\tilde{Z}) \geq E[U(Y + \tilde{Z})]$$

provided that $U''(\ ) < 0$. This is a direct consequence of a standard mathematical result known as Jensen's inequality (see Box 3-1).

To put it differently, if an uncertain payoff is available for sale, a risk-averse agent will only be willing to buy it at a price less than its expected payoff. This statement leads to a pair of useful definitions. The (maximal) certain sum of money a person is willing to pay to acquire an uncertain opportunity defines his **certainty equivalent** (*CE*) for that risky prospect; the difference between the *CE* and the expected value of the prospect

---

BOX 3-1

Jensen's Inequality

Theorem 3.1 (Jensen's Inequality):
Let $g(\ )$ be a convex function on the interval (a, b), and $\tilde{x}$ be a random variable such that

$$\text{Prob}\{\tilde{x} \in (a, b)\} = 1.$$

Suppose the expectations $E(\tilde{x})$ and $Eg(\tilde{x})$ exist; then

$$E[g(\tilde{x})] \geq g[E(\tilde{x})].$$

Furthermore, if $g(\ )$ is strictly convex and $\text{Prob}\{\tilde{x} = E(\tilde{x})\} \neq 1$, then the inequality is strict.

This theorem applies whether the interval (a, b) on which $g(\ )$ is defined is finite or infinite and, if a and b are finite, the interval can be open or closed at either endpoint. If $g(\ )$ is concave, the inequality is reversed. See De Groot (1970).

is a measure of the uncertain payoff's **"risk premium."** It represents the maximum amount the agent would be willing to pay to avoid the investment or gamble.

Let us make this notion more precise. The context of the discussion is as follows. Consider an agent with current wealth Y and utility function $U(\ )$ who has the opportunity to acquire an uncertain investment $\tilde{Z}$ with expected value $E\tilde{Z}$. The certainty equivalent, $CE(Y, Z)$, and the risk premium, $\Pi(Y, \tilde{Z})$, are the solutions to the following equations:

$$EU(Y + \tilde{Z}) = U(Y + CE(Y, \tilde{Z})) \tag{3.6}$$
$$= U(Y + E\tilde{Z} - \Pi(Y, \tilde{Z})), \tag{3.7}$$

which, of course, implies

$$CE(\tilde{Z}, Y) = E\tilde{Z} - \Pi(Y, \tilde{Z}) \text{ or, } \Pi(Y, \tilde{Z}) = E\tilde{Z} - CE(\tilde{Z}, Y).$$

These concepts are illustrated in Figure 3-3.

It is intuitively clear that there is a direct relationship between the size of the risk premium and the degree of risk aversion of a particular individual. The link can be made quite easily in the spirit of the derivations of the previous section. For simplicity, the derivation that follows applies to the case of an actuarially fair prospect $\tilde{Z}$, one for which $E\tilde{Z} = 0$. Using Taylor series approximations we can develop the left-hand side (LHS) and right-hand side (RHS) of the definitional Equations (3.6) and (3.7)

$$\text{LHS: } EU(Y + \tilde{Z}) = EU(Y) + E[\tilde{Z}U'(Y)] + E\left[\frac{1}{2}\tilde{Z}^2U''(Y)\right] + \underbrace{EH(\tilde{Z}^3)}_{\substack{\text{terms of order} \\ \text{at least } Z^3}}$$

$$= U(Y) + \frac{1}{2}\sigma_{\tilde{z}}^2 U''(Y) + EH(\tilde{Z}^3)$$

$$\text{RHS: } U(Y - \Pi(Y, \tilde{Z})) = U(Y) - \Pi(Y, \tilde{Z})U'(Y) + \underbrace{H(\Pi^2)}_{\substack{\text{terms of order} \\ \text{at least } \Pi^2}}$$

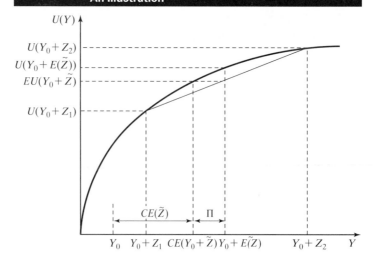

FIGURE 3-3 Certainty Equivalent and Risk Premium: An Illustration

or, ignoring the terms of order $\tilde{Z}^3$ or Π^2 or higher,

$$\Pi(Y, \tilde{Z}) \cong \frac{1}{2} \sigma_z^2 \left(\frac{-U''(Y)}{U'(Y)} \right) = \frac{1}{2} \sigma_z^2 R_A(Y).$$

This approximation can be accurate even if the standard deviation of the uncertain investment is quite large. To illustrate, consider our earlier example in which $U(Y) = Y^{1-\gamma}/1 - \gamma$, and suppose $\gamma = 3$, $Y = \$500,000$, and

$$\tilde{Z} = \begin{cases} \$100,000 & \text{probability} = \frac{1}{2} \\ -\$100,000 & \text{probability} = \frac{1}{2}. \end{cases}$$

For this case the approximation specializes to

$$\pi(Y, \tilde{Z}) = \frac{1}{2} \sigma_z^2 \frac{\gamma}{Y} = \frac{1}{2} (100,000)^2 \left(\frac{3}{500,000} \right) = \$30,000.$$

To confirm that this approximation is a good one, we must show that:

$$U(Y - \pi(Y, \tilde{Z})) = U(500,000 - 30,000)$$
$$= \frac{1}{2} U(600,000) + \frac{1}{2} U(400,000) = EU(Y + \tilde{Z}), \text{ or}$$
$$(4.7)^{-2} = \frac{1}{2}(6)^{-2} + \frac{1}{2}(4)^{-2}, \text{ or}$$
$$.0452694 = .04513; \text{ confirmed.}$$

Note also that for this preference class, the insurance premium is directly proportional to the parameter γ.

Can we convert these ideas into statements about rates of return? Let the equivalent risk-free return be defined by $U(Y(1 + r_f)) = U(Y + CE(\tilde{Z}, Y))$. The random payoff $\tilde{Z}$ can also be converted into a rate of return distribution via $\tilde{Z} = \tilde{r}Y$, or, $\tilde{r} = \tilde{Z}/Y$. Therefore, r_f is defined by the equation

$$U(Y(1 + r_f)) \equiv EU(Y(1 + \tilde{r})).$$

By risk aversion, $E\tilde{r} > r_f$. We thus define the rate of return risk premium Π' as $\Pi' = E\tilde{r} - r_f$, or $E\tilde{r} = r_f + \Pi'$, where Π' depends on the degree of risk aversion of the agent in question. Let us conclude this section by computing the rate of return premium in a particular case. Suppose $U(Y) = \ln Y$, and that the random payoff $\tilde{Z}$ satisfies

$$\tilde{Z} = \begin{cases} \$100,000 & \text{probability} = \frac{1}{2} \\ -\$50,000 & \text{probability} = \frac{1}{2} \end{cases}$$

from a base of $Y = \$500,000$. The risky rate of return implied by these numbers is clearly

$$\tilde{r} = \begin{cases} 20\% & \text{probability} = \frac{1}{2} \\ -10\% & \text{probability} = \frac{1}{2} \end{cases}$$

with an expected return of 5%. The certainty equivalent $CE(Y, \tilde{Z})$ must satisfy

$$\ln(500,000 + CE(Y, \tilde{Z})) = \frac{1}{2} \ln(600,000) + \frac{1}{2} \ln(450,000), \text{ or}$$
$$CE(Y, \tilde{Z}) = e^{\frac{1}{2} \ln(600,000) + \frac{1}{2} \ln(450,000)} - 500,000$$
$$CE(Y, \tilde{Z}) = 19,618, \text{ so that}$$
$$(1 + r_f) = \frac{519,618}{500,000} = 1.0392.$$

The rate of return risk premium is thus 5% minus 3.92% = 1.08%. Let us be clear: This rate of return risk premium does *not* represent a market or equilibrium premium. Rather it reflects personal preference characteristics and corresponds to the premium over the risk-free rate necessary to compensate, utility-wise, a specific individual, with the postulated preferences and initial wealth, for engaging in the risky investment.

3.5 ASSESSING AN INVESTOR'S LEVEL OF RELATIVE RISK AVERSION

Suppose that agents' utility functions are of the form $U(Y) = Y^{1-\gamma}/1 - \gamma$ class. As noted earlier, a quick calculation informs us that $R_R(Y) \equiv \gamma$, and we say that $U(\ )$ is of the constant relative risk aversion class. To get a feeling as to what this measure means, consider the following uncertain payoff:

$$\pi = \frac{1}{2} \qquad \$50,000$$
$$\pi = \frac{1}{2} \qquad \$100,000$$

Assuming your utility function is of the type just noted, what would you be willing to pay for such an opportunity (i.e., what is the certainty equivalent for this uncertain prospect) if your current wealth were Y? The interest in asking such a question resides in the fact that, given the amount you are willing to pay, it is possible to infer your coefficient of relative risk aversion $R_R(Y) = \gamma$, provided your preferences are adequately represented by the postulated functional form. This is achieved with the following calculation.

The CE, the maximum amount you are willing to pay for this prospect, is defined by the equation

$$\frac{(Y + CE)^{1-\gamma}}{1 - \gamma} = \frac{\frac{1}{2}(Y + 50{,}000)^{1-\gamma}}{1 - \gamma} + \frac{\frac{1}{2}(Y + 100{,}000)^{1-\gamma}}{1 - \gamma}$$

Assuming zero initial wealth ($Y = 0$), we obtain the following sample results (clearly, $CE > 50{,}000$):

$\gamma = 0$	$CE = 75{,}000$ (risk neutrality)
$\gamma = 1$	$CE = 70{,}711$
$\gamma = 2$	$CE = 66{,}246$
$\gamma = 5$	$CE = 58{,}566$
$\gamma = 10$	$CE = 53{,}991$
$\gamma = 20$	$CE = 51{,}858$
$\gamma = 30$	$CE = 51{,}209$

Alternatively, if we suppose a current wealth of $Y = \$100{,}000$ and a degree of risk aversion of $\gamma = 5$, the equation results in a $CE = \$66{,}530$.

We will use this notion in future chapters.

3.6 THE CONCEPT OF STOCHASTIC DOMINANCE

In response to dissatisfaction with the standard ranking of risky prospects based on mean and variance, a theory of choice under uncertainty with general applicability has been developed. In this section we show that the postulates of expected utility lead to a definition of two weaker concepts of dominance with wider applicability than the concept of state-by-state dominance. These are of interest because they circumscribe the situations in which rankings among risky prospects are preference free, or, can be defined independently of the specific trade-offs (among return, risk, and other characteristics of probability distributions) represented by an agent's utility function.

We start with an illustration. Consider two investment alternatives, Z_1 and Z_2, with the characteristics outlined in Table 3-1:

TABLE 3-1 Sample Investment Alternatives			
States of Nature	*1*	*2*	*3*
Probabilities	.4	.4	.2
Investment Z_1	10	100	100
Investment Z_2	10	100	2000
	$EZ_1 = 64, \sigma_{z_1} = 44$		
	$EZ_2 = 444, \sigma_{z_2} = 779$		

First observe that under standard mean-variance analysis, these two investments cannot be ranked: Although investment Z_1 has the greater mean, it also has the greater variance. Yet, all of us would clearly prefer to own investment 2. It at least matches investment 1 and has a positive probability of exceeding it.

To formalize this intuition, let us examine the cumulative probability distributions associated with each investment, $F_1(\bar{Z})$ and $F_2(\bar{Z})$ where $F_i(\bar{Z}) = \text{Prob}(Z_i \le \bar{Z})$.

In Figure 3-4 we see that $F_1(.)$ always lies above $F_2(.)$. This observation leads to Definition 3.1.

Definition 3.1:

Let $F_A(\tilde{x})$ and $F_B(\tilde{x})$, respectively, represent the cumulative distribution functions of two random variables (cash payoffs) that, without loss of generality assume values in the interval $[a, b]$. We say that $F_A(\tilde{x})$ first order stochastically dominates (FSD) $F_B(\tilde{x})$ if and only if $F_A(x) \le F_B(x)$ for all $x \in [a, b]$.

Distribution A in effect assigns more probability to higher values of x, in other words, "higher payoffs are more likely." That is, the distribution functions of A and B generally conform to the following pattern: if F_A FSD F_B, then F_A is everywhere below and to the right of F_B as represented in Figure 3-5.

By this criterion, investment 2 in Figure 3-5 stochastically dominates investment 1. It should, intuitively, be preferred. Theorem 3.2 summarizes our intuition in this latter regard.

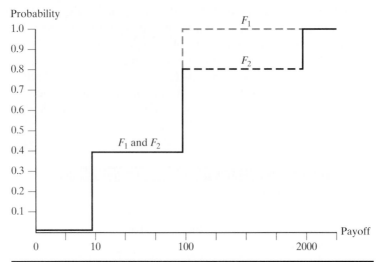

FIGURE 3-4   An Example of First Order Stochastic Dominance

Theorem 3.2:
Let $F_A(\tilde{x})$, $F_B(\tilde{x})$, be two cumulative probability distributions for random pay-offs $\tilde{x} \in [a, b]$. Then $F_A(\tilde{x})$ FSD $F_B(\tilde{x})$ if and only if $E_A U(\tilde{x}) \geq E_B U(\tilde{x})$ for all nondecreasing utility functions $U(\ )$.

Proof:
See Appendix.

FIGURE 3-5   First Order Stochastic Dominance: A More General Representation

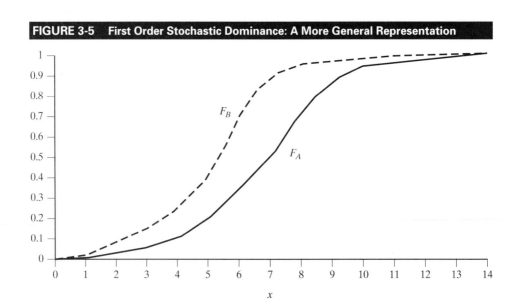

Although it is not equivalent to state-by-state dominance, FSD is an extremely strong condition. As is the case with the former, it is so strong a concept that it induces only a very incomplete ranking among uncertain prospects. Can we find a broader measure of comparison, for instance, which would make use of the hypothesis of risk aversion as well?

Consider the two independent investments in Table 3-2.[1]

Which of these investments is better? Clearly, neither investment (first order) stochastically dominates the other as Figure 3-6 confirms. The probability distribution function corresponding to investment 3 is not everywhere below the distribution function of investment 4. Yet, we would probably prefer investment 3. Can we formalize this intuition (without resorting to the mean/variance criterion, which in this case accords with intuition: $ER_4 = 5$, $ER_3 = 6.5$; $\sigma_4 = 10.25$, and $\sigma_3 = 7$)? This question leads to a weaker notion of stochastic dominance that explicitly compares distribution functions.

TABLE 3-2	Two Independent Investments		
Investment 3		*Investment 4*	
Payoff	*Prob.*	*Payoff*	*Prob.*
4	0.25	1	0.33
5	0.50	6	0.33
12	0.25	8	0.33

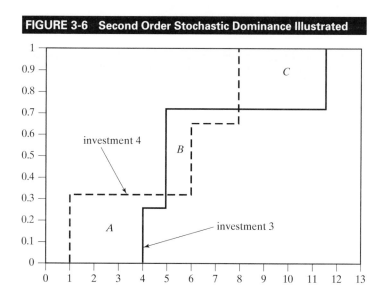

FIGURE 3-6   Second Order Stochastic Dominance Illustrated

Definition 3.2: Second Order Stochastic Dominance (SSD).

Let $F_A(\tilde{x})$, $F_B(\tilde{x})$, be two cumulative probability distributions for random payoffs in $[a, b]$. We say that $F_A(\tilde{x})$ second order stochastically dominates (SSD) $F_B(\tilde{x})$ if and only if for any x:

$$\int_{-\infty}^{x} [F_B(t) - F_A(t)]\, dt \geq 0.$$

(with strict inequality for some meaningful interval of values of t).

The calculations in Table 3-3 reveal that, in fact, investment 3 second order stochastically dominates investment 4 (let $f_i(x)$, $i = 3,4$, denote the density functions corresponding to the cumulative distribution function $F_i(x)$). In geometric terms (Figure 3-6), this would be the case as long as area B is smaller than area A.

As Theorem 3.3 shows, this notion makes sense, especially for risk-averse agents:

Theorem 3-3:

Let $F_A(\tilde{x})$, $F_B(\tilde{x})$, be two cumulative probability distributions for random payoffs $\tilde{x}$ defined on $[a, b]$. Then, $F_A(\tilde{x})$ SSD $F_B(\tilde{x})$ if and only if $E_A U(\tilde{x}) \geq E_B U(\tilde{x})$ for all nondecreasing and concave U.

Proof:

See Laffont (1989), Chapter 2, Section 2.5.

TABLE 3-3 Investment 3 Second Order Stochastically Dominates Investment 4

Values of x	$\int_0^x f_3(t)dt$	$\int_0^x F_3(t)dt$	$\int_0^x f_4(t)dt$	$\int_0^x F_4(t)dt$	$\int_0^x [F_4(t) - F_3(t)]dt$
0	0	0	0	0	0
1	0	0	1/3	1/3	1/3
2	0	0	1/3	2/3	2/3
3	0	0	1/3	1	1
4	.25	.25	1/3	4/3	13/12
5	.75	1	1/3	5/3	2/3
6	.75	1.75	2/3	7/3	7/12
7	.75	2.5	2/3	3	1/2
8	.75	3.25	1	4	3/4
9	.75	4	1	5	1
10	.75	4.75	1	6	5/4
11	.75	5.5	1	7	3/2
12	1	6.5	1	8	3/2
13	1	7.5	1	9	3/2

That is, all risk-averse agents will prefer the second-order stochastically dominant asset. Of course, FSD implies SSD: If for two investments Z_1 and Z_2, Z_1 FSD Z_2, then it is also true that Z_1 SSD Z_2. But the converse is not true.

3.7 MEAN PRESERVING SPREAD

Theorems 3.2 and 3.3 attempt to characterize the notion of "better/worse" relevant for probability distributions or random variables (representing investments). But there are two aspects to such a comparison: the notion of "more or less risky" and the trade-off between risk and return. Let us now attempt to isolate the former effect by comparing only those probability distributions with identical means. We will then review Theorem 3.3 in the context of this latter requirement.

The concept of "more or less risky" is captured by the notion of a mean preserving spread. In our context, this notion can be informally stated as follows: Let $f_A(x)$ and $f_B(x)$ describe, respectively, the probability density functions on payoffs to assets A and B. If $f_B(x)$ "can be obtained" from $f_A(x)$ by removing some of the probability weight from the center of $f_A(x)$ and distributing it to the tails in such a way as to leave the mean unchanged, we say that $f_B(x)$ is related to $f_A(x)$ via a **"mean preserving spread."** Figure 3-7 suggests what this notion would mean in the case of normal-type distributions with identical mean, yet different variances.

How can this notion be made both more intuitive and more precise? Consider a set of possible payoffs $\tilde{x}_A$ that are distributed according to $F_A(\ )$. We "further randomize" these payoffs to obtain a new random variable $\tilde{x}_B$ according to

$$\tilde{x}_B = \tilde{x}_A + \tilde{z} \qquad\qquad (3.8)$$

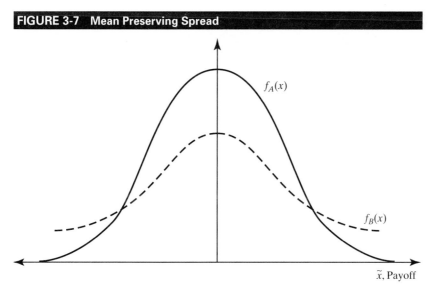

FIGURE 3-7   Mean Preserving Spread

$\int x f_A(x)dx = \int x f_B(x)dx$

where, for any x_A value, $E(\tilde{z}) = \int z dH_{x_A}(\tilde{z}) = 0$; in other words, we add some pure randomness to $\tilde{x}_A$. Let $F_B(\ )$ be the distribution function associated with $\tilde{x}_B$. We say that $F_B(\ )$ is a mean preserving spread of $F_B(\ )$.

A simple example of this is as follows. Let

$$\tilde{x}_A = \begin{cases} 5 & \text{prob } \frac{1}{2} \\ 2 & \text{prob } \frac{1}{2} \end{cases},$$

and suppose $\tilde{z} = \begin{cases} +1 & \text{prob } \frac{1}{2} \\ -1 & \text{prob } \frac{1}{2} \end{cases}$. Then,

$$\tilde{x}_B = \begin{cases} 6 & \text{prob } \frac{1}{4} \\ 4 & \text{prob } \frac{1}{4} \\ 3 & \text{prob } \frac{1}{4} \\ 1 & \text{prob } \frac{1}{4} \end{cases}.$$

Clearly, $E\tilde{x}_A = E\tilde{x}_B = 3.5$; we would also all agree that $F_B(\ )$ is intuitively riskier.

Our final theorem (Theorem 3.4) relates the sense of a mean preserving spread, as captured by Equation (3.8), to our earlier results.

Theorem 3.4:

Let $F_A(\ )$ and $F_B(\ )$ be two distribution functions defined on the same state space with identical means. If this is true, the following statements are equivalent:

$F_A(\tilde{x})$ SSD $F_B(\tilde{x})$
$F_B(\tilde{x})$ is a mean preserving spread of $F_A(\tilde{x})$ in the sense of Equation (3.8).

Proof:
See Rothschild and Stiglitz (1970, p. 237).

But what about distributions that are not stochastically dominant under either definition and for which the mean-variance criterion does not give a relative ranking? For example, consider (independent) investments 5 and 6 in Table 3-4.

In this case we are left to compare distributions by computing their respective expected utilities. That is to say, the ranking between these two investments is preference dependent. Some risk-averse individuals will prefer investment 5 while other risk-

TABLE 3-4	Two Investments: No Dominance		
Investment 5		*Investment 6*	
Payoff	*Prob.*	*Payoff*	*Prob.*
1	0.25	3	0.33
7	0.5	5	0.33
12	0.25	8	0.34

averse individuals will prefer investment 6. This is not bad. There remains a systematic basis of comparison. The task of the investment advisor is made more complex, however, as she will have to elicit more information on the preferences of her client if she wants to be in position to provide adequate advice.

3.8 CONCLUSIONS

The main topic of this chapter was the VNM expected utility representation specialized to admit risk aversion. Two measures of the degree of risk aversion were presented. Both are functions of an investor's current level of wealth and, as such, we would expect them to change as wealth changes. Is there any systematic relationship between $R_A(Y)$, $R_R(Y)$, and Y which it is reasonable to assume?

In order to answer that question we must move from the somewhat artificial setting of this chapter. As we will see in Chapter 4, systematic relationships between wealth and the measures of absolute and relative risk aversion are closely related to investors' portfolio behavior.

References

Arrow, K. J., *Essays in the Theory of Risk Bearing*, Chicago: Markham, 1971.

De Groot, M., *Optimal Statistical Decisions*, New York: McGraw Hill, 1970.

Laffont, Jean-Jacques, *The Economics of Uncertainty and Information*, Cambridge, MA: MIT Press, 1989.

Pratt, J., "Risk Aversion in the Small and the Large," *Econometrica,* 32 (1964): 122–136.

Rothschild, M., and J. E. Stiglitz, "Increasing Risk: I. A Definition," *Journal of Economic Theory,* 2 (1970): 225–243.

A P P E N D I X

Proof of Theorem 3-2

⇒ We assert that there is no loss in generality by assuming $U(\ )$ is differentiable, with $U'(\ ) > 0$.

Suppose $F_A(x)$ FSD $F_B(x)$, and let $U(\ )$ be a utility function defined on $[a, b]$ for which $U'(\ ) > 0$. We need to show that

$$E_A U(\tilde{x}) = \int_a^b U(\tilde{x}) dF_A(\tilde{x})$$

$$> \int_a^b U(\tilde{x}) dF_B(\tilde{x}) = E_B U(\tilde{x}).$$

This result follows from "integration by parts" (recall the relationship $\int_a^b u\,dv = uv\big|_a^b - \int_a^b v\,du$).

$$\int_a^b U(\tilde{x}) dF_A(\tilde{x}) - \int_a^b U(\tilde{x}) dF_B(\tilde{x})$$

$$= U(b)F_A(b) - U(a)F_A(a)$$

$$- \int_a^b F_A(\tilde{x}) U'(\tilde{x}) d\tilde{x}$$

$$- \left\{ U(b)F_B(b) - U(a)F_B(a) \right.$$

$$\left. - \int_a^b F_B(\tilde{x}) U'(\tilde{x}) d\tilde{x} \right\}$$

$$= \int_a^b F_A(\tilde{x}) U'(\tilde{x}) d\tilde{x}$$

$$+ \int_a^b F_B(\tilde{x}) U'(\tilde{x}) d\tilde{x},$$

(since $F_A(b) = F_B(b) = 1$,

and $F_A(a) = F_B(a) = 0$)

$$= \int_a^b [F_B(\tilde{x}) - F_A(\tilde{x})] U'(\tilde{x}) d\tilde{x} \geq 0.$$

The desired inequality follows since, by the definition of FSD and the assumption that the marginal utility is always positive, both terms within the integral are positive. If there is some subset $(c, a) \subset [a, b]$ on which $F_A(x) > F_B(x)$, the final inequality is strict.

⇐ Proof by contradiction. If $F_A(\tilde{x}) \leq F_B(\tilde{x})$ is false, then there must exist an $\bar{x} \in [a, b]$ for which $F_A(\bar{x}) > F_B(\bar{x})$. Define the following nondecreasing function $\hat{U}(x)$ by

$$\hat{U}(x) = \begin{cases} 1 & \text{for } b \geq x > \bar{x} \\ 0 & \text{for } a \leq x < \bar{x} \end{cases}.$$

We'll use integration by parts again to obtain the required contradiction.

$$\int_a^b \hat{U}(\tilde{x}) dF_A(\tilde{x}) - \int_a^b \hat{U}(\tilde{x}) dF_B(\tilde{x})$$

$$= \int_a^b \hat{U}(\tilde{x}) [dF_A(\tilde{x}) - F_B(\tilde{x})]$$

$$= \int_{\bar{x}}^b 1[dF_A(\tilde{x}) - F_B(\tilde{x})]$$

$$= F_A(b) - F_B(b) - [F_A(\bar{x}) - F_B(\bar{x})]$$

$$- \int_{\bar{x}}^b [F_A(\tilde{x}) - F_B(\tilde{x})](0) d\tilde{x}$$

$$= F_B(\bar{x}) - F_A(\bar{x}) < 0.$$

Thus we have exhibited an increasing function $\hat{U}(x)$ for which $\int_a^b \hat{U}(\tilde{x}) dF_A(\tilde{x}) < \int_a^b U(\tilde{x}) dF_B(\tilde{x})$, a contradiction.

CHAPTER 4

RISK AVERSION AND INVESTMENT DECISIONS, PART I

4.1   INTRODUCTION

Chapters 2 and 3 provided a systematic procedure for assessing an investor's relative preference for various investment payoffs: Rank them according to expected utility using a VNM utility representation constructed to reflect the investor's preferences over random payments. The subsequent postulate of risk aversion further refined this idea. It is natural to hypothesize that the utility-of-money function entering the investor's VNM index is concave ($U''(\ ) < 0$). Two widely used measures were introduced, each permitting us to assess an investor's degree of risk aversion. In the setting of a zero-cost investment paying either ($+h$) or ($-h$), these measures were shown to be linked with the minimum probability of success above one half necessary for a risk-averse investor to take on such a prospect willingly. They differ only as to whether (h) measures an absolute amount of money or a proportion of the investors' initial wealth.

In this chapter we begin to use these ideas with a view toward understanding an investor's demand for assets of different risk classes and, in particular, his or her demand for risk-free versus risky assets. This is an essential aspect of the investor's portfolio allocation decision.

4.2   RISK AVERSION AND PORTFOLIO ALLOCATION: RISK FREE VS. RISKY ASSETS

4.2.1   THE CANONICAL PORTFOLIO PROBLEM

Consider an investor with wealth level Y_0, who is deciding what amount, a, to invest in a risky portfolio with uncertain rate of return $\tilde{r}$. We can think of the risky asset as being, in fact, the market portfolio under the "old" Capital Asset Pricing Model (CAPM), to be reviewed in Chapter 6. His alternative is to invest in a risk-free asset that pays a certain rate of return r_f. The time horizon is one period. The investor's wealth at the end of the period is given by

$$\tilde{Y}_1 = (1 + r_f)(Y_0 - a) + a(1 + \tilde{r}) = Y_0(1 + r_f) + a(\tilde{r} - r_f)$$

The choice problem he must solve can be expressed as

$$(P) \qquad \max_a EU(\tilde{Y}_1) = \max EU(Y_0(1 + r_f) + a(\tilde{r} - r_f)),$$

where $U(\ )$ is his utility-of-money function, and E the expectations operator.

This formulation of the investor's problem is fully in accord with the lessons of the prior chapter. Each choice of a leads to a different uncertain payoff distribution, and we want to find the choice that corresponds to the most preferred such distribution. By construction of his VNM representation, this is the payoff pattern that maximizes his expected utility.

Under risk aversion ($U''(\ ) < 0$), the necessary and sufficient first-order condition for problem (P) is given by:

$$E[U'(Y_0(1 + r_f) + a(\tilde{r} - r_f))(\tilde{r} - r_f)] = 0. \qquad \textbf{(4.1)}$$

Analyzing Equation (4.1) allows us to describe the relationship between the investor's degree of risk aversion and his portfolio's composition as per Theorem 4.1.

Theorem 4.1:

Assume $U'(\ ) > 0$, and $U''(\ ) < 0$ and let $\hat{a}$ denote the solution to problem (P). Then

$$\hat{a} > 0 \quad \text{if and only if } E\tilde{r} > r_f$$
$$\hat{a} = 0 \quad \text{if and only if } E\tilde{r} = r_f$$
$$\hat{a} < 0 \quad \text{if and only if } E\tilde{r} < r_f.$$

Proof:

Since this is a fundamental result, it is worthwhile to make clear its (straightforward) justification. We follow the argument presented in Arrow (1971), Chapter 2.

Define $W(a) = E\{U(Y_0(1 + r_f) + a(\tilde{r} - r_f))\}$. The First Order Condition (FOC) (4.1) can then be written $W'(a) = E[U'(Y_0(1 + r_f) + a(\tilde{r} - r_f))(\tilde{r} - r_f)] = 0$. By risk aversion ($U'' < 0$), $W''(a) = E[U''(Y_0(1 + r_f) + a(\tilde{r} - r_f))(\tilde{r} - r_f)^2] < 0$; that is, $W'(a)$ is everywhere decreasing. It follows that $\hat{a}$ will be positive if and only if $W'(0) = U'(Y_0(1 + r_f))E(\tilde{r} - r_f) > 0$ (since then a will have to be increased from its value of 0 to achieve equality in the FOC). Since U' is always strictly positive, this implies $\hat{a} > 0$ if and only if $E(\tilde{r} - r_f) > 0$. The other assertion follows in a similar manner.

Theorem 4.1 asserts that a risk-averse agent will invest in the risky asset or portfolio only if the expected return on the risky asset exceeds the risk-free rate. On the other hand, a risk-averse agent will *always* participate (possibly via an arbitrarily small stake) in a risky investment when the odds are favorable. We will henceforth assume this is true, and that $U'(\ ) > 0$, $U''(\ ) < 0$.

4.2.2   ILLUSTRATION AND EXAMPLES

It is worth pursuing this result to get a sense of how large a is relative to Y_0. Our findings will, of course, be preference dependent. Let us begin with the fairly standard and highly tractable utility function $U(Y) = \ln Y$. For added simplicity let us also assume that the risky asset is forecast to pay either of two returns (corresponding to an "up" or "down" stock market), r_2 and r_1, with probabilities π and $1 - \pi$ respectively. It makes sense (why?) to assume $r_2 > r_f > r_1$, and

$$E\tilde{r} = \pi r_2 + (1 - \pi)r_1 > r_f.$$

Under this specification, the FOC (4.1) becomes

$$E\left\{\frac{\tilde{r} - r_f}{Y_0(1 + r_f) + a(\tilde{r} - r_f)}\right\} = 0.$$

Writing out the expectation explicitly yields

$$\frac{\pi(r_2 - r_f)}{Y_0(1 + r_f) + a(r_2 - r_f)} + \frac{(1 - \pi)(r_1 - r_f)}{Y_0(1 + r_f) + a(r_1 - r_f)} = 0,$$

which, after some straightforward algebraic manipulation, gives:

$$\frac{a}{Y_0} = \frac{-(1 + r_f)[E\tilde{r} - r_f]}{(r_1 - r_f)(r_2 - r_f)} > 0. \tag{4.2}$$

This is an intuitive sort of expression: The fraction of wealth invested in risky assets increases with the return premium paid by the risky asset $(E\tilde{r} - r_f)$ and decreases with an increase in the return dispersion around r_f as measured by $(r_2 - r_f)(r_f - r_1)$.[1]

Suppose $r_f = .05$, $r_2 = .40$, and $r_1 = -.20$, and $\pi = 1/2$ (the latter information guarantees $E\tilde{r} = .10$). In this case $a/Y_0 = .6$: 60% of the investor's wealth turns out to be invested in the risky asset. Alternatively, suppose $r_2 = .30$ and $r_1 = -.10$ (same r_f, π and $E\tilde{r}$); here we find that $a/Y_0 = 1.4$. This latter result must be interpreted to mean that an investor would prefer to invest at least his full wealth in the risky portfolio. If possible, he would even want to borrow an additional amount, equal to 40% of his initial wealth, at the risk-free rate and invest this amount in the risky portfolio as well. In comparing these two examples, we see that the return dispersion is much smaller in the second case (lower risk in a mean-variance sense) with an unchanged return premium. With less risk and unchanged mean returns, it is not surprising that the proportion invested in the risky asset increases very substantially. We will see in Section 4.5, however, that, somewhat surprisingly, this result does not generalize without further assumption on the form of the investor's preferences.

4.3   PORTFOLIO COMPOSITION, RISK AVERSION, AND WEALTH

In this section we consider how an investor's portfolio decision is affected by his degree of risk aversion and his wealth level. A natural first exercise is to compare the portfolio composition across individuals of differing risk aversion. The answer to this first

[1]That this fraction is independent of the wealth level is not a general result, as we shall find out in Section 3.

question conforms with intuition: If John is more risk averse than Amos, he optimally invests a smaller fraction of his wealth in the risky asset. This is the essence of our next two theorems.

> **Theorem 4.2 (Arrow, 1971):**
> Suppose, for all wealth levels Y, $R_A^1(Y) > R_A^2(Y)$ where $R_A^i(Y)$ is the measure of absolute risk aversion of investor i, $i = 1,2$. Then $\hat{a}_1(Y) < \hat{a}_2(Y)$.

That is, the more risk averse agent, as measured by his absolute risk aversion measure, will always invest less in the risky asset, given the same level of wealth. This result does not depend on measuring risk aversion via the absolute Arrow-Pratt measure. Indeed, since $R_A^1(Y) > R_A^2(Y) \Leftrightarrow R_R^1(Y) > R_R^2(Y)$, Theorem 4.2 can be restated as Theorem 4.3.

> **Theorem 4.3:**
> Suppose, for all wealth levels $Y > 0$, $R_R^1(Y) > R_R^2(Y)$ where $R_R^i(Y)$ is the measure of relative risk aversion of investor i, $i = 1,2$. Then $\hat{a}_1(Y) < \hat{a}_2(Y)$.

Continuing with the example of Section 4.2.2, suppose now that the investor's utility function has the form $U(Y) = Y^{1-\gamma}/1 - \gamma$. For $\gamma > 1$, this utility function displays both greater absolute and greater relative risk aversion than $U(Y) = \ln Y$ (you are invited to prove this statement). From Theorems 4.2 and 4.3, we would expect this greater risk aversion to manifest itself in a reduced willingness to invest in the risky portfolio. Let us see if this is the case.

For these preferences the expression corresponding to Equation (4.2) is

$$\frac{a}{Y_0} = \frac{(1 + r_f)\{[(1-\pi)(r_f - r_1)]^{1/\gamma} - (\pi(r_2 - r_f))^{1/\gamma}\}}{(r_1 - r_f)\{\pi(r_2 - r_f)\}^{1/\gamma} - (r_2 - r_f)\{(1-\pi)(r_f - r_1)\}^{1/\gamma}} \quad (4.3)$$

In the case of our first example, but with $\gamma = 3$, we obtain, by simple direct substitution, $a/Y_0 = .24$; indeed, only 24% of the investor's asset are invested in the risky portfolio, down from 60%.

The next logical question is to ask how the investment in the risky asset varies with the investor's total wealth as a function of his degree of risk aversion. Let us begin with statements appropriate to the absolute measure of risk aversion.

> **Theorem 4.4 (Arrow, 1971):**
> Let $\hat{a} = \hat{a}(Y_0)$ be the solution to problem (P); then:
>
> (i) $R_A'(Y) < 0$ (DARA) implies $\hat{a}'(Y_0) > 0$
> (ii) $R_A'(Y) = 0$ (CARA) implies $\hat{a}'(Y_0) = 0$
> (iii) $R_A'(Y) > 0$ (IARA) implies $\hat{a}'(Y_0) < 0$.

Case (i) is referred to as declining absolute risk aversion (DARA). Agents with this property become more willing to accept greater bets as they become wealthier. Theorem 4.3 says that such agents will also increase the amount invested in the risky asset $(\hat{a}'(Y_0) > 0)$. To state matters slightly differently, an agent with the indicated declining absolute risk aversion will, if he becomes wealthier, be willing to put some of that additional wealth at risk. Utility functions of this form are quite common: Those considered in the example, $U(Y) = \ln Y$ and $U(Y) = Y^{1-\gamma}/1 - \gamma, \gamma > 0$, display this property. It also makes intuitive sense.

Under constant absolute risk aversion (CARA), case (ii), the amount invested in the risky asset is unaffected by the agent's wealth. This result is somewhat counterintuitive. One might have expected that a CARA decision maker, say with little risk aversion, would invest some of his or her increase in initial wealth in the risky asset. Theorem 4.4 disproves this intuition.

An example of a CARA utility function is $U(Y) = -e^{-\alpha Y}$. Indeed,

$$R_A(Y) = \frac{-U''(Y)}{U'(Y)} = \frac{-(-\alpha^2)e^{-\alpha Y}}{\alpha e^{-\alpha Y}} = \alpha$$

Let's verify the claim of Theorem 4.2 for this utility function. Consider

$$\max_a E(-e^{-\alpha(Y_0(1+r_f)+a(\tilde{r}-r_f))})$$

FOC $\qquad E[\alpha(\tilde{r} - r_f)e^{-\alpha(Y_0(1+r_f)+a(\tilde{r}-r_f))}] = 0$

Now compute da/dY_0; by differentiating the equation, we obtain:

$$E\left[\alpha(\tilde{r} - r_f)e^{-\alpha(Y_0(1+r_f)+a(\tilde{r}-r_f))}\left(1 + r_f + (\tilde{r} - r_f)\frac{da}{dY_0}\right)\right] = 0$$

$$(1 + r_f)\underbrace{E[\alpha(\tilde{r} - r_f)e^{-\alpha(Y_0(1+r_f)+a(\tilde{r}-r_f))}]}_{= 0\text{(by the F.O.C.)}} + E\left[\underbrace{\alpha(\tilde{r} - r_f)^2}_{>0} \frac{da}{dY_0} \underbrace{e^{-\alpha(Y_0(1+r_f)+a(\tilde{r}-r_f))}}_{>0}\right] = 0;$$

therefore, $da/dY_0 \equiv 0$.

For the preference ordering, and our original two-state risky distribution,

$$\hat{a} = \frac{1}{\alpha}\left(\frac{1}{r_1 - r_2}\right)\ln\left(\frac{(1 - \pi)}{\pi}\left(\frac{r_f - r_1}{r_2 - r_f}\right)\right)$$

Note that in order for $\hat{a}$ to be positive, it must be that

$$0 < \frac{(1 - \pi)}{\pi}\left(\frac{r_f - r_1}{r_2 - r_f}\right) < 1.$$

A sufficient condition is $\pi > \frac{1}{2}$.

Case (iii) is one with increasing absolute risk aversion (IARA). It says that as an agent becomes wealthier, he reduces his investments in risky assets. This does not make much sense and we will generally ignore this possibility. Note, however, that the quadratic utility function, which is of some significance as we will see later on, possesses this property.

Let us now think in terms of the relative risk aversion measure. Because it is defined for bets expressed as a *proportion of wealth*, it is appropriate to think in terms of *elasticities*, or of how the fraction invested in the risky asset changes as wealth changes. Define $\eta(Y, \hat{a}) = d\hat{a}/\hat{a}/dY/Y = Y/\hat{a} \times d\hat{a}/dY$, i.e., the wealth elasticity of investment in the risky asset. For example, if $\eta(Y, \hat{a}) > 1$, this says that as wealth Y increases, the **percentage** increase in the amount optimally invested in the risky portfolio exceeds the percentage increase in Y. Or as wealth increases, the **proportion** optimally invested in the risky asset increases. Analogous to Theorem 4.4 is Theorem 4.5.

Theorem 4.5 (Arrow 1971):

If, for all wealth levels Y,

(i) $R'_R(Y) = 0$ (CRRA) then $\eta = 1$
(ii) $R'_R(Y) < 0$ (DRRA) then $\eta > 1$
(iii) $R'_R(Y) > 0$ (IRRA) then $\eta < 1$.

In his article, Arrow gives support for the hypothesis that the rate of relative risk aversion should be constant and CRRA ≈ 1. In particular it can be shown that if an investor's utility of wealth is to be bounded above as wealth tends to ∞, then $\lim_{Y \mapsto \infty} R_R(Y) \geq 1$; similarly, if $U(Y)$ is to be bounded below as Y tends to zero, then $\lim_{Y \mapsto \infty} R_R(Y) \leq 1$;. These results suggest that if we wish to assume CRRA, then CRRA $= 1$ is the appropriate value.[2] Utility functions of the CRRA class include $U(Y) = Y^{1-\gamma}/1 - \gamma$, where $R_R(Y) = \gamma, R_A(Y) = \gamma/Y$.

4.4   SPECIAL CASE OF RISK-NEUTRAL INVESTORS

As noted in Chapter 3, a risk-neutral investor is one who does not care about risk; he ranks investments solely on the basis of their expected returns. The utility function of such an agent is necessarily of the form $U(Y) = c + dY$, where c and d are constants and $d > 0$ (check that U'' is effectively 0 in this case).

What proportion of his wealth will such an agent invest in the risky asset? The answer is: provided $E\tilde{r} > r_f$ (as we have assumed), **all** of his wealth will be invested in the risky asset. This is clearly seen from the following. Consider the agent's portfolio problem:

$$\max_a E(c + d(Y_0(1 + r_f) + a(\tilde{r} - r_f))) = \max_a c + d(Y_0(1 + r_f)) + da(E\tilde{r} - r_f)$$

With $E\tilde{r} > r_f$ and, consequently, $d(E\tilde{r} - r_f) > 0$, this expression is increasing in a. This means that if the risk-neutral investor is unconstrained, he will attempt to borrow as much as possible at r_f and reinvest the proceeds in the risky portfolio. He is willing, without bound, to exchange certain payments for uncertain claims of greater expected value. As such he stands willing to absorb all of the economy's financial risk. If we specify that the investor is prevented from borrowing, then the maximum will occur at $a = Y_0$.

---

[2]Note that the above comments also suggest the appropriateness of weakly increasing relative risk aversion as an alternative working assumption.

4.5 RISK AVERSION AND RISKY PORTFOLIO COMPOSITION

So far we have considered the question of how an investor should allocate his wealth between a risk-free asset and a risky asset or portfolio. We now go one step further and ask the following question: When is the *composition* of the portfolio (i.e., the percentage of the portfolio's value invested in each of the J risky assets that compose it) independent of the agent's wealth level? This question is particularly relevant in light of current investment practices whereby portfolio decisions are usually taken in steps. Step 1, often associated with the label *asset allocation,* is the choice of instruments: stocks, bonds, and riskless assets. Step 2 is the country allocation decision and Step 3 is the individual stock picking decisions made on the basis of information provided by financial analysts. The issuing of asset and country allocation grids by all major financial institutions, tailored to the risk profiles of different clients, but independent of their wealth levels (and of changes in their wealth), is predicated on the hypothesis that changes in wealth do not require adjustments in portfolio composition provided risk tolerance is unchanged.

Let us illustrate the issue in more concrete terms; take the example of an investor with invested wealth equal to $12,000 and optimal portfolio proportions of $a_1 = \frac{1}{2}$, $a_2 = \frac{1}{3}$, and $a_3 = \frac{1}{6}$ (only 3 assets are considered). In other words, this individual's portfolio holdings are $6,000 in asset 1, $4,000 in asset 2, and $2,000 in asset 3. The implicit assumption behind the most common asset management practice is that, were the investor's wealth to double to $24,000, the new optimal portfolio would naturally be:

$$
\begin{aligned}
\text{Asset 1:} \quad &\tfrac{1}{2}(\$24{,}000) = \$12{,}000 \\
\text{Asset 2:} \quad &\tfrac{1}{3}(\$24{,}000) = \$8{,}000 \\
\text{Asset 3:} \quad &\tfrac{1}{6}(\$24{,}000) = \$4{,}000.
\end{aligned}
$$

The question we pose in the present section is: Is this hypothesis supported by theory?

The answer is generally no, in the sense that it is only for very specific preferences (utility functions) that the asset allocation is optimally left unchanged in the face of changes in wealth levels. Fortunately, these specific preferences include some of the major utility representations. The principal result in this regard is found in Theorem 4.6.

Theorem 4.6 (Cass and Stiglitz, 1970):

Let the vector

$$
\begin{bmatrix}
\hat{a}_1(Y_0) \\
\cdot \\
\cdot \\
\hat{a}_J(Y_0)
\end{bmatrix}
$$

denote the amount optimally invested in the J risky assets if the wealth level is Y_0. Then

(continued)

Theorem 4.6 (*continued*)

$$\begin{bmatrix} \hat{a}_1(Y_0) \\ \cdot \\ \cdot \\ \hat{a}_J(Y_0) \end{bmatrix} = \begin{bmatrix} a_1 \\ \cdot \\ \cdot \\ a_J \end{bmatrix} f(Y_0)$$

if and only if either

(i) $U'(Y_0) = (\theta Y_0 + \kappa)^\Delta$ or
(ii) $U'(Y_0) = \xi e^{-\nu Y_0}$.

There are, of course, implicit restrictions on the choice of $\theta, \kappa, \Delta, \xi$, and ν to ensure, in particular, that $U''(Y_0) < 0$.[3]

Integrating (i) and (ii), respectively, in order to recover the utility functions corresponding to these marginal utilities, one finds, significantly, that the first includes the CRRA class of functions:

$$U(Y_0) = \frac{1}{1-\gamma} Y_0^{(1-\gamma)}, \gamma \neq 1, \text{ and } U(Y_0) = \ln(Y_0),$$

while the second corresponds to the CARA class:

$$U(Y_0) = \frac{\xi}{-\nu} e^{-\nu Y_0}.$$

In essence, Theorem 4.6 states that it is only in the case of utility functions satisfying constant absolute or constant relative risk aversion preferences (and some generalization of these functions of minor interest) that the relative composition of the risky portion of an investor's optimal portfolio is not tied to changes in his wealth.[4] Only in these cases, should the investor's portfolio composition be left unchanged as invested wealth increases or decreases. It is only with such utility specifications that the standard *grid* approach to portfolio investing is formally justified.[5]

4.6 RISK AVERSION AND SAVINGS BEHAVIOR

4.6.1 SAVINGS AND THE RISKINESS OF RETURNS

We have thus far considered the relationship between an agent's degree of risk aversion and the composition of his portfolio. A related, though significantly different, ques-

---

[3]For (i), we must have **either**

$$\theta > 0, \Delta < 0 \text{ and } Y_0 \text{ such that } \theta Y_0 + \gamma \geq 0 \text{ or } \theta < 0, \gamma < 0, \Delta > 0, \text{ and } Y_0 \leq -\frac{\gamma}{\theta}.$$

For (ii), $\xi \geq 0, -\nu < 0$ and $Y_0 \geq 0$.
[4]As noted earlier, the constant absolute risk aversion class of preferences has the property that the total amount invested in risky assets is independent of the level of wealth. It is not surprising, therefore, that the proportionate allocation among the available risky assets is similarly invariant as this theorem asserts.
[5]Theorem 4.6 does not mean, however, that the fraction of initial wealth invested in the risk free asset vs. the risky mutual fund is invariant to changes in Y_0. The CARA class of preferences discussed in the previous footnote is a case in point.

tion is to ask how an agent's *savings rate* is affected by an increase in the degree of risk facing him. It is to be expected that the answer to this question will be influenced, in a substantial way, by the agent's degree of risk aversion.

Consider first an agent solving the following two-period consumption-savings problem:

$$\max_s E\{U(Y_0 - s) + \delta U(s\tilde{R})\},$$

$$\text{s.t. } s \geq 0 \tag{4.4}$$

where Y_0 is initial (period zero) wealth, s is the amount saved and entirely invested in a risky portfolio with uncertain gross risky return, $\tilde{R} = 1 + \tilde{r}$, $U(\ )$ is the agent's period utility-of-consumption function, and δ his subjective discount factor.[6] Note that this is the first occasion where we have explicitly introduced a time dimension into the analysis (i.e., where the important trade-off involves the present vs. the future): The discount rate $\delta < 1$ captures the extent to which the investor values consumption in the future less than current consumption.

BOX 4-1

Thinking About the Discount Factor δ

In this chapter, and indeed throughout this text, the subjective time discount factor δ is assumed to be exogenous and fixed. In Chapter 10 more specifically, we present arguments for fixing the annual discount factor of a representative or average individual at $\delta = .96$, which implies a quarterly $\delta = .99$. It is well known, however, that some individuals have discount factors that are "too low for their own good." Individuals who save nothing for retirement, or individuals who allow themselves to become addicted to some life-shortening substance are cases in point. Both examples suggest a low weighting of the utility of future consumption; i.e., a low δ. This tendency is sometimes attributed to a lack of imagination: It is thought that such individuals simply are unable to imagine all the utility benefits possible in the future, and thus make no preparations to enjoy them.

But resources can be expended on activities that increase the depth of our imagination. Education and travel can be seen as contributing to this purpose. Becker and Mul-

ligan (1997) consider precisely this latter issue. In a two-period certainty version of their model, agents solve

$$\max_{\{s,\,c_0\}} U(c_0) + \delta(s)U((Y_0 - s - c_0)(1 + r_f))$$

$$\text{s.t. } c_0 + s \leq Y_0,$$

where s are the resources devoted to expanding the imagination and $\delta = \delta(s)$ is the resulting subjective discount factor; they assume $\delta'(s) > 0, \delta''(s) < 0$.

Under standard preferences (e.g., CRRA), wealthier individuals (those with larger Y_0) will have higher subjective discount factors since they save more in the absolute. This, in turn, implies that they will, in this context, save *proportionately* more in contradiction to the corresponding assertion of Theorem 4.5. It is observed that wealthy individuals indeed tend to save a larger fraction of their incomes. This could be due, in part, to a greater time discount factor reflecting greater exposure to the world with the attendant richer imagination.

---

[6]Note that this $U(c)$ is, in principle, different from the (indirect) utility-of-wealth function considered earlier in the chapter. Assuming a single consumption good with price identically equal to one, however, these notions are equivalent.

The first-order condition for this problem (assuming an interior solution) is given by:

$$U'(Y_0 - s) = \delta E\{U'(s\tilde{R})\tilde{R}\} \tag{4.5}$$

It is clear from the Equation (4.5) that the properties of the return distribution $\tilde{R}$ will influence the optimal level of s. One is particularly interested to know how optimal savings is affected by the riskiness of returns.

To be concrete, let us think of two return distributions $\tilde{R}_A$, $\tilde{R}_B$ such that $\tilde{R}_B$ is riskier than $\tilde{R}_A$ and $E\tilde{R}_A = E\tilde{R}_B$. From our previous work (Theorem 3.4), we know this can be made precise by stating that $\tilde{R}_A$ SSD $\tilde{R}_B$ or that $\tilde{R}_B$ is a mean-preserving spread of $\tilde{R}_A$. In other words, one can write $\tilde{R}_B = \tilde{R}_A + \tilde{\varepsilon}$ where $\tilde{\varepsilon}$ is a random variable with zero mean uncorrelated with $\tilde{R}_A$. Let s_A and s_B be, respectively, the savings out of Y_0 corresponding to the return distributions $\tilde{R}_A$ and $\tilde{R}_B$. The issue is whether s_A is larger than s_B or if the converse is true. In other words, can one predict that a representative risk-averse agent *will save more or less* when confronted with riskier returns on his or her savings?

Let us try to think intuitively about this issue. On the one hand, one may expect that more risk will mean a decrease in savings because "a bird in the hand is worth two in the bush." This can be viewed as a substitution effect: A riskier return can be likened to an increase in the cost of future consumption. A rational individual may then opt to consume more today. On the other hand, a risk-averse individual may want to increase savings in the face of uncertainty, as a precautionary measure, in order to insure a minimum standard of living in the future. This reaction is indeed associated with the notion of *precautionary savings*. The reader is invited to verify that, in a mean-variance world, this ambiguity is resolved in favor of the first argument. In that context, riskier returns imply a decrease in the RHS of Equation (4.5), or a decrease in the expected future marginal utility of consumption weighted by the gross return. For the equality to be restored, consumption today must increase and, consequently, savings must decrease.

It is important to realize, however, that the mean-variance response is not representative of the reactions of all risk-averse agents. Indeed, observers seeking to explain the increase in savings registered in many Western countries in the first half of the nineties have regularly pointed to the rising uncertainties surrounding the macroeconomic situation in general and the pace of economic growth in particular.[7] As our discussion suggests, the key technical issue is whether the RHS of Equation (4.5) is increased or decreased by an increase in risk. Applying reasoning similar to that used when discussing risk aversion (see Section 4.3.2), it is easy to see that this issue, in fact, revolves around whether the RHS of Equation (4.5), (i.e., $\delta U'(sR)R \equiv \delta g(R)$), is convex (in which case it increases) or concave (in which case it decreases) in R.

Suppose, to take an extreme case, that the latter is linear in R; we know that linearity means that the RHS of Equation (4.5) can be written as $\delta E(g(R)) = \delta g(ER)$. But since R_A and R_B have the same mean, this implies that the RHS of Equation (4.5), and consequently optimal savings, are unaffected by an increase in risk. If on the other hand, $g(R)$ is concave, then $E(g(R)) < g(E(R))$; the reverse is true if $g(\ )$ is convex. The latter inequality is an application of Jensen's inequality, a result we have used, implicitly, on several occasions.

Note that in the all-important case where $U(c) = \ln(c)$, $g(R)$ is in fact a constant function of R, with the obvious result that the savings decision is not affected by the in-

---

crease in the riskiness of the return distribution. This difference in results between two of the workhorses of finance (mean variance and log utility) is worth underlining.

Let us now compute the second derivative of $g(R)$:[8]

$$g''(R) = 2U''(sR)s + s^2RU'''(sR) \qquad (4.6)$$

Using Equation (4.6) one can express the sign of g'' in terms of the relative rate of risk aversion as in Theorem 4.7.

Theorem 4.7 (Rothschild and Stiglitz, 1971):
Let $\tilde{R}_A, \tilde{R}_B$ be two return distributions with identical means such that $\tilde{R}_A$ SSD $\tilde{R}_B$, and let s_A and s_B be, respectively, the savings out of Y_0 corresponding to the return distributions $\tilde{R}_A$ and $\tilde{R}_B$.

$$\text{If } R'_R(Y) \leq 0 \text{ and } R_R(Y) > 1, \text{ then } s_A < s_B;$$
$$\text{If } R'_R(Y) \geq 0 \text{ and } R_R(Y) < 1, \text{ then } s_A > s_B.$$

Proof:
To prove this assertion we need Lemma 4.7.

Lemma 4.7:
$R'_R(Y)$ has the same sign as $-[U'''(Y)Y + U''(Y)(1 + R_R(Y)]$.

Proof:
Since $R_R(Y) = \dfrac{-YU''(Y)}{U'(Y)}$,

$$R'_R(Y) = \frac{[-U'''(Y)Y - U''(Y)]U'(Y) - [-U''(Y)Y]U''(Y)}{[U'(Y)]^2}.$$

Since $U'(Y) > 0$, $R'_R(Y)$ has the same sign as

$$\frac{[-U'''(Y)Y - U''(Y)]U'(Y) - [-U''(Y)Y]U''(Y)}{U'(Y)}$$

$$= -U'''(Y)Y - U''(Y) - \left[\frac{-U''(Y)Y}{U'(Y)}\right]U''(Y)$$
$$= -\{U'''(Y)Y + U''(Y)[1 + R_R(Y)]\}.$$

Now we can proceed with the theorem. We'll show only the first implication as the second follows similarly.

By the earlier remarks, we need to show that $R'_R(Y) < 0$ and $R_R(Y) > 1$ guarantee that $g''(R) > 0$ ($g(\ )$ is convex).

Since $g''(R) > 0 \Leftrightarrow 2U''(sR)s + s^2RU'''(sR) > 0$
$$\Leftrightarrow 2U''(sR) + sRU'''(sR) > 0,$$

we need to show this latter inequality is satisfied.

(continued)

Theorem 4.7 (*continued*)

By the lemma, since $R'_R(Y) < 0$

$$-\{U'''(Y)Y + U''(Y)[1 + R_R(Y)]\} < 0, or$$
$$\{U'''(Y)Y + U''(Y)[1 + R_R(Y)]\} > 0.$$

Since $U''(Y) < 0$, and $R_R(Y) > 1$,

$$U''(Y)Y + U''(Y)(2) > \{U'''(Y)Y + U''(Y)[1 + R_R(Y)]\} > 0.$$

This is true for all Y; hence

$$2U''(sR) + sRU'''(sR) > 0 \text{ as required.}$$

Theorem 4.7 implies that for the class of constant relative risk aversion utility functions, or, functions of the form

$$U(c) = (1 - \gamma)^{-1}c^{1-\gamma}$$

$(\gamma > 0), (\gamma \neq 1)$, an increase in risk increases savings if $\gamma > 1$ and decreases it if $\gamma < 1$, with the $U(c) = \ln(c)$ case being the watershed for which savings is unaffected. For broader classes of utility functions, this theorem provides a partial characterization only, suggesting different investors react differently according to whether they display declining or increasing relative risk aversion.

A more complete characterization of the issue of interest is afforded if we introduce the concept of prudence, first proposed by Kimball (1990). Let

$$P(c) = \frac{-U'''(c)}{U''(c)}$$

be a measure of Absolute Prudence, while by analogy with relative risk aversion,

$$P(c)c = \frac{-cU'''(c)}{U''(c)}$$

then measures Relative Prudence. Theorem 4.7 can now be restated as Theorem 4.8.

Theorem 4.8:
Let $\tilde{R}_A, \tilde{R}_B$ be two return distributions such that $\tilde{R}_A$ SSD $\tilde{R}_B$, and let s_A and s_B be, respectively, the savings out of Y_0 corresponding to the return distributions $\tilde{R}_A$ and $\tilde{R}_B$. Then,

$$s_A \geq s_B \quad \text{iff } cP(c) \leq 2, \text{ and conversely,}$$
$$s_A < s_B \quad \text{iff } cP(c) > 2.$$

In other words, risk-averse individuals with Relative Prudence lower than 2 decrease savings while those with Relative Prudence above 2 increase savings in the face of an increase in the riskiness of returns.

Proof:

We have seen that $s_A < s_B$ if and only if $g''(R) < 0$. From Equation (4.6), this means

$$sRU'''(sR) < -2, \text{ or}$$

$$cP(c) = \frac{sRU'''(sR)}{-U''(sR)} < 2, \text{ as claimed.}$$

The other part of the proposition is proved similarly.

BOX 4-2

Hours Worked and Wage Uncertainty

An issue similar in spirit to that considered in Theorems 4.7 and 4.8 is whether individuals work harder (supply more hours) or less hard (fewer hours) if there is a (mean-preserving) increase in their wage uncertainty. This turns out to be a fairly difficult question to answer with any generality.

Consider an individual whose utility depends upon his consumption level and the number of leisure hours he is able to enjoy; in other words,

$$U(\ ) = U(c, L - n),$$

where L denotes the total available hours and n the hours of work supplied. The labor market is presumed to be competitive and workers must commit to supplying a fixed number of hours before the uncertain wage, $\tilde{w}$, is determined. In this simplest possible formulation of the problem, workers solve

$$\max_{0 \le n \le L} EU(\tilde{w}n, L - n).$$

Suppose the workers' utility function is of the form $c^\gamma(L-n)^{1-\gamma}$. Then

$$\max_{0 \le n \le L} EU(\tilde{w}n, L - n)$$
$$= \max_{0 \le n \le L} E(\tilde{w}n)^\gamma(L - n)^{1-\gamma}$$
$$= \max E(\tilde{w})^\gamma\{n^\gamma(L - n)^{1-\gamma}\},$$

that is, hours supplied are independent of any statistical properties of the wage whatsoever. This is in the spirit of Theorem 4.7 when utility is logarithmic.

In the case where $U(c, L-n) = [a(c)^{1-\gamma} + b(L-n)^{1-\gamma}]^{-1/\gamma}$, Hartwick (2000) demonstrates that for small initial wage uncertainty and $\gamma < 0$, greater wage uncertainty induces the agent to supply more hours. He obtains this result via numerical analysis.

4.6.2 ILLUSTRATING PRUDENCE

The relevance of the concept of prudence can be illustrated in the simplest way if we turn to a slightly different problem, where one ignores uncertainty in returns (assuming, in effect, that the net return is identically zero) while asking how savings in period zero is affected by uncertain labor income in period 1. Our remarks in this context are drawn from Kimball (1990).

Let us write the agent's second-period labor income, Y, as $Y = \bar{Y} + \tilde{Y}$ where $\bar{Y}$ is the mean labor income and $\tilde{Y}$ measures deviations from the mean (of course, $E\tilde{Y} = 0$). The simplest form of the decision problem facing the agent is thus:

$$\max_s E\{U(Y_0 - s) + \delta U(s + \bar{Y} + \tilde{Y})\},$$

where $s = s_i$ satisfies the first-order condition

$$\text{(i)}\ U'(Y_0 - s_i) = \delta E\{U'(s_i + \bar{Y} + \tilde{Y})\}.$$

It will be of interest to compare the solution s_i to the previous FOC with the solution to the analogous decision problem, noted s_{ii}, in which the uncertain labor income component is absent. The latter FOC is simply

$$\text{(ii)}\ U'(Y_0 - s_{ii}) = \delta U'(s_{ii} + \bar{Y})$$

The issue, once again, is whether and to what extent s_i differs from s_{ii}.

One approach to this question, which gives content to the concept of prudence, is to ask what the agent would need to be paid (what compensation is required in terms of period 2 income) to ignore labor income risk, in other words, for his first-period consumption and savings decision to be unaffected by uncertainty in labor income. The answer to this question leads to the definition of the *compensating precautionary premium*, $\psi = \psi(\bar{Y}, \tilde{Y}, s)$, as the amount of additional second-period wealth (consumption) that must be given to the agent in order that the solution to (i) coincides with the solution to (ii). That is, the compensatory precautionary premium $\psi(\bar{Y}, \tilde{Y}, s)$ is defined as the solution of

$$U'(Y_0 - s_{ii}) = \delta E\{U'(s_{ii} + \bar{Y} + \tilde{Y} + \psi(\bar{Y}, \tilde{Y}, s))\}.$$

Kimball (1990) proves the results shown in Theorem 4.9.

Theorem 4.9:
Let $U(\ )$ be three times continuously differentiable and $P(s)$ be the index of Absolute Prudence. Then

(i) $\psi(\bar{Y}, \tilde{Y}, s) \approx \frac{1}{2}\sigma_{\tilde{Y}}^2 P(s + \bar{Y})$
(ii) Let $U_1(\ )$ and $U_2(\ )$ be two second-period utility functions for which

$$P_1(s) = \frac{-U_1'''(s)}{U_1''(s)} < \frac{-U_2'''(s)}{U_2''(S)} = P_2(s), \text{for all } s.$$

Then $\psi_2(\bar{Y}, \tilde{Y}, s) > \psi_1(\bar{Y}, \tilde{Y}, s)$ for all $s, \bar{Y}, \tilde{Y}$.

The result of Theorem 4.9 (i) shows that investors' precautionary premia are directly proportional to the product of their prudence index and the variance of their uncertain income component, a result analogous to the characterization of the measure of absolute risk aversion obtained in Section 3.3. The result of Theorem 4.9 (ii) confirms the intuition that the more prudent the agent, the greater the compensating premium.

4.6.3 THE JOINT SAVING-PORTFOLIO PROBLEM

Although, for conceptual reasons, we have so far distinguished the consumption-savings and the portfolio allocation decisions, it is obvious that the two decisions should really be considered jointly. We now formalize the consumption-savings-portfolio allocation problem:

$$\max_{\{a, s\}} U(Y_0 - s) + \delta EU(s(1 + r_f) + a(\tilde{r} - r_f)), \tag{4.7}$$

where s denotes the total amount saved and a is the amount invested in the risky asset. Specializing the utility function to the form $U(Y) = Y^{1-\gamma}/1 - \gamma$, the first-order conditions for this joint decision problem are

$$s: \quad (Y_0 - s)^{-\gamma}(-1) + \delta E([s(1 + r_f) + a(\tilde{r} - r_f)]^{-\gamma}(1 + r_f)) = 0$$
$$a: \quad E[(s(1 + r_f) + a(\tilde{r} - r_f)^{-\gamma}(\tilde{r} - r_f)] = 0$$

The first equation spells out the condition to be satisfied at the margin for the savings level—and by corollary, consumption—to be optimal. It involves comparing the marginal utility today with the expected marginal utility tomorrow, with the rate of transformation between consumption today and consumption tomorrow being the product of the discount factor and the gross risk-free return. This FOC need not occupy us any longer here. The interesting element is the solution to the second first-order condition: it has exactly the same form as Equation (4.1) with the endogenous (optimal) s replacing the exogenous initial wealth level Y_0. Let us rewrite this equation as

$$s^{-\gamma}E\left[\left((1 + r_f) + \frac{a}{s}(\tilde{r} - r_f)\right)^{-\gamma}(\tilde{r} - r_f)\right] = 0,$$

which implies:

$$E\left[\left((1 + r_f) + \frac{a}{s}(\tilde{r} - r_f)\right)^{-\gamma}(\tilde{r} - r_f)\right] = 0.$$

This equation confirms the lessons of Equations (4.2) and (4.3): For the selected utility function, the proportion of savings invested in the risky asset is independent of s, the amount saved. This is an important result that does not generalize to other utility functions, but opens up the possibility of a straightforward extension of the savings-portfolio problem to a many-period problem. We pursue this important extension in Section 4.8.

4.7   SEPARATING RISK AND TIME PREFERENCES

In the context of a standard consumption-savings problem such as Equation (4.4), let us suppose once again that the agent's period utility function has been specialized to have the standard CRRA form,

$$U(c) = \frac{c^{1-\gamma}}{1 - \gamma}, \gamma > 0.$$

For this utility function, the single parameter γ captures not only the agent's sensitivity to risk, but also his sensitivity to consumption variation across time periods and, equivalently, his willingness to substitute consumption in one period for consumption in another. A high γ signals a strong desire for a very smooth inter-temporal consumption profile and, simultaneously, a strong reluctance to substitute consumption in one period for consumption in another. To see this more clearly, consider a deterministic version of Equation (4.4) where $\delta < 1, \tilde{x} \equiv 1$:

$$\max_{s \leq Y_0} E\{U(Y_0 - s) + \delta U(s)\}$$

with $U(c) = c^{1-\gamma}/1 - \gamma, \gamma > 0$.

The necessary and sufficient first-order condition is

$$-(Y_0 - s)^{-\gamma} + \delta s^{-\gamma} = 0, \text{ or } \left(\frac{1}{\delta}\right)^{1/\gamma} = \left(\frac{Y_0 - s}{s}\right).$$

With $\delta < 1$, as the agent becomes more and more risk averse $(\gamma \mapsto \infty), (Y_0 - s)/s \mapsto 1$; in other words, $c_0 \approx c_1$. For this preference structure, a highly risk-averse agent will also seek an inter-temporal consumption profile that is very smooth.

While in an atemporal setting, the desire for smooth consumption (across states of nature) is the very definition of risk aversion (Chapter 1, Boxes 1-1 and 1-2), in a multi-period environment, risk aversion and inter-temporal consumption smoothing need not be similarly related. After all, one may speak of inter-temporal consumption smoothing in a no-risk, deterministic setting, and one may speak of risk aversion in an uncertain, atemporal environment. This situation, where the same parameters determine both, is thus restrictive. Empirical studies, furthermore, tend to suggest that typical individuals are more averse to inter-temporal substitution (they desire very smooth consumption inter-temporally) than they are averse to risk *per se*. This latter fact cannot be captured in the aforementioned, single-parameter setting.

Is it possible to generalize the standard utility specification and break this coincidence of time and risk preferences? Epstein and Zin (1989, 1991) answer positively and propose a class of utility functions that allows each dimension to be parametrized separately while still preserving the time consistency property discussed in Section 2.7 of Chapter 2. They provide, in particular, the axiomatic basis for preferences over lotteries leading to the Kreps and Porteus (1978)-like utility representation (see Chapter 2):

$$U_t = U(c_t, c_{t+1}, c_{t+2}, \ldots) = W(c_t, CE(\tilde{U}_{t+1})), \tag{4.8}$$

where $CE(\tilde{U}_{t+1})$ denotes the certainty equivalent in terms of period t consumption of the uncertain utility in all future periods. Epstein and Zin (1991) and others (e.g., Weil (1989)) explore the following CES-like specialized version:

$$U(c_t, CE_{t+1}) = [(1 - \kappa)c_t^\rho + \kappa CE_{t+1}^\rho]^{1/\rho}, 0 \neq \rho < 1, \text{ or} \tag{4.9i}$$
$$U(c_t, CE_{t+1}) = (1 - \kappa)\log c_t + \kappa \log CE_{t+1}, \rho = 0, \tag{4.9ii}$$

where $CE_{t+1} = CE(\tilde{U}_{t+1})$ is the certainty equivalent of future utility and is calculated according to

$$[CE(\tilde{U}_{t+1})]^{1-\gamma} = E_t(\tilde{U}_{t+1})^{1-\gamma}, 1 \neq \gamma > 0, \text{ or} \tag{4.10i}$$
$$\log CE(\tilde{U}_{t+1}) = E_t(\log \tilde{U}_{t+1}), \gamma = 1 \tag{4.10ii}$$

Epstein and Zin (1989) show that γ can be viewed as a measure of risk aversion in the sense that as γ declines (becomes more negative) the agent indeed exhibits a more risk-averse behavior. Similarly, when the time preference parameter ρ becomes smaller, the agent becomes less willing to substitute consumption inter-temporally. If $\gamma = \rho$, recursive substitution to eliminate U_t yields

$$U_t = \left[(1 - \kappa) E_t \sum_{j=0}^{\infty} \kappa^j c_{t+j}^{1-\gamma} \right]^{1/1-\gamma}$$

which represents the same preference as

$$E_t \sum_{j=0}^{\infty} \kappa^j c_{t+j}^{1-\gamma},$$

and is thus equivalent to the usual time separable case with CRRA utility.

Although seemingly complex, this utility representation turns out to be surprisingly easy to work with in consumption-savings contexts. We will provide an illustration of its use in Chapter 10 when discussing the equity premium puzzle. Note, however, that Equations (4.9) and (4.10) do not lead to an expected utility representation, as the probabilities do not enter linearly. If one wants to extricate time and risk preferences, the expected utility framework must be abandoned.

4.8   MULTIPERIOD PORTFOLIO CHOICE

The consumption-savings-portfolio problem that is at the core of our attention in this chapter is fundamentally a multiperiod problem. Yet, our canonical problem so far has been cast in the one-period, static, now-and-then setting, a setting that also characterizes Modern Portfolio Theory and the CAPM to which we will turn in the following two chapters. Before doing so, we close the present one by casting the portfolio problem in its natural multiperiod mode, thus alerting the reader to an important dimension in which these core theories of modern finance are fundamentally lacking. We do it with the sole ambition of illustrating a broader perspective, as a full coverage of this most important topic appears, at this stage, beyond the scope of this text.

Let us go back to the joint saving-portfolio problem of Section 4.6.3 and propose the following multiperiod version of this problem:

$$\max_{\{s_t, a_t\}} E\left(\sum_{t=0}^{T} \delta^t U(c_t) \right) \text{ s.t.}$$

$$c_T = s_{T-1}(1 + r_f) + a_{T-1}(\tilde{r}_T - r_f)$$

$$c_t + s_t \leq s_{t-1}(1 + r_f) + a_{t-1}(\tilde{r}_t - r_f)$$

$$c_0 + s_0 \leq Y_0.$$

Now suppose the property obtained in Section 4.6.3, the independence of the a/s ratio from the savings level, does not hold. The previous problem would then become seriously complex. Depending on specific future events, in particular, variations in the risk-free rate and realizations of the risky return, the agent's level of income and thus of savings would vary widely. So would portfolio choices since they would not be invariant to changes in beginning-of-period wealth. This is indeed the general case and its solution is detailed in Merton (1971). As a first approach it is realistic to try to maintain the independence property. Let us thus make the CRRA utility hypothesis, and in addition assume that the return environment is not changing through time, in other words, that r_f is constant through time and $\{\tilde{r}_t\}$ is independently and identically distributed (i.i.d.). The latter assumptions guarantee that future return prospects always look the same. Combined with the CRRA hypothesis it indeed produces the desired result, which is summarized in Theorem 4.10.

Theorem 4.10 (Merton, 1971):

Consider the canonical multiperiod consumption-saving-portfolio allocation problem. Suppose $U(\ )$ displays CRRA, r_f is constant, and $\{\tilde{r}_t\}$ is i.i.d. Then the ratio a_t/s_t is time invariant.

This is an important result in the following sense: It delineates the conditions under which a pure static portfolio choice analysis will be generalizable to a multiperiod context. The optimal portfolio choice—in the sense of the allocation decision between the risk-free and the risky asset—defined in a static one-period context, will continue to characterize the optimal portfolio decision in the more natural multiperiod environment. The conditions that are imposed are easy to understand: If the returns on the risky asset were not independently distributed, today's realization of the risky return observation made today would provide information about future returns that would almost surely affect the allocation decision. Suppose, for example, that returns are positively correlated. Then a good realization today would suggest high returns are more likely again tomorrow. It would then be natural to take this into account by, say, increasing the share of the risky asset in the portfolio (beware, however, that, as the first sections of the present chapter illustrate, without extra assumption on the shape of the utility function (beyond risk aversion) the more intuitive result may not generally occur). The same can be said if the risk-free rate was changing through time. In a period of high risk-free rates, the riskless asset would be more attractive, all other things equal.

The need for the other assumption—the CRRA utility specification—is a direct consequence of Theorem 4.5. With a utility form other than CRRA, Theorem 4.5 tells us that the share of wealth invested in the risky asset varies with the initial wealth level. But in a multiperiod context, the investable wealth, that is the savings level, is sure to be changing over time, increasing when realized returns are favorable and decreasing otherwise. With a non-CRRA utility function, optimal portfolio allocations would consistently be affected by these changes.

Now let us illustrate the power of these ideas to evaluate an important practical problem. Consider the problem of an individual investor saving for retirement. At each period he must decide what fraction of his already accumulated wealth should be invested in stocks (understood to mean a well-diversified portfolio of risky assets) and risk-free bonds for the next investment period. Popular wisdom in this area can be summarized in the following three assertions:

1. Early in life the investor should invest nearly all of his wealth in stocks (stocks have historically outperformed risk-free assets over long (20-year periods), while gradually shifting almost entirely into risk-free instruments as retirement approaches in order to avoid the possibility of a catastrophic loss.

2. If an investor is saving for a target level of wealth (such as, in the U.S., college tuition payments for children), he should gradually reduce his holdings in stocks as

his wealth approaches the target level in order to minimize the risk of a short fall due to an unexpected market downturn.

3. Investors who are working and saving from their labor income should rely more heavily on stocks early in their working lives, not only because of the historically higher returns that stocks provide, but also because bad stock market returns, early on, can be offset by increased saving out of labor income.

Following Jagannathan and Kocherlakota (1996), we wish to subject these assertions to the discipline of the ideas presented in this chapter. Let us maintain the assumptions of Theorem 4.10 and hypothesize that the risk-free rate is constant, that stock returns $\{r_t\}$ are i.i.d. (that they are at least independently distributed is a good first approximation of the empirical evidence), and that the investor's utility function assumes the standard CRRA form.

To evaluate assertion 1, let us appeal to Theorem 4.1 while abstracting away from the consumption-savings problem. This amounts to assuming that the investor seeks to maximize the utility of his terminal wealth W_T in period T, the planned conclusion of his working life. Under CRRA we know that the investor should invest the same fraction of his wealth in risky assets every period (disproving the assertion), but it is worthwhile to see how this comes about in a simple multiperiod setting.

Let S_t and B_t denote, respectively, the investment in stocks and bonds in period t, and let $\tilde{r}$ denote the (invariant) risky return distribution; the investor solves:

$$\underset{\{S_t, B_t\}_{t=0}^{T-1}}{\text{Max }} E\left\{\frac{(W_T)^{1-\gamma}}{1-\gamma}\right\} \quad \text{s.t.}$$
$$W_T = S_{T-1}(1+\tilde{r}) + B_{T-1}(1+r_f) \qquad t = T$$
$$S_t + B_t \le S_{t-1}(1+\tilde{r}) + B_{t-1}(1+r_f) \quad 1 \le t \le T-1$$
$$S_0 + B_0 \le W_0$$

Problems of this type are most appropriately solved by working backward: first solving for the $T-1$ decision, then solving for the $T-2$ decision conditional on the $T-1$ decision, and so on. Let $s_{T-1} = S_{T-1}/W_{T-1}$ represent the fraction of the investor's period $T-1$ wealth invested in stocks. In period $T-1$, the investor solves:

$$\underset{s_{T-1}}{\max} \, E\{(1-\gamma)^{-1}[s_{T-1}W_{T-1}(1+\tilde{r}) + (1-s_{T-1})W_{T-1}(1+r_f)]^{1-\gamma}\}$$

The solution to this problem, $s_{T-1} = \hat{s}$, satisfies the first-order condition:

$$E\{[\hat{s}(1+\tilde{r}) + (1-\hat{s})(1+r_f)]^{-\gamma}(\tilde{r} - r_f)\} = 0$$

As expected, because of the CRRA assumption, the optimal fraction invested in stocks is independent of the period $T-1$ wealth level. Given this result, we can work backward. In period $T-2$, the investor rebalances his portfolio, knowing that in $T-1$ he will invest the fraction $\hat{s}$ in stocks. As such, his problem becomes:

$$\underset{s_{T-2}}{\max} \, E\langle(1-\gamma)^{-1}\{[s_{T-2}W_{T-2}(1+\tilde{r}) + (1-s_{T-2})W_{T-2}(1+r_f)][\hat{s}(1+\tilde{r}) + (1-\hat{s})(1+r_f)]\}^{1-\gamma}\rangle$$

Because stock returns are i.i.d., this objective function may be written as a product of the expectations as per

$$E[\hat{s}(1+\tilde{r}) + (1-\hat{s})(1+r_f)]^{1-\gamma} \underset{s_{T-2}}{\max} \, E\{(1-\gamma)^{-1}[s_{T-2}W_{T-2}(1+\tilde{r}) + (1-s_{T-2})W_{T-2}(1+r_f)]^{1-\gamma}\}$$

Written in this way the structure of the problem is no different than the prior one, and the solution is again $s_{T-2} = \hat{s}$. Repeating the same argument, it must be the case that $s_t = \hat{s}$ in every period, a result that depends, critically, not only on the CRRA assumption (wealth factors out of the first-order condition) but also on the independence. The risky return realized in any period does not alter our belief about the future return distributions. There is no meaningful difference between the long (many periods) run and the short run (one period): agents invest the same fraction in stocks irrespective of their portfolio's performance history. Assertion 1 is clearly not generally valid.

To evaluate our second assertion, and again following Jagannathan and Kocherlakota (1996), let us modify the agent's utility function to be of the form

$$U(W_T) = \begin{cases} \dfrac{(W_T - \bar{W})^{1-\gamma}}{1 - \gamma} & \text{if } W_T \geq \bar{W} \\ -\infty & \text{if } W_T < \bar{W} \end{cases}$$

where $\bar{W}$ is the target level of wealth. Under this formulation it is absolutely essential that the target be achieved: As long as there exists a positive probability of failing to achieve the target the investor's expected utility of terminal wealth is $-\infty$. Accordingly, we must also require that

$$W_0(1 + r_f)^T > \bar{W}; \text{ in other words,}$$

that the target can be attained by investing everything in risk-free assets. If such an inequality were not satisfied, then every strategy would yield an expected utility of $-\infty$, with the optimal strategy thus being indeterminate.

A straightforward analysis of this problem yields the following two-step solution:

Step 1: Always invest sufficient funds in risk-free assets to achieve the target wealth level with certainty, and

Step 2: Invest a constant share s^* of any additional wealth in stock, where s^* is time invariant.

By this solution, the investor invests less in stocks than he would in the absence of a target, but since he invests in both stocks and bonds, his wealth will accumulate, on average, more rapidly than it would if invested solely at the risk-free rate, and the stock portion of his wealth will, on average, grow faster. As a result, the investor will typically use proportionately less of his resources to guarantee achievement of the target. And, over time, targeting will tend to increase the share of wealth in stocks, again contrary to popular wisdom!

In order to evaluate assertion 3, we must admit savings from labor income into the analysis. Let $\{Y_t\}$ denote the stream of savings out of labor income. The investor's problem is now:

$$\max_{\{S_t, B_t\}_{t=0}^{T-1}} E\left\{\frac{(W_T)^{1-\gamma}}{1-\gamma}\right\} \text{ s.t.}$$
$$W_T = Y_T + S_{T-1}(1 + \tilde{r}) + B_{T-1}(1 + r_f) \qquad t = T$$
$$S_t + B_t \leq Y_t + S_{t-1}(1 + \tilde{r}) + B_{t-1}(1 + r_f) \quad 1 \leq t \leq T - 1$$
$$S_0 + B_0 \leq W_0; \{Y_t\}_{t=0}^{T} \text{ given}$$

(again abstracting away from the consumption-savings problem).

In any period, the investor now has two sources of wealth: financial wealth, FW_t, defined as

$$FW_t = Y_t + (1 + \hat{r})S_{t-1} + (1 + r_f)B_{t-1},$$

($\hat{r}$ is the realized value of $\tilde{r}$) and labor income wealth as measured by the present value of the future stream of labor income. For simplicity, assume this income stream is risk free with present value,

$$PV(Y_{t+}) = \frac{Y_{t+1}}{(1 + r_f)} + \cdots + \frac{Y_T}{(1 + r_f)^{T-t}}$$

Since the investor continues to have CRRA preferences, he will, in every period, invest a constant fraction of his total wealth $\vec{s}$ in stocks, where $\vec{s}$ depends only upon his CRRA and the characteristics of the return distributions $\tilde{r}$ and r_f; in other words,

$$S_t = \vec{s}(FW_t + PV(Y_{t+})).$$

As the investor approaches retirement, the $PV(Y_{t+})$ declines. In order to maintain the same fraction of wealth invested in risk-free assets, the fraction of financial wealth invested in stocks,

$$\frac{S_t}{FW_t} = \vec{s}\left(1 + \frac{PV(Y_t)}{FW_t}\right)$$

must decline on average. Here, at least the assertion has theoretical support, but for a reason different from that commonly believed.

4.9 CONCLUSIONS

We have considered, in a very simple context, the relationship between an investor's degree of risk aversion, on the one hand, and his desire to save and the composition of his portfolio on the other. Most of the results were intuitively acceptable and that, in itself, makes us more confident of the VNM representation.

Are there any lessons here for portfolio managers? At least three are suggested.

1. Irrespective of the level of risk, some investment in risky assets is warranted, even for the most risk-averse of clients (provided $E\tilde{r} > r_f$). This is the substance of Theorem 4.1.
2. As the value of a portfolio changes significantly, it should be restructured vis-à-vis its risk-free/risky asset composition. How that should be done depends critically on the client's attitudes toward risk. This is the substance of Theorems 4.2 to 4.6.
3. Investors are willing, in general, to pay to reduce income (consumption risk), and would like to enter into mutually advantageous transactions with institutions less risk-averse than themselves. This is the substance of Section 4.4.

We went on to consider how greater return uncertainty influences savings behavior. On this score and in some other instances, this chapter has illustrated the fact that, somewhat surprisingly, risk aversion is not always a sufficient hypothesis to recover intuitive behavior in the face of risk. The third derivative of the utility function often plays a role. The notion of prudence helps provide elegant characterization in these situations.

In many ways, this chapter has aimed at providing a broad perspective so that Modern Portfolio Theory and its underlying assumptions can be placed in their proper context. We are now ready to revisit this pillar of modern finance.

References

Arrow, K. J., *Essays in the Theory of Risk Bearing*, Chicago: Markham (1971).

Becker, G., and C. Mulligan, "The Endogenous Determination of Time Preferences," *Quarterly Journal of Economics*, 112 (1997), 729–758.

Cass, D., and J. E. Stiglitz, "The Structure of Investor Preference and Asset Returns and Separability in Portfolio Allocation: A Contribution to the Pure Theory of Mutual Funds," *Journal of Economic Theory*, 2 (1970), 122–160.

Epstein, L. G., and S. E. Zin, "Substitution, Risk Aversion, and the Temporal Behavior of Consumption Growth and Asset Returns I: Theoretical Framework," *Econometrica*, 57 (1989), 937–969.

Epstein, L. G., and S. E. Zin, "Substitution, Risk Aversion, and the Temporal Behavior of Consumption Growth and Asset Returns II: An Empirical Analysis," *Journal of Political Economics*, 99 (1991), 263–286.

Hartwick, J., "Labor Supply Under Wage Uncertainty," *Economics Letters*, 68 (2000), 319–325.

Jagannathan, R., and N. R. Kocherlakota, "Why Should Older People Invest Less in Stocks than Younger People?" *Fed. Reserve Bank of Minneapolis Quarterly Review*, summer (1996), 11–23.

Kimball, M. S., "Precautionary Savings in the Small and in the Large," *Econometrica*, 58 (1990), 53–73.

Kreps, P., and E. Porteus, "Temporal Resolution of Uncertainty and Dynamic Choice Theory," *Econometrica*, 461 (1978), 185–200.

Merton, R.C., "Optimum Consumption and Portfolio Rules in a Continuous-Time Model," *Journal of Economic Theory*, 3 (1971), 373–413.

Rothschild, M., and J. Stiglitz, "Increasing Risk II: Its Economic Consequences," *Journal of Economic Theory*, 3 (1971), 66–84.

Weil, Ph., "The Equity Premium Puzzle and the Riskfree Rate Puzzle," *Journal of Monetary Economics*, 24 (1989), 401–421.

CHAPTER 5

RISK AVERSION AND INVESTMENT DECISIONS, PART II: MODERN PORTFOLIO THEORY

5.1 INTRODUCTION

In the context of the previous chapter, we encountered the following canonical portfolio problem:

$$\max_{a} EU(\tilde{Y}) = \max_{a} EU[Y_0(1 + r_f) + a(\tilde{r} - r_f)]. \tag{5.1}$$

Here the portfolio choice is limited to allocating investable wealth, Y_0, between a risk-free and a risky asset, a being the amount invested in the latter.

Slightly more generally, we can admit N risky assets, with returns $(\tilde{r}_1, \tilde{r}_2, \ldots, \tilde{r}_N)$, as in the Cass-Stiglitz theorem. The above problem in this case becomes:

$$\max_{\{a_1, a_2, \ldots, a_N\}} EU\left(Y_0(1 + r_f) + \sum_{i=1}^{N} a_i(\tilde{r}_i - r_f)\right)$$

$$= \max_{\{w_1, w_2, \ldots, w_N\}} EU\left(Y_0(1 + r_f) + \sum_{i=1}^{N} w_i Y_0(\tilde{r}_i - r_f)\right) \tag{5.2}$$

where w_i is the proportion of wealth invested in the risky asset i. The latter expression may further be written as

$$\max_{\{w_1, w_2, \ldots, w_N\}} EU\left\{Y_0\left[(1 + r_f) + \sum_{i=1}^{N} w_i(\tilde{r}_i - r_f)\right]\right\}$$

$$= EU\{Y_0[1 + \tilde{R}]\} = EU\{\tilde{Y}_1\} \tag{5.3}$$

where $\tilde{Y}$ denotes the end of period wealth and $\tilde{R}$ the rate of return on the overall portfolio of assets held.

Modern Portfolio Theory (MPT) explores the details of a similar portfolio choice (Problem 5.3) under the mean-variance utility hypothesis, and (2) for an arbitrary number of risky investments, with or without a risk-free asset. The goal of this chapter is to review the fundamentals underlying this theory. We first draw the connection between the mean-variance utility hypothesis and our earlier utility development.

5.2 MORE ABOUT UTILITY FUNCTIONS

What provides utility? As noted in Chapter 2, financial economics assumes that the ultimate source of a consumer's satisfaction is the consumption of the goods and services he is able to purchase.[1] Preference relations and utility functions are accordingly defined on bundles of consumption goods:

$$u(c_1, c_2, \ldots, c_n), \tag{5.4}$$

where the indexing $i = 1, \ldots, n$ is across date-state commodities: goods characterized not only by their identity as a product or service but also by the time and state in which they may be consumed. States of nature, however, are mutually exclusive. For each date and state of nature (θ) there is a traditional budget constraint

$$p_{1\theta} c_{1k} + p_{2\theta} c_{2\theta} + \ldots + p_{m\theta} c_{m\theta} \leq Y_\theta \tag{5.5}$$

where the indexing runs across goods only, in other words, the m consumption goods $c_{i\theta}$, $i = 1, \ldots, m$, prices $p_{i\theta}$, $i = 1, \ldots, m$ are for the m goods available in state of nature θ, and Y_θ is the ("end period") wealth level available in that same state. We quite naturally assume that the number of goods available in each state is constant.[2]

In this context, and in some sense summarizing what we did in our last chapter, it is quite natural to think of an individual's decision problem as being undertaken sequentially, in three steps.

STEP 1: THE CONSUMPTION-SAVINGS DECISION

Here, the issue is deciding how much to consume versus how much to save today: how to split period zero income I_0 between current consumption now c_0 and saving Y_0 for consumption in the future where

$$C_0 + Y_0 = I_0.$$

STEP 2: THE PORTFOLIO PROBLEM

At this second step, the problem is to choose assets in which to invest one's savings so as to obtain the desired pattern of end-of-period wealth across the various states of nature. This means, in particular, allocating Y_0 between the risk-free and the N risky assets with $(1 - \sum_{i=1}^{N} w_i) Y_0$ representing the investment in the risk-free asset, and $(w_1 Y_0, w_2 Y_0, \ldots, w_N Y_0)$, representing the vector of investments in the various risky assets.

---

[1]Of course this doesn't mean that nothing else in life provides utility or satisfaction (!) but the economist's inquiry is normally limited to the realm of market phenomena and economic choices.
[2]This is purely formal: if a good is not available in a given state of nature, it is said to exist but with a total economy-wide endowment of the good being zero.

STEP 3: TOMORROW'S CONSUMPTION CHOICE

Given the realized state of nature and the wealth level obtained, there remains the issue of choosing consumption bundles to maximize the utility function [Equation (5.4)] subject to Equation (5.5) where $Y_\theta = Y_0[(1 + r_f) + \sum_{i=1}^{N} w_i(r_{i\theta} - r_f)]$ and $r_{i\theta}$ denotes the ex-post return to asset i in state θ.

In such problems, it is fruitful to work by backward induction, starting from the end (step 3). Step 3 is a standard microeconomic problem and for our purpose its solution can be summarized by a utility-of-money function $U(Y_\theta)$ representing the (maximum) level of utility that results from optimizing in step 3 given that the wealth available in state θ is Y_θ. In other words,

$$U(Y_\theta) \equiv_{\text{def}} \max_{(c_{1k}, \ldots, c_{m\theta})} u(c_{1\theta}, \ldots, c_{m\theta})$$
$$\text{s.t., } p_{1\theta} c_{1\theta} + \ldots + p_{m\theta} c_{m\theta} \leq Y_\theta.$$

Naturally enough, maximizing the expected utility of Y_θ across all states of nature becomes the objective of step 2:

$$\max_{\{w_1, w_2, \ldots, w_N\}} EU(\tilde{Y}) = \sum_\theta \pi_\theta U(Y_\theta).$$

Here, π_θ is the probability of state of nature θ. The end-of-period wealth (a random variable) can now be written as $\tilde{Y} = Y_0(1 + \tilde{R})$, with Y_0 the initial wealth net of date 0 consumption and $\tilde{R} = \{(1 + r_f) + \sum_{i=1}^{N} w_i(\tilde{r}_i - r_f)\}$, the rate of return on the portfolio of assets in which Y_0 is invested. This brings us back to Equation (5.3).

Clearly with an appropriate redefinition of the utility function,

$$\max EU(\tilde{Y}) = \max EU(Y_0(1 + \tilde{R})) =_{\text{def}} \max E\hat{U}(\tilde{R})$$

where in all cases the decision variables are portfolio proportions (or amounts) invested in the different available assets. The level of investable wealth, Y_0, becomes a parameter of the $\hat{U}(.)$ representation. Note that restrictions on the form of the utility function do not have the same meaning when imposed on $U(.)$ or on $\hat{U}(.)$, or for that matter on $u(.)$ [(as in Equation (5.4)].

Finally, given the characteristics (e.g., expected return, standard deviation) of the optimally chosen portfolio, the optimal consumption and savings levels can be selected. We are back in step 1 of the decision problem.

From now on in this chapter we shall work with utility functions defined on the overall portfolio's rate of return $\tilde{R}$. This utility index can be further constrained to be a function of the *mean and variance* (or standard deviation) of the probability distribution of $\tilde{R}$. This latter simplification can be accepted either as a working approximation or it can be seen as resulting from two further (alternative) hypotheses made within the expected utility framework: It must be assumed that the decision maker's utility function is quadratic or that asset returns are normally distributed.

The main justification for using a mean-variance approximation is its tractability. As already noted, probability distributions are cumbersome to manipulate and difficult to estimate empirically. Summarizing them by their first two moments is appealing and leads to a rich set of implications that can be tested empirically.

Using a simple Taylor series approximation, one can also see that the mean and variance of an agent's wealth distribution are critical to the determination of his expected utility for any distribution. Let $\tilde{Y}$ denote an investor's end period wealth, an uncertain quantity, and $U(.)$ his utility-of-money function. The Taylor series approximation for his utility of wealth around $E(\tilde{Y})$ yields:

$$U(\tilde{Y}) = U[E(\tilde{Y})] + U'[E(\tilde{Y})][\tilde{Y} - E(\tilde{Y})]$$
$$+ \tfrac{1}{2} U''[E(\tilde{Y})][\tilde{Y} - E(\tilde{Y})]^2 + H_3 \quad \textbf{(5.6)}$$

where

$$H_3 = \sum_{j=3}^{\infty} \frac{1}{j!} U^{(j)}[E(\tilde{Y})][\tilde{Y} - E(\tilde{Y})]^j.$$

Now let us compute expected utility using this approximation:

$$EU(\tilde{Y}) = U[E(\tilde{Y})] + U'[E(\tilde{Y})]\underbrace{[E(\tilde{Y}) - E(\tilde{Y})]}_{=0} + \tfrac{1}{2} U''[E(\tilde{Y})]\underbrace{E[\tilde{Y} - E(\tilde{Y})]^2}_{=\sigma^2(\tilde{Y})} + EH_3$$

$$= U[E(\tilde{Y})] + \tfrac{1}{2} U''[E(\tilde{Y})]\sigma^2(\tilde{Y}) + EH_3.$$

If EH_3 is small, to a first approximation only, $E(\tilde{Y})$ and $\sigma^2(\tilde{Y})$ are central to determining $EU(\tilde{Y})$.

If $U(Y)$ is quadratic, U'' is a constant and, as a result, $EH_3 \equiv 0$, so $E(\tilde{Y})$ and $\sigma^2(\tilde{Y})$ are all that matter. If $\tilde{Y}$ is normally distributed, EH_3 can be expressed in terms of $E(\tilde{Y})$ and $\sigma^2(\tilde{Y})$, so the approximation is exact in this case as well. These well-known assertions are detailed in Appendix 5.1 where it is also shown that, under either of the above hypotheses, indifference curves in the mean-variance space are increasing and convex to the origin.

Assuming the utility objective function is quadratic, however, is not fully satisfactory since the preference representation would then possess an attribute we deemed fairly implausible in the previous chapters, increasing absolute risk aversion (IARA). On this ground, supposing all or most investors have a quadratic utility function is very restrictive. The normality hypothesis on the rate of return processes is easy to verify directly, but we know it cannot, in general, be satisfied exactly. Limited liability instruments such as stocks can pay at worst a negative return of −100% (complete loss of the investment). Even more clearly at variance with the normality hypothesis, default-free (government) bonds always yield a positive return (abstracting from inflation). These remarks suggest that our analysis to follow must be viewed as an (useful and productive) approximation.

BOX 5-1

About the Probability Distribution on Returns

As noted in the text, the assumption that period returns (e.g., daily, monthly, annual) are normally distributed is inconsistent with the limited liability feature of most financial instruments; i.e., $\tilde{r}_{it} \geq -1$ for most securities i. It furthermore presents a problem for computing compounded cumulative returns: The product of normally distributed random variables (returns) is not itself normally distributed.

(*continued*)

BOX 5-1 (*continued*)

These objectives are made moot if we assume that it is the continuously compounded rate of return, r_{it}^c, that is normally distributed where $\tilde{r}_{it}^c = \log(1 + \tilde{r}_{it})$.

This is consistent with limited liability since $Y_0 e^{\tilde{r}_{it}^c} \geq 0$ for any $\tilde{r}_{it}^c \in (-\infty, +\infty)$. It has the added feature that cumulative continuously compounded returns are normally distributed since the sum of normally distributed random variables is normally distributed.

The working assumption in empirical financial economics is that continuously compounded equity returns are i.i.d. normal; in other words, for all times t,

$$\tilde{r}_{it}^c \approx N(\mu_i, \sigma_i).$$

By way of language we say that the discrete period returns $\tilde{r}_{it}^c$ are lognormally distributed because their logarithm is normally distributed. There is substantial statistical evidence to support this assumption, subject to a number of qualifications.

1. First, while the normal distribution is perfectly symmetric about its mean, daily stock returns are frequently skewed to the right. Conversely, the returns to certain stock indices appear

(*continued*)

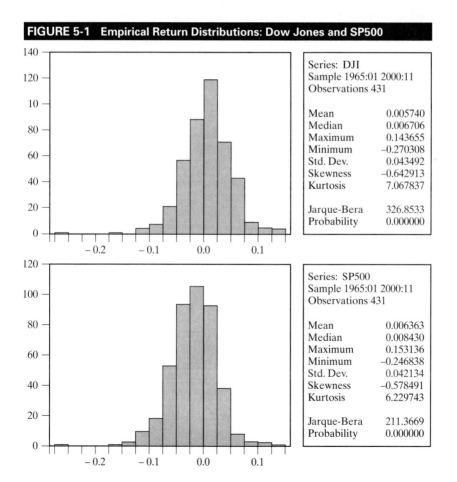

FIGURE 5-1   Empirical Return Distributions: Dow Jones and SP500

Series: DJI
Sample 1965:01 2000:11
Observations 431

Mean	0.005740
Median	0.006706
Maximum	0.143655
Minimum	−0.270308
Std. Dev.	0.043492
Skewness	−0.642913
Kurtosis	7.067837
Jarque-Bera	326.8533
Probability	0.000000

Series: SP500
Sample 1965:01 2000:11
Observations 431

Mean	0.006363
Median	0.008430
Maximum	0.153136
Minimum	−0.246838
Std. Dev.	0.042134
Skewness	−0.578491
Kurtosis	6.229743
Jarque-Bera	211.3669
Probability	0.000000

BOX 5-1 (*continued*)

skewed to the left.[3] Figure 5-1 illustrates for the returns on the Dow Jones and the S&P 500. Both indices display negative skewness and a significant degree of kurtosis.

2. Second, the sample daily return distributions for many individual stocks exhibit "excess kurtosis" or "fat tails"; i.e., there is more probability in the tails than would be justified by the normal distribution. The same is true of stock indices. The extent of

this excess kurtosis diminishes substantially, however, when monthly data is used.[4]

There is one further complication. Even if individual stock returns are lognormally distributed, the returns to a portfolio of such stocks need not be lognormal (log of a sum is not equal to the sum of the logs). The extent of the error introduced by assuming lognormal portfolio returns is usually not great if the return period is short (e.g., daily).

Note also that in this chapter we are assuming the investor knows and takes as exogenously given the vector of return random variables $(\tilde{r}_1, \tilde{r}_2, \ldots, \tilde{r}_N)$. We have not yet discussed how these rate of return distributions are determined. We are at the stage of identifying demand curves, and not yet attempting to describe equilibrium prices or returns.

5.3 DESCRIPTION OF THE OPPORTUNITY SET IN THE MEAN-VARIANCE SPACE: THE GAINS FROM DIVERSIFICATION AND THE EFFICIENT FRONTiER

The main idea of this section is as follows: The expected return to a portfolio is the *weighted* average of the expected returns of the assets composing the portfolio. The same result is not generally true for the variance. The variance of a portfolio is generally *smaller* than the weighted average of the variances of individual asset returns corresponding to this portfolio. Therein lies the gain from diversification.

Let us illustrate this assertion, starting with the case of a portfolio of two assets only. The typical investor's objective is to maximize a function $U(\mu_R, \sigma_R)$, where $U_1 > 0$ and $U_2 < 0$: he likes expected return (μ_R) and dislikes standard deviation (σ_R). In this context, one recalls that an asset (or portfolio) A is said to **mean-variance dominate** an asset (or portfolio) B if $\mu_A \geq \mu_B$ and simultaneously $\sigma_A < \sigma_B$, or if $\mu_A > \mu_B$ while $\sigma_A \leq \sigma_B$. We can then define the **efficient frontier** as the locus of all non-dominated portfolios in the mean-standard deviation space. By definition, no ("rational") mean-variance investor would choose to hold a portfolio not located on the efficient frontier. The shape of the efficient frontier is thus of primary interest.

Let us examine the efficient frontier in the two-asset case for a variety of possible asset return correlations. The basis for the results of this section is the formula for the

---

[3]Skewness: The extent to which a distribution is "pushed left or right" off symmetry is measured by the skewness statistic $S(\tilde{r}_{it})$, defined by $S(\tilde{r}_{it}) = E((r_{it} - \mu_i)^3/\sigma_i^3)$. $S(\tilde{r}_{it}) \equiv 0$ if $\tilde{r}_{it}$ is normally distributed. $S(\tilde{r}_{it}) > 0$ suggests a rightward bias, and conversely if $S(\tilde{r}_{it}) < 0$.
[4]Kurtosis is measured as the normalized fourth moment: $K(\tilde{r}_{it}) = E((r_{it} - \mu_i)^4/\sigma_i^4)$. If $\tilde{r}_{it}$ is normal then $K(\tilde{r}_{it}) = 3$, but fat-tailed distribution with extra probability weight in the tail areas have higher kurtosis measures.

variance of a portfolio of two assets, 1 and 2, defined by their respective expected returns, $\bar{r}_1, \bar{r}_2$, standard deviations, σ_1 and σ_2, and their correlation $\rho_{1,2}$:

$$\sigma_R^2 = w_1^2 \sigma_1^2 + (1 - w_1)^2 \sigma_2^2 + 2w_1(1 - w_1)\sigma_1\sigma_2\rho_{1,2},$$

where w_1 is the proportion of the portfolio allocated to asset 1. The following results, detailed in Appendix 5.2, are of importance.

CASE 1 (REFERENCE)

In the case of two risky assets with perfectly positively correlated returns, the efficient frontier is linear. In that extreme case the two assets are essentially identical, there is no gain from diversification, and the portfolio's standard deviation is nothing other than the average of the standard deviations of the component assets:

$$\sigma_R = w_1\sigma_1 + (1 - w_1)\sigma_2.$$

As a result, the equation of the efficient frontier is

$$\mu_R = \bar{r}_1 + \frac{\bar{r}_2 - \bar{r}_1}{\sigma_2 - \sigma_1}(\sigma_R - \sigma_1),$$

as depicted in Figure 5-2. It assumes positive amounts of both assets are held.

CASE 2

In the case of two risky assets with imperfectly correlated returns, the standard deviation of the portfolio is necessarily smaller than it would be if the two component assets were perfectly correlated. By the previous result, one must have $\sigma_R < w_1\sigma_1 + (1 + w_1)\sigma_2$, provided the proportions are not 0 or 1. Thus, the efficient frontier must stand left of the straight line in Figure 5-2. This is illustrated in Figure 5-3 for different values of $\rho_{1,2}$.

The smaller the correlation (the further away it is from +1), the more to the left is the efficient frontier as demonstrated formally in Appendix 5.2. Note that the diagram makes clear that in this case, some portfolios made up of assets 1 and 2 are, in fact, dominated by other portfolios. Unlike in Case 1, not all portfolios are efficient. In view of future developments, it is useful to distinguish the **minimum variance frontier** from the efficient frontier. In the present case, all portfolios between A and B belong to the minimum variance frontier, that is, they correspond to the combination of assets with minimum variance for all arbitrary levels of expected returns. However, certain levels of expected returns are not efficient targets since higher levels of returns can be obtained

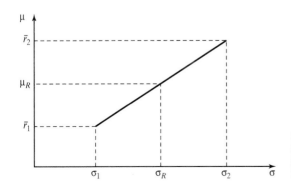

FIGURE 5-2   The Efficient Frontier: Two Perfectly Correlated Risky Assets

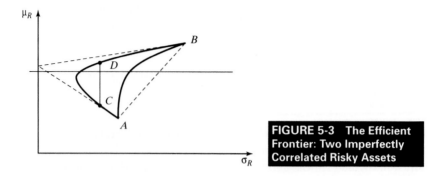

FIGURE 5-3 The Efficient Frontier: Two Imperfectly Correlated Risky Assets

for identical levels of risk. Thus portfolio C is minimum variance, but it is not efficient, being dominated by portfolio D, for instance. Figure 5-3 again assumes positive amounts of both assets (A and B) are held.

CASE 3

If the two risky assets have returns that are perfectly negatively correlated, one can show that the minimum variance portfolio is risk free while the frontier is once again linear. Its graphical representation in that case is in Figure 5-4, with the corresponding demonstration placed in Appendix 5.2.

CASE 4

If one of the two assets is risk free, then the efficient frontier is a straight line originating on the vertical axis at the level of the risk-free return. In the absence of a short sales restriction, that is, if it is possible to borrow at the risk-free rate to leverage one's holdings of the risky asset, then, intuitively enough, the overall portfolio can be made riskier than the riskiest among the existing assets. In other words, it can be made riskier than the one risky asset and it must be that the efficient frontier is projected to the right of the $(\bar{r}_2, \sigma_2)$ point (defining asset 1 as the risk-free asset). This situation is depicted in Figure 5-5 with the corresponding results demonstrated in Appendix 5.2.

FIGURE 5-4 The Efficient Frontier: Two Perfectly Negatively Correlated Risky Assets

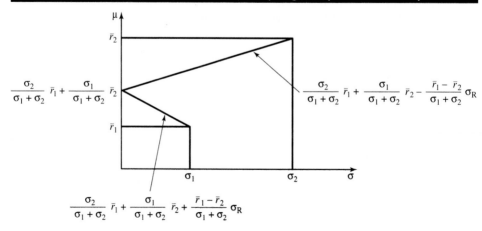

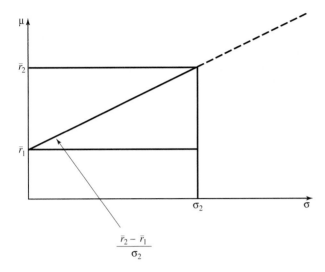

FIGURE 5-5   The Efficient Frontier: One Risky and One Risk Free Asset

CASE 5 (*n* RISKY ASSETS)

It is important to realize that a portfolio is also an asset, fully defined by its expected return, its standard deviation, and its correlation with other existing assets or portfolios. Thus, the previous analysis with two assets is more general than it appears: It can easily be repeated with one of the two assets being a portfolio. In that way, one can extend the analysis from two to three assets, from three to four, etc. If there are *n* risky, imperfectly correlated assets, then the efficient frontier will have the bullet shape of Figure 5-6. Adding an extra asset to the two-asset framework implies that the diversification possibilities are improved and that, in principle, the efficient frontier is displaced to the left.

CASE 6

If there are *n* risky assets and a risk-free one, the efficient frontier is a straight line once again. To arrive at this conclusion, let us arbitrarily pick one portfolio on the efficient frontier when there are *n* risky assets only, say portfolio *E* in Figure 5-6, and make up all possible portfolios combining *A* and the risk-free asset.

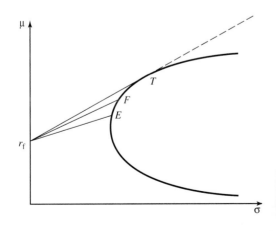

FIGURE 5-6   The Efficient Frontier: One Risky and *n* Risky Assets

What we just learned tells us that the set of such portfolios is the straight line join-ing the point $(0, r_f)$ to E. Now we can quickly check that all portfolios on this line are dominated by those we can make by combining the risk-free asset with portfolio F. Con-tinuing our reasoning in this way and searching for the highest similar line joining $(0, r_f)$ with the risky asset bullet-shaped frontier, we obtain, as the truly efficient frontier, the straight line originating from $(0, r_f)$, tangent to the risky asset frontier. Let T be the tan-gency portfolio. As before, if we allow short position in the risk-free asset, the efficient frontier extends beyond T as represented by the broken line in Figure 5-6.

Formally, with n assets (possibly one of them risk free), the efficient frontier is ob-tained as the relevant (non-dominated) portion of the minimum variance frontier, the latter being the solution, for all possible expected return μ, to the following quadratic program (QP):

$$\min_{w_i's} \sum_i \sum_j w_i w_j \sigma_{ij}$$

$$\text{(QP)} \qquad \text{s.t.} \sum_i w_i \bar{r}_i = \mu$$

$$\sum_i w_i = 1$$

In (QP) we search for the vector of weights that minimizes the variance of the port-folio (verify that you understand the writing of the portfolio variance in the case of n assets) under the constraint that the expected return on the portfolio must be μ. This defines one point on the minimum variance frontier. One can then change the set value of μ to equal all plausible levels of portfolio expected return to effectively draw the minimum variance frontier.[5] Program (QP) is the simplest version of a family of simi-lar quadratic programs used in practice. This is because (QP) includes the minimal set of constraints. The first is only an artifice in that it defines the expected return to be reached, but μ is a parameter; the second constraint is simply the assertion that the vec-tor of $w_i's$ defines a portfolio (and thus that they add up to unity).

Many other constraints can be added to customize the portfolio selection process without altering the basic structure of problem (QP). Probably the most common implicit or explicit constraint for an investor involves limiting her investment universe. The well-known *home bias puzzle* reflects the difficulty in explaining, from the MPT viewpoint, why investors do not invest a larger fraction of their portfolios in stocks quoted "away from home," that is, in international, or emerging, markets. This can be viewed as the re-sult of an unconscious limitation of the investment universe considered by the investor. Self-limitation may also be fully conscious and explicit as in the case of "ethical" mutual funds that exclude arms manufacturers or companies with a tarnished ecological record from their investment universe. These constraints are easily accommodated in our setup, as they simply appear or do not appear in the list of the N assets under consideration.

Other common constraints are non-negativity constraints ($w_i \geq 0$), indicating the impossibility of short selling some or all assets under consideration. Short selling may be impossible for feasibility reasons (exchanges or brokers may not allow it for certain instruments) or, more frequently, for regulatory reasons applying to specific types of in-vestors, for example, pension funds.

---

[5] While in principle one could as well maximize the portfolio's expected return for given levels of standard deviation, it turns out to be more efficient computationally to do the reverse.

An investor may also wish to construct an efficient portfolio subject to the constraint that his holdings of some stocks should not, in value terms, fall below a certain level (perhaps because of potential tax liabilities or because ownership of a large block of this stock affords some degree of managerial control). This requires a constraint of the form

$$w_j \geq \frac{V_j}{V_p},$$

where V_j is the current value of his holdings of stock j and V_p is the overall value of his portfolio.

Other investors may wish to obtain the lowest risk subject to a required expected return constraint and/or be subject to a constraint that limits the number of stocks in their portfolio (in order, possibly, to economize on transaction costs). An investor may, for example, wish to hold at most 3 out of a possible 10 stocks, yet to hold those 3 which give the minimum risk subject to a required return constraint. With certain modifications, this possibility can be accommodated into (QP) as well. Appendix 5.3 details how Microsoft Excel® can be used to construct the portfolio efficient frontier under these and other constraints.

5.4   THE OPTIMAL PORTFOLIO: A SEPARATION THEOREM

The optimal portfolio is naturally defined as that portfolio maximizing the investor's (mean-variance) utility, in other words, that portfolio for which he is able to reach the highest indifference curve, which we know to be increasing and convex from the origin. If the efficient frontier has the shape described in Figure 5-5, that is, if there is a risk-free asset, then all tangency points must lie on the same efficient frontier, irrespective of the rate of risk aversion of the investor. In other words, let there be two investors sharing the same perceptions as to expected returns, variances, and return correlations but differing in their willingness to take risks. The relevant efficient frontier will be identical for these two investors, although their optimal portfolios will be represented by different points on the same line. This is because with differently shaped indifference curves the tangency points must differ. See Figure 5-7.

However, it is a fact that our two investors will invest in the same two funds, the risk-free asset on the one hand, and the risky portfolio (T) identified by the tangency point between the straight line originating from the vertical axis and the bullet-shaped frontier of risky assets, on the other. This is the **two-fund theorem,** also known as the **separation theorem,** because it implies the optimal portfolio of risky assets can be identified separately from the knowledge of the risk preference of an investor. This result will play a significant role in the next section when constructing the Capital Asset Pricing Model.

5.5   CONCLUSIONS

First, it is important to keep in mind that everything said so far applies, regardless of the (possibly normal) probability distributions of returns representing the *subjective* expectations of the particular investor upon whom we are focusing. Market equilibrium considerations are next.

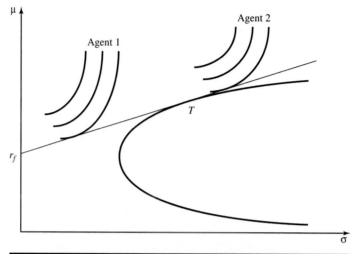

FIGURE 5-7 The Optimal Portfolios of Two Differently Risk Averse Investors

Second, although initially conceived in the context of descriptive economic theories, the success of portfolio theory arose primarily from the possibility of giving it a normative interpretation; that is, of seeing the theory as providing a guide on how to proceed to identify a potential investor's optimal portfolio. In particular it points to the information requirements to be fulfilled (ideally). Even if we accept the restrictions implied by mean-variance analysis, one cannot identify an optimal portfolio without spelling out expectations on mean returns, standard deviations of returns, and correlations among returns. One can view the role of the financial analyst as providing plausible figures for the relevant statistics or offering alternative scenarios for consideration to the would-be investor. This is the first step in the search for an optimal portfolio. The computation of the efficient frontier is the second step and it essentially involves solving the quadratic programming problem (QP) possibly in conjunction with constraints specific to the investor. The third and final step consists of defining, at a more or less formal level, the investor's risk tolerance and, on that basis, identifying the optimal portfolio.

References

Markowitz, H. M., "Portfolio Selection," *Journal of Finance* 7 (1952): 77–91.

Tobin, J., "Liquidity Preference as Behavior Towards Risk," *Review of Economic Studies* 26 (1958): 65–86.

A P P E N D I X   5 . 1

Indifference Curves Under Quadratic Utility or Normally Distributed Returns

In this appendix we first demonstrate that if an investor's utility function is quadratic or if returns are normally distributed, then the investor's expected utility of the portfolio's rate of return is a function only of the portfolio's mean return and standard deviation (Part I). We subsequently show that in either case, investor's indifference curves are convex to the origin (Part II).

PART I

If the utility function is **quadratic,** it can be written as:

$$U(\tilde{R}) = a + b\tilde{R} + c\tilde{R}^2$$

where $\tilde{R}$ denotes a portfolio's rate of return.

Expected utility is then of the following form:

$$\begin{aligned} E(U(\tilde{R})) &= a + bE(\tilde{R}) + c(E(\tilde{R}^2)) \\ &= a + b\mu_R + c\mu_R^2 + c\sigma_R^2 \\ &= g(\sigma_R, \mu_R). \end{aligned}$$

Graphically (Figure A5-1): $U(\tilde{R}) = a + b\tilde{R} + c\tilde{R}^2$ where $a > 0$ and $c < 0$

$$U'(\tilde{R}) = b + 2c\tilde{R} \qquad U''(\tilde{R}) = 2c < 0$$

This function is strictly concave. It allows, however, for negative marginal utility for $\tilde{R} > -b/2c$. Moreover, the coefficient of absolute risk aversion is increasing (increasing absolute risk aversion, $R'_A > 0$). These two characteristics are unpleasant, and more or less disqualify the quadratic utility function from further consideration.

Alternatively, if the individual asset returns $\tilde{r}_i$ are normally distributed, $\tilde{R} = \sum_i w_i \tilde{r}_i$ is normally distributed as well. Let $\tilde{R}$ have density $f(\tilde{R})$, where

$$f(\tilde{R}) = N(\tilde{R}; \mu_R, \sigma_R)$$

The standard normal variate $\tilde{Z}$ is defined by:

$$\tilde{Z} = \frac{\tilde{R} - \mu_R}{\sigma_R} \sim N(\tilde{Z}; 0, 1) \quad \text{Thus}$$
$$\tilde{R} = \sigma_R \tilde{Z} + \mu_R$$

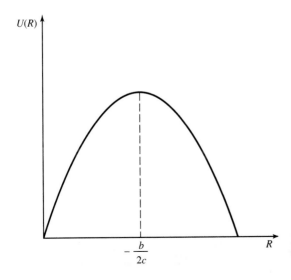

FIGURE A5-1   The Graph of a Quadratic Utility Function

$$E(U(\tilde{R})) = \int_{-\infty}^{+\infty} U(R)f(R)\,dR$$

$$= \int_{-\infty}^{+\infty} U(\sigma_R Z + \mu_R)N(Z;0,1)\,dZ \ (*)$$

The quantity $E(U(\tilde{R}))$ is thus a function of σ_R and μ_R only. Max $E(U(\tilde{R}))$ amounts to choosing w_i so that the corresponding σ_R and μ_R maximize the integral (*).

PART II

Construction of indifference curves in the mean-variance space. There are again two cases.

U IS QUADRATIC

An indifference curve in mean-variance space is defined as the set:

$$\{(\sigma_R, \mu_R)\,|\,E(U(\tilde{R}))$$
$$= a + b\mu_R + c\mu_R^2 + c\sigma_R^2 = k\},$$
$$\textit{for some utility level } k.$$

This can be rewritten as

$$\sigma_R^2 + \mu_R^2 + \frac{b}{c}\mu_R + \frac{b^2}{4c^2} = \frac{k}{c} - \frac{a}{c} + \frac{b^2}{4c^2}$$

$$\sigma_R^2 + \left(\mu_R + \frac{b}{2c}\right)^2 = \frac{k}{c} - \frac{a}{c} + \frac{b^2}{4c^2}$$

This equation defines the set of points (σ_R, μ_R) located in the circle of radius $\sqrt{k/c - a/c + b^2/4c^2}$ of center $(0, -b/2c)$ as in Figure A5-2.

In the relevant portion of the (σ_R, μ_R) space, indifference curves have positive slope and are convex to the origin.

THE DISTRIBUTION OF R IS NORMAL

One wants to describe

$$\{(\sigma_R, \mu_R)\,|\int_{-\infty}^{+\infty} U(\sigma_R Z + \mu_R)N(Z;0,1)dZ = k\}$$

Differentiating totally yields:

$$\int_{-\infty}^{+\infty} U'(\sigma_R Z + \mu_R) \times$$
$$(Zd\sigma_R + d\mu_R)N(Z;0,1)dZ = 0$$

$$d\mu_R/d\sigma_R =$$
$$-\int_{-\infty}^{+\infty} U'(\sigma_R Z + \mu_R)ZN(Z;0,1)dZ$$
$$\div \int_{-\infty}^{+\infty} U'(\sigma_R Z + \mu_R)N(Z;0,1)dZ$$

if $\sigma_R = 0$ (in other words, at the origin) $d\mu_R/d\sigma_R = -\int_{-\infty}^{+\infty} ZN(Z;0,1)dZ/\int_{-\infty}^{+\infty} N(Z;0,1)dZ = 0$

if $\sigma_R > 0$ $\qquad d\mu_R/d\sigma_R > 0$

Indeed, the denominator is positive since $U'(.)$ is positive by assumption, and $N(Z;0,1)$ is a probability density function, hence always positive.

The expression

$$\int_{-\infty}^{+\infty} U'(\sigma_R Z + \mu_R)ZN \times (Z;0,1)dZ$$

is negative under the hypothesis that the investor is risk averse; in other words, that $U(.)$ is strictly concave. If this hypothesis is verified, the marginal utility of each negative value of Z is larger than the marginal utility associated with positive values. This is illustrated in Figure A5-3. Since this is true for all pairs of $\pm Z$, the integral on the numerator is negative.

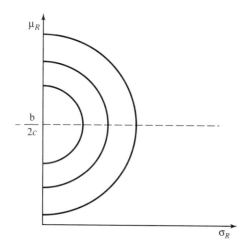

μ_R

$-\dfrac{b}{2c}$

σ_R

FIGURE A5-2 The Indifference Curves of a Quadratic Utility Agent

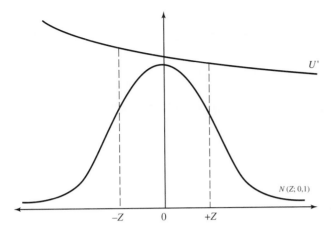

FIGURE A5-3   The Marginal Utility For Negative Values of Z Is Higher Than For Positive Ones

PROOF OF THE CONVEXITY OF INDIFFERENCE CURVES

Let two points (σ_R, μ_R) and $(\sigma_{R'}, \mu_{R'})$ lie on the same indifference curve offering the same level of expected utility $\hat{U}$.

Let us consider the point $(\sigma_{R''}, \mu_{R''})$ where:

$$\sigma_{R''} = \alpha\sigma_R + (1 - \alpha)\sigma_{R'}, \text{ and}$$
$$\mu_{R''} = \alpha\mu_R + (1 - \alpha)\mu_{R'}$$

One would like to prove that: $E(U(\sigma_{R''}\tilde{Z} + \mu_{R''})) > \alpha E(U(\sigma_R\tilde{Z} + \mu_R)) + (1 - \alpha)E(U(\sigma_{R'}\tilde{Z} + \mu_{R'})) = \hat{U}$.

By the strict concavity of U, the inequality

$$U(\sigma_{R''}\tilde{Z} + \mu_{R''}) > \alpha U(\sigma_R\tilde{Z} + \mu_R) \\ + (1 - \alpha)U(\sigma_{R'}\tilde{Z} + \mu_{R'})$$

is verified for all (σ_R, μ_R) and $(\sigma_{R'}, \mu_{R'})$.

One may thus write:

$$\int_{-\infty}^{+\infty} U(\sigma_{R''}Z + \mu_{R''})N(Z; 0, 1)dZ > \\ \alpha\int_{-\infty}^{+\infty} U(\sigma_R Z + \mu_R)N(Z; 0, 1)dZ + \\ (1 - \alpha)\int_{-\infty}^{+\infty} U(\sigma_{R'} Z + \mu_{R'})N(Z; 0, 1)dZ$$

or: $$E(U(\sigma_{R''}\tilde{Z} + \mu_{R''})) > \\ \alpha E(U(\sigma_R\tilde{Z} + \mu_R)) + \\ (1 - \alpha)E(U(\sigma_{R'}\tilde{Z} + \mu_{R'}))$$
$$E(U(\sigma_{R''}\tilde{Z} + \mu_{R''})) > \\ \alpha\hat{U} + (1 - \alpha)\hat{U} = \hat{U}$$

as illustrated in Figure A5-4.

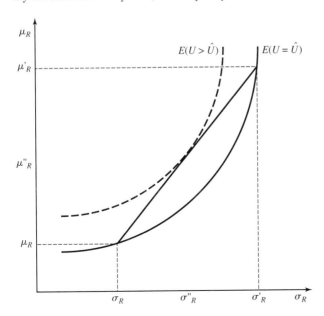

FIGURE A5-4   Indifference Curves Are Convex-Shaped

A P P E N D I X 5 . 2

The Shape of the Efficient Frontier; Two Assets; Alternative Hypotheses

PERFECT POSITIVE CORRELATION (FIGURE 5-2)

$$\rho_{12} = 1$$
$$\sigma_R = w_1\sigma_1 + (1 - w_1)\sigma_2$$

the weighted average of the SD of individual asset returns.

$$\rho_{1,2} = 1$$
$$\begin{aligned}
\mu_R &= w_1\bar{r}_1 + (1 - w_1)\bar{r}_2 \\
&= \bar{r}_1 + (1 - w_1)(\bar{r}_2 - \bar{r}_1)
\end{aligned}$$
$$\begin{aligned}
\sigma_R^2 &= w_1^2\sigma_1^2 + (1 - w_1)^2\sigma_2^2 + 2w_1w_2\sigma_1\sigma_2\rho_{1,2} \\
&= w_1^2\sigma_1^2 + (1 - w_1)^2\sigma_2^2 + 2w_1w_2\sigma_1\sigma_2 \\
&= (w_1\sigma_1 + (1 - w_1)\sigma_2)^2 \text{ [perfect square]}
\end{aligned}$$
$$\sigma_R = \pm(w_1\sigma_1 + (1 - w_1)\sigma_2)$$

$$\Rightarrow w_1 = \frac{\sigma_R - \sigma_2}{\sigma_1 - \sigma_2}; 1 - w_1 = \frac{\sigma_1 - \sigma_R}{\sigma_1 - \sigma_2}$$

$$\begin{aligned}
\mu_R &= \bar{r}_1 + \frac{\sigma_1 - \sigma_R}{\sigma_1 - \sigma_2}(\bar{r}_2 - \bar{r}_1) \\
&= \bar{r}_1 + \frac{\bar{r}_2 - \bar{r}_1}{\sigma_2 - \sigma_1}(\sigma_R - \sigma_1)
\end{aligned}$$

IMPERFECTLY CORRELATED ASSETS (FIGURE 5-3)

$$-1 < \rho_{1,2} < 1$$

Reminder: $\mu_R = w_1\bar{r}_1 + (1 - w_1)\bar{r}_2$

$$\sigma_R^2 = w_1^2\sigma_1^2 + (1 - w_1)^2\sigma_2^2 + 2w_1w_2\sigma_1\sigma_2\rho_{1,2}$$

Thus

$$\frac{\partial\sigma_R^2}{\partial\rho_{1,2}} = 2w_1w_2\sigma_1\sigma_2 > 0$$

which implies: $\sigma_R < w_1\sigma_1 + (1 - w_1)\sigma_2$. σ_R is smaller than the weighted average's gain from diversifying.

Fix μ_R, hence w_1, and observe: as one decreases $\rho_{1,2}$ (from +1 to −1), σ_R^2 diminishes (and thus also σ_R). Hence the opportunity set for $\rho = \bar{\rho} < 1$ must be to the left of the line $AB(\rho_{1,2} = 1)$ except for the extremes.

$$w_1 = 0 \Rightarrow \mu_R = \bar{r}_2 \text{ and } \sigma_R^2 = \sigma_2^2$$
$$w_1 = 1 \Rightarrow \mu_R = \bar{r}_1 \text{ and } \sigma_R^2 = \sigma_1^2$$

PERFECT NEGATIVE CORRELATION (FIGURE 5-4)

$$\rho_{1,2} = -1$$
$$\begin{aligned}
\sigma_R^2 &= w_1^2\sigma_1^2 + (1 - w_1)^2\sigma_2^2 \\
&\quad - 2w_1w_2\sigma_1\sigma_2 \ (w_2 = (1 - w_1)) \\
&= (w_1\sigma_1 - (1 - w_1)\sigma_2)^2 \\
&\quad \text{[perfect square again]}
\end{aligned}$$
$$\begin{aligned}
\sigma_R &= \pm[w_1\sigma_1 - (1 - w_1)\sigma_2] \\
&= \pm[w_1(\sigma_1 + \sigma_2) - \sigma_2]
\end{aligned}$$
$$w_1 = \frac{\pm\sigma_R + \sigma_2}{\sigma_1 + \sigma_2}$$

$$\sigma_R = 0 \Leftrightarrow w_1 = \frac{\sigma_2}{\sigma_1 + \sigma_2}$$

$$\begin{aligned}
\mu_R &= \frac{\pm\sigma_R + \sigma_2}{\sigma_1 + \sigma_2}\bar{r}_1 + \left(1 - \frac{\pm\sigma_R + \sigma_2}{\sigma_1 + \sigma_2}\right)\bar{r}_2 \\
&= \frac{\pm\sigma_R + \sigma_2}{\sigma_1 + \sigma_2}\bar{r}_1 + \frac{\sigma_1 \mp \sigma_R}{\sigma_1 + \sigma_2}\bar{r}_2 \\
&= \frac{\sigma_2}{\sigma_1 + \sigma_2}\bar{r}_1 + \frac{\sigma_1}{\sigma_1 + \sigma_2}\bar{r}_2 + \frac{\bar{r}_1 - \bar{r}_2}{\sigma_1 + \sigma_2}\sigma_R
\end{aligned}$$

ONE RISKLESS AND ONE RISKY ASSET (FIGURE 5-5)

Asset 1: $\bar{r}_1, \sigma_1 = 0$

Asset 2: $\bar{r}_2, \sigma_2$

$\bar{r}_1 < \bar{r}_2$

$$\tilde{R} = w_1\tilde{r}_1 + (1 - w_1)\tilde{r}_2$$

$$\mu_R = w_1\bar{r}_1 + (1 - w_1)\bar{r}_2$$

$$\sigma_R^2 = w_1^2\sigma_1^2 + (1 - w_1)^2\sigma_2^2$$
$$+ 2w_1(1 - w_1)\text{cov}_{1,2}$$
$$= (1 - w_1)^2\sigma_2^2 \text{ since } \sigma_1^2 = 0$$
$$\text{and cov}_{1,2} = \rho_{1,2}\sigma_1\sigma_2 = 0$$

Thus,

$$\sigma_R = (1 - w_1)\sigma_2, \text{ and}$$

$$w_1 = 1 - \frac{\sigma_R}{\sigma_2}$$

The opportunity frontier (μ_R, σ_R) is the locus of points (μ_R, σ_R) that can be reached when varying w_1 from 0 to 1. The equation of this frontier is obtained by replacing w_1 by $1 - (\sigma_R/\sigma_2)$ in the definition of μ_R:

$$\mu_R = \left(1 - \frac{\sigma_R}{\sigma_2}\right)\bar{r}_1 + \frac{\sigma_R}{\sigma_2}\bar{r}_2 = \bar{r}_1 + \frac{\bar{r}_2 - \bar{r}_1}{\sigma_2}\sigma_R$$

A P P E N D I X   5 . 3

Constructing the Efficient Frontier

In this Appendix we outline how Excel's "SOLVER" program may be used to construct an efficient frontier using historical data on returns. Our method does not require the explicit computation of means, standard deviations, and return correlations for the various securities under consideration; they are implicitly obtained from the data directly.[6]

THE BASIC PORTFOLIO PROBLEM

Let us, for purposes of illustration, assume that we have assembled a time series of four data points (monthly returns) for each of three stocks, and let us further assume that these four realizations fully describe the relevant return distributions. We also assign equal probability to the events underlying these realizations.

Table A5-1 presents this hypothetical data.

Following our customary notation, let w_i represent the fraction of wealth invested in asset i, $i = 1, 2, 3$, and let $r^P_{\theta_j}$ represent the return for a portfolio of these assets in the case of event θ_j, $j = 1, 2, 3, 4$. The Excel formulation analogous to problem (QP) of the text is found in Table A5-2, where (A1) through (A3) define the portfolio's

return in each of the four states; (A5) defines the portfolio's average return; (A6) places a bound on the expected return; by varying μ, it is possible to trace out the efficient frontier; (A7) defines the standard deviation when each state is equally probable; and (A8) is the *budget constraint*.

The Excel-based solution to this problem is

$$w_1 = .353$$
$$w_2 = .535$$
$$w_3 = .111,$$

when μ is fixed at $\mu = 3.0\%$. The corresponding portfolio mean and standard deviation are $\bar{r}_p = 3.00$, and $\sigma_P = 1.67$. Screen 1 describes the Excel setup for this case.

Notice that this approach does not require the computation of individual security expected returns, variances, or correlations, but it is fundamentally no different than problem (QP) in the text which does require them. Notice also that by recomputing "min SD" for a number of different values of μ, the efficient frontier can be well approximated.

GENERALIZATIONS

The approach described above is very flexible and accommodates a number of variations,

TABLE A5-1   Hypothetical Return Data

	Prob	Stock 1	Stock 2	Stock 3
Event 1	.25	6.23%	5.10%	7.02%
Event 2	.25	−.68%	4.31%	.79%
Event 3	.25	5.55%	−1.27%	−.21%
Event 4	.25	−1.96%	4.52%	10.30%

---

[6]This is the method taught in the Decision Models course offered at the Graduate School of Business, Columbia University. We are indebted to the Management Science Division and especially to Professor Mark Broadie for calling it to our attention.

TABLE A5-2 The Excel Formulation of the (QP) Problem

$$\min_{\{w_1, w_2, w_3, w_4\}} SD$$

(minimize portfolio standard deviation)

Subject to:

(A1) $r_1^P = 6.23w_1 + 5.10w_2 + 7.02w_3$

(A2) $r_2^P = -.68w_1 + 4.31w_2 + .79w_3$

(A3) $r_3^P = 5.55w_1 - 1.27w_2 - .21w_3$

(A4) $r_4^P = -1.96w_1 + 4.52w_2 + 10.30w_3$

(A5) $\bar{r}_p = .25r_1^P + .25r_2^P + .25r_3^P + .25r_4^P$

(A6) $\bar{r}_p \geq \mu = 3$

(A7) $SD = SQRT(SUMPRODUCT(r_1^P, r_2^P, r_3^P, r_4^P))$

(A8) $w_1 + w_2 + w_3 = 1$

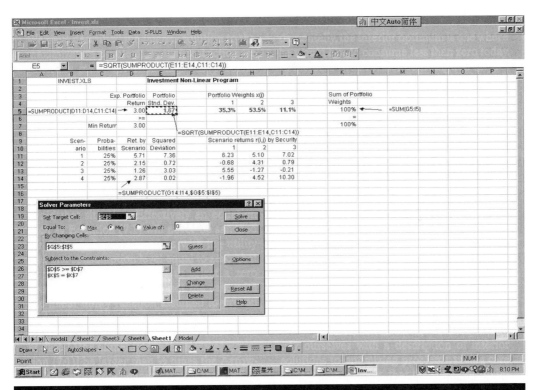

Screen 1

all of which amount to specifying further constraints.

NON-NEGATIVITY CONSTRAINTS

These amount to restrictions on short selling. It is sufficient to specify the additional constraints

$w_1 \geq 0$

$w_2 \geq 0$

$w_3 \geq 0.$

The functioning of SOLVER is unaffected by these added restrictions (although more constraints must be added), and for the example above the solution remains unchanged. (This is intuitive since the solutions were all positive.) See Screen 2.

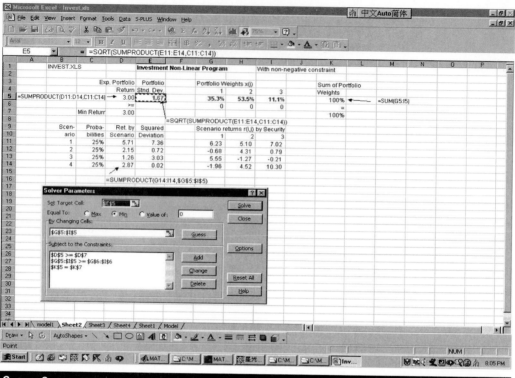

Screen 2

COMPOSITION CONSTRAINTS

Let us enrich the scenario. Assume the market prices of stocks 1, 2, and 3 are, respectively, $25, $32, and $17, and that the current composition of the portfolio consists of 10,000 shares of stock 1, 10,000 shares of stock 2, and 30,000 shares of stock 3, with an aggregate market value of $1,080,000. You wish to obtain the lowest SD for a given expected return subject to the constraints that you retain 10,000 shares of stock 1 and 10,000 shares of stock 3. Equivalently, you wish to constrain portfolio proportions as follows:

$$w_1 \geq \frac{10,000 \times \$25}{\$1,080,000} = .23$$

$$w_3 \geq \frac{10,000 \times \$17}{\$1,080,000} = .157;$$

while w_2 is free to vary. Again SOLVER easily accommodates this. We find $w_1 = .23$, $w_2 = .453$, and $w_3 = .157$, yielding $\bar{r}_p = 3.03\%$ and $\sigma_P = 1.70\%$. Both constraints are binding. See Screen 3.

ADJUSTING THE DATA (MODIFYING THE MEANS)

On the basis of the information in Table A5-1,

$$\bar{r}_1 = 2.3\%$$
$$\bar{r}_2 = 3.165\%$$
$$\bar{r}_3 = 4.47\%.$$

Suppose, either on the basis of fundamental analysis or an SML-style calculation, other information became available suggesting that, over the next portfolio holding period, the returns on stocks 1 and 2 would be 1% higher than their historical mean and the return on stock 3 would be 1% lower. This supplementary information can be incorporated into min SD by modifying Table A5-1. In particular, each return entry for stocks 1 and 2 must be increased by 1% while each entry of stock 3 must be decreased by 1%. Such changes do not in any way alter the standard deviations or correlations implicit in the data. The new input table for SOLVER is found in Table A5-3.

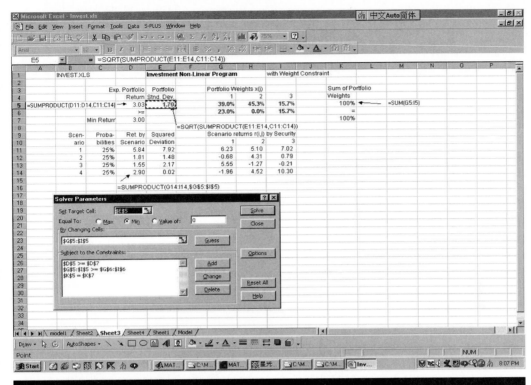

Screen 3

Solving the same problem, min SD without additional constraints yields $w_1 = .381$, $w_2 = .633$, and $w_3 = -0.013$, yielding $\bar{r}_p = 3.84$ and $\sigma_P = 1.61$. See Screen 4.

CONSTRAINTS ON THE NUMBER OF SECURITIES IN THE PORTFOLIO

Transactions costs may be substantial. In order to economize on these costs, suppose an investor wished to solve min SD subject to the constraint that his portfolio would contain at most two of the three securities. To accommodate this change, it is necessary to introduce three new bi-

nary variables that we will denote x_1, x_2, x_3, corresponding to stocks 1, 2, and 3, respectively. For all x_i, $i = 1, 2, 3$, $x_i \in \{0, 1\}$. The desired result is obtained by adding the following constraints to the problem min SD:

$$w_1 \le x_1$$
$$w_1 \le x_2$$
$$w_1 \le x_3$$
$$x_1 + x_2 + x_3 \le 2,$$
$$x_1, x_2, x_3 \text{ are binary}$$

In the previous example the solution is to include only securities one and two with proportions $w_1 = .188$, and $w_2 = .812$. See Screen 5.

TABLE A5-3	Modified Return Data			
	Prob	*Stock 1*	*Stock 2*	*Stock 3*
Event 1	.25	7.23%	6.10%	6.02%
Event 2	.25	.32%	5.31%	−.21%
Event 3	.25	6.55%	−.27%	−1.21%
Event 4	.25	−.96%	5.52%	9.30%

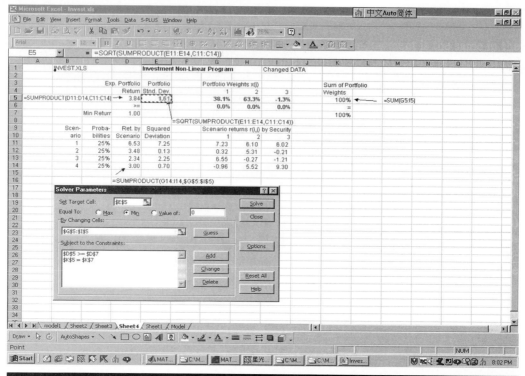

Screen 4

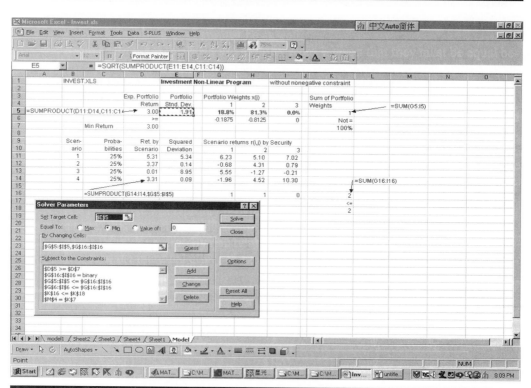

Screen 5

CHAPTER 6

THE CAPITAL ASSET PRICING MODEL: ANOTHER VIEW ABOUT RISK

6.1 INTRODUCTION

The CAPM is an equilibrium theory built on the premises of Modern Portfolio Theory. It is, however, an equilibrium theory with a somewhat peculiar structure. This is true for a number of reasons:

1. First, the CAPM is a theory of financial equilibrium only. Investors take the various statistical quantities—means, variances, covariances—that characterize a security's return process as given. There is no attempt within the theory to link the return processes with events in the *real* side of the economy. In future model contexts we shall generalize this feature.
2. Second, as a theory of financial equilibrium it makes the assumption that the supply of existing assets is equal to the demand for existing assets and, as such, that the currently observed asset prices are equilibrium ones. There is no attempt, however, to compute asset supply and demand functions explicitly. Only the equilibrium price vector is characterized. Let us elaborate on this point.

   Under the CAPM, portfolio theory informs us about the demand side. If individual i invests a fraction w_{ij} of his initial wealth W_{oi} in asset j, the value of his asset j holding is $w_{ij}W_{oi}$. Absent any information that he wishes to alter these holdings, we may interpret the quantity $w_{ij}W_{oi}$ as his demand for asset j at the prevailing price vector. If there are I individuals in the economy, the total value of all holdings of asset j is $\Sigma_i^I w_{ij}W_{0i}$; by the same remark we may interpret this quantity as aggregate demand. At equilibrium one must have $\Sigma_i^I w_{ij}W_{0i} = p_j Q_j$ where p_j is the prevailing equilibrium price per share of asset j, Q_j is the total number of shares outstanding and, consequently, $p_j Q_j$ is the market capitalization of asset j. The CAPM derives the implications for valuation of the assumption that the actual economy-wide asset holdings are investors' aggregate optimal asset holdings.

3. Third, the CAPM expresses equilibrium in terms of relationships between the return distributions of individual assets and the return characteristics of the portfolio of all assets. We may view the CAPM as informing us, via modern Portfolio Theory, as to what asset return interrelationships must be in order for equilibrium asset prices to coincide with the observed asset prices.

In what follows we first present an overview of the traditional approach to the CAPM. This is followed by a more general presentation that permits at once a more complete and more general characterization.

6.2 THE TRADITIONAL APPROACH TO THE CAPM

To get useful results in this complex world of many assets we have to make simplifying assumptions. The CAPM approach essentially hypothesizes (1) that all agents have the *same beliefs* about future returns (i.e., homogenous expectations and in its simplest form), and (2) that there is a risk-free asset, paying a safe return r_f. These assumptions guarantee that the mean-variance efficient frontier is the same for every investor, and furthermore, by the separation theorem, that all investors' optimal portfolios have an identical structure: a fraction of initial wealth is invested in the risk-free asset, the rest in the (identical) tangency portfolio (two-fund separation). It is then possible to derive a few key characteristics of equilibrium asset and portfolio returns without detailing the underlying equilibrium structure, that is, the demand for and supply of assets, or discussing their prices.

Because all investors acquire shares in the same risky tangency portfolio T, and make no other risky investments, by definition of equilibrium, all existing risky assets must belong to T. By contradiction, if some asset k were not found in T, there would be no demand for it; yet, it is assumed to exist in positive supply. Supply would then exceed demand, which is inconsistent with assumed financial market equilibrium. The same reasoning implies that the share of any asset j in portfolio T must correspond to the ratio of the market value of that asset $p_j Q_j$ to the market value of all assets $\sum_{j=1}^{J} p_j Q_j$. This, in turn, guarantees that tangency portfolio T must be nothing other than the market portfolio M, the portfolio of all existing assets where each asset appears in a proportion equal to the ratio of its market value to the total market capitalization.

This simple reasoning leads to a number of useful conclusions:

a. The market portfolio is efficient since it is on the efficient frontier.

b. All individual optimal portfolios are located on the half-line originating at point $(0, r_f)$ and going through $(\sigma_M, \bar{r}_M)$, which is also the locus of all efficient portfolios (see Figure 6-1). This locus is usually called the Capital Market Line or CML.

c. The slope of the CML is $(\bar{r}_M - r_f)/\sigma_M$. It tells us that an investor considering a marginally riskier efficient portfolio would obtain, in exchange, an increase in expected return of $(\bar{r}_M - r_f)/\sigma_M$. This is the price of, or reward for, risk taking—the price of risk as applicable to efficient portfolios. In other words, for efficient portfolios, we have the simple linear relationship in Equation (6.1).

$$\bar{r}_p = r_f + \frac{\bar{r}_M - r_f}{\sigma_M} \sigma_p \tag{6.1}$$

The CML applies only to efficient portfolios. What can be said of an arbitrary asset j not belonging to the efficient frontier? To discuss this essential part of the CAPM we

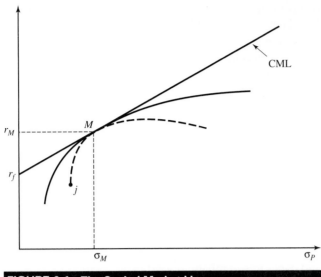

FIGURE 6-1 The Capital Market Line

first rely on Equation (6.2), formally derived in Appendix 6.1, and limit our discussion to its intuitive implications:

$$\bar{r}_j = r_f + (\bar{r}_M - r_f)\frac{\sigma_{jM}}{\sigma_M^2} \tag{6.2}$$

Let us define $\beta_j = \sigma_{jM}/\sigma_M^2$, that is the ratio of the covariance between the returns on asset j and the returns on the market portfolio over the variance of the market returns. We can thus rewrite Equation (6.2) as Equation (6.3).

$$\bar{r}_j = r_f + \left(\frac{\bar{r}_M - r_f}{\sigma_M}\right)\beta_j\sigma_M = r_f + \left(\frac{\bar{r}_M - r_f}{\sigma_M}\right)\rho_{jM}\sigma_j \tag{6.3}$$

Comparing Equations (6.1) and (6.3), we obtain one of the major lessons of the CAPM: Only a portion of the total risk of an asset j, σ_j, is remunerated by the market. Indeed, the risk premium on a given asset is the market price of risk, $(\bar{r}_M - r_f)/\sigma_M$, multiplied by the relevant measure of the quantity of risk for that asset. In the case of an ineffi-cient asset or portfolio j, this measure of risk differs from σ_j. The portion of total risk that is priced is measured by $\beta_j\sigma_M$ or $\rho_{jM}\sigma_j$. This is the **systematic risk** of asset j (also re-ferred to as market risk or undiversifiable risk). The intuition for this fundamental re-sult is as follows.

Every investor holds the market portfolio ($T = M$). The relevant risk for the in-vestor is thus the variance of the market portfolio. Consequently, what is important to him is the contribution of asset j to the risk of the market portfolio; that is, the extent to which the inclusion of asset j into the overall portfolio increases the latter's variance. This marginal contribution of asset j to the overall portfolio risk is appropriately mea-sured by $\rho_{jM}\sigma_j$ ($=\beta_j\sigma_M$). Equation (6.3) says that investors must be compensated to persuade them to hold an asset with high covariance with the market, and that this com-pensation takes the form of a higher expected return.

The comparison of Equations (6.1) and (6.3) also leads us to conclude that an efficient portfolio is one for which all diversifiable risks have been eliminated. For an efficient portfolio, total risk and systematic risk are thus one and the same. This result is made clear from writing, without loss of generality, the return on asset j as a linear function of the market return with a random error term that is independent of the market return,[1]

$$\tilde{r}_j = \alpha + \beta_j \tilde{r}_M + \varepsilon_j \tag{6.4}$$

and looking at the implication of this general regression equation for variances

$$\sigma_j^2 = \beta_j^2 \sigma_M^2 + \sigma_{\varepsilon_j}^2, \tag{6.5}$$

this regression equation provides us with the justification for the "beta" label. The standard regression estimator of the market return coefficient in Equation (6.4) will indeed be of the form

$$\hat{\beta}_j = \frac{\hat{\sigma}_{ij}}{\hat{\sigma}_M^2}$$

Equation (6.3) can equivalently be rewritten as

$$\bar{r}_j - r_f = (\bar{r}_M - r_f)\beta_j \tag{6.6}$$

which says that the expected excess return or the risk premium on an asset j is proportional to its β_j. Equation (6.6) defines the **security market line** or SML. It is depicted in Figure 6-2.

The SML has two key features. The beta of asset j, β_j, is the sole specific determinant of the excess return on asset j. Adopting a terminology that we shall justify later, we can say that the beta is the only explanatory factor of returns; in other words, the CAPM is a single-factor model. Furthermore, the relation between excess returns on different assets and their betas is linear.

In the sections that follow, we first generalize the analysis of the efficient frontier presented in Chapter 5 to the $N \geq 2$ asset case. Such a generalization will require the

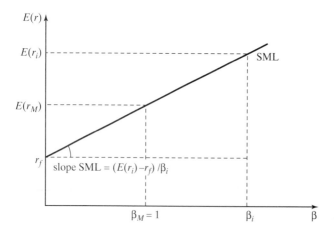

FIGURE 6-2   The Security Market Line

---

[1]The "market model" is based on this same regression equation. It makes the additional hypothesis that $\text{cor}(\varepsilon_i, \varepsilon_j) = 0$ for all $i \neq j$. The market model is reviewed in Chapter 12.

use of elementary matrix algebra and is one of those rare situations in economic science where a more general approach yields a greater specificity of results. We will, for instance, be able to detail a version of the CAPM without a risk-free asset. This is then followed by the derivation of the standard CAPM where a risk-free asset is present.

As noted in the introduction, the CAPM is essentially an interpretation that we are able to apply to the efficient frontier. Not surprisingly, therefore, we begin this task with a return to characterizing that frontier.

6.3 THE MATHEMATICS OF THE PORTFOLIO FRONTIER: MANY RISKY ASSETS AND NO RISK-FREE ASSET

Notation Assume $N \geq 2$ risky assets; assume further that no asset has a return that can be expressed as a linear combination of the returns to a subset of the other assets (the returns are linearly independent). Let V denote the variance-covariance matrix, in other words, $V_{ij} = \text{cov}(r_i, r_j)$; by construction V is symmetric. Linear independence in this sense implies that V^{-1} exists. Let w represent a column vector of portfolio weights for the N assets. The expression $w^T V w$ then represents the portfolio's return variance: $w^T V w$ is always positive (i.e., V is positive definite).

Let us illustrate this latter assertion in the two-asset case

$$
w^T V w = (w_1 \quad w_2) \begin{pmatrix} \sigma_1^2 & \sigma_{12} \\ \sigma_{21} & \sigma_2^2 \end{pmatrix} \begin{pmatrix} w_1 \\ w_2 \end{pmatrix}
$$

$$
= (w_1\sigma_1^2 + w_2\sigma_{21} \quad w_1\sigma_{12} + w_2\sigma_2^2) \begin{pmatrix} w_1 \\ w_2 \end{pmatrix}
$$

$$
= w_1^2\sigma_1^2 + w_1 w_2\sigma_{21} + w_1 w_2\sigma_{12} + w_2^2\sigma_2^2
$$

$$
= w_1^2\sigma_1^2 + w_2^2\sigma_2^2 + 2w_1 w_2\sigma_{12} \geq 0,
$$

since $\sigma_{12} \geq -\sigma_1\sigma_2$.

Definition 6.1 formalizes the notion of a portfolio lying on the efficient frontier. Note that every portfolio is ultimately defined by the weights that determine its composition.

Definition 6.1:
A frontier portfolio is one that displays minimum variance among all feasible portfolios with the same $E(\tilde{r}_p)$.

A portfolio P, characterized by w_p, is a frontier portfolio, if and only if w_p solves.[2]

$$
\min_{w} \tfrac{1}{2} w^T V w
$$

$$
(\lambda) \quad \text{s.t. } w^T e = E \qquad \left(\sum_{i=1}^{N} w_i E(\tilde{r}_i) = E \right)
$$

$$
(\gamma) \quad \quad w^T \mathbf{1} = 1 \qquad \left(\sum_{i=1}^{N} w_i = 1 \right)
$$

---

[2]The problem below is, in vector notation, problem (QP) of Chapter 5.

where the superscript T stands for *transposed,* i.e. transforms a column vector into a line vector and reciprocally, e denotes the column vector of expected returns to the N assets, **1** represents the column vector of ones, and λ, γ are Lagrange multipliers. Short sales are permitted (no non-negativity constraints are present). The solution to this problem can be characterized as the solution to $\min_{\{w,\lambda,\gamma\}} L$ where L is the Lagrangian:

$$L = \tfrac{1}{2}w^T Vw + \lambda(E - w^T e) + \gamma(1 - w^T \mathbf{1}) \tag{6.7}$$

Under these assumptions, w_p, λ and γ must satisfy Equations (6.8) through (6.10), which are the necessary and sufficient first order conditions:

$$\frac{\partial L}{\partial w} = Vw - \lambda e - \gamma \mathbf{1} = 0 \tag{6.8}$$

$$\frac{\partial L}{\partial \lambda} = E - w^T e = 0 \tag{6.9}$$

$$\frac{\partial L}{\partial \gamma} = 1 - w^T \mathbf{1} = 0 \tag{6.10}$$

In the lines that follow, we manipulate these equations to provide an intuitive characterization of the optimal portfolio proportions [Equation (6.15)]. From Equation (6.8), $Vw_p = \lambda e + \lambda \mathbf{1}$, or

$$w_p = \lambda V^{-1}e + \gamma V^{-1}\mathbf{1}, \text{ and}$$
$$e^T w_p = \lambda(e^T V^{-1}e) + \gamma(e^T V^{-1}\mathbf{1}), \tag{6.11}$$

since $e^T w_p = w_p^T e$. We also have, from Equation (6.9), that

$$E(\tilde{r}_p) = \lambda(e^T V^{-1}e) + \gamma(e^T V^{-1}\mathbf{1}) \tag{6.12}$$

From Equation (6.11), we have:

$$\mathbf{1}^T w_p = w_p^T \mathbf{1} = \lambda(\mathbf{1}^T V^{-1}e) + \gamma(\mathbf{1}^T V^{-1}\mathbf{1}) = 1 \quad \text{[by Equation (6.10)]}$$
$$1 = \lambda(\mathbf{1}^T V^{-1}e) + \gamma(\mathbf{1}^T V^{-1}\mathbf{1}) \tag{6.13}$$

Notice that Equations (6.12) and (6.13) are two *scalar* equations in the unknowns λ and γ (since such terms as $e^T V^{-1}e$ are pure numbers!). Solving this system of two equations in two unknowns, we obtain:

$$\lambda = \frac{CE - A}{D} \text{ and } \gamma = \frac{B - AE}{D} \tag{6.14}$$

where $A = \mathbf{1}^T V^{-1}e = e^T V^{-1}\mathbf{1}$; $B = e^T V^{-1}e > 0$; $C = \mathbf{1}^T V^{-1}\mathbf{1}$; $D = BC - A^2$. Here we have used the fact that the inverse of a positive definite matrix is itself positive definite. It can be shown that D is also strictly positive. Substituting Equation (6.14) into Equation (6.11) we obtain:

$$w_p = \underbrace{\frac{CE - A}{D}}_{\substack{\lambda \\ \text{scalar}}}\underbrace{V^{-1}e}_{\text{vector}} + \underbrace{\frac{B - AE}{D}}_{\substack{\gamma \\ \text{scalar}}}\underbrace{V^{-1}\mathbf{1}}_{\text{vector}}$$

$$= \frac{1}{D}[B(V^{-1}\mathbf{1}) - A(V^{-1}e)] + \frac{1}{D}[C(V^{-1}e) - A(V^{-1}\mathbf{1})]E$$

$$w_p = \underbrace{g}_{\text{vector}} + \underbrace{h}_{\text{vector}} \underbrace{E}_{\text{scalar}} \tag{6.15}$$

Since the FOCs [Equations (6.8) through (6.10)] are a necessary and sufficient characterization for w_p to represent a frontier portfolio with expected return equal to E, any frontier portfolio can be represented by Equation (6.15). This is a very nice expression; pick the desired expected return E and it straightforwardly gives the weights of the corresponding frontier portfolio with E as its expected return. The portfolio's variance follows as $\sigma_p^2 = w_p^T V w_p$, which is also straightforward. Efficient portfolios are those for which E exceeds the expected return on the minimum risk, risky portfolio. Our characterization thus applies to efficient portfolios as well: Pick an efficient E and Equation (6.15) gives its exact composition. See Appendix 6.2 for an example.

Can we further identify the vectors g and h in Equation (6.15); in particular, do they somehow correspond to the weights of easily recognizable portfolios? The answer is yes. Since, if $E = 0$, $g = w_p$, g then represents the weights that define the frontier portfolio with $E(\tilde{r}_p) = 0$. Similarly, $g + h$ corresponds to the weights of the frontier portfolio with $E(\tilde{r}_p) = 1$, since $w_p = g + hE(\tilde{r}_p) = g + h1 = g + h$.

The simplicity of the relationship in Equation (6.15) allows us to make two claims.

Proposition 6.1:
The entire set of frontier portfolios can be generated by (are convex combinations of) g and $g + h$.

Proof:
To see this, let q be an arbitrary frontier portfolio with $E(\tilde{r}_q)$ as its expected return. Consider portfolio weights (proportions) $\pi_g = 1 - E(\tilde{r}_q)$ and $\pi_{g+h} = E(\tilde{r}_q)$; then, as asserted,

$$[1 - E(\tilde{r}_q)]g + E(\tilde{r}_q)(g + h) = g + hE(\tilde{r}_q) = w_q.$$

The prior remark is generalized in Proposition 6.2.

Proposition 6.2:
The portfolio frontier can be described as convex combinations of any two frontier portfolios, not just the frontier portfolios g and $g + h$.

Proof:
To confirm this assertion, let p_1 and p_2 be any two distinct frontier portfolios, since the frontier portfolios are different, $E(\tilde{r}_{p_1}) \neq E(\tilde{r}_{p_2})$. Let q be an arbitrary frontier portfolio, with expected return equal to $E(\tilde{r}_q)$. Since $E(\tilde{r}_{p_1}) \neq E(\tilde{r}_{p_2})$, there must exist a unique number α such that

$$E(\tilde{r}_q) = \alpha E(\tilde{r}_{p_1}) + (1 - \alpha)E(\tilde{r}_{p_2}) \qquad (6.16)$$

Now consider a portfolio of p_1 and p_2 with weights $\alpha, 1 - \alpha$, respectively, as determined by Equation (6.16). We must show that $w_q = \alpha w_{p_1} + (1 - \alpha)w_{p_2}$.

$$\begin{aligned}
\alpha w_{p_1} + (1 - \alpha)w_{p_2} &= \alpha[g + hE(\tilde{r}_{p_1})] + (1 - \alpha)[g + hE(\tilde{r}_{p_2})] \\
&= g + h[\alpha E(\tilde{r}_{p_1}) + (1 - \alpha)E(\tilde{r}_{p_2})] \\
&= g + hE(\tilde{r}_q), \text{ by construction} \\
&= w_q, \text{ since } q \text{ is a frontier portfolio.}
\end{aligned}$$

What does the set of frontier portfolios, which we have calculated so conveniently, look like? Can we identify, in particular, the minimum variance portfolio? Locating that portfolio is surely key to a description of the set of all frontier portfolios. Fortunately, given our results thus far, the task is straightforward.

For any portfolio on the frontier, $\sigma^2(\tilde{r}_p) = [g + hE(\tilde{r}_p)]^T V[g + hE(\tilde{r}_p)]$, with g and h as defined earlier.

Multiplying all this out (very messy), yields:

$$\sigma^2(\tilde{r}_p) = \frac{C}{D}\left(E(\tilde{r}_p) - \frac{A}{C}\right)^2 + \frac{1}{C}, \qquad (6.17)$$

where A, C, and D are the constants defined earlier. We can immediately identify the following: since $C > 0, D > 0$,

(i) the expected return of the minimum variance portfolio is A/C;
(ii) the variance of the minimum variance portfolio is given by $1/C$;
(iii) Equation (6.17) is the equation of a parabola with vertex $(1/C, A/C)$ in the expected return/variance space and of a hyperbola in the expected return/standard deviation space. See Figures 6-3 and 6-4.

The extended shape of this set of frontier portfolios is due to the allowance for short sales as underlined in Figure 6-5.

What has been accomplished thus far? First and foremost, we have a much richer knowledge of the set of frontier portfolios: Given a level of desired expected return, we can easily identify the relative proportions of the constituent assets that must be combined to create a portfolio with that expected return. This was illustrated in Equation (6.15), and it is key. We then used it to identify the minimum risk portfolio and to describe the graph of all frontier portfolios.

All of these results apply to portfolios of any arbitrary collection of assets. So far, nothing has been said about financial market equilibrium. As a next step toward that goal, however, we need to identify the set of frontier portfolios that is efficient. Given Equation (6.15) this is a straightforward task.

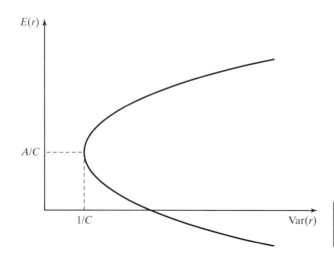

FIGURE 6-3   The Set of Frontier Portfolios: Mean/Variance Space

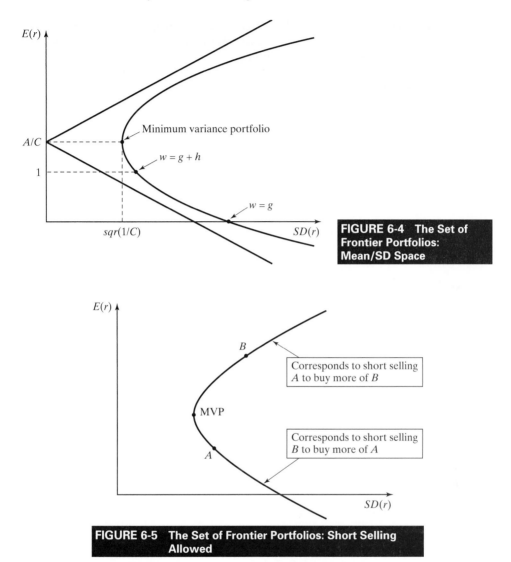

FIGURE 6-4   The Set of Frontier Portfolios: Mean/SD Space

FIGURE 6-5   The Set of Frontier Portfolios: Short Selling Allowed

6.4   CHARACTERIZING EFFICIENT PORTFOLIOS— (NO RISK-FREE ASSETS)

Our first order of business is a definition.

Definition 6.2:
Efficient portfolios are those frontier portfolios for which the expected return exceeds A/C, the expected return of the minimum variance portfolio.

Since Equation (6.15) applies to all frontier portfolios, it applies to efficient ones as well. Fortunately, we also know the $E(\tilde{r})$ of the minimum variance portfolio. As a first step, let us prove the converse of Proposition 6.2.

Proposition 6.3:
Any convex combination of frontier portfolios is also a frontier portfolio.

Proof:
Let $(\bar{w}_1 \ldots \bar{w}_N)$, define N frontier portfolios ($\bar{w}_i$ represents the vector defining the composition of the ith portfolios) and let α_i, $i = 1, \ldots, N$ be real numbers such that $\sum_{i=1}^{N} \alpha_i = 1$. Lastly, let $E(\tilde{r}_i)$ denote the expected return of portfolio with weights $\bar{w}_i$.

Thus $\sum_{i=1}^{N} \alpha_i \bar{w}_i$ is a frontier portfolio with $E(\tilde{r}) = \sum_{i=1}^{N} \alpha_i E(\tilde{r}_i)$.

The weights corresponding to a linear combination of the N portfolios are:

$$\sum_{i=1}^{N} \alpha_i \bar{w}_i = \sum_{i=1}^{N} \alpha_i(g + hE(\tilde{r}_i))$$
$$= \sum_{i=1}^{N} \alpha_i g + h\sum_{i=1}^{N} \alpha_i E(\tilde{r}_i)$$
$$= g + h\left[\sum_{i=1}^{N} \alpha_i E(\tilde{r}_i)\right]$$

Thus $\sum_{i=1}^{N} \alpha_i \bar{w}_i$ is a frontier portfolio with $E(\tilde{r}) = \sum_{i=1}^{N} \alpha_i E(\tilde{r}_i)$.

A corollary to the previous result is:

Proposition 6.4:
The set of efficient portfolios is a convex set.[3]

Proof:
Suppose each of the N portfolios under consideration was efficient; then $E(\tilde{r}_i) \geq A/C$, for every portfolio i. However, $\sum_{i=1}^{N} \alpha_i E(\tilde{r}_i) \geq \sum_{i=1}^{N} \alpha_i(A/C) = A/C$; thus, the convex combination is efficient as well. So the set of efficient portfolios, *as characterized by their portfolio weights,* is a convex set.

It follows from Proposition 6.4 that if every investor holds an efficient portfolio, the market portfolio, being a weighted average of all individual portfolios, is also efficient. This is a key result.

The next section further refines our understanding of the set of frontier portfolios and, more especially, the subset of them that is efficient. Observe, however, that as yet we have said nothing about equilibrium.

---

[3]This does not mean, however, that the frontier of this set is convex-shaped in the risk-return space.

6.5   BACKGROUND FOR DERIVING THE ZERO-BETA CAPM: NOTION OF A ZERO COVARIANCE PORTFOLIO

Proposition 6.5:
For any frontier portfolio p, except the minimum variance portfolio, there exists a unique frontier portfolio with which p has zero covariance.

We will call this portfolio the *zero covariance portfolio relative to* p, and denote its vector of portfolio weights by $ZC(p)$.

Proof:
To prove this claim it will be sufficient to exhibit the (unique) portfolio that has this property. As we shall demonstrate shortly [see Equation (6.23) and the discussion following it], the covariance of any two frontier portfolios p and q is given by the following general formula:

$$\text{cov}(\tilde{r}_p, \tilde{r}_q) = \frac{C}{D}\left[E(\tilde{r}_p) - \frac{A}{C}\right]\left[E(\tilde{r}_q) - \frac{A}{C}\right] + \frac{1}{C} \qquad (6.18)$$

where A, C, and D are uniquely defined by e, the vector of expected returns and V, the matrix of variances and covariances. These are, in fact, the same quantities A, C, and D defined earlier. If it exists, $ZC(p)$ must therefore satisfy,

$$\text{cov}(\tilde{r}_p, \tilde{r}_{ZC(p)}) = \frac{C}{D}\left[E(\tilde{r}_p) - \frac{A}{C}\right]\left[E(\tilde{r}_{ZC(p)}) - \frac{A}{C}\right] + \frac{1}{C} = 0 \qquad (6.19)$$

Since A, C, and D are all numbers, we can solve for $E(\tilde{r}_{ZC(p)})$

$$E(\tilde{r}_{ZC(p)}) = \frac{A}{C} - \frac{\dfrac{D}{C^2}}{E(\tilde{r}_p) - \dfrac{A}{C}} \qquad (6.20)$$

Given $E(\tilde{r}_{ZC(p)})$, we can use Equation (6.15) to uniquely define the portfolio weights corresponding to it.

From Equation (6.20), since $A > 0$, $C > 0$, $D > 0$, if $E(\tilde{r}_p) > A/C$ (i.e., is efficient), then $E(\tilde{r}_{ZC(p)}) < A/C$ (i.e., is inefficient), and vice versa. The portfolio $ZC(p)$ will turn out to be crucial to what follows. It is possible to give a more complete geometric identification to the zero covariance portfolio if we express the frontier portfolios in the context of $E(\tilde{r}) \times \sigma^2(\tilde{r})$ space (Figure 6-6).

The equation of the line through the chosen portfolio p and the minimum variance portfolio can be shown to be the following [it has the form $(y = b + mx)$]:

$$E(\tilde{r}) = \frac{A}{C} - \frac{\dfrac{D}{C^2}}{E(\tilde{r}_p) - \dfrac{A}{C}} + \frac{E(\tilde{r}_p) - \dfrac{A}{C}}{\sigma^2(\tilde{r}_p) - \dfrac{1}{C}}\sigma^2(\tilde{r}).$$

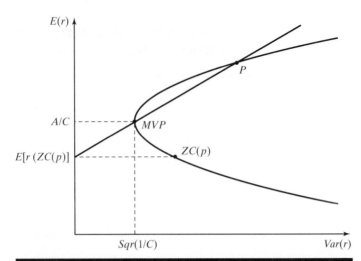

FIGURE 6-6 **The Set of Frontier Portfolios: Location of the Zero-Covariance Portfolio**

If $\sigma^2(\tilde{r}) = 0$, then $E(\tilde{r}) = \dfrac{A}{C} - \dfrac{\dfrac{D}{C^2}}{E(\tilde{r}_p) - \dfrac{A}{C}} = E(\tilde{r}_{ZC(p)})$ [by Equation (6.20)].

That is, the intercept of the line joining p and the minimum variance portfolio is the expected return on the zero-covariance portfolio. This identifies the zero-covariance portfolio to p geometrically. We already know how to determine its precise composition.

Our next step is to describe the expected return on any portfolio in terms of frontier portfolios. After some manipulations this yields Equation (6.27). The specialization of this relationship will give the zero-beta CAPM, which is a version of the CAPM when there is no risk-free asset. Recall that thus far we have not included a risk-free asset in our collection of assets from which we construct portfolios. Let q be any portfolio (which might not be on the portfolio frontier) and let p be any frontier portfolio.

$$\operatorname{cov}(\tilde{r}_p, \tilde{r}_q) \underset{\text{by definition}}{=} w_p^T V w_q$$

$$= [\lambda V^{-1}e + \gamma V^{-1}1]^T V w_q$$

$$= \lambda e^T V^{-1} V w_q + \gamma 1^T V^{-1} V w_q$$

$$= \lambda e^T w_q + \gamma \left(\text{since } 1^T w_q = \sum_{i=1}^{N} w_q^i \equiv 1 \right) \qquad \textbf{(6.21)}$$

$$\operatorname{cov}(\tilde{r}_p, \tilde{r}_q) = \lambda E(\tilde{r}_q) + \gamma \left(\text{since } e^T w_q = \sum_{i=1}^{N} E(\tilde{r}_i) w_q^i \equiv E(\tilde{r}_q) \right) \qquad \textbf{(6.22)}$$

where $\lambda = (CE(\tilde{r}_p) - A)/D$ and $\gamma = (B - AE(\tilde{r}_p))/D$, as per earlier definitions. Substituting these expressions into Equation (6.22) gives

$$\operatorname{cov}(\tilde{r}_p, \tilde{r}_q) = \frac{CE(\tilde{r}_p) - A}{D} E(\tilde{r}_q) + \frac{B - AE(\tilde{r}_p)}{D} \qquad \textbf{(6.23)}$$

Equation (6.23) is a short step from Equation (6.18): Collect all terms involving expected returns, add and subtract A^2C/DC^2 to get the first term in Equation (6.18) with a remaining term equal to $(+1/C)((BC/D) - (A^2/D))$. But the latter is simply $1/C$ since $D = BC - A^2$.

Let us go back to Equation (6.22) and apply it to the case where q is $ZC(p)$; one gets

$$0 = \text{cov}(\tilde{r}_p, \tilde{r}_{ZC(p)}) = \lambda E(\tilde{r}_{ZC(p)}) + \gamma \quad \text{or} \quad \gamma = -\lambda E(\tilde{r}_{ZC(p)}); \qquad \textbf{(6.24)}$$

hence Equation (6.22) becomes

$$\text{cov}(\tilde{r}_p, \tilde{r}_q) = \lambda[E(\tilde{r}_q) - E(\tilde{r}_{ZC(p)})]. \qquad \textbf{(6.25)}$$

Apply the later to the case $p = q$ to get

$$\sigma_p^2 = \text{cov}(\tilde{r}_p, \tilde{r}_p) = \lambda[E(\tilde{r}_p) - E(\tilde{r}_{ZC(p)})]. \qquad \textbf{(6.26)}$$

and divide Equation (6.25) by Equation (6.26) and rearrange to obtain

$$E(\tilde{r}_q) = E(\tilde{r}_{ZC(p)}) + \beta_{pq}[E(\tilde{r}_p) - E(\tilde{r}_{ZC(p)})]. \qquad \textbf{(6.27)}$$

This equation bears more than a passing resemblance to the *security market line* implication of the capital asset pricing model. But as yet it is simply a statement about the various portfolios that can be created from arbitrary collections of assets: (1) pick any frontier portfolio p; (2) this defines an associated zero-covariance portfolio $ZC(p)$; (3) any other portfolio q's expected return can be expressed in terms of the returns to those portfolios and the covariance of q with the arbitrarily chosen frontier portfolio. Equation (6.27) would *very closely* resemble the security market line (SML) if, in particular, we could choose $p = M$, the market portfolio of existing assets. The circumstances under which it is possible to do this form the subject to which we now turn.

6.6   THE ZERO-BETA CAPITAL ASSET PRICING MODEL

We would like to explain asset expected returns *in equilibrium*. The relationship in Equation (6.27), however, is not the consequence of an equilibrium theory because it was derived for a *given* particular vector of expected asset returns, e, and a given covariance-variance matrix, V. In fact, it is the vector of returns e that we would like, in equilibrium, to understand. We need to identify a particular portfolio as being a frontier portfolio without specifying a priori the (expected) return vector and variance-covariance matrix of its constituent assets. The zero-beta CAPM tells us that under certain assumptions, this desired portfolio can be identified as the market portfolio M.

We may assume one of the following:

 (i) agents maximize expected utility with increasing and strictly concave utility of money functions and asset returns are multivariate normally distributed, or
 (ii) each agent chooses a portfolio with the objective of maximizing a derived utility function of the form $W(e, \sigma^2)$, $W_1 > 0$, $W_2 < 0$, W concave.

In addition, we assume that all investors have a common time horizon and homogeneous beliefs about e and V.

Under either set of assumptions, investors will only hold mean-variance efficient frontier portfolios.[4] But this implies that, **in equilibrium,** the market portfolio, which is a convex combination of individual portfolios is also on the efficient frontier.[5]

Therefore, in Equation (6.21), p can be chosen to be M, the portfolio of all risky assets, and Equation (6.27) can, therefore, be expressed as:

$$E(\tilde{r}_q) = E(\tilde{r}_{ZC(M)}) + \beta_{Mq}[E(\tilde{r}_M) - E(\tilde{r}_{ZC(M)})] \qquad \textbf{(6.28)}$$

The relationship in Equation (6.28) holds for any portfolio q, whether it is a frontier portfolio or not. This is the zero-beta CAPM.

An individual asset j is also a portfolio, so Equation (6.28) applies to it as well:

$$E(\tilde{r}_j) = E(\tilde{r}_{ZC(M)}) + \beta_{Mj}[E(\tilde{r}_M) - E(\tilde{r}_{ZC(M)})] \qquad \textbf{(6.29)}$$

The zero-beta CAPM (and the more familiar *Sharpe-Lintner-Mossin* CAPM)[6] is an equilibrium theory: The relationships in Equations (6.28) and (6.29) hold in equilibrium. In equilibrium, investors will not be maximizing utility unless they hold efficient portfolios. Therefore, the market portfolio is efficient; we have identified one efficient frontier portfolio, and we can apply Equation (6.28). By contrast, Equation (6.27) is a pure mathematical relationship with no economic content; it simply describes relationships between frontier portfolio returns and the returns from any other portfolio of the same assets.

As noted in the introduction, the zero-beta CAPM does not, however, describe the process to or by which equilibrium is achieved. In other words, the process by which agents buy and sell securities in their desire to hold efficient portfolios, thereby altering security prices and thus expected returns, and requiring further changes in portfolio composition. When this process ceases and all agents are optimizing given the prevailing prices, then all will be holding efficient portfolios given the equilibrium expected returns e and covariance-variance matrix V. Thus M is also efficient.

Since, in equilibrium, agents desired holdings of securities coincide with their actual holdings, we can identify M as the actual portfolio of securities held in the marketplace. There are many convenient approximations to M—the S&P 500 index of stocks being the most popular in the United States. The usefulness of these approximations, which are needed to give empirical content to the CAPM, is, however, debatable as discussed in our concluding comments.

As a final remark, let us note that the name "zerobeta CAPM" comes from the fact that $\beta_{ZC(M),M} = \text{cov}(\tilde{r}_M, \tilde{r}_{ZC(M)})/\sigma_M^2 = 0$, by construction of $ZC(M)$; in other words, the beta of $ZC(M)$ is zero.

6.7 THE STANDARD CAPM

Our development thus far did not admit the option of a risk-free asset. We need to add this if we are to achieve the standard form CAPM. On a purely formal basis, of course, a risk-free asset has zero covariance with M and thus $E(\tilde{r}_{ZC(M)})$. Hence we could replace

---

[4]Recall the demonstration in Section 5.3
[5]Note that, in the standard version of the CAPM, the analogous claim crucially depended on the existence of a risk-free asset.
[6]Sharpe (1964), Lintner (1965), and Mossin (1966).

$E(\tilde{r}_{ZC(M)})$ with r_f in Equation (6.29) to obtain the standard representation of the CAPM, the SML. But this approach is not entirely appropriate since the derivation of Equation (6.29) presumed the absence of any such risk-free asset.

More formally, the addition of a risk-free asset substantially alters the shape of the set of frontier portfolios in $E(\tilde{r}) \times \sigma(\tilde{r})$ space. Let us briefly outline the development here, which closely resembles what is previously done. Consider N risky assets with expected return vector e, and one risk-free asset, with *expected* return $\equiv r_f$. Let p be a frontier portfolio and let w_p denote the N vector of portfolio weights on the risky assets of p; w_p in this case is the solution to:

$$\min_{w} \tfrac{1}{2} w^T V w$$

$$\text{s.t. } w^T e + (1 - w^T \mathbf{1}) r_f = E$$

Solving this problem gives

$$w_p = V^{-1}(e - r_f \mathbf{1}) \frac{E - r_f}{H}$$

where $H = B - 2Ar_f + Cr_f^2$, and A, B, and C are defined as before.

Let us examine this expression for w_p more carefully:

$$w_p = \underbrace{V^{-1}}_{\text{nxn}} \underbrace{(e - r_f \mathbf{1})}_{\text{nx1}} \underbrace{\frac{E(\tilde{r}_p) - r_f}{H}}_{\text{a number}} \qquad (6.30)$$

$$\underbrace{\phantom{V^{-1}(e-r_f\mathbf1)}}_{\text{nx1}}$$

This expression tells us that if we wish to have a higher expected return, we invest proportionally the same amount more in each risky asset so that the relative proportions of the risky assets remain unchanged. These proportions are defined by the $V^{-1}(e - r_f \mathbf{1})$ term. This is exactly the result we were intuitively expecting: Graphically, we are back to the linear frontier represented in Figure 6-1.

The weights w_p uniquely identify the tangency portfolio T. Also,

$$\sigma^2(\tilde{r}_p) = w_q^T V w_p = \frac{[E(\tilde{r}_p) - r_f]^2}{H}, \text{ and} \qquad (6.31)$$

$$\text{cov}(\tilde{r}_q, \tilde{r}_p) = w_q^T V w_p = \frac{[E(\tilde{r}_q) - r_f][E(\tilde{r}_p) - r_f]}{H} \qquad (6.32)$$

for any portfolio q and any frontier portfolio p. Note how all this parallels what we did before. Solving Equation (6.32) for $E(\tilde{r}_q)$ gives:

$$E(\tilde{r}_q) - r_f = \frac{H \, \text{cov}(\tilde{r}_q, \tilde{r}_p)}{E(\tilde{r}_p) - r_f} \qquad (6.33)$$

Substituting for H via Equation (6.30) yields

$$E(\tilde{r}_q) - r_f = \frac{\text{cov}(\tilde{r}_q, \tilde{r}_p)}{E(\tilde{r}_p) - r_f} \frac{[E(\tilde{r}_p) - r_f]^2}{\sigma^2(\tilde{r}_p)} \text{ or}$$

$$E(\tilde{r}_q) - r_f = \frac{\text{cov}(\tilde{r}_q, \tilde{r}_p)}{\sigma^2(\tilde{r}_p)} [E(\tilde{r}_p) - r_f] \qquad (6.34)$$

Again, since T is a frontier portfolio, we can choose $p \equiv T$. But in equilibrium $T = M$; in this case, Equation (6.34) gives:

$$E(\tilde{r}_q) - r_f = \frac{\text{cov}(\tilde{r}_q, \tilde{r}_M)}{\sigma^2(\tilde{r}_M)}[E(\tilde{r}_M) - r_f], \text{ or}$$

$$E(\tilde{r}_q) = r_f + \beta_{qM}[E(\tilde{r}_M) - r_f] \tag{6.35}$$

for any asset (or portfolio) q. This is the standard CAPM.

Again, let us review the flow of logic that led to this conclusion. First, we identified the efficient frontier of risk-free and risky assets. This efficient frontier is fully characterized by the risk-free asset and a specific tangency frontier portfolio. The latter is identified in Equation (6.30). We then observed that all investors, in equilibrium under homogeneous expectations, would hold combinations of the risk-free asset and that portfolio. Thus it must constitute the *market*—the portfolio of all risky assets. It is these latter observations that give the CAPM its empirical content.

6.8 CONCLUSIONS

Understanding and identifying the determinants of equilibrium asset returns is inherently an overwhelmingly complex problem. In order to make some progress, we have made, in the present chapter, a number of simplifying assumptions that we will progressively relax in the future.

1. Rather than deal with fully described probability distributions on returns, we consider only the first two moments, $E(\tilde{r}_p)$ and $\sigma^2(\tilde{r}_p)$. When returns are at least approximately normally distributed, it is natural to think first of characterizing return distributions by their means and variances, since $\text{Prob}(\mu_r - 2\sigma_r \leq \tilde{r} \leq \mu_r + 2\sigma_r) = 0.95$, for the normal distribution: plus or minus two standard deviations from the mean will encompass nearly all of the probability. It is also natural to try to estimate these distributions and their moments from historical data. To do this naively would be to assign equal probability to each past observation. Yet, we suspect that more recent observations should contain more relevant information concerning the true distribution than observations in the distant past. Indeed the entire distribution may be shifting through time; that is, it may be nonstationary. Much current research is devoted to studying what and how information can be extracted from historical data in this setting.
2. The model is static; in other words, only one period of returns are measured and analyzed. The defined horizon is assumed to be equally relevant for all investors.
3. Homogeneous expectations: all investors share the same information. We know this assumption cannot, in fact, be true. Anecdotally, different security analysts produce reports on the same stock that are wildly different. More objectively, the observed volume of trade on the stock exchanges is much higher than is predicted by trading models with assumed homogeneous expectations.

The CAPM is at the center of modern financial analysis. As with modern portfolio theory, its first and foremost contribution is conceptual: It has played a major role in helping us to organize our thoughts on the key issue of equilibrium asset pricing. Beyond that, it is also a testable theory, and indeed, a huge amount of resources has been devoted to testing it. Since the just-mentioned assumptions do not hold up in practice, it is not surprising that empirical tests of the CAPM often yield disappointing results.[7] One example is the Roll (1977) critique. Roll reminds us that the CAPM's view of the market portfolio is that it contains every asset. Yet data on asset returns is not available for many assets. For example, no systematic data is available on real estate and, in the United States at least, approximately one-half of total wealth is invested in real estate. Thus it is customary to use proxies for the true M in conducting tests of CAPM. Roll demonstrates, however, that even if two potential proxies for M are correlated greater than 0.9, the beta estimates obtained using each may be very different. This suggests that the empirical implications of the model are very sensitive to the choice of proxy. With no theory to inform us as to what proxy to use, the applicability of the theory is suspect.

Furthermore, beginning in the late 1970s and continuing to the present, more and more evidence has come to light suggesting that firm characteristics beyond beta provide explanatory power for mean equity returns. In particular, various studies have demonstrated that a firm's average equity returns are significantly related to its size (as measured by the aggregate market value of equity), the ratio of book value per share to market value per share for its common equity, its equity price to earnings ratio, its cash flow per share to price per share ratio, and its historical sales growth. These relationships contradict strict CAPM, which argues that only a stock's systematic risk should matter for its returns; as such they are referred to as anomalies. In addition, even in models that depart from the CAPM assumptions, there is little theoretical evidence as to why these particular factors should be significant.

We close this chapter by illustrating these ideas with brief summaries of two especially prominent recent papers. Fama and French (1992) showed that the relationship between market betas and average returns is essentially flat for their sample period (1963 to 1990). In other words, their results suggest that the single factor CAPM can no longer explain the cross-sectional variation in equity returns. They also find that for this sample period the univariate (single factor) relationship between average stock returns and size (market value of equity), leverage, earnings-to-price ratio, and book-to-market value of equity per share are strong. More specifically, there is a negative relationship between size and average return, which is robust to the inclusion of other variables. There is also a consistent positive relationship between average returns and book-to-market ratio, which is not swamped by the introduction of other variables. They find that the combination of size and the book-to-market ratio as explanatory variables appears, for their sample period, to subsume the explanatory roles of leverage and the price-to-earnings ratio.

In a related paper, Fama and French (1993) formalize their size and book-to-market ratio factors more precisely by artificially constructing two-factor portfolios to which they assign acronyms, HML (high-medium-low) and SMB (small-medium-big). Both portfolios consist of a joint long and short position and have net asset value zero. The HML portfolio represents a combination of a long position in high book-to-market stocks with a short position in low book-to-market stocks. The SMB portfolio is one consisting of a

---

[7]We have chosen not to systematically review this literature. Standard testing procedures and their results are included in the introductory finance manuals which are prerequisites for the present text. Advanced issues properly belong to financial econometrics courses. The student wishing to invest in this area should consult Jensen (1979) and Friend, Westerfield, and Granito (1979) for early surveys; Ferson and Jagannathan (1996) and Shanken (1996) for more recent ones.

long position in small capitalization stocks and a short position in large capitalization stocks. These designations are, of course, somewhat arbitrary.[8] In conjunction with the excess (above the risk-free rate) return on a broad-based index, Fama and French study the ability of these factors to explain cross-sectional stock returns. They find that their explanatory power is highly significant.

References

Fama, E., and K. French, "The Cross Section of Expected Stock Returns," *Journal of Finance,* 47 (1992): 427–465.

Fama, E., and K. French, "Common Risk Factors in the Returns on Stocks and Bonds," *Journal of Financial Economics,* 33 (1993): 3–56.

Ferson, W. E., and R. Jagannathan, "Econometric Evaluation of Asset Pricing Models," in *Statistical Methods in Finance, Handbook of Statistics*, 14, G. S. Maddala and C. R. Rao, eds., 1996.

Friend, I., R. Westerfield, and M. Granito, "New Evidence on the Capital Asset Pricing Mode, l," in *Handbook of Financial Economics*, J. L. Bicksler, ed., Amsterdam: North Holland, 1979.

Jensen, M., "Tests of Capital Market Theory and Implications of the Evidence," in *Handbook of Financial Economics*, J. L. Bicksler, ed., Amsterdam: North Holland, 1979.

Lintner, J., "The Valuation of Risk Assets and the Selection of Risky Investments in Stock Portfolio and Capital Budgets," *Review of Economics and Statistics,* 47(1), (1965): 13–37.

Mossin, J., "Equilibrium in a Capital Asset Market," *Econometrica,* 34(4), (1966): 768–783.

Roll, R., "A Critique of the Asset Pricing Theory's Test—Part I: On Past and Potential Testability of the Theory," *Journal of Financial Economics,* 4 (1977): 129–176.

Shanken, J. "Statistical Methods in Tests of Portfolio Efficiency: A Synthesis," in *Statistical Methods in Finance, Handbook of Statistics*, 14, G. S. Maddala and C. R. Rao, ed., Amsterdam: North Holland, 1996.

Sharpe, W. F. "Capital Asset Prices: A Theory of Market Equilibrium under Conditions of Risk," *Journal of Finance*, 19(3), 1964.

---

[8]Short description on how to construct SMB, HML:
In June each year, all NYSE stocks are ranked by size. The medium NYSE size is used to split all NYSE, AMEX, and NASDAQ firms into two groups, small and big. All NYSE, AMEX, and NASDAQ stocks are also broken into three BE/ME equity groups based on the breakpoints for the bottom 30% (low), middle 40% (medium), and top 30% (high) of the ranked values of BE/ME for NYSE stocks. Fama and French (1993) then construct six portfolios (S/L, S/M, S/H, B/L, B/M, B/H) from the intersection of the two ME groups and the three BE/ME groups. SMB is the difference between the simple average of returns on three small stock portfolios (S/L, S/M, S/H) and the three big stock portfolios (B/L, B/M, B/H). SMB mimics the risk factor in return related to size. Accordingly, HML is the difference of the simple average of the returns on the two high BE/ME portfolios (S/H, B/H) and the average of the returns on the two low BE/ME portfolios (S/L, B/L). HML mimics the risk factor in returns that is related to BE/ME.

A P P E N D I X   6 . 1

Proof of the CAPM Relationship

Refer to Figure 6-1. Consider a portfolio with a fraction $1 - \alpha$ of wealth invested in an arbitrary security j and a fraction in the market portfolio.

$$\bar{r}_p = \alpha \bar{r}_M + (1 - \alpha)\bar{r}_j$$
$$\sigma_p^2 = \alpha^2 \sigma_M^2 + (1 - \alpha)^2 \sigma_j^2 + 2\alpha(1 - \alpha)\sigma_{jM}$$

As α varies we trace a locus that

- passes through M
- (and through j)
- cannot cross the CML (why?)
- hence must be tangent to the CML at M

Tangency $= (d\bar{r}_p/d\sigma_p)/_{\alpha=1} =$ slope of the locus at $M =$ slope of $CML = (\bar{r}_M - r_f)/\sigma_M$

$$\frac{d\bar{r}_p}{d\sigma_p} = \frac{d\bar{r}_p/d\alpha}{d\sigma_p/d\alpha}$$

$$\frac{d\bar{r}_p}{d\alpha} = \bar{r}_M - \bar{r}_j$$

$$2\sigma_p \frac{d\sigma_p}{d\alpha} = 2\alpha\sigma_M^2 - 2(1 - \alpha)\sigma_j^2 + 2(1 - 2\alpha)\sigma_{jM}$$

$$\frac{d\bar{r}_p}{d\sigma_p} = \frac{(\bar{r}_M - \bar{r}_j)\sigma_p}{\alpha\sigma_M^2 - (1 - \alpha)\sigma_j^2 + (1 - 2\alpha)\sigma_{jM}}$$

$$\frac{d\bar{r}_p}{d\sigma_p}\bigg/_{\alpha=1} = \frac{(\bar{r}_M - \bar{r}_j)\sigma_M}{\sigma_M^2 - \sigma_{jM}} = \frac{\bar{r}_M - \bar{r}_f}{\sigma_M}$$

$$(\bar{r}_M - \bar{r}_j) = \frac{(\bar{r}_M - r_f)(\sigma_M^2 - \sigma_{jM})}{\sigma_M^2}$$

$$(\bar{r}_M - \bar{r}_j) = (\bar{r}_M - r_f)\left(1 - \frac{\sigma_{jM}}{\sigma_M^2}\right)$$

$$\bar{r}_j = r_f + (\bar{r}_M - r_f)\frac{\sigma_{jM}}{\sigma_M^2}$$

A P P E N D I X   6 . 2

The Mathematics of the Portfolio Frontier: An Example

Assume $e = \begin{pmatrix} \bar{r}_1 \\ \bar{r}_2 \end{pmatrix} = \begin{pmatrix} 1 \\ 2 \end{pmatrix}$; $V = \begin{pmatrix} 1 & -1 \\ -1 & 4 \end{pmatrix}$

i.e., $\rho_{12} = \rho_{21} = -1/2$

Therefore,

$V^{-1} = \begin{pmatrix} 4/3 & 1/3 \\ 1/3 & 1/3 \end{pmatrix}$;

check: $\begin{pmatrix} 1 & -1 \\ -1 & 4 \end{pmatrix} \begin{pmatrix} 4/3 & 1/3 \\ 1/3 & 1/3 \end{pmatrix}$

$= \begin{pmatrix} 4/3 - 1/3 & 1/3 - 1/3 \\ -4/3 + 4/3 & -1/3 + 4/3 \end{pmatrix} = \begin{pmatrix} 1 & 0 \\ 0 & 1 \end{pmatrix}$

$A = 1^T V^{-1} e = (1 \quad 1) \begin{pmatrix} 4/3 & 1/3 \\ 1/3 & 1/3 \end{pmatrix} \begin{pmatrix} 1 \\ 2 \end{pmatrix}$

$= \left(\underbrace{4/3 + 1/3}_{5/3} \quad \underbrace{1/3 + 1/3}_{2/3} \right) \begin{pmatrix} 1 \\ 2 \end{pmatrix}$

$= 5/3 + 2(2/3) = 3$

$B = e^T V^{-1} e = (1 \quad 2) \begin{pmatrix} 4/3 & 1/3 \\ 1/3 & 1/3 \end{pmatrix} \begin{pmatrix} 1 \\ 2 \end{pmatrix}$

$= (4/3 + 2/3 \quad 1/3 + 2/3) \begin{pmatrix} 1 \\ 2 \end{pmatrix}$

$= 6/3 + 6/3 = 4$

$C = 1^T V^{-1} 1 = (1 \quad 1) \begin{pmatrix} 4/3 & 1/3 \\ 1/3 & 1/3 \end{pmatrix} \begin{pmatrix} 1 \\ 1 \end{pmatrix}$

$= (5/3 \quad 2/3) \begin{pmatrix} 1 \\ 1 \end{pmatrix}$

$= 5/3 + 2/3 = 7/3$

$D = BC - A^2 = 4(7/3) - 9$
$= 28/3 - 27/3 = 1/3$

Now we can compute g and h:

1. $g = \dfrac{1}{D} [B(V^{-1}1) - A(V^{-1}e)]$

$= \dfrac{1}{1/3} \left[4 \begin{pmatrix} 4/3 & 1/3 \\ 1/3 & 1/3 \end{pmatrix} \begin{pmatrix} 1 \\ 1 \end{pmatrix} \right.$

$\left. - 3 \begin{pmatrix} 4/3 & 1/3 \\ 1/3 & 1/3 \end{pmatrix} \begin{pmatrix} 1 \\ 2 \end{pmatrix} \right]$

$= 3 \left[4 \begin{pmatrix} 5/3 \\ 2/3 \end{pmatrix} - 3 \begin{pmatrix} 6/3 \\ 3/3 \end{pmatrix} \right]$

$= 3 \left[\begin{pmatrix} 20/3 \\ 8/3 \end{pmatrix} - \begin{pmatrix} 18/3 \\ 9/3 \end{pmatrix} \right]$

$= \left[\begin{pmatrix} 20 \\ 8 \end{pmatrix} - \begin{pmatrix} 18 \\ 9 \end{pmatrix} \right] = \begin{pmatrix} 2 \\ -1 \end{pmatrix}$

2. $h = \dfrac{1}{D} [C(V^{-1}e) - A(V^{-1}1)]$

$= \dfrac{1}{1/3} \left[\dfrac{7}{3} \begin{pmatrix} 4/3 & 1/3 \\ 1/3 & 1/3 \end{pmatrix} \begin{pmatrix} 1 \\ 2 \end{pmatrix} \right.$

$\left. - 3 \begin{pmatrix} 4/3 & 1/3 \\ 1/3 & 1/3 \end{pmatrix} \begin{pmatrix} 1 \\ 2 \end{pmatrix} \right]$

$= 3 \left[\dfrac{7}{3} \begin{pmatrix} 2 \\ 1 \end{pmatrix} - 3 \begin{pmatrix} 5/3 \\ 2/3 \end{pmatrix} \right]$

$= 7 \begin{pmatrix} 2 \\ 1 \end{pmatrix} - 3 \begin{pmatrix} 5/3 \\ 2/3 \end{pmatrix}$

$= \begin{pmatrix} 14 \\ 7 \end{pmatrix} - \begin{pmatrix} 15 \\ 6 \end{pmatrix} = \begin{pmatrix} -1 \\ 1 \end{pmatrix}$

Check by recovering the two initial assets; suppose $E(\tilde{r}_p) = 1$

$\begin{pmatrix} w_1 \\ w_2 \end{pmatrix} = \begin{pmatrix} 2 \\ -1 \end{pmatrix} + \begin{pmatrix} -1 \\ 1 \end{pmatrix} E(\tilde{r}_p)$

$= \begin{pmatrix} 2 \\ -1 \end{pmatrix} + \begin{pmatrix} -1 \\ 1 \end{pmatrix} = \begin{pmatrix} 1 \\ 0 \end{pmatrix} \Rightarrow \text{OK}$

suppose $E(\tilde{r}_p) = 2$

$\begin{pmatrix} w_1 \\ w_2 \end{pmatrix} = \begin{pmatrix} 2 \\ -1 \end{pmatrix} + \begin{pmatrix} -1 \\ 1 \end{pmatrix} 2$

$= \begin{pmatrix} 2 \\ -1 \end{pmatrix} + \begin{pmatrix} -2 \\ 2 \end{pmatrix} = \begin{pmatrix} 0 \\ 1 \end{pmatrix} \Rightarrow \text{OK}$

The equation corresponding to Equation (6.15) thus reads:

$$\begin{pmatrix} w_1^p \\ w_2^p \end{pmatrix} = \begin{pmatrix} 2 \\ -1 \end{pmatrix} + \begin{pmatrix} -1 \\ 1 \end{pmatrix} E(\tilde{r}_p)$$

Let us compute the minimum variance portfolio for these assets.

$$E(\tilde{r}_{p,\ \text{min variance}}) = \frac{A}{C} = \frac{9}{7}$$

$$\sigma^2(\tilde{r}_{p,\ \text{min variance}}) = \frac{1}{C} = \frac{3}{7} < \min\{1, 4\}$$

$$w^p = \begin{pmatrix} 2 \\ -1 \end{pmatrix} + \begin{pmatrix} -1 \\ 1 \end{pmatrix} \frac{9}{7} = \begin{pmatrix} 2 \\ -1 \end{pmatrix} + \begin{pmatrix} -9/7 \\ 9/7 \end{pmatrix}$$

$$= \begin{pmatrix} 14/7 \\ -7/7 \end{pmatrix} + \begin{pmatrix} -9/7 \\ 9/7 \end{pmatrix} = \begin{pmatrix} 5/7 \\ 2/7 \end{pmatrix}$$

Let's check $\sigma^2(\tilde{r}_p)$ by computing it another way:

$$\sigma_p^2 = (5/7 \quad 2/7) \begin{pmatrix} 1 & -1 \\ -1 & 4 \end{pmatrix} \begin{pmatrix} 5/7 \\ 2/7 \end{pmatrix}$$

$$= (3/7 \quad 3/7) \begin{pmatrix} 5/7 \\ 2/7 \end{pmatrix} = 3/7 \Rightarrow \text{OK}$$

CHAPTER 7

ARROW-DEBREU PRICING

7.1 INTRODUCTION

As interesting and popular as it is, the CAPM is a very limited theory of equilibrium pricing and we will devote the next chapters to reviewing alternative theories, each of which goes beyond the CAPM in one direction or another. The Arrow-Debreu pricing theory discussed in this chapter is a full general equilibrium theory as opposed to the partial equilibrium static view of the CAPM. Although also static in nature, it is applicable to a multi-period setup and can be generalized to a broad set of situations. In particular, it is free of any preference restrictions, and of distributional assumptions on returns. The Consumption CAPM considered subsequently (Chapter 10) is a fully dynamic construct. It is also an equilibrium theory, though of a somewhat specialized nature. The Risk Neutral Valuation Model and the Arbitrage Pricing Theory (APT), taken up in Chapters 9, 11, and 12, are arbitrage-based theories in contrast to the equilibrium approach of Arrow-Debreu. We will, in due time, develop further the comparisons among these approaches.

The Arrow-Debreu model takes a more standard equilibrium view than the CAPM: It is explicit in stating that equilibrium means supply equals demand in every market. It is a very general theory accommodating production and, as already stated, very broad hypotheses on preferences. Moreover, no restriction on the distribution of returns is necessary. We will not, however, fully exploit the generality of the theory: In keeping with the objective of this text, we shall often limit ourselves to illustrating the theory with examples.

We will be interested to apply it to the equilibrium pricing of securities, especially the pricing of complex securities that pay returns in many different time periods and states of nature, such as common stocks or 30-year government coupon bonds. The theory will, as well, enrich our understanding of project valuation. To see this connection, recall from elementary finance that it is customary to model a project simply as an uncertain future cash flow stream:

$$
\begin{array}{cccccc}
t = 0 & 1 & 2 & 3 & \dots & T \\
-I_0 & \tilde{C}F_1 & \tilde{C}F_2 & \tilde{C}F_3 & \dots & \tilde{C}F_T
\end{array}
$$

To decide if the firm should undertake the project, the latter's Net Present Value (NPV) is usually calculated:

$$NPV = -I_0 + \underbrace{\frac{EC\tilde{F}_1}{(1 + r_f + \Pi)} + \frac{EC\tilde{F}_2}{(1 + r_f + \Pi)^2} + \cdots + \frac{EC\tilde{F}_T}{(1 + r_f + \Pi)^T}}_{PV \left(\substack{\text{future cash flows discounted at a rate of return that reflects} \\ \text{their systematic (non-diversifiable) risk, } \Pi \text{ the risk premium}} \right)}$$

The risk premium is estimated as the risk premium on traded stocks or securities that represents title to cash flows similar (i.e., of similar systematic risk) to that of the project.

Now, let us reflect for a moment on what we are really doing when we compute the risk-adjusted PV. We are, in effect, asking the question: If this project's cash flow was traded as though it was a security, at what price would it sell given that it should pay the prevailing rate for securities of that same systematic risk level? We compare its worth, estimated in this way, with its cost, I_0. Evaluating a project is thus a special case of evaluating a complex security and the theory developed in this chapter will help us in that objective as well.

7.2 SETTING: AN ARROW-DEBREU ECONOMY

In the basic setting that we shall use, the following parameters apply:

1. There are two dates: 0, 1. This setup, however, is fully generalizable to multiple periods; see the later remark.
2. There are N possible states of nature at date 1, which we index by $\theta = 1, 2, \ldots, N$ with probabilities π_θ;
3. There is one perishable (non-storable) consumption good.
4. There are K agents, indexed by $k = 1, \ldots, K$, with preferences:

$$U_0^k(c_0^k) + \delta^k \sum_{\theta=1}^{N} \pi_\theta U^k(c_\theta^k);$$

5. Agent k's endowment is described by the vector $\{e_0^k, (e_\theta^k)_{\theta=1,2,\ldots,N}\}$.

In this description, c_θ^k denotes agent k's consumption of the sole consumption good in state θ, U is the real-valued utility representation of agent k's period preferences, and δ^k is the agent's time discount factor. In fact, the theory allows for more general preferences than the time-additive expected utility form. Specifically, we could adopt the following representation of preferences:

$$u^k(c_0^k, c_{\theta_1}^k, c_{\theta_2}^k, \ldots, c_{\theta_N}^k).$$

This formulation allows not only for a different way of discounting the future (implicit in the relative taste for present consumption relative to all future consumptions), but it also permits heterogeneous, subjective views on the state probabilities (again implicit in the representation of relative preference for, say, $c_{\theta_2}^k$ and $c_{\theta_3}^k$). In addition, it assumes neither time-additivity, nor an expected utility representation. Since our main objective is not generality, we choose to work with the less general, but easier to manipulate time-additive expected utility form.

In this economy, the only traded securities are of the following form: One unit of security θ, with price q_θ, pays one unit of consumption if state θ occurs and nothing otherwise. Its payout can thus be summarized by a vector with all entries equal to zero except for column θ where the entry is 1: $(0 \ldots 0\, 1\, 0 \ldots 0)$. These primitive securities are called **Arrow-Debreu securities,**[1] or *state contingent claims* or simply *state claims.* Of course, the consumption of any individual k if state θ occurs equals the number of units of security θ that he holds. This is because buying the relevant contingent claims is the only way for a consumer to secure purchasing power at a future date-state (recall that the good is perishable). An agent's decision problem can then be characterized by:

$$\max_{(c_0^k, c_1^k, \ldots, c_N^k)} U_0^k(c_0^k) + \delta^k \sum_{\theta=1}^{N} \pi_\theta U^k(c_\theta^k)$$

$$\text{s.t.} \qquad\qquad\qquad\qquad\qquad\qquad\qquad\qquad\text{(P)}$$

$$c_0^k + \sum_{\theta=1}^{N} q_\theta c_\theta^k \le e_0^k + \sum_{\theta=1}^{N} q_\theta e_\theta^k$$

$$c_0^k, c_1^k, \ldots, c_N^k \ge 0$$

Note that the first inequality constraint will typically hold with equality in a world of non-satiation. That is, the total value of goods and security purchases made by the agent (the left-hand side of the inequality) will exhaust the total value of his endowments (the right-hand side).

Equilibrium for this economy is a set of contingent claim prices $(q_1, q_2, \ldots, q_N)$ such that

1. at those prices $(c_0^k, \ldots, c_N^k)$ solve problem (P), for all k, and
2. $\sum_{k=1}^{K} c_0^k = \sum_{k=1}^{K} e_0^k$, $\sum_{k=1}^{K} c_\theta^k = \sum_{k=1}^{K} e_\theta^k$, for every θ.

Note that here the agents are solving for desired future and present consumption holdings rather than holdings of Arrow-Debreu securities. This is appropriate because, as just noted, there is a one-to-one relationship between the amount consumed by an individual in a given state θ and his holdings of the Arrow-Debreu security corresponding to that particular state θ, the latter being a promise to deliver one unit of the consumption good if that state occurs.

Note also that there is nothing in this formulation that inherently restricts matters to two periods, if we define our notion of a state somewhat more richly, as a *date-state* pair. Consider three periods, for example. There are N possible states in date one and J possible states in date two, irrespective of the state achieved in date 1. Define $\hat{\theta}$ new states to be of the form $\hat{\theta}_s = (j, \theta_k^j)$, where j denotes the state in date 1 and θ_k^j denotes the state k in date 2, conditional that state j was observed in date 1 (Refer to Figure 7-1). So $(1, \theta_5^1)$ would be a state and $(2, \theta_3^2)$ another state. Under this interpretation, the number of *states* expands to $1 + NJ$, with:

> 1: the date 0 state
> N: the number of date-1 states
> J: the number of date-2 states

With minor modifications, we can thus accommodate many periods and states. In this sense, our model is fully general and can represent as complex an environment as we might desire. In this case, the real productive side of the economy is in the back-

---

[1]So named after the originators of modern equilibrium theory; see Arrow (1951) and Debreu (1959).

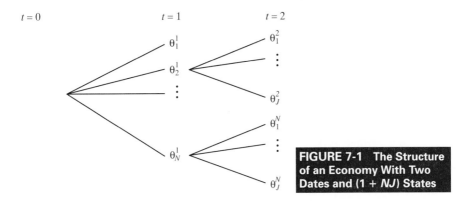

FIGURE 7-1   The Structure of an Economy With Two Dates and (1 + NJ) States

ground. We are, in effect, viewing that part of the economy as invariant to securities trading. The unusual and unrealistic aspect of this economy is that all trades occur at $t = 0$.[2] We will relax this assumption in Chapter 10.

7.3   COMPETITIVE EQUILIBRIUM AND PARETO OPTIMALITY ILLUSTRATED

Let us now develop an example. The essentials are found in Table 7-1.

There are thus two dates and, at the future date, two possible states of nature with probabilities ⅓ and ⅔. It is an exchange economy and the issue is to share the existing endowments between the two individuals. Their preferences are linear in date 0 consumption with constant marginal utility equal to ½. This choice is made for ease of computation, but great care must be exercised in interpreting the results obtained in such a simplified framework. Date 1 preferences are concave and identical. The discount factor is .9. Let q_1 be the price of a unit of consumption in date 1 state 1, q_2 the price of one unit of consumption good (the numeraire) in date 1 state 2. We will solve for optimal consumption directly, knowing that these will define the equilibrium holdings of the securities. The prices of these consumption goods coincide with the prices of the corresponding state-contingent claims; Period 0 consumption is taken as the numeraire and its price is 1. This means that all prices are expressed in units of period 0 consumption: q_1, q_2 are prices for the consumption good at date 1, in states 1 and 2, respectively, measured in units of date 0 consumption. They can thus be used to add up or compare units

TABLE 7-1 Endowments and Preferences in Our Reference Example				
Agents	*Endowments*			*Preferences*
	t = 0	*t = 1*		
		θ_1	θ_2	
Agent 1	10	1	2	$\frac{1}{2} c_0^1 + 0.9(\frac{1}{3} \ln(c_1^1) + \frac{2}{3} \ln(c_2^1))$
Agent 2	5	4	6	$\frac{1}{2} c_0^2 + 0.9(\frac{1}{3} \ln(c_1^2) + \frac{2}{3} \ln(c_2^2))$
Total	15	5	8	

[2]Interestingly, this is less of a problem for project valuation than for asset pricing.

of consumption at different dates and in different states, making it possible to add different date cash flows, with the q_i being the appropriate weights. This, in turn, permits computing an individual's wealth. Thus, in the previous problem, agent 1's wealth, which equals the present value of his current and future endowments, is $10 + 1q_1 + 2q_2$ while agent 2's wealth is $5 + 4q_1 + 6q_2$.

The respective agent problems are:

Agent 1:
$$\max \tfrac{1}{2}(10 + 1q_1 + 2q_2 - c_1^1 q_1 - c_2^1 q_2) + 0.9(\tfrac{1}{3}\ln(c_1^1) + \tfrac{2}{3}\ln(c_2^1))$$
$$\text{s.t. } c_1^1 q_1 + c_2^1 q_2 \leq 10 + q_1 + 2q_2, c_1^1, c_2^1 \geq 0$$

Agent 2:
$$\max \tfrac{1}{2}(5 + 4q_1 + 6q_2 - c_1^2 q_1 - c_2^2 q_2) + 0.9(\tfrac{1}{3}\ln(c_1^2) + \tfrac{2}{3}\ln(c_2^2))$$
$$\text{s.t. } c_1^2 q_1 + c_2^2 q_2 \leq 5 + 4q_1 + 6q_2, c_1^2, c_2^2 \geq 0$$

Note that in this formulation, we have substituted out for the date 0 consumption, in other words, the first term in the max expression stands for $\tfrac{1}{2}(c_0)$ and for c_0 we have substituted its value from the constraint: $c_0 + c_1^1 q_1 + c_2^1 q_2 = 10 + 1q_1 + 2q_2$. With this trick, the only constraints remaining are the non-negativity constraints requiring consumption to be nonnegative in all date-states.

The FOCs state that the intertemporal rate of substitution between future (in either state) and present consumption (i.e. the ratio of the relevant marginal utilities), should equal the price ratio. The latter is effectively measured by the price of the Arrow-Debreu security, the date 0 price of consumption being the numeraire. These FOCs (assuming interior solutions) are

Agent 1: $\begin{cases} c_1^1: \dfrac{q_1}{2} = 0.9(\tfrac{1}{3})\dfrac{1}{c_1^1} \\[2ex] c_2^1: \dfrac{q_2}{2} = 0.9(\tfrac{2}{3})\dfrac{1}{c_2^1} \end{cases}$ Agent 2: $\begin{cases} c_1^2: \dfrac{q_1}{2} = 0.9(\tfrac{1}{3})\dfrac{1}{c_1^2} \\[2ex] c_2^2: \dfrac{q_2}{2} = 0.9(\tfrac{2}{3})\dfrac{1}{c_2^2} \end{cases}$

while the market clearing conditions read: $c_1^1 + c_1^2 = 5$ and $c_2^1 + c_2^2 = 8$. Each of these conditions is of the form $q_\theta/1 = [(.9)(\tfrac{1}{3})(1/c_\theta^k)]/(\tfrac{1}{2})$, $k, \theta = 1, 2$, or

$$q_\theta = \dfrac{\delta \pi_\theta \dfrac{\partial U^k}{\partial c_\theta^k}}{\dfrac{\partial U_0^k}{\partial c_0^k}}, k, \theta = 1, 2 \tag{7.1}$$

Together with the market clearing conditions, Equation (7.1) reveals the determinants of the equilibrium Arrow-Debreu security prices. It is of the form:

$$\frac{\text{price of the good if state } \theta \text{ is realized}}{\text{price of the good today}} = \frac{MU_\theta^k}{MU_0^k};$$

in other words, the ratio of the price of the Arrow-Debreu security to the price of the date 0 consumption good must equal (at an interior solution) the ratio of the marginal utility of consumption tomorrow if state θ is realized to the marginal utility of today's consumption (the latter being constant at $\tfrac{1}{2}$). This is the marginal rate of substitution between the contingent consumption in state θ and today's consumption. From this system of equations, one clearly gets $c_1^1 = c_1^2 = 2.5$ and $c_2^1 = c_2^2 = 4$ from which one, in turn, obtains:

$$q_1 = \frac{1}{\frac{1}{2}}(0.9)(\frac{1}{3})\left(\frac{1}{c_1^1}\right) = \frac{1}{\frac{1}{2}}(0.9)(\frac{1}{3})(\frac{1}{2.5}) = (0.9)(\frac{1}{3})(\frac{4}{5}) = 0.24$$

$$q_2 = \frac{1}{\frac{1}{2}}(0.9)(\frac{2}{3})\left(\frac{1}{c_2^1}\right) = \frac{1}{\frac{1}{2}}(0.9)(\frac{2}{3})(\frac{1}{4}) = (0.9)(\frac{2}{3})(\frac{4}{8}) = 0.3$$

Notice how the Arrow-Debreu state-contingent prices reflect probabilities, on the one hand, and marginal rates of substitution (taking the time discount factor into account and computed at consumption levels compatible with market clearing) and thus relative scarcities, on the other. The just computed prices differ in that they take account of the different state probabilities ($\frac{1}{3}$ for state 1, $\frac{2}{3}$ for state 2) and because the marginal utilities differ as a result of the differing total quantities of the consumption good available in state 1 (5 units) and in state 2 (8 units). In our particular formulation, the total amount of goods available at date 0 is made irrelevant by the fact that date 0 marginal utility is constant. Note that if the date 1 marginal utilities were constant, as would be the case with linear (risk neutral) utility functions, the goods endowments would not influence the Arrow-Debreu prices, which would then be exactly proportional to the state probabilities.

The date 0 consumptions, at those equilibrium prices, are given by

$$c_0^1 = 10 + 1(.24) + 2(.3) - 2.5(.24) - 4(.3) = 9.04$$
$$c_0^2 = 5 + 4(.24) + 6(.3) - 2.5(.24) - 4(.3) = 5.96$$

So, post trade, the equilibrium consumptions are found in Table 7-2.

This allocation is the best each agent can achieve at the given prices $q_1 = .24$ and $q_2 = .3$. Furthermore, at those prices, supply equals demand in each market, in every state and time period. These are the characteristics of a (general) competitive equilibrium.

In light of this example, it is interesting to return to some of the concepts discussed in our introductory chapter. In particular, let us confirm the (Pareto) optimality of the allocation emerging from the competitive equilibrium. Indeed, we have assumed as many markets as there are states of nature, so assumption H1 is satisfied. We have *de facto* assumed competitive behavior on the part of our two consumers (they have taken prices as given when solving their optimization problems), so H2 is satisfied (of course, in reality such behavior would not be privately optimal if indeed there were only two agents). Our example would not have changed materially had we assumed a large number of agents, but the notation would have become much more cumbersome.

TABLE 7-2 Post-Trade Equilibrium Consumptions			
	$t = 0$	$t = 1$	
		θ_1	θ_2
Agent 1	9.04	2.5	4
Agent 2	5.96	2.5	4
Total	15.00	5.0	8

In order to guarantee the existence of an equilibrium, we need hypotheses H3 and H4 as well. H3 is satisfied in a weak form (no curvature in date 0 utility). Finally, ours is an exchange economy where H4 does not apply (or, if one prefers, it is trivially satisfied). Once the equilibrium is known to exist, as is the case here, H1 and H2 are sufficient to guarantee the optimality of the resulting allocation of resources. Thus, we expect to find that the competitive allocation is Pareto optimal (PO), that is, it is impossible to rearrange the allocation of consumptions so that the utility of one agent is higher without diminishing the utility of the other agent.

One way to verify the optimality of the competitive allocation is to establish the precise conditions that must be satisfied for an allocation to be Pareto optimal in the exchange economy context of our example. It is intuitively clear that the Pareto superior reallocations will be impossible if the initial allocation maximizes the weighted sum of the two agents' utilities. That is, an allocation is optimal in our example if, for some weight λ, it solves the following maximization problem.[3]

$$\max_{\{c_0^1, c_1^1, c_2^1\}} u^1(c_0^1, c_1^1, c_2^1) + \lambda u^2(c_0^2, c_1^2, c_2^2)$$

s.t.

$$c_0^1 + c_0^2 = 15; c_1^1 + c_1^2 = 5; c_2^1 + c_2^2 = 8,$$
$$c_0^1, c_1^1, c_2^1, c_0^2, c_1^2, c_2^2 \geq 0$$

This problem can be interpreted as the problem of a benevolent central planner constrained by an economy's total endowment $(15, 5, 8)$ and weighting the two agents utilities according to a parameter λ, possibly equal to 1. The decision variables at his disposal are the consumption levels of the two agents in the two dates and the two states. With u_i^k denoting the derivative of agent k's utility function with respect to c_i^k $(i = 1, 2, 3)$, the FOCs for an interior solution to the problem are found in Equation (7.3).

$$\frac{u_0^1}{u_0^2} = \frac{u_1^1}{u_1^2} = \frac{u_2^1}{u_2^2} = \lambda \tag{7.3}$$

This condition states that, in a Pareto optimal allocation, the ratio of the two agents' marginal utilities with respect to the three goods (i.e., the consumption good at date 0, the consumption good at date 1 if state 1, and the consumption good at date 1 if state 2) should be identical.[4] In an exchange economy this condition, properly extended to take account of the possibility of corner solution, together with the condition that the agents' consumption adds up to the endowment in each date-state, is necessary and sufficient.

It remains to check that Equation (7.3) is satisfied at the equilibrium allocation. We can rewrite Equation (7.3) for the parameters of our example:

$$\frac{\frac{1}{2}}{\frac{1}{2}} = \frac{(0.9)\frac{1}{3}\dfrac{1}{c_1^1}}{(0.9)\frac{1}{3}\dfrac{1}{c_1^2}} = \frac{(0.9)\frac{2}{3}\dfrac{1}{c_2^1}}{(0.9)\frac{2}{3}\dfrac{1}{c_2^2}}$$

---

[3] It is just as easy here to work with the most general utility representation.
[4] Check that Equation (7.3) implies that the MRS between any two pair of goods is the same for the two agents and refer to the definition of the contract curve (the set of PO allocations) in the appendix of Chapter 1.

It is clear that the condition in Equation (7.3) is satisfied since $c_1^1 = c_2^1; c_2^1 = c_2^2$ at the competitive equilibrium, which thus corresponds to the Pareto optimum with equal weighting of the two agents' utilities: $\lambda = 1$ and all three ratios of marginal utilities are equal to 1. Note that other Pareto optima are feasible, for example, one where $\lambda = 2$. In that case, only the latter two equalities can be satisfied, however. This is because the date 1 marginal utilities are constant which implies that no matter how agent consumptions are redistributed by the market or by the central planner, the first ratio of marginal utilities in Equation (7.3) cannot be made equal to 2. This is an example of a corner solution to the maximization problem leading to equation (7.3).

BOX 7-1

Interior vs. Corner Solutions

We have described the *interior* solution to the maximization problem. By that restriction we generally mean the following: The problem under maximization is constrained by the condition that consumption at all dates should be nonnegative. There is no interpretation given to a negative level of consumption, and, generally, even a zero consumption level is precluded. Indeed, when we make the assumption of a log utility function, the marginal utility at zero is infinity, meaning that by construction the agent will do all that is in his power to avoid that situation. Effectively an equation such as Equation (7.1) will never be satisfied for finite and nonzero prices with log utility and one consumption level equal to zero; that is, it will never be optimal to select a zero consumption level. Such is not the case with the linear utility function assumed to prevail at date 0. Here it is conceivable that, no matter what, the marginal utility in either state at date 1 [the numerator in the RHS of Equation (7.1)] be larger than ½ times the Arrow-Debreu price [the denominator of the RHS in Equation (7.1) multiplied by the state price]. Intuitively, this would be a situation where the agent derives more utility from the good tomorrow than from consuming today, even when his consumption level today is zero. Fun-

damentally, the interior optimum is one where he would like to consume less than zero today to increase even further consumption tomorrow, something that is impossible. Thus the only solution is at a corner, that is at the boundary of the feasible set, with $c_0^k = 0$ and the condition in Equation (7.1) taking the form of an inequality.

In the present case we can argue that corner solutions cannot occur with regard to future consumption (because of the log utility assumption). The full and complete description of the FOCs for problem (P) spelled out in Section 7.2 is then

$$q_\theta \frac{\partial U_0^k}{\partial c_0^k} \leq \delta \pi_\theta \frac{\partial U^k}{\partial c_\theta^k},$$
$$= \text{if } c_0^k > 0, k, \theta = 1, 2 \quad \textbf{(7.2)}$$

In line with our goal of being as transparent as possible, we will often, in the sequel, satisfy ourselves with a description of interior solutions to optimizing problems, taking care to ascertain, ex post, that the solutions do indeed occur at the interior of the choice set. This can be done in the present case by verifying that the optimal c_0^k is strictly positive for both agents at the interior solutions, so that Equation (7.1) must indeed apply.

In this example, agents are able to purchase consumption in any date-state of nature. This is the case because there are enough Arrow-Debreu securities; specifically there is an Arrow-Debreu security corresponding to each state of nature. If this were

TABLE 7-3	The Post-Trade Allocation		
	$t = 0$	$t = 1$	
		θ_1	θ_2
Agent 1	9.64	2.5	2
Agent 2	5.36	2.5	6
Total	15.00	5.0	8

not the case, the attainable utility levels would decrease: At least one agent, possibly both of them, would be worse off. If we assume that only the state θ_1 Arrow-Debreu security is available, then there is no way to make the state θ_2 consumption of the agents differ from their endowments. It is easy to check that this constraint does not modify their demand for the state θ_1-contingent claim, nor its price. The post-trade allocation, in that situation, is found in Table 7-3.

The resulting post-trade utilities are

$$\text{Agent 1: } \tfrac{1}{2}(9.64) + .9(\tfrac{1}{3}\ln(2.5) + \tfrac{2}{3}\ln(2)) = 5.51$$
$$\text{Agent 2: } \tfrac{1}{2}(5.36) + .9(\tfrac{1}{3}\ln(2.5) + \tfrac{2}{3}\ln(6)) = 4.03$$

In the case with two state-contingent claim markets, the post-trade utilities are both higher (illustrating a reallocation of resources that is said to be *Pareto superior* to the no-trade allocation):

$$\text{Agent 1: } \tfrac{1}{2}(9.04) + .9(\tfrac{1}{3}\ln(2.5) + \tfrac{2}{3}\ln(4)) = 5.62$$
$$\text{Agent 2: } \tfrac{1}{2}(5.96) + .9(\tfrac{1}{3}\ln(2.5) + \tfrac{2}{3}\ln(4)) = 4.09.$$

When there is an Arrow-Debreu security corresponding to each state of nature, one says that the securities markets are complete.

7.4 PARETO OPTIMALITY AND RISK SHARING

In this section and the next we further explore the nexus between a competitive equilibrium in an Arrow-Debreu economy and Pareto optimality. We first discuss the risk-sharing properties of a Pareto optimal allocation. We remain in the general framework of the example of the previous two sections but start with a different set of parameters. In particular, let the endowment matrix for the two agents be as shown in Table 7-4.

Assume further that each state is now equally likely, that is, has probability $\tfrac{1}{2}$. As before, consumption in period 0 cannot be stored and carried over into period 1. In the absence of trade, agents clearly experience widely differing consumption and utility levels in period 1, depending on what state occurs (see Table 7-5).

TABLE 7-4	The New Endowment Matrix		
	$t = 0$	$t = 1$	
		θ_1	θ_2
Agent 1	4	1	5
Agent 2	4	5	1

TABLE 7-5 Agents' Utility in the Absence of Trade		
	State-Contingent Utility	*Expected Utility in Period 1*
	θ_1	θ_2	
Agent 1	$\ln(1) = 0$	$\ln(5) = 1.609$	$\frac{1}{2}\ln(1) + \frac{1}{2}\ln(5) = .8047$
Agent 2	$\ln(5) = 1.609$	$\ln(1) = 0$	$\frac{1}{2}\ln(1) + \frac{1}{2}\ln(5) = .8047$

How could agents' utility be improved? By concavity (risk aversion), this must be accomplished by reducing the spread of the date 1 income possibilities, in other words, lowering the risk associated with date 1 income. Because of symmetry, all date 1 income fluctuations can, in fact, be eliminated if agent 2 agrees to transfer two units of the good in state 1 against the promise to receive two units from agent 1 if state 2 is realized (see Table 7-6).

Now we can compare expected second period utility levels before and after trade for both agents:

Before	*After*
.8047	$\frac{1}{2}\ln(3) + \frac{1}{2}\ln(3) = 1.099 \cong 1.1$

in other words, expected utility has increased quite significantly as anticipated.[5]

This feasible allocation is, in fact, *Pareto optimal*. In conformity with Equation (7.3), the ratios of the two agents' marginal utilities are indeed equalized across states. More is accomplished in this perfectly symmetrical and equitable allocation: Consumption levels and MU are equated across agents and states, but this is a coincidence resulting from the symmetry of the initial data.

Suppose the initial allocation was that illustrated in Table 7-7.

TABLE 7-6 The Desirable Trades and Post-Trade Consumptions				
Date 1	*Endowments Pre-Trade*		*Consumption Post-Trade*	
	θ_1	θ_2	θ_1	θ_2
Agent 1	1	5 [⇓2]	3	3
Agent 2	5 [⇑2]	1	3	3

TABLE 7-7 Another Set of Initial Allocations			
	$t = 0$	$t = 1$	
		θ_1	θ_2
Agent 1	4	1	3
Agent 2	4	5	3

---

[5]With the selected utility function, it has increased by 37%. Such quantification is not, however, compatible with the observation that expected utility functions are defined only up to a linear transformation. Instead of using ln c for the period utility function, we could equally well have used $(b + \ln c)$ to represent the same preference ordering. The quantification of the increased in utility pre- and post-trade would be affected.

Once again there is no aggregate risk: The total date 1 endowment is the same in the two states, but one agent is now richer than the other. Now consider the plausible trade outlined in Table 7-8.

Check that the new post-trade allocation is also Pareto optimal: Although consumption levels and marginal utilities are not identical, the ratio of marginal utilities is the same across states (except at date 0 where, as before, we have a corner solution since the marginal utilities are given constants). Note that this PO allocation features perfect risk sharing as well. By that we mean that the two agents have constant date 1 consumption (two units for agent 1, four units for agent 2) independent of the realized state. This is a general characteristic of PO allocations in the absence of aggregate risk (and with risk-averse agents). If there is no aggregate risk, all PO allocations necessarily feature full mutual insurance.

This statement can be demonstrated, using the data of our problem. Equation (7.3) states that the ratio of the two agents' marginal utilities should be equated across states. This also implies, however, that the Marginal Rate of Substitution (MRS) between state 1 and state 2 consumption must be the same for the two agents. In the case of log period utility:

$$\frac{\frac{1}{c_1^1}}{\frac{1}{c_1^2}} = \frac{\frac{1}{c_2^1}}{\frac{1}{c_2^2}} \Rightarrow \frac{\frac{1}{c_1^1}}{\frac{1}{c_2^1}} = \frac{\frac{1}{c_1^2}}{\frac{1}{c_2^2}}$$

But the latter equality implies:

1. If one of the two agents is fully insured—no variation in his date 1 consumption (i.e., MRS = 1)—the other must be as well.
2. More generally, if the MRS are to differ from 1, given that they must be equal between them, the low consumption-high MU state must be the same for both agents and similarly for the high consumption-low MU state. But this is impossible if there is no aggregate risk and total endowment is constant. Thus, as asserted, in the absence of aggregate risk, a PO allocation features perfectly insured individuals and MRS identically equal to 1.
3. If there is aggregate risk, however, the reasoning also implies that, at a Pareto optimum, it is shared "proportionately." This is literally true if agents' preferences are homogeneous. Refer to the competitive equilibrium of Section 7.3 for an example.
4. Finally, if agents are differentially risk averse, in a Pareto optimal allocation the less risk averse will typically provide some insurance services to the more risk averse. This is most easily illustrated by assuming that one of the two agents, say agent 1, is risk neutral. By risk neutrality, agent one's marginal utility is constant. But then the marginal utility of agent 2 should also be constant across states. For

TABLE 7-8 Plausible Trades And Post-Trade Consumptions

Date 1	Endowments Pre-Trade		Consumption Post-Trade	
	θ_1	θ_2	θ_1	θ_2
Agent 1	1	3 [⇓1]	2	2
Agent 2	5 [⇑1]	3	4	4

this to be the case, however, agent two's income uncertainty must be fully absorbed by agent 1, the risk-neutral agent.

5. More generally, optimal risk sharing dictates that the agent most tolerant of risk bears a disproportionate share of it.

7.5   IMPLEMENTING PARETO OPTIMAL ALLOCATIONS: ON THE POSSIBILITY OF MARKET FAILURE

Although to achieve the desired allocations, the agents of our previous section could just effect a handshake trade, real economic agents typically interact only through impersonal security markets or through deals involving financial intermediaries. One reason is that, in an organized security market, the contracts implied by the purchase or sale of a security are enforceable. This is important: Without an enforceable contract, if state θ_1 occurs, agent 2 might retreat from his ex-ante commitment and refuse to give up the promised consumption to agent 1, and vice versa if state θ_2 occurs. Accordingly, we now address the following question: What securities could empower these agents to achieve the optimal allocation for themselves?

Consider the Arrow-Debreu security with payoff in state θ_1 and call it security Q to clarify the notation below. Denote its price by q_Q, and let us compute the demand by each agent for this security denoted z_Q^i, $i = 1, 2$. The price is expressed in terms of period 0 consumption. We otherwise maintain the setup of the preceding section. Thus,

(i) Agent 1 solves: $\max (4 - q_Q z_Q^1) + [\frac{1}{2} \ln(1 + z_Q^1) + \frac{1}{2} \ln(5)]$

$$q_Q z_Q^1 \le 4$$

(ii) Agent 2 solves: $\max (4 - q_Q z_Q^2) + [\frac{1}{2} \ln(5 + z_Q^2) + \frac{1}{2} \ln(1)]$

$$q_Q z_Q^2 \le 4$$

Assuming an interior solution, the FOCs are

$$(i)': \quad -q_Q + \frac{1}{2}\left(\frac{1}{1 + z_Q^1}\right) = 0;$$

$$(ii)': \quad -q_Q + \frac{1}{2}\left(\frac{1}{5 + z_Q^2}\right) = 0 \Rightarrow \frac{1}{1 + z_Q^1} = \frac{1}{5 + z_Q^2};$$

also $z_Q^1 + z_Q^2 = 0$ in equilibrium, hence, $z_Q^1 = 2$; $z_Q^2 = -2$; these represent the holdings of each agent and $q_Q = (\frac{1}{2})(\frac{1}{3}) = \frac{1}{6}$. In effect, agent 1 gives up $q_Q z_Q^1 = \frac{1}{6}(2) = \frac{1}{3}$ unit of consumption at date 0 to agent 2 in exchange for 2 units of consumption at date 1 if state 1 occurs. Both agents are better off as revealed by the computation of their expected utilities post-trade:

Agent 1 expected utility: $4 - \frac{1}{3} + \frac{1}{2} \ln 3 + \frac{1}{2} \ln 5 = 5.013$

Agent 2 expected utility: $4 + \frac{1}{3} + \frac{1}{2} \ln 3 + \frac{1}{2} \ln 1 = 4.879$,

though agent 2 only slightly so. Clearly agent 1 is made proportionately better off because security Q pays off in the state where his MU is highest. We may view agent 2 as the issuer of this security as it entails, for him, a future obligation.[6]

---

[6]In a noncompetitive situation, it is likely that agent 2 could extract a larger portion of the rent. Remember, however, that we maintain, throughout, the assumption of price-taking behavior for our two agents who are representatives of larger classes of similar individuals.

Let us denote R as the other conceivable Arrow-Debreu security paying in state θ_2. By symmetry, it would also have a price of $\frac{1}{6}$, and the demand at this price would be $z_R^1 = -2, z_R^2 = +2$, respectively. Agent 2 would give up $\frac{1}{3}$ unit of period 1 consumption to agent 1 in exchange for 2 units of consumption in state 2.

Thus, if both security Q and R are traded, the market allocation will replicate the optimal allocation of risks, as seen in Table 7-9.

In general, it will be possible to achieve the optimal allocation of risks provided the number of linearly independent securities equals the number of states of nature. By linearly independent we mean, again, that there is no security whose payoff pattern across states and time periods can be duplicated by a portfolio of other securities. This important topic will be discussed at length in the next section. Here let us simply take stock of the fact that clearly our securities Q, R are the simplest pair of securities with this property.

Although a complete set of Arrow-Debreu securities is sufficient for optimal risk sharing, it is not necessary in the sense that it is possible, by coincidence, for the desirable trades to be effected with a simplified asset structure. For our simple example, one security would allow the agents to achieve that goal because of the essential symmetry of the problem. Consider security Z with payoffs:

	θ_1	θ_2
Z	2	-2

Clearly, if agent 1 purchases one unit of this security ($z_Z^1 = 1$) and agent 2 sells one unit of this security ($z_Z^2 = -1$), optimal risk sharing is achieved. (At what price would this security sell?)

So far we have implicitly assumed that the creation of these securities is costless. In reality, the creation of a new security is an expensive proposition: Disclosure documents, promotional materials, etc., must be created, and the agents most likely to be interested in the security contacted. In this example, issuance will occur only if the cost of issuing Q and R does not exceed the (expected) utility gained from purchasing them. In this margin lies the investment banker's fee.

In the previous discussion we imagined each agent as issuing securities to the other simultaneously. More realistically, perhaps, we could think of the securities Q and R as being issued in sequence, one after the other (but both before period 1 uncertainty is resolved). Is there an advantage or disadvantage of going first, that is, of issuing the *first* security? Alternatively, we might be preoccupied with the fact that, although both agents benefit from the issuance of new securities, only the individual issuer pays the

TABLE 7-9	Market Allocation When Both Securities Are Traded			
	$t = 0$		$t = 1$	
			θ_1	θ_2
Agent 1	4		3	3
Agent 2	4		3	3

cost of establishing a new market. In this perspective it is interesting to measure the net gains to trade for each agent. These quantities are summarized in Table 7-10.

This computation tells us that, in our example, the issuer of the security gains less than the other party in the future trade. If agent 2 goes first and issues security Q, his net expected utility gain is 0.0733, which also represents the most he would be willing to pay his investment bank in terms of period 0 consumption to manage the sale for him. By analogy, the marginal benefit to agent 1 of *then* issuing security R is 0.0856. The reverse assignments would have occurred if agent 1 had gone first, due to symmetry in the agent endowments. That these quantities represent the upper bounds on possible fees comes from the fact that period 0 utility of consumption is the level of consumption itself.

The impact of all this is that each investment bank will, out of desire to maximize its fee potential, advise its client to issue his security second. No one will want to go first. Alternatively, if the effective cost of setting up the market for security Q is anywhere between 0.0733 and 0.28, there is a possibility of *market failure,* unless agent 2 finds a way to have agent 1 share in the cost of establishing the market. We speak of market failure because the social benefit of setting up the market would be positive 0.28 minus the cost itself—while the market might not go ahead if the private cost to agent 2 exceeds his own private benefit, measured at 0.0733 units of date 0 consumption. Of course, it might also be the case that the cost exceeds the total benefit. This is another reason for the market not to exist and, in general, for markets to be incomplete. But in this case, one would not talk of market failure. Whether the privately motivated decisions of individual agents lead to the socially optimal outcome—in this case the socially optimal set of securities—is a fundamental question in finance and economics.

There is no guarantee that private incentives will suffice to create the social optimal set of markets. We have identified a problem of sequencing (the issuer of a security may not be the most important beneficiary of the creation of the market) and as a result there may be a waiting game with suboptimal results. There is also a problem linked with the sharing of the cost of setting up a market. The benefits of a new market often are widely spread among a large number of potential participants and it may be difficult to find an appropriate mechanism to have them share the initial setup cost, for example, because of free rider or coordination problems. Note that in both these cases, as well as in the situation where the cost of establishing a market exceeds the total benefit for individual agents, we anticipate that technical innovations leading to decreases in the cost of establishing markets will help alleviate the problem and foster a convergence toward a more complete set of markets.

TABLE 7-10	The Net Gains from Trade Expected Utility Levels and Net Trading Gains (Gain to issuer in bold)					
	No Trade		*Trade Only Q*		*Trade Both Q and R*	
	EU		*EU*	$\Delta EU^{(i)}$	*EU*	$\Delta EU^{(ii)}$
Agent 1	4.8057		5.013	0.2073	5.0986	**0.0856**
Agent 2	4.8057		4.879	**0.0733**	5.0986	0.2186
Total				0.2806		0.3042

(i) Difference in EU when trading Q only relative to no trade.

(ii) Difference in EU when trading both Q and R relative to trading Q only.

7.6 MARKET COMPLETENESS AND COMPLEX SECURITIES

In this section we pursue, more systematically, the important issue of market completeness touched upon in the two preceding sections when discussing the optimality property of a general competitive equilibrium. Let us start with two definitions.

1. **Completeness.** Financial markets are said to be *complete* if, for each state of nature θ, there exists a market for contingent claim or Arrow-Debreu security θ, in other words, for a claim promising delivery of one unit of the consumption good (or, more generally, the numeraire) if state θ is realized, and nothing otherwise. Note that this definition takes a form specifically appropriate to models where there is only one consumption good and several date states. This is the usual context in which financial issues are addressed.

2. **Complex security.** A complex security is one that pays off in more than one state of nature. For example, suppose $N = 4$; a complex security example is $S = (5, 2, 0, 6)$ with payoffs 5, 3, 0, and 6, respectively, in states of nature 1, 2, 3, and 4. If markets are complete, we can immediately price such a security since

$$(5, 2, 0, 6) = 5(1, 0, 0, 0) + 2(0, 1, 0, 0) + 0(0, 0, 1, 0) + 6(0, 0, 0, 1),$$

in other words, since the complex security can be replicated by a portfolio of Arrow-Debreu securities. Therefore (appealing to the law of one price[7] or to a condition of no arbitrage; see Chapter 12 for an elaboration), the price of security S, p_S, must be

$$P_S = 5q_1 + 2q_2 + 6q_4$$

Effectively, the argument can be stated in the following proposition.

> **Proposition 7.1:**
> If markets are complete, any complex security or any cash flow stream can be replicated as a portfolio of Arrow-Debreu securities.

A "no arbitrage" condition then implies that the complex security or the cash flow can also be priced using the relevant Arrow-Debreu prices as fundamental elements. The portfolio, which is easily priced using the (Arrow-Debreu) prices of its individual components, is essentially the same good as the cash flow or the security it replicates: It pays the same amount of the consumption good in each and every state. Therefore it should bear the same price. This is a key result underlying much of what we do in the remainder of this chapter and our interest in Arrow-Debreu pricing.

Suppose now that only complex securities are traded and that there are M of them (N states). The following is true.

---

[7]This is stating that the equilibrium prices of two separate units of what is essentially the same good should be identical. If this were not the case, a riskless and costless arbitrage opportunity would open up: Buy extremely large amounts at the low price and sell them at the high price, forcing the two prices to converge. When applied across two different geographical locations (which is not the case here: our world is a point in space), the law of one price may not hold because of transport costs rendering the arbitrage costly.

> **Proposition 7.2:**
> If $M = N$, and all the M complex securities are linearly independent, then (i) it is possible to infer the prices of the Arrow-Debreu state-contingent claims from the complex securities' prices and (ii) markets are effectively complete.[8]

The hypothesis of linear independence can be interpreted as a requirement that there exists N truly different securities for completeness to be achieved. Thus it is easy to understand that if among the N complex securities available, one security A pays $(1, 2, 3)$ in the three states of nature, and the other B pays $(2, 4, 6)$, only $N - 1$ truly different securities are available: B does not permit any different redistribution of purchasing power across states that A does not permit. More generally, the linear independence hypothesis requires that no one complex security can be replicated as a portfolio of some of the other complex securities. You will remember that we made the same hypothesis at the beginning of Section 6.3.

Suppose the following securities are traded:

$$(3, 2, 0) \qquad (1, 1, 1) \qquad (2, 0, 2)$$

at equilibrium prices $1.00, $0.60, and $0.80, respectively. It is easy to verify that these three securities are linearly independent. We can then construct the Arrow-Debreu prices as follows. Consider, for example, the security $(1, 0, 0)$:

$$(1, 0, 0) = w_1(3, 2, 0) + w_2(1, 1, 1) + w_3(2, 0, 2)$$

Thus,
$$1 = 3w_1 + w_2 + 2w_3$$
$$0 = 2w_1 + w_2$$
$$0 = w_2 + 2w_3$$

Solve: $w_1 = \frac{1}{3}$, $w_2 = -\frac{2}{3}$, $w_3 = \frac{1}{3}$, and $q_{(1,0,0)} = \frac{1}{3}(1.00) + (-\frac{2}{3})(.60) + \frac{1}{3}(.80) = .1966$. Similarly, we could replicate $(0, 1, 0)$ and $(0, 0, 1)$ with portfolios $(w_1 = 0, w_2 = 1, w_3 = -\frac{1}{2})$ and $(w_1 = -\frac{1}{3}, w_2 = \frac{2}{3}, w_3 = \frac{1}{6})$, respectively, and price them accordingly.

Expressed in a more general way, the reasoning just completed amounts to searching for a solution of the following system of equations:

$$\begin{pmatrix} 3 & 1 & 2 \\ 2 & 1 & 0 \\ 0 & 1 & 2 \end{pmatrix} \begin{pmatrix} w_1^1 & w_1^2 & w_1^3 \\ w_2^1 & w_2^2 & w_2^3 \\ w_3^1 & w_3^2 & w_3^3 \end{pmatrix} = \begin{pmatrix} 1 & 0 & 0 \\ 0 & 1 & 0 \\ 0 & 0 & 1 \end{pmatrix}$$

Of course, this system has solution $\begin{pmatrix} 3 & 1 & 2 \\ 2 & 1 & 0 \\ 0 & 1 & 2 \end{pmatrix}^{-1} \begin{pmatrix} 1 & 0 & 0 \\ 0 & 1 & 0 \\ 0 & 0 & 1 \end{pmatrix}$ only if the matrix of security payoffs can be inverted, which requires that it be of full rank, or that its determinant be nonzero, or that all its lines or columns be linearly independent.

Now suppose the number of linearly independent securities is strictly less than the number of states (such as in the final, no-trade, example of Section 7.3 where we assume

---

[8]When we use the language "linearly dependent," we are implicitly regarding securities as N-vectors of payoffs.

only a risk-free asset is available). Then the securities markets are fundamentally incomplete: There may be some assets that cannot be accurately priced. Furthermore, risk sharing opportunities are less than if the securities markets were complete and, in general, social welfare is lower than what it would be under complete markets. This is because some gains from exchange cannot be exploited due to the lack of instruments permitting these exchanges to take place.

We conclude this section by revisiting the project valuation problem of our introductory section. How should we, in the light of the Arrow-Debreu pricing approach, value an uncertain cash flow stream such as:

$$
\begin{array}{cccccc}
t = 0 & 1 & 2 & 3 & \ldots & T \\
-I_0 & \tilde{C}F_1 & \tilde{C}F_2 & \tilde{C}F_3 & \ldots & \tilde{C}F_T
\end{array}
$$

This cash flow stream is akin to a complex security since it pays in multiple states of the world. Let us specifically assume that there are N states at each date $t, t = 1, \ldots, T$ and let us denote $q_{t,\theta}$ as the price of the Arrow-Debreu security promising delivery of one unit of the numeraire if state θ is realized at date t. Similarly, let us identify as $CF_{t,\theta}$ the cash flow associated with the project in the same occurrence. Then pricing the complex security à la Arrow-Debreu means valuing the project as in Equation (7.4).

$$
NPV = -I_0 + \sum_{t=1}^{T} \sum_{\theta=1}^{N} q_{t,\theta} CF_{t,\theta}. \tag{7.4}
$$

Although this is a demanding procedure, this pricing approach is fully general and involves no approximation. For this reason it constitutes an extremely useful reference.

In a risk-free setting, the concept of state contingent claim has a very familiar real-world counterpart. In fact, the notion of the term structure is simply a reflection of "state-date" contingent claims prices. We pursue this idea in the next section.

7.7   CONSTRUCTING STATE CONTINGENT CLAIMS PRICES IN A RISK-FREE WORLD: DERIVING THE TERM STRUCTURE

Suppose we are considering risk-free investments and risk-free securities exclusively. In this setting—where we ignore risk—the "states of nature" that we have been speaking of simply correspond to *future time periods*. This section shows that the process of computing the term structure from the prices of coupon bonds is akin to recovering Arrow-Debreu prices from the prices of complex securities.

Under this interpretation, the Arrow-Debreu state contingent claims correspond to risk-free discount bonds of various maturities, as seen in Table 7-11. These are Arrow-Debreu securities because they pay off in one state (the period of maturity), and zero for all other time periods (states).

In the United States at least, securities of this type are not issued for maturities longer than one year. Rather, only interest bearing or coupon bonds are issued for longer maturities. These are complex securities by our definition: They pay off in many states of nature. But we know that if we have enough distinct complex securities we can compute the prices of the Arrow-Debreu securities even if they are not explicitly

TABLE 7-11 Risk-Free Discount Bonds as Arrow-Debreu Securities

Current Bond Price						Future Cash Flows
$t=0$	1	2	3	4	...	T
$-q_1$	$1,000					
$-q_2$		$1,000				
...						
$-q_T$						$1,000

where the cash flow of a "j-period discount bond" is just

$t=0$	1	...	j	$j+1$	...	T
$-q_j$	0	0	$1,000	0	0	0

traded. So we can also compute the prices of these zero coupon or discount bonds from the prices of the coupon or interest-bearing bonds.

For example, suppose we wanted to price a 5 year discount bond coming due in November of 2005, and that we observe two coupon bonds being traded that mature at the same time:

(i) 7⅞% bond priced at 109²⁵/₃₂, or $1,097.8125/$1,000 face value
(ii) 5⅝% bond priced at 100⁹/₃₂, or $1,002.8125/$1,000 face value

The coupons of these bonds are respectively,

$$.07875 * \$1,000 = \$78.75/\text{year}$$
$$.05625 * \$1,000 = \$56.25/\text{year}$$

The cash flows of these two bonds are seen in Table 7-12. Note that we want somehow to eliminate the interest payments (to get a discount bond) and that $78.75/56.25 = 1.4$. So, consider the following strategy: Sell one 7⅞% bond while simultaneously buying 1.4 unit of 5⅝% bonds. The corresponding cash flows are found in Table 7-13.

TABLE 7-12 Present and Future Cash Flows for Two Coupon Bonds

Bond Type		Cash Flow at Time t				
	$t=0$	1	2	3	4	5
7⅞ bond:	−1,097.8125	78.75	78.75	78.75	78.75	1,078.75
5⅝ bond:	−1,002.8125	56.25	56.25	56.25	56.25	1,056.25

TABLE 7-13 Eliminating Intermediary Payments

Bond		Cash Flow at Time t				
	$t=0$	1	2	3	4	5
−1×7⅞ bond:	+1,097.8125	−78.75	−78.75	−78.75	−78.75	−1,078.75
+1.4×5⅝ bond:	−1,403.9375	78.75	78.75	78.75	78.75	1,478.75
Difference:	−306.125	0	0	0	0	400.00

The net cash flow associated with this strategy thus indicates that the $t = 0$ price of a $400 payment in 5 years is $306.125. This price is implicit in the pricing of our two original coupon bonds. Consequently, the price of $1,000 in 5 years must be

$$306.125 \times \frac{1000}{400} = 765.3125$$

Alternatively, the price today of $1.00 in 5 years is $.7653125. In the notation of our earlier discussion we have the following securities:

$$
\begin{matrix} \theta_1 \\ \theta_2 \\ \theta_3 \\ \theta_4 \\ \theta_5 \end{matrix}
\begin{bmatrix} 78.75 \\ 78.75 \\ 78.75 \\ 78.75 \\ 1078.75 \end{bmatrix}
\text{ and }
\begin{bmatrix} 56.25 \\ 56.25 \\ 56.25 \\ 56.25 \\ 1056.25 \end{bmatrix}
\text{ and we consider }
$$

$$
-\frac{1}{400}
\begin{bmatrix} 78.75 \\ 78.75 \\ 78.75 \\ 78.75 \\ 1078.75 \end{bmatrix}
+ \frac{1.4}{400}
\begin{bmatrix} 56.25 \\ 56.25 \\ 56.25 \\ 56.25 \\ 1056.25 \end{bmatrix}
=
\begin{bmatrix} 0 \\ 0 \\ 0 \\ 0 \\ 1 \end{bmatrix}
$$

This is an Arrow-Debreu security in the riskless context we are considering in this section.

So, if there are enough coupon bonds with different maturities with pairs coming due at the same time and with different coupons, we can construct a complete set of Arrow-Debreu securities and their implicit prices. Notice that the payoff patterns of the two bonds are fundamentally different: They are linearly independent of one another. This is a requirement, as per our earlier discussion, for being able to use them to construct a fundamentally new payoff pattern, in this case, the discount bond.

We can more systematically recover the term structure from coupon bond prices provided we know the prices of coupon bonds of all different maturities. Suppose we observe risk-free government bonds of 1-, 2-, 3-, and 4-year maturities all selling at par[9] with coupons, respectively, of 6%, 6.5%, 7.2%, and 9.5%. We can construct the term structure as follows:

r_1: Since the 1-year bond sells at par, we have $r_1 = 6\%$;
r_2: By definition, we know that the 2-year bond is priced such that

$$1000 = \frac{65}{(1 + r_1)} + \frac{1065}{(1 + r_2)^2}$$

which, given that $r_1 = 6\%$, solves for $r_2 = 6.5113\%$
r_3: is derived accordingly as the solution to

$$1000 = \frac{72}{(1 + r_1)} + \frac{72}{(1 + r_2)^2} + \frac{1072}{(1 + r_3)^3}.$$

___
[9]That is, selling at their issuing or face value, typically of $1,000.

TABLE 7-14   Date Claim vs. Discount Bond Prices

	Price of a N year claim	Analogous Discount Bond Price ($1,000 Denomination)
$N=1$	$q_1 = 1/1.06 = .94340$	$943.40
$N=2$	$q_2 = 1/(1.065113)^2 = .88147$	$881.47
$N=3$	$q_3 = 1/(1.072644)^3 = .81028$	$810.28
$N=4$	$q_4 = 1/1.09935)^4 = .68463$	$684.63

With $r_1 = 6\%$ and $r_2 = 6.5113\%$, the solution is $r_3 = 7.2644\%$. Finally, given these values for r_1 to r_3,

$$r_4 \text{ solves: } 1000 = \frac{95}{(1+r_1)} + \frac{95}{(1+r_2)^2} + \frac{95}{(1+r_3)^3} + \frac{1095}{(1+r_4)^4}, \text{ i.e., } r_4 = 9.935\%.$$

Note that these rates are the counterpart of the date contingent claims. Of course, once we have the discount bond prices (the prices of the Arrow-Debreu claims) we can clearly price all other risk-free securities; for example, suppose we wished to price a 4-year 8% bond:

$$
\begin{array}{cccccc}
t = 0 & 1 & 2 & 3 & 4 \\
-p_0(?) & 80 & 80 & 80 & 1080
\end{array}
$$

and suppose also that we had available the discount bonds corresponding to Table 7-14 as in Table 7-15. Then the portfolio of discount bonds (Arrow-Debreu claims) which replicates the 8% bond cash flow is (Table 7-16):

$$\{.08 \times 1\text{-yr bond}, .08 \times 2\text{-yr bond}, .08 \times 3\text{-yr bond}, 1.08 \times 4\text{-yr bond}\}$$

Thus: $p_{4yr.8\% \text{ bond}} = .08(943.39) + .08(881.47) + .08(810.27) + 1.08(684.63) = \$950.21$

Notice that we are emphasizing, in effect, the equivalence of the term structure of interest rates with the prices of date contingent claims. Each defines the other. This is especially apparent in Table 7-14.

Let us now extend this discussion to consider the evaluation of arbitrary risk-free cash flows: any such cash flow can be evaluated as a portfolio of Arrow-Debreu securities; for example:

$$
\begin{array}{cccccc}
t = 0 & 1 & 2 & 3 & 4 \\
& 60 & 25 & 150 & 300
\end{array}
$$

TABLE 7-15   Discount Bonds as Arrow-Debreu Claims

Bond	Price (t = 0)	CF Pattern			
		t = 1	2	3	4
1-yr discount	−943.39	$1,000			
2-yr discount	−881.47		$1,000		
3-yr discount	−810.27			$1,000	
4-yr discount	−684.63				$1,000

TABLE 7-16 Replicating the Discount Bond Cash Flow					
Bond	*Price (t = 0)*	*CF Pattern*			
		t = 1	*2*	*3*	*4*
.08 1-yr discount	(.08)(−943.39) = −75.47	$80			(80 state 1 A-D claims)
.08 2-yr discount	(.08)(−881.47) = −70.52		$80		(80 state 2 A-D claims)
.08 3-yr discount	(.08)(−810.27) = −64.82			$80	. . .
1.08 4-yr discount	(1.08)(−684.63) = −739.40				$1,080

We want to price this cash flow today ($t = 0$) using the Arrow-Debreu prices we have calculated in Table 7-13.

$$p = (\$60 \text{ at } t = 1)\left(\frac{.94339 \text{ at } t = 0}{\$1 \text{ at } t = 1}\right) + (\$25 \text{ at } t = 2)\left(\frac{.88147 \text{ at } t = 0}{\$1 \text{ at } t = 2}\right) + \cdots$$

$$= (\$60)\frac{1.00}{1 + r_1} + (\$25)\frac{1.00}{(1 + r_2)^2} + \cdots$$

$$= (\$60)\frac{1.00}{1.06} + (\$25)\frac{1.00}{(1.065113)^2} + \cdots$$

The second equality underlines the fact that evaluating risk-free projects as portfolios of Arrow-Debreu state contingent securities is equivalent to discounting at the term structure:

$$= \frac{60}{(1 + r_1)} + \frac{25}{(1 + r_2)^2} + \frac{150}{(1 + r_3)^3} + \cdots \text{ etc.}$$

In effect, we treat a risk-free project as a risk-free coupon bond with (potentially) differing coupons.

7.8 FORWARD PRICES AND FORWARD RATES

There is an analogous notion of forward prices and its more familiar counterpart, the forward rate. These correspond to the prices of (rates of return earned by) securities to be issued in the future.

Let $_k f_1$ denote the (compounded) rate of return on a risk-free discount bond to be issued at a future date k and maturing at date $k + 1$. These forward rates are defined by the equations:

$$(1 + r_1)(1 + {}_1 f_1) = (1 + r_2)^2$$
$$(1 + r_1)(1 + {}_1 f_2)^2 = (1 + r_3)^3$$
$$(1 + r_2)^2(1 + {}_2 f_1) = (1 + r_3)^3, \text{ etc.}$$

We emphasize that the forward rates are *implied* forward rates, in the sense that the corresponding contracts are typically not traded. However, it is feasible to *lock in* these forward rates; that is, guarantee their availability in the future. Suppose we wished to lock in the 1-year forward rate 1 year from now. This amounts to creating a new security "synthetically" as a portfolio of existing securities, and is accomplished by simply

TABLE 7-17   Locking in a Forward Rate

t =	0	1	2
Buy a 2-yr bond	−1,000	65	1,065
Sell short a 1-yr bond	+1,000	−1,060	
	0	−995	1,065

TABLE 7-18   Creating a $1,000 Payoff

t =	0	1	2
Buy .939 × 2-yr bonds	−939	61.0	1,000
Sell short .939 × 1-yr bonds	+939	−995.34	
	0	−934.34	1,000

undertaking a series of *long* and *short* transactions today. For example, take as given the implied discount bond prices of Table 7-14 and consider the transactions in Table 7-17. The portfolio we have constructed has a zero cash flow at date 0, requires an investment of $995 at date 1, and pays $1,065 at date 2. The gross return on the date 1 investment is

$$\frac{1065}{995} = 1.07035.$$

That this is exactly equal to the corresponding forward rate can be seen from the forward rate definition:

$$1 + {}_1f_1 = \frac{(1 + r_2)^2}{(1 + r_1)} = \frac{(1.065163)^2}{1.06} = 1.07035.$$

Let us scale back the previous transactions to create a $1,000 payoff for the forward security. This amounts to multiplying all of the indicated transactions by $1000/1065 = .939$ (Table 7-18).

This price ($934.34) is the no arbitrage price of this forward bond, no arbitrage in the sense that if there were any other contract calling for the delivery of such a bond at a price different from $934.34, an arbitrage opportunity would exist.[10]

7.9   THE VALUE ADDITIVITY THEOREM[11]

In this section we present an important result illustrating the power of the Arrow-Debreu pricing apparatus to generate one of the main lessons of the CAPM. Let there be two assets (complex securities) a and b with date 1 payoffs $\tilde{z}_a$ and $\tilde{z}_b$, respectively, and let their equilibrium prices be p_a and p_b. Suppose a third asset, c, turns out to be a linear combination of a and b. By that we mean that the payoff to c can be replicated by a portfolio of a and b. One can thus write

$$\tilde{z}_c = A\tilde{z}_a + B\tilde{z}_b, \text{ for some constant coefficients } A \text{ and } B. \tag{7.5}$$

---

[10]The approach of this section can, of course, be generalized to more distant forward rates.
[11]See Varian (1987) for further discussion.

Then the proposition known as the Value Additivity Theorem asserts that the same linear relationship must hold for the date 0 prices of the three assets:

$$p_c = Ap_a + Bp_b.$$

Let us first prove this result and then discuss its implications. The proof easily follows from our discussion in Section 7.6 on the pricing of complex securities in a complete market Arrow-Debreu world. Indeed, for our two securities a, b, one must have:

$$p_i = \sum_s q_s z_{si} \qquad i = a, b \tag{7.6}$$

where q_s is the price of an Arrow-Debreu security that pays one unit of consumption in state s and z_{si} is the payoff of asset i in state s.

But then, the pricing of c must respect the following relationships:

$$p_c = \sum_s q_s z_{sc} = \sum_s q_s(Az_{sa} + Bz_{sb}) = \sum_s Aq_s z_{sa} + Bq_s z_{sb} = Ap_a + Bp_b$$

The first equality follows from the fact that c is itself a complex security and can thus be priced using Arrow-Debreu prices [i.e., an equation such as Equation (7.6) applies]; the second directly follows from Equation (7.5); the third is a pure algebraic expansion that is feasible because our pricing relationships are fundamentally linear; and the fourth follows from Equation (7.6) again.

Now this is easy enough. Why is this interesting? Think of a and b as being two stocks with negatively correlated returns; we know that c, a portfolio of these two stocks, is much less risky than either one of them. But p_c is a linear combination of p_a and p_b. Thus, the fact that they can be combined in a less risky portfolio has implications for the pricing of the two independently riskier securities and their equilibrium returns. Specifically, it cannot be the case that p_c would be *high* because it corresponds to a desirable, riskless, claim while the p_a and p_b would be *low* because they are risky.

To see this more clearly, let us take an extreme example. Suppose that a and b are *perfectly* negatively correlated. For an appropriate choice of A and B, say A^* and B^*, the resulting portfolio, call it d, will have zero risk; i.e., it will pay a constant amount in each and every state of nature. What should the price of this riskless portfolio be? Intuitively, its price must be such that purchasing d at p_d will earn the riskless rate of return. But how could the risk of a and b be remunerated while simultaneously d would earn the riskless rate and the value additivity theorem hold? The answer is that this is not possible. Therefore, there cannot be any remuneration for risk in the pricing of a and b. The prices p_a and p_b must be such that the expected return on a and b is the riskless rate. This is true despite the fact that a and b are two risky assets (they do not pay the same amount in each state of nature).

In formal terms, we have just asserted that the two terms of the Value Additivity Theorem $\tilde{z}_c = A\tilde{z}_a + B\tilde{z}_p$ and $p_d = A * p_a + B * p_b$, together with the fact that d is risk-free, $E\tilde{z}_d/p_d = 1 + r_f$, force $E\tilde{z}_a/p_a = E\tilde{z}_b/p_b = 1 + r_f$.

What we have obtained in this very general context is a confirmation of one of the main results of the CAPM: Diversifiable risk is not priced. If risky assets a and b can be combined in a riskless portfolio, that is, if their risk can be diversified away, their return cannot exceed the risk-free return. Note that we have made no assumption here on utility functions nor on the return expectations held by agents. On the other hand we have explicitly assumed that markets are complete and that consequently each and every complex security can be priced (by arbitrage) as a portfolio of Arrow-Debreu securities.

7.10 CONCLUSIONS

The asset pricing theory presented in this chapter is in some sense the father of all asset pricing relationships. It is fully general and constitutes an extremely valuable reference. Conceptually its usefulness is unmatched and this justifies us investing more in its associated apparatus. At the same time, it is one of the most abstract theories and its usefulness in practice is impaired by the difficulty in identifying individual states of nature and by the fact that, even when a state (or a set of states) can be identified, its realization cannot always be verified. This is an issue because it makes it difficult to write the appropriate conditional contracts. These problems go a long way in explaining why we do not see Arrow-Debreu securities being traded, a fact that does not strengthen the immediate applicability of the theory. In addition, as already mentioned, the static setting of the Arrow-Debreu theory is unrealistic for most applications. For all these reasons we cannot stop here and we will explore a set of alternative, sometimes closely related, avenues for pricing assets in the following chapters.

References

Arrow, K., "An Extension of the Basic Theorems of Classical Welfare Economics," in J. Neyman (ed.), *Proceedings of the Second Berkeley Symposium on Mathematical Statistics and Probability,* Berkeley: University of California Press (1951): 507–532.

Debreu, G., *Theory of Value*, New York: John Wiley & Sons, 1959.

Varian, H., "The Arbitrage Principle in Financial Economics," *Journal of Economic Perspectives* 1(2), (1987): 55–72.

CHAPTER 8

OPTIONS AND MARKET COMPLETENESS

8.1 INTRODUCTION

In the previous chapter we argued that any *risk-free* cash flow can be easily and straightforwardly priced as an equivalent portfolio of date-contingent claims. These latter instruments are, in effect, discount bonds of various maturities. Our main interest, of course, is to extend this approach to the evaluation of *risky* cash flows. To do so requires, by analogy, that for each future date-state the corresponding contingent cash flow be priced. This, in turn, requires that we know, for each future date-state, the price today of a security that pays off in that date-state and only in that date-state. This latter statement is equivalent to the assumption of market completeness.

In this chapter, we take on the issue of completeness in the context of securities known as options. Our goal is twofold. First, we want to give the reader an opportunity to review an important element of financial theory—the theory of options. The appendix to this chapter describes the essentials for the reader in need of a refresher. Second, we want to provide a concrete illustration of the view that the recent expansion of derivative markets constitutes a major step in the quest for the "holy grail" of achieving a complete securities market structure. We will see, indeed, that options can, in principle, be used relatively straightforwardly to complete the markets. Furthermore, even in situations where this is not practically the case, we can use option pricing theory to value risky cash flows in a manner as though the financial markets were complete. Our discussion will follow the outline suggested by the following two questions.

1. How can options be used to complete the financial markets? We will first answer this question in a simple, highly abstract setting. Our discussion closely follows Ross (1976).
2. What is the link between the prices of market quoted options and the prices of Arrow-Debreu securities? We will see that it is indeed possible to infer Arrow-Debreu prices from option prices in a practical setting conducive to the valuation of an actual cash flow stream. Here our discussion follows Banz and Miller (1978) and Breeden and Litzenberger (1978).

8.2 USING OPTIONS TO COMPLETE THE MARKET: AN ABSTRACT SETTING

As is our custom we illustrate the relevant ideas in the context of examples. We assume a finite number of possible future date-states indexed $i = 1, 2, \ldots, N$. Suppose, for a start, that three states of the world are possible in date $T = 1$, yet only one security (a stock) is traded. The single security's payoffs are as follows:

State	Payoff
θ_1	$\begin{bmatrix} 1 \\ 2 \\ 3 \end{bmatrix}.$
θ_2	
θ_3	

Clearly this unique asset is not equivalent to a complete set of state-contingent claims. Note that we can identify the payoffs with the ex post price of the security in each of the three states: the security pays two units of the numeraire commodity in state 2 and we decide that its price then is $2.00. This amounts to normalizing the ex post, date 1, price of the commodity to $1, much as we have done at date 0. On that basis, we can consider call options written on this asset with exercise prices $1 and $2, respectively. These securities are contracts giving the right (but not the obligation) to purchase the underlying security at prices $1 and $2, respectively, tomorrow. They are contingent securities in the sense that the right they entail is valuable only if the price of the underlying security exceeds the exercise price at expiration, and they are valueless otherwise. We think of the option expiring at $T = 1$, that is, when the state of nature is revealed.[1] The *states of nature* structure enables us to be specific regarding what these contracts effectively promise to pay. Take the call option with exercise price 1. If state 1 is realized, that option is a right to buy at $1 the underlying security whose value is exactly $1. The option is said to be *at the money* and, in this case, the right in question is valueless. If state 2 is realized, however, the stock is worth $2. The right to buy, at a price of $1, something one can immediately resell for $2 naturally has a market value of $1. In this case, the option is said to be *in the money*. In other words, at $T = 1$, when the state of nature is revealed, an option is worth the difference between the value of the underlying asset and its exercise price, if this difference is positive, and zero otherwise. The complete payoff vectors of these options at expiration are as follows:

$$C_T([1, 2, 3]; 1) = \begin{bmatrix} 0 \\ 1 \\ 2 \end{bmatrix} \begin{matrix} \theta_1 \\ \theta_2 \\ \theta_3 \end{matrix} \left\{ \begin{matrix} \text{at the money} \\ \text{in the money} \\ \text{in the money} \end{matrix} \right\}.$$

Similarly,

$$C_T([1, 2, 3]; 2) = \begin{bmatrix} 0 \\ 0 \\ 1 \end{bmatrix} \begin{matrix} \theta_1 \\ \theta_2 \\ \theta_3 \end{matrix}.$$

---

[1] In our simple two-date world there is no difference between an American option, which can be exercised at any date before the expiration date, and a European option, which can be exercised only at expiration.

In our notation, $C_T(S; E)$ is the payoff to a call option written on security S with exercise price E at expiration date T. We use $C_t(S; E)$ to denote the option's market price at time $t \leq T$. We frequently drop the time subscript to simplify notation when there is no ambiguity.

It remains now to convince ourselves that the three traded assets (the underlying stock and the two call options, each denoted by its payoff vector at T)

$$
\begin{array}{c} \theta_1 \\ \theta_2 \\ \theta_3 \end{array}
\begin{bmatrix} 1 \\ 2 \\ 3 \end{bmatrix},
\begin{bmatrix} 0 \\ 1 \\ 2 \end{bmatrix},
\begin{bmatrix} 0 \\ 0 \\ 1 \end{bmatrix}
$$

constitute a complete set of securities markets for states $(\theta_1, \theta_2, \theta_3)$. This is so because we can use them to create all the state claims. Clearly

$$
\begin{bmatrix} 0 \\ 0 \\ 1 \end{bmatrix} \text{ is present. To create } \begin{bmatrix} 0 \\ 1 \\ 0 \end{bmatrix}, \text{ observe that } \begin{bmatrix} 0 \\ 1 \\ 0 \end{bmatrix} = w_1 \begin{bmatrix} 1 \\ 2 \\ 3 \end{bmatrix} + w_2 \begin{bmatrix} 0 \\ 1 \\ 2 \end{bmatrix} + w_3 \begin{bmatrix} 0 \\ 0 \\ 1 \end{bmatrix},
$$

where $w_1 = 0$, $w_2 = 1$, and $w_3 = -2$.

The vector $\begin{bmatrix} 1 \\ 0 \\ 0 \end{bmatrix}$ can be similarly created.

We have thus illustrated one of the main ideas of this chapter, and we need to discuss how general and applicable it is in more realistic settings. A preliminary issue is why trading call option securities $C([1, 2, 3]; 1)$ and $C([1, 2, 3]; 2)$ might be the preferred approach to completing the market, relative to the alternative possibility of directly issuing the Arrow-Debreu securities $[1, 0, 0]$ and $[0, 1, 0]$? In the simplified world of our example, in the absence of transactions costs, there is, of course, no advantage to creating the options markets. In the real world, however, if a new security is to be issued, its issuance must be accompanied by costly disclosure as to its characteristics; in our parlance, the issuer must disclose as much as possible about the security's payoff in the various states. As there may be no agreement as to what the relevant future states are—let alone what the payoffs will be—this disclosure is difficult. And if there is no consensus as to its payoff pattern (i.e., its basic structure of payoffs), investors will not want to hold it, and it will not trade. But the payoff pattern of an option on an already-traded asset is obvious and verifiable to everyone. For this reason, it is, in principle, a much less expensive new security to issue. Another way to describe the advantage of options is to observe that it is useful conceptually, but difficult in practice, to define and identify a single state of nature. It is more practical to define contracts contingent on a well-defined range of states. The fact that these states are themselves defined in terms of, or revealed via, market prices is another facet of the superiority of this type of contract.

Note that options are by definition in zero net supply, that is, in this context

$$
\sum_k C^k([1, 2, 3]; j) = 0,
$$

where $C^k([1, 2, 3]; j)$ is the value of call options with exercise price j, held by agent k at time $t \leq T$. This means that there must exist a group of agents with negative positions serving as the counter-party to the subset of agents with positive holdings. We naturally interpret those agents $\hat{k}$ for which $C_t^{\hat{k}}([1, 2, 3]; j) < 0$ as agents who have *written* the call options.

We have illustrated the property that markets can be completed using call options. Now let us explore the generality of this result. Can call options always be used to complete the market in this way? The answer is not necessarily. It depends on the payoff to the underlying fundamental assets. Consider the asset:

$$\begin{array}{c} \theta_1 \\ \theta_2 \\ \theta_3 \end{array} \begin{bmatrix} 2 \\ 2 \\ 3 \end{bmatrix}.$$

For any exercise price E, all options written on this security must have payoffs of the form:

$$C_T([2, 2, 3]; E) = \begin{cases} \begin{bmatrix} 2 - E \\ 2 - E \\ 3 - E \end{bmatrix} & \text{if } E \leq 2 \\ \\ \begin{bmatrix} 0 \\ 0 \\ 3 - E \end{bmatrix} & \text{if } 2 < E \leq 3 \end{cases}.$$

Clearly, for any E, $\begin{bmatrix} 2 \\ 2 \\ 3 \end{bmatrix}$ and $\begin{bmatrix} 2 - E \\ 2 - E \\ 3 - E \end{bmatrix}$ have identical payoffs in state θ_1 and θ_2, and, there-

fore, they cannot be used to generate Arrow-Debreu securities $\begin{bmatrix} 1 \\ 0 \\ 0 \end{bmatrix}$ and $\begin{bmatrix} 0 \\ 1 \\ 0 \end{bmatrix}$.

There is no way to complete the markets with options in the case of this underlying asset. This illustrates the following truth: We cannot generally write options that distinguish between two states if the underlying assets pay identical returns in those states.

The problem just illustrated can sometimes be solved *if we permit options to be written on **portfolios** of the basic underlying assets.* Consider the case of four possible states at $T = 1$, and suppose that the only assets currently traded are

$$\begin{array}{c} \theta_1 \\ \theta_2 \\ \theta_3 \\ \theta_4 \end{array} \begin{bmatrix} 1 \\ 1 \\ 2 \\ 2 \end{bmatrix} \text{ and } \begin{bmatrix} 1 \\ 2 \\ 1 \\ 2 \end{bmatrix}.$$

It can be shown that it is not possible, using call options, to generate a complete set of securities markets using only these underlying securities. Consider, however, the portfolio composed of 2 units of the first asset and 1 unit of the second:

$$2 \begin{bmatrix} 1 \\ 1 \\ 2 \\ 2 \end{bmatrix} + 1 \begin{bmatrix} 1 \\ 2 \\ 1 \\ 2 \end{bmatrix} = \begin{bmatrix} 3 \\ 4 \\ 5 \\ 6 \end{bmatrix}.$$

This portfolio pays a different return in each state of nature. Options written on the portfolio alone can thus be used to construct a complete set of traded Arrow-Debreu securities. The example illustrates a second general truth, which we will enumerate as Proposition 8.1.

Proposition 8.1:
A necessary as well as sufficient condition for the creation of a complete set of Arrow-Debreu securities is that there exists a single portfolio with the property that options can be written on it and such that its payoff pattern distinguishes among all states of nature.

Going back to our last example, it is easy to see that the created portfolio and the three natural calls to be written on it:

$$\begin{bmatrix} 3 \\ 4 \\ 5 \\ 6 \end{bmatrix} \text{ plus } \underset{(E\,=\,3)}{\begin{bmatrix} 0 \\ 1 \\ 2 \\ 3 \end{bmatrix}} \text{ and } \underset{(E\,=\,4)}{\begin{bmatrix} 0 \\ 0 \\ 1 \\ 2 \end{bmatrix}} \text{ and } \underset{(E\,=\,5)}{\begin{bmatrix} 0 \\ 0 \\ 0 \\ 1 \end{bmatrix}}$$

are sufficient (i.e., constitute a complete set of markets in our four-state world). Combinations of the $(E = 5)$ and $(E = 4)$ vectors can create:

$$\begin{bmatrix} 0 \\ 0 \\ 1 \\ 0 \end{bmatrix}.$$

Combinations of this vector, and the $(E = 5)$ and $(E = 3)$ vectors can then create:

$$\begin{bmatrix} 0 \\ 1 \\ 0 \\ 0 \end{bmatrix}, \text{ etc.}$$

Probing further we may inquire if *the writing of* calls *on the underlying assets is always sufficient*, or whether there are circumstances under which other types of options may be necessary. Again, suppose there are four states of nature, and consider the following set of *primitive* securities:

$$\begin{matrix} \theta_1 \\ \theta_2 \\ \theta_3 \\ \theta_4 \end{matrix} \begin{bmatrix} 0 \\ 0 \\ 0 \\ 1 \end{bmatrix} \begin{bmatrix} 1 \\ 1 \\ 0 \\ 1 \end{bmatrix} \begin{bmatrix} 0 \\ 1 \\ 1 \\ 1 \end{bmatrix}.$$

Because these assets pay either one or zero in each state, calls written on them will either replicate the asset itself, or give the zero payoff vector. The writing of call options will not help because they cannot further discriminate among states. But suppose we write a put option on the first asset with exercise price 1. A put is a contract giving the right, but not the obligation, to *sell* an underlying security at a pre-specified exercise price on a given expiration date. The put option with exercise price 1 has positive value at $T = 1$ in those states where the underlying security has value less than 1. The put on the first asset with exercise price = \$1 thus has the following payoff:

$$\begin{bmatrix} 1 \\ 1 \\ 1 \\ 0 \end{bmatrix} = P_T([0, 0, 0, 1]; 1).$$

You can confirm that the securities plus the put are sufficient to allow us to construct (as portfolios of them) a complete set of Arrow-Debreu securities for the indicated four states. In general, one can prove Proposition 8.2.

Proposition 8.2:

If it is possible to create, using options, a complete set of traded securities, simple put and call options written on the underlying assets are sufficient to accomplish this goal.

That is, portfolios of options are not required.

8.3   SYNTHESIZING STATE-CONTINGENT CLAIMS: A FIRST APPROXIMATION

The abstract setting of the previous discussion aimed at conveying the message that options are natural instruments for completing the markets. In this section, we show how we can directly create a set of state-contingent claims, *as well as their equilibrium prices,* using option prices or option pricing formulae in a more realistic setting. The interest in doing so is, of course, to exploit the possibility, inherent in Arrow-Debreu prices, of pricing any complex security. In this section we first approach the problem under the hypothesis that the price of the underlying security or portfolio can take only discrete values.

Assume that a risky asset is traded with current price S and future price S_T. It is assumed that S_T discriminates across all states of nature so that Proposition 8.1 applies; without loss of generality, we may assume that S_T takes the following set of values:

$$S_1 < S_2 < \ldots < S_\theta < \ldots < S_N,$$

where S_θ is the price of this complex security if state θ is realized at date T. Assume also that call options are written on this asset with all possible exercise prices, and that these options are traded. Let us also assume that $S_\theta = S_{\theta-1} + \delta$ for every state θ. (This is not so unreasonable as stocks, say, are traded at prices that can differ only in multiples of a minimum price change).[2] Throughout the discussion we will fix the time to expiration and will not denote it notationally.

---

[2]Until recently, the minimum price change was equal to \$1/16 on the NYSE. At the end of 2000, the exchange had begun to phase in *decimal pricing* where the prices are quoted to the nearest \$1/100 (1 cent).

Consider, for any state $\hat{\theta}$, the following portfolio P:

> Buy one call with $E = S_{\hat{\theta}-1}$
> Sell two calls with $E = S_{\hat{\theta}}$
> Buy one call with $E = S_{\hat{\theta}+1}$.

At any point in time, the value of this portfolio, V_P, is

$$V_P = C(S, E = S_{\hat{\theta}-1}) - 2C(S, E = S_{\hat{\theta}}) + C(S, E = S_{\hat{\theta}+1}).$$

To see what this portfolio represents, let us examine its payoff *at expiration* (refer to Figure 8-1).

For $S_T \leq S_{\hat{\theta}-1}$, the value of our options portfolio, P, is obviously zero. The same is true for $S_T \geq S_{\hat{\theta}+1}$ since the loss on the 2 written calls with $E = S_{\hat{\theta}}$ exactly offsets the gains on the other two calls. In state $\hat{\theta}$, the value of the portfolio is δ, corresponding to the value of $C_T(S_{\hat{\theta}}, E = S_{\hat{\theta}-1})$, the other two options being out of the money when the underlying security takes value $S_{\hat{\theta}}$. The payoff from such a portfolio thus equals:

$$\text{Payoff to } P = \begin{cases} 0 & \text{if} \quad S_T < S_{\hat{\theta}} \\ \delta & \text{if} \quad S_T = S_{\hat{\theta}} \\ 0 & \text{if} \quad S_T > S_{\hat{\theta}} \end{cases}$$

in other words, it pays a positive amount δ in state $\hat{\theta}$, and nothing otherwise. In other words, it replicates the payoff of the Arrow-Debreu security associated with state θ up to a factor (in the sense that it pays δ instead of 1). Consequently, the current price of the state $\hat{\theta}$ contingent claim (i.e., one that pays \$1.00 if state $\hat{\theta}$ is realized and nothing otherwise) is

$$q_{\hat{\theta}} = \tfrac{1}{\delta}[C(S, E = S_{\hat{\theta}-1}) + C(S, E = S_{\hat{\theta}+1}) - 2C(S, E = S_{\hat{\theta}})].$$

Even if these calls are not traded, if we identify our relevant states with the prices of some security—say the market portfolio—then we can use readily available option pricing formulas (such as the famous Black-Scholes formula; see the Appendix to this chapter) to obtain the necessary call prices and, from them, compute the price of the state-contingent claim. We explore this idea further in the next section.

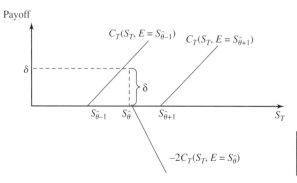

FIGURE 8-1 Payoff Diagram for All Options in the Portfolio *P*

8.4   RECOVERING ARROW-DEBREU PRICES FROM OPTIONS PRICES: A GENERALIZATION

By the CAPM, the only relevant risk is systematic risk. We may interpret this to mean that the only states of nature that are economically or financially relevant are those that can be identified with different values of the market portfolio.[3] Thus, the market portfolio may be selected to be the complex security on which we write options, portfolios of which will be used to replicate our state-contingent payoffs. The conditions of Proposition 8.1 are satisfied, guaranteeing the possibility of completing the market structure.

In Section 8.3 we considered the case for which the underlying asset assumed a discrete set of values. If the underlying asset is the market portfolio M, however, this cannot be strictly valid: As an index it can essentially assume an infinite number of possible values. How is this added feature accommodated?

1. Suppose that S_T, the price of the underlying portfolio (we may think of it as a proxy for M), assumes a *continuum* of possible values. We want to price an Arrow-Debreu security that pays \$1.00 if $S_T \in [-\frac{\delta}{2} + \hat{S}_T, \hat{S}_T + \frac{\delta}{2}]$, in other words, if S_T assumes any value in a range of width δ, centered on $\hat{S}_T$. We are thus identifying our states of nature with **ranges of possible values** for the market portfolio. Here the subscript T refers to the future date at which the Arrow-Debreu security pays \$1.00 if the relevant state is realized.

2. Let us construct the following portfolio[4] for some small positive number $\varepsilon > 0$,

$$\text{Buy one call with} \quad E = \hat{S}_T - \tfrac{\delta}{2} - \varepsilon$$
$$\text{Sell one call with} \quad E = \hat{S}_T - \tfrac{\delta}{2}$$
$$\text{Sell one call with} \quad E = \hat{S}_T + \tfrac{\delta}{2}$$
$$\text{Buy one call with} \quad E = \hat{S}_T + \tfrac{\delta}{2} + \varepsilon.$$

Let us see what this portfolio pays *at expiration* (Figure 8-2).

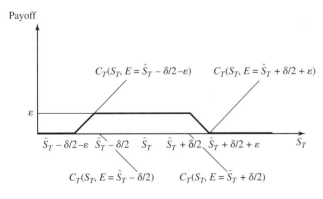

$C_T(S_T, E = \hat{S}_T - \delta/2 - \varepsilon)$ $C_T(S_T, E = \hat{S}_T + \delta/2 + \varepsilon)$

$\hat{S}_T - \delta/2 - \varepsilon$ $\hat{S}_T - \delta/2$ $\hat{S}_T$ $\hat{S}_T + \delta/2$ $\hat{S}_T + \delta/2 + \varepsilon$ S_T

$C_T(S_T, E = \hat{S}_T - \delta/2)$ $C_T(S_T, E = \hat{S}_T + \delta/2)$

FIGURE 8-2   Payoff Diagram: Portfolio of Options

—— Value of the portfolio at expiration

---

[3]That is, diversifiable risks have zero market value (see Chapters 6 and 7). At an individual level, personal risks are, of course, also relevant. They can, however, be insured or diversified away. Insurance contracts are often the most appropriate to cover these risks. Recall our discussion of this issue in Chapter 1.
[4]The option position corresponding to our portfolio P is known as a *butterfly spread* in the jargon.

Observe that our portfolio pays ε on a range of states and 0 almost everywhere else. By purchasing $1/\varepsilon$ units of the portfolio, we will mimic the payoff of an Arrow-Debreu security, except for the two small diagonal sections of the payoff line where the portfolio pays something between 0 and ε. This undesirable feature (since our objective is to replicate an Arrow-Debreu security) will be taken care of by using a standard mathematical trick involving taking limits.

3. Let us thus consider buying $\frac{1}{\varepsilon}$ units of the portfolio. The total payment, when $\hat{S}_T - \frac{\delta}{2} \le S_T \le \hat{S}_T + \frac{\delta}{2}$, is $\varepsilon \cdot \frac{1}{\varepsilon} \equiv 1$, for any choice of ε. We want to let $\varepsilon \mapsto 0$, so as to eliminate payments in the ranges $S_T \in (\hat{S}_T - \frac{\delta}{2} - \varepsilon, \hat{S}_T - \frac{\delta}{2})$ and $S_T \in (\hat{S}_T + \frac{\delta}{2}, \hat{S}_T + \frac{\delta}{2} + \varepsilon)$. The value of $\frac{1}{\varepsilon}$ units of this portfolio is:

$$\frac{1}{\varepsilon}\{C(S, E = \hat{S}_T - \frac{\delta}{2} - \varepsilon) - C(S, E = \hat{S}_T - \frac{\delta}{2}) \\ - [C(S, E = \hat{S}_T + \frac{\delta}{2}) - C(S, E = \hat{S}_T + \frac{\delta}{2} + \varepsilon)]\},$$

where a minus sign indicates that the call was sold (thereby reducing the cost of the portfolio by its sale price). On balance the portfolio will have a positive price as it represents a claim on a positive cash flow in certain states of nature. Let us assume that the pricing function for a call with respect to changes in the exercise price can be differentiated (this property is true, in particular, in the case of the Black-Scholes option pricing formula). We then have:

$$\lim_{\varepsilon \mapsto 0} \frac{1}{\varepsilon}\{C(S, E = \hat{S}_T - \frac{\delta}{2} - \varepsilon) - C(S, E = \hat{S}_T - \frac{\delta}{2}) \\ - [C(S, E = \hat{S}_T + \frac{\delta}{2}) - C(S, E = \hat{S}_T + \frac{\delta}{2} + \varepsilon)]\}$$

$$= -\lim_{\varepsilon \mapsto 0}\left\{\underbrace{\frac{C(S, E = \hat{S}_T - \frac{\delta}{2} - \varepsilon) - C(S, E = \hat{S}_T - \frac{\delta}{2})}{-\varepsilon}}_{\le 0}\right\}$$

$$+ \lim_{\varepsilon \mapsto 0}\left\{\underbrace{\frac{C(S, E = \hat{S}_T + \frac{\delta}{2} + \varepsilon) - C(S, E = \hat{S}_T + \frac{\delta}{2})}{\varepsilon}}_{\le 0}\right\}$$

$$= C_2(S, E = \hat{S}_T + \frac{\delta}{2}) - C_2(S, E = \hat{S}_T - \frac{\delta}{2}).$$

Here the subscript 2 indicates the partial derivative with respect to the second argument (E), evaluated at the indicated exercise prices. In summary, the limiting portfolio has a payoff at expiration as represented in Figure 8-3 and a (current) price $C_2(S, E = \hat{S}_T + \frac{\delta}{2}) - C_2(S, E = \hat{S}_T - \frac{\delta}{2})$ that is positive since the payoff is positive. We have thus priced an Arrow-Debreu state-contingent claim, given that we define states of the world as coincident with ranges of a proxy for the market portfolio.

4. Suppose, for example, we have an uncertain payment with the following payoff at time T:

$$CF_T = \left\{ \begin{array}{l} 0 \text{ if } S_T \notin [\hat{S}_T - \frac{\delta}{2}, \hat{S}_T + \frac{\delta}{2}] \\ 50000 \text{ if } S_T \in [\hat{S}_T - \frac{\delta}{2}, \hat{S}_T + \frac{\delta}{2}] \end{array} \right\}.$$

The value today of this cash flow is:

$$50000 \cdot [C_2(S, E = \hat{S}_T + \frac{\delta}{2}) - C_2(S, E = \hat{S}_T - \frac{\delta}{2})].$$

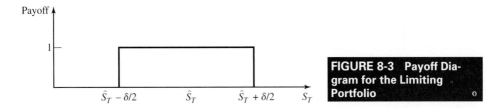

FIGURE 8-3 Payoff Diagram for the Limiting Portfolio

The formula we have developed is really very general. In particular, for any arbitrary values S_T^1 and S_T^2, the price of an Arrow-Debreu contingent claim that pays off $1.00 if the underlying market portfolio assumes a value $S_T \in [S_T^1, S_T^2]$, is given by

$$q(S_T^1, S_T^2) = C_2(S, E = S_T^2) - C_2(S, E = S_T^1). \qquad (8.1)$$

We value this quantity in Box 8-1 for a particular set of parameters making explicit use of the Black-Scholes option pricing formula.

Suppose we wished to price an uncertain cash flow to be received in one period from now, where a period corresponds to a duration of time T. What do we do? Choose several ranges of the value of the market portfolio corresponding to the various states of nature that may occur—say three states: "recession," "slow growth," and "boom" and estimate the cash flow in each of these states (see Figure 8-4). It would be unusual to

---

BOX 8-1

Pricing A-D Securities with Black-Scholes

For calls priced according to the Black-Scholes option pricing formula, Breeden and Litzenberger (1978) prove that

$$AD(S_T^1, S_T^2) = C_2(S, E = S_T^2)$$
$$- C_2(S, E = S_T^1)$$
$$= e^{-rT}\{N(d_2(S_T^1)) - N(d_2(S_T^2))\}$$

where $d_2(S_T^i) = [\ln(S_0/S_T^i) + (r_f - \delta - (\sigma^2/2)T]/\sigma\sqrt{T}$. In this expression, T is the time to expiration, r_f the annualized continuously compounded riskless rate over that period, δ the continuous annualized portfolio dividend yield, σ the standard deviation of the continuously compounded rate of return on the underlying index portfolio, $N(\ )$ the standard normal distribution, and S_0 the current value of the index.

Suppose the not-continuously compounded risk-free rate is .06, the not-continuously compounded dividend yield is $\delta = .02$, $T = .5$ year, $S_0 = 1,500$, $S_T^2 = 1,700$, $S_T^1 = 1,600$, $\sigma = .20$; then

$$d_2(S_T^1) = \left\{\ln\left(\frac{1500}{1600}\right) + \left[\ln(1.06)\right.\right.$$
$$\left.\left. - \ln(1.02) - \frac{(.20)^2}{2}\right](.5)\right\}\Big/.20\sqrt{.5}$$
$$= \{-.0645 + (.0583 - .0198$$
$$- .02)(.5)\}/.1414$$
$$= -.391$$

$$d_2(S_T^2) = \left\{\ln\left(\frac{1500}{1700}\right)\right.$$
$$\left. + (.0583 - .0198 - .02)(.5)\right\}\Big/.1414$$
$$= \{-.1252 + .00925\}/.1414$$
$$= -.820$$

$$AD(S_T^1 - S_T^2) = e^{-\ln(1.06)(.5)}$$
$$\times \{N(-.391) - N(-.820)\}$$
$$= .9713\{.2939 - .1517\}$$
$$= .1381,$$

or about $.14.

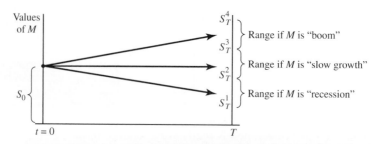

FIGURE 8-4   Constructing "States" as Ranges of the Future Value of M

have a large number of states as the requirement of having to estimate the cash flows in each of those states is likely to exceed our forecasting abilities.

Suppose the cash flow estimates are, respectively, CF_B, CF_{SG}, CF_R, where the subscripts denote, respectively, "boom," "slow growth," and "recession." Then,

$$\text{Value of the } CF = V_{CF} = CF_B q(S_T^3, S_T^4) + CF_{SG} q(S_T^2, S_T^3) + CF_R q(S_T^1, S_T^2),$$

where $S_T^1 < S_T^2 < S_T^3 < S_T^4$, and the Arrow-Debreu prices are estimated from option prices or option pricing formulas according to Equation (8.1).

We can go one (final) step further if we assume for a moment that the cash flow we wish to value can be described by a continuous function of the value of the market portfolio.

In principle, for a very fine partition of the range of possible values of the market portfolio, say $\{S_1, \ldots, S_N\}$, where $S_i < S_{i+1}$, $S_N = \max S_T$, and $S_1 = \min S_T$, we could price the Arrow-Debreu securities that pay off in each of these $N - 1$ states defined by the partition:

$$q(S_1, S_2) = C_2(S, S_2) - C_2(S, S_1)$$
$$q(S_2, S_3) = C_2(S, S_3) - C_2(S, S_2) \ldots \text{etc.}$$

Simultaneously, we could approximate a cash flow function $CF(S_T)$ by a function that is constant in each of these ranges of S_T (a so-called "step function"), in other words, $C\hat{F}(S_T) = CF_i$, for $S_{i-1} \le S_T \le S_i$. For example,

$$C\hat{F}(S_T) = CF_i = \frac{CF(S, S_T = S_i) + CF(S, S_T = S_{i-1})}{2} \text{ for } S_{i-1} \le S_T \le S_i.$$

This particular approximation is represented in Figure 8-5. The value of the approximate cash flow would then be

$$V_{CF} = \sum_{i=2}^{N} C\hat{F}_i \cdot q(S_{i-1}, S_i)$$
$$= \sum_{i=2}^{N} C\hat{F}_i [C_2(S, S_T = S_i) - C_2(S, S_T = S_{i-1})]. \tag{8.2}$$

Our approach is now clear. The value of the uncertain cash flow will be the sum of the approximate cash flows evaluated at the Arrow-Debreu prices as the norm of the partition (the size of the interval $S_i - S_{i-1}$) tends to zero. It can be shown (and it is intu-

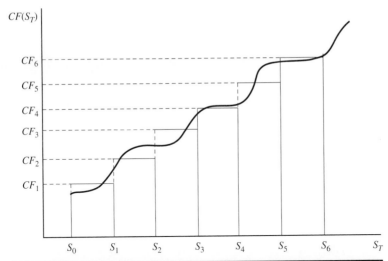

FIGURE 8-5   A Discrete Approximation to a Continuous Cash Flow Function

itively plausible) that the limit of Equation (8.2) as $\max_i |S_{i+1} - S_i| \mapsto 0$ is the integral of the cash flow function multiplied by the second derivative of the call's price with respect to the exercise price. The latter is the infinitesimal counterpart to the difference in the first derivatives of the call prices entering in Equation (8.1):

$$\lim_{\max_i |S_{i+1} - S_i| \mapsto 0} \sum_{i=2}^{N} C\hat{F}_i [C_2(S, S_T = S_{i+1}) - C_2(S, S_T = S_i)]$$

$$= \int CF(S_T) C_{22}(S, S_T) dS_T. \quad \textbf{(8.3)}$$

As a particular case of a constant cash flow stream, a risk-free bond paying $1.00 in every state is then priced as per

$$p^{r_f} = \frac{1}{(1 + r_f)} = \int_0^{\infty} C_{22}(S, S_T) dS_T.$$

BOX 8-2

Extracting Arrow-Debreu Prices from Option Prices: A Numerical Illustration

Let us now illustrate the power of the approach adopted in this and the previous section. For that purpose, Table 8-1 [adapted from Pirkner, Weigend, and Zimmermann (1999)] starts by recording call prices, obtained from the Black-Scholes formula for a call option, on an underlying index portfolio, currently valued at $S = 10$, for a range of strike prices going from $E = 7$ to $E = 13$ (columns 1 and 2). Column 3 computes the value of portfolio P of Section 8.3. Given that the difference between the exercise prices is

(*continued*)

BOX 8-2 (*continued*)

TABLE 8-1 Pricing an Arrow-Debreu State Claim

E	C(S, E)	Cost of Position	Payoff if S_T = 7	8	9	10	11	12	13	ΔC	$\Delta(\Delta C) = q_\theta$
7	3.354										
										−0.895	
8	2.459										0.106
										−0.789	
9	1.670	+1.670	0	0	0	1	2	3	4		0.164
										−0.625	
10	1.045	−2.090	0	0	0	0	−2	−4	−6		**0.184**
										−0.441	
11	0.604	+0.604	0	0	0	0	0	1	2		0.162
										−0.279	
12	0.325										0.118
										−0.161	
13	0.164										
		0.184	0	0	0	1	0	0	0		

always 1 (i.e., $\delta = 1$), holding exactly one unit of this portfolio replicates the $1.00 payoff of the Arrow-Debreu security associated with $E = 10$. This is shown in column 4. From column 2, we learn that the price of this Arrow-Debreu security, which must be equal to the value of the replicating portfolio, is $0.184. Finally, columns 5 and 6 approximate the first and second derivatives of the call price with respect to the exercise price. In the current context this is naturally done by computing the first and second differences (the price increments and the increments of the increments as the exercise price varies) from the price data given in column 2. This is a literal application of Equation (8.1). One thus obtains the full series of Arrow-Debreu prices for states of nature identified with values of the underlying market portfolios ranging from 8 to 12, confirming that the $0.184 price occurs when the state of nature is identified as $S = 10$ (or $9.5 < S < 10.5$).

8.5 ARROW-DEBREU PRICING IN A MULTIPERIOD SETTING

The fact that the Arrow-Debreu pricing approach is static makes it most adequate for the pricing of one-period cash flows and it is, quite naturally, in this context that most of our discussion has been framed. But as we have emphasized previously, it is formally equally appropriate for pricing multiperiod cash flows. The estimation (for instance via option pricing formulas and the methodology introduced in the last two sections) of Arrow-Debreu prices for several periods ahead is inherently more difficult, however, and relies on more perilous assumptions than in the case of one period ahead prices. (This parallels the fact that the assumptions necessary to develop closed form option pricing formulae are more questionable when they are used in the context of pricing long-term options). Pricing long-term assets, whatever the approach adopted, requires making hypotheses to the effect that the recent past tells us something about the future, which, in ways to be defined and which vary from one model to the next, translates into hypotheses that some form of stationarity prevails. Completing the Arrow-Debreu pricing approach with an additional stationarity hypothesis provides an interesting perspective on the pricing of multiperiod cash flows. This is the purpose of the present section.

For notational simplicity, let us first assume that the same two states of nature (ranges of value of M) can be realized in each period, and that all future state-contingent cash flows have been estimated. The structure of the cash flow is found in Figure 8-6.

Suppose also that we have estimated, using our formulae derived earlier, the values of the one-period state-contingent claims as follows:

Tomorrow

$$\text{Today} \quad \begin{array}{c} 1 \\ 2 \end{array}\begin{bmatrix} .54 & .42 \\ .46 & .53 \end{bmatrix} = q$$

where q_{11} (= .54) is the price today of an Arrow-Debreu claim paying $1 if state 1 (a boom) occurs tomorrow, given we are in state 1 (boom) today. Similarly, q_{12} is the price today of an Arrow-Debreu claim paying $1 if state 2 (recession) occurs tomorrow given we are in state 1 today. Note that these prices differ because the distribution of the value of M tomorrow differs depending on the state today.

Now let us introduce our stationarity hypothesis. Suppose that q, the matrix of values, is invariant through time.[5] That is, the same two states of nature describe the possible futures at all future dates and the contingent one-period prices remain the same. This allows us to interpret the power of the q matrix, $q^2, q^3, \ldots$ in a particularly useful way. Consider q^2 (see also Figure 8-7):

$$q^2 = \begin{bmatrix} .54 & .42 \\ .46 & .53 \end{bmatrix} \cdot \begin{bmatrix} .54 & .42 \\ .46 & .53 \end{bmatrix} = \begin{bmatrix} (.54)(.54) + (.42)(.46) & (.54)(.42) + (.42)(.53) \\ (.46)(.54) + (.53)(.46) & (.46)(.42) + (.53)(.53) \end{bmatrix}$$

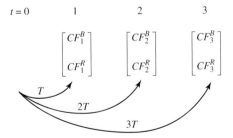

FIGURE 8-6   A Multiperiod Cash Flow: Two States of Nature Every Period

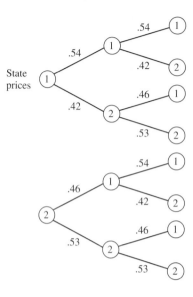

FIGURE 8-7   The Evolution of State Prices Through Time

Note there are two ways to be in state 1 two periods from now, given we are in state 1 today. Therefore, the price today of $1.00, if state 1 occurs in two periods, given we are in state 1 today is:

$$\underbrace{(.54)(.54)}_{\substack{\text{value of \$1 in two periods if state 1 occurs} \\ \text{and the intermediate state is 1}}} + \underbrace{(.42)(.46)}_{\substack{\text{value of \$1.00 in two periods if state 1 occurs} \\ \text{and the intermediate state is 2}}}$$

Similarly, $q^2_{22} = (.46)(.42) + (.53)(.53)$ is the price today, if today's state is 2, of $1.00 contingent on state 2 occurring in two periods. In general, for powers N of the matrix q, we have the following interpretation for q^N_{ij}: Given that we are in state i today, it gives the price today of $1.00, contingent on state j occurring in N periods. Of course, if we hypothesized three states, then the Arrow-Debreu matrices would be 3×3 and so forth.

How can this information be used in a "capital budgeting" problem? First we must estimate the cash flows. Suppose they were as outlined in Table 8-2.

Then the present value (PV) of the cash flows, contingent on state 1 or state 2 are given by:

$$
PV = \begin{bmatrix} PV_1 \\ PV_2 \end{bmatrix} = \begin{bmatrix} .54 & .42 \\ .46 & .53 \end{bmatrix}\begin{bmatrix} 42 \\ 65 \end{bmatrix} + \begin{bmatrix} .54 & .42 \\ .46 & .53 \end{bmatrix}^2\begin{bmatrix} 48 \\ 73 \end{bmatrix} + \begin{bmatrix} .54 & .42 \\ .46 & .53 \end{bmatrix}^3\begin{bmatrix} 60 \\ 58 \end{bmatrix}
$$

$$
= \begin{bmatrix} .54 & .42 \\ .46 & .53 \end{bmatrix}\begin{bmatrix} 42 \\ 65 \end{bmatrix} + \begin{bmatrix} .4848 & .4494 \\ .4922 & .4741 \end{bmatrix}\begin{bmatrix} 48 \\ 73 \end{bmatrix} + \begin{bmatrix} .4685 & .4418 \\ .4839 & .4580 \end{bmatrix}\begin{bmatrix} 60 \\ 58 \end{bmatrix}
$$

$$
= \begin{bmatrix} 49.98 \\ 53.77 \end{bmatrix} + \begin{bmatrix} 56.07 \\ 58.23 \end{bmatrix} + \begin{bmatrix} 53.74 \\ 55.59 \end{bmatrix} = \begin{bmatrix} 159.79 \\ 167.59 \end{bmatrix}.
$$

This procedure can be expanded to include as many states of nature as we may wish to define. This amounts to choosing as fine a partition of the range of possible values of M that one wishes to choose. It makes no sense to construct a finer partition, however, if we have no real basis for estimating different cash flows in those states. For most practical problems, three or four states are probably sufficient. But an advantage of this

TABLE 8-2   State Contingent Cash Flows

$t = 0$	1	2	3
state 1	$\begin{bmatrix} 42 \\ 65 \end{bmatrix}$	$\begin{bmatrix} 48 \\ 73 \end{bmatrix}$	$\begin{bmatrix} 60 \\ 58 \end{bmatrix}$
state 2			

method is that it forces one to think carefully about what a project cash flow will be in each state, and what the relevant states, in fact, are.

One may wonder whether this methodology implicitly assumes that the states are equally probable. That is not the case. Although the probabilities, which would reflect the likelihood of the value of M lying in the various intervals, are not explicit, they are built into the prices of the state-contingent claims.

We close this chapter by suggesting a way to tie the approach proposed here with our work in the previous chapter. Risk-free cash flows are special (degenerate) examples of risky cash flows. It is thus easy to use the method of this section to price risk-free flows. The comparison with the results obtained with the method of Chapter 7 then provides a useful check of the appropriateness of the assumptions made in the present context.

Consider our earlier example with Arrow-Debreu prices given by:

$$\text{states} \begin{array}{c} \\ 1 \\ 2 \end{array} \begin{array}{cc} 1 & 2 \\ \begin{bmatrix} .54 & .42 \\ .46 & .53 \end{bmatrix} \end{array}.$$

If we are in state 1 today, the price of $1.00 in each state tomorrow (i.e., a risk-free cash flow tomorrow of $1.00) is $.54 + .42 = .96$. This implies a risk-free rate of:

$$(1 + r_f^1) = \frac{1.00}{.96} = 1.0416 \text{ or } 4.16\%.$$

To put it differently, $.54 + .42 = .96$ is the price of a one-period discount bond paying $1.00 in one period, given that we are in state 1 today. More generally, we would evaluate the following risk-free cash flow as:

$$
\begin{array}{ccccc}
t = 0 & 0 & 1 & 2 & 3 \\
 & & 100 & 100 & 100
\end{array}
$$

$$PV = \begin{bmatrix} PV_1 \\ PV_2 \end{bmatrix} = \begin{bmatrix} .54 & .42 \\ .46 & .53 \end{bmatrix}\begin{bmatrix} 100 \\ 100 \end{bmatrix} + \begin{bmatrix} .54 & .42 \\ .46 & .53 \end{bmatrix}^2\begin{bmatrix} 100 \\ 100 \end{bmatrix} + \begin{bmatrix} .54 & .42 \\ .46 & .53 \end{bmatrix}^3\begin{bmatrix} 100 \\ 100 \end{bmatrix}$$

$$= \begin{bmatrix} .54 & .42 \\ .46 & .53 \end{bmatrix}\begin{bmatrix} 100 \\ 100 \end{bmatrix} + \begin{bmatrix} .4848 & .4494 \\ .4922 & .4741 \end{bmatrix}\begin{bmatrix} 100 \\ 100 \end{bmatrix} + \begin{bmatrix} .4685 & .4418 \\ .4839 & .4580 \end{bmatrix}\begin{bmatrix} 100 \\ 100 \end{bmatrix}$$

So $PV_1 = [.54 + .42]100 + [.4848 + .4494]100 + [.4685 + .4418]100$

$= [.96]100 + [.9342]100 + [.9103]100$

$= 280.45$

where $[.96] =$ price of a one-period discount bond, given state 1 today,
$[.9342] =$ price of a two-period discount bond, given state 1 today,
$[.9103] =$ price of a three-period discount bond, given state 1 today.

The PV given state 2 is computed analogously. Now this provides us with a **verification test:** If the price of a discount bond using this method does not coincide with the prices using the approach developed in the preceding chapter (which relies on quoted coupon bond prices), then this must mean that our states are not well defined or numerous enough or that the assumptions of the option pricing formulae used to compute Arrow-Debreu prices are inadequate.

8.6   CONCLUSIONS

This chapter has served two main purposes. First, it has provided us with a platform to think more in depth about the all-important notion of market completeness. Our demonstration that, in principle, a portfolio of simple calls and puts written on the market portfolio might suffice to reach a complete market structure suggests the "holy grail" may not be totally out of reach. Caution must be exercised, however, in interpreting the necessary assumptions. Can we indeed assume that the market portfolio—and what do we mean by the latter—is an adequate reflection of all the economically relevant states of nature? And the time dimension of market completeness should not be forgotten. The most relevant state of nature for a Swiss resident of 40 years of age may be the possibility of a period of prolonged depression with high unemployment in Switzerland 25 years from now (i.e., when he is nearing retirement).[6] Now extreme aggregate economic conditions would certainly be reflected in the Swiss Market Index (SMI), but options with 20-year maturities are not customarily traded. Is it because of a lack of demand (our assumption as to the most relevant state is not borne out), or because the structure of the financial industry is such that the supply of securities for long horizons is deficient?[7]

   The second part of the chapter discussed how Arrow-Debreu prices can be extracted from option prices (in the case where the relevant option is actively traded) or option pricing formulas (in the case where they are not). This discussion helps make Arrow-Debreu securities a less abstract concept. In fact, in specific cases the detailed procedure is fully operational and may indeed be the wiser route to evaluating risky cash flows. The key hypotheses are similar to those we have just discussed: The relevant states of nature are adequately distinguished by the market portfolio, a hypothesis that may be deemed appropriate if the context is limited to the valuation of risky cash flows. Moreover, in the case where options are not traded, the quality of the extracted Arrow-Debreu prices depends on the appropriateness of the various hypotheses imbedded in the option pricing formulas to which one has recourse. This issue has been abundantly discussed in the relevant literature.

References

Banz, R., and M. Miller, "Prices for State-Contingent Claims: Some Estimates and Applications," *Journal of Business*, 51 (1978): 653–672.

---

[6]The predominant pension regime in Switzerland is a defined benefit scheme with the benefits defined as a fraction of the most recent salary.

[7]A forceful statement in support of a similar claim is found in Shiller (1993) (see also the conclusions to Chapter 1). For the particular example discussed here, it may be argued that shorting the SMI would provide the appropriate hedge. Is it conceivable to take a short SMI position with a 20-year horizon?

Breeden, D., and Litzenberger, R. H., "Prices of State-Contingent Claims Implicit in Option Prices," *Journal of Business*, 51 (1978): 621–651.

Pirkner, C. D., A. S. Weigend, and H. Zimmermann, "Extracting Risk-Neutral Densities from Option Prices Using Mixture Binomial Trees." University of St-Gallen. Mimeographed (1999).

Ross, S., "Options and Efficiency," *Quarterly Journal of Economics*, 90 (1976): 75–89.

Shiller, R. J., *Macro Markets—Creating Institutions for Managing Society's Largest Economic Risks*, Oxford: Clarendon Press, 1993.

A P P E N D I X

Review of Basic Options, Concepts, and Terminology

A8.1 INTRODUCTION

The purchase of an options contract gives the buyer the right to buy (call options contract) or sell (put options contract) some other asset under pre-specified terms and circumstances. This *underlying* asset, as it is called, can, in principle, be anything with a well-defined price. For example, options on individual stocks, portfolios of stocks (i.e., indices such as the S&P 500), futures contracts, bonds, and currencies are actively traded. Note that options contracts do not represent an obligation to buy or sell and, as such, must have a positive, or at worst zero, price.

"American" style options allow the right to buy or sell (the so-called "right of exercise") at any time on or before a pre-specified future date (the "expiration" date). "European" options allow the right of exercise only at the pre-specified expiration date. Most of our discussion will be in the context of European call options. If the underlying asset does not provide any cash payments during the time to expiration (no dividends in the case of individual stocks), however, it can be shown that it is never wealth maximizing to exercise an American call option prior to expiration (its market price will at least equal and likely exceed its value if exercised). In this case, American and European call options are essentially the same, and are priced identically. The same statement is not true for puts.

In all applied options work it is presumed that the introduction of options trading does not influence the price process of the underlying asset on which they are written. In full general equilibrium in the presence of incomplete markets, however, this will not generally be the case.

A8.2 CALL AND PUT OPTIONS ON INDIVIDUAL STOCKS

EUROPEAN CALL OPTIONS

1. Definition: A European call options contract gives the owner the right to buy a pre-specified number of shares of a pre-specified stock (the underlying asset) at a pre-specified price (the "strike" or "exercise" price) on a pre-specified future date (the expiration date). American options allow exercise "on or before" the expiration date. A contract typically represents 100 options with the cumulative right to buy 100 shares.

2. Payoff diagram: It is customary to describe the payoff to an individual call option by its value at expiration, seen in Figure A8-1, where S_T denotes the possible values of the underlying stock at expiration date T, E the exercise price, and C_T the corresponding call value at expiration. Algebraically, we would write

$$C_T = \max\{0, S_T - E\}$$

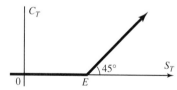

FIGURE A8-1 Payoff Diagram: European Call Option

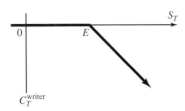

FIGURE A8-2   Payoff Diagram: Call Writer's Perspective

The diagram in Figure A8-1 assumes the perspective of the buyer; the payoff to the seller (the so-called "writer" of the option) is exactly opposite to that of the buyer, as seen in Figure A8-2.

Note that options give rise to exactly offsetting wealth transfers between the buyer and the seller. The options-related wealth positions of buyers and sellers must thus always sum to zero. As such we say that options are in zero net supply, and thus are not elements of M, the market portfolio of the classic CAPM.

3. Remarks: The purchaser of a call option is essentially buying the expected price appreciation of the underlying asset in excess of the exercise price. As we will make explicit in a later chapter, a call option can be thought of as very highly leveraged position in the underlying stock, which makes it an ideal vehicle for speculation. For relatively little money (as call option price will typically be much less than the underlying share's price) the buyer can acquire the upward potential.

There will, of course, be no options market without substantial diversity of expectations regarding the future price behavior of the underlying stock.

EUROPEAN PUT OPTIONS

1. Definition: A European put options contract gives the buyer the right to sell a pre-specified number of shares of the

underlying stock at a pre-specified price (the "exercise" or "strike" price) on a pre-specified future date (the expiration date). American puts allow for the sale on or before the expiration date. A typical contract represents 100 options with the cumulative right to sell 100 shares.

2. Payoff diagram: In the case of a put, the payoff at expiration of an individual option is represented as in Figure A8-3.

Here P_T denotes the put's value at expiration; otherwise, the notation is the same as for calls. The algebraic equivalent to the payoff diagram is

$$P_T = \max\{0, E - S_T\}$$

The same comments about wealth transfers apply equally to the put as to the call; puts are thus also not included in the market portfolio M.

3. Remarks: Puts pay off when the underlying asset's price falls below the exercise price at expiration. This makes puts ideal financial instruments for *insuring,* in a sense, against price declines. Let us consider the payoff to the simplest *fundamental hedge* portfolio:

$$\left\{ \begin{array}{ll} 1 \text{ share of stock,} & 1 \text{ put written on the stock} \\ & \text{with exercise price } E \end{array} \right\}$$

To see how these two securities interact with one another, let us consider their net total value at expiration (Table A8-1).

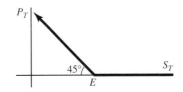

FIGURE A8-3   Payoff Diagram for a Put

TABLE A8-1	Payoff Table: Fundamental Hedge	
Payoffs: Fundamental Hedge		
Events:	$S_T \leq E$	$S_T > E$
Stock	S_T	S_T
Put	$E - S_T$	0
Hedge Port.	E	S_T

The diagrammatic equivalent is found in Figure A8-4.

The introduction of the put effectively bounds the share price to fall no lower than E. Such insurance costs money, of course, and its price is the price of the put.

Puts and calls are fundamentally different securities: calls pay off when the underlying asset's price at expiration exceeds E; puts pay off when its price falls short of E. Although the payoff patterns of puts and calls are individually simple, virtually any payoff pattern can be replicated by a properly constructed portfolio of these instruments.

A8.3 THE BLACK-SCHOLES FORMULA FOR A EUROPEAN CALL OPTION

Assumptions: The probability distribution on the possible payoffs to call ownership will depend upon the underlying stock's price process. The Black-Scholes formula gives the price of a European call under the following assumptions:

1. The underlying stock pays no dividends over the time to expiration.
2. The risk-free rate of interest is constant over the time to expiration.

3. The continuously compounded rate of return on the underlying stock is governed by a geometric Brownian motion with constant mean and variance over the time to expiration.

This model of rate of return evolution essentially presumes that the rate of return on the underlying stock—its rate of price appreciation since there are no dividends—over any small interval of time $\Delta t \in [0, T]$ is given by

$$r_{t,t+\Delta t} = \frac{\Delta S_{t,t+1}}{S_t} = \hat{\mu}\Delta t + \hat{\sigma}\tilde{\varepsilon}\sqrt{\Delta t} \quad \text{(A.8.1)}$$

where $\tilde{\varepsilon}$ is the standard normal distribution and $\hat{\mu}$, $\hat{\sigma}$, are, respectively, the annualized continuously compounded mean return and the standard deviation of the continuously compounded return on the stock. Under this abstraction the rate of return over any small interval of time Δt is distributed $N(\hat{\mu}\Delta t, \hat{\sigma}\sqrt{\Delta t})$; furthermore, these returns are independently distributed from interval to interval t. Recall (Chapter 2) that these are the two basic statistical properties of stock returns. More precisely, equation (A.8.1) describes the discrete time approximation to geometric Brownian motion.

True geometric Brownian motion presumes continuous trading, and its attendant continuous compounding of returns. Of course, continuous trading presumes an uncountably large number of *trades* in any finite interval of time, which is impossible. It should be thought of as a very useful mathematical abstraction.

Under continuous trading the expression analogous to (A.8.1) is

$$\frac{dS}{S} = \hat{\mu}dt + \hat{\sigma}\tilde{\varepsilon}\sqrt{dt} \quad \text{(A.8.2)}$$

Much more will be said about this price process in subsequent chapters.

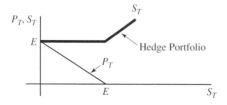

FIGURE A8-4 Payoff Diagram: Fundamental Hedge

THE FORMULA

The Black-Scholes formula is given by

$$C_T(S, E) = SN(d_1) - e^{\hat{r}_f T}EN(d_2)$$

where
$$d_1 = \frac{\ln(S/E) + (\hat{r} - \frac{1}{2}\hat{\sigma}^2)T}{\sigma\sqrt{T}}$$

$$d_2 = d_1 - \hat{\sigma}\sqrt{T}.$$

In this formula:

S = the price of the stock "today" (at the time the call valuation is being undertaken);

E = the exercise price;

T = the time to expiration, measured in years;

$\hat{r}_f$ = the estimated continuously compounded annual risk-free rate;

$\hat{\sigma}$ = the estimated standard deviation of the continuously compounded rate of return on the underlying asset annualized; and

$N(\ )$ is the standard normal distribution.

In any practical problem, of course, $\hat{\sigma}$ must be estimated. The risk-free rate is usually unambiguous, as normally there is a T-bill coming due on approximately the same date as the options contracts expire (U.S. markets).

AN EXAMPLE

Suppose $S = \$68$
$E = \$60$
$$T = 88 \text{ days} = \frac{88}{365} = 241 \text{ years}$$
$r_f = 6\%$ (not continuously compounded)
$\hat{\sigma} = .40$

The r_f inserted into the formula is that rate which is, when continuously compounded, equivalent to the actual 6% annual rate; this must satisfy

$$e^{\hat{r}_f} = 1.06, \text{ or } \hat{r}_f = \ln(1.06) = .058.$$

Thus,

$$d_1 = \frac{\ln{}^{68}\!/_{60} + (.058 + \frac{1}{2}(.4)^2).241}{(.40)\sqrt{.241}} = .806$$

$$d_2 = .806 - (.40)\sqrt{.241} = .610$$

$$N(d_1) = N(.806) \approx .79$$

$$N(d_2) = N(.610) \approx .729.$$
$$C = \$.68(.79) - e^{-(.058)(.241)}(\$60)(.729)$$
$$= \$10.60$$

ESTIMATING σ

We gain intuition about the Black-Scholes model if we understand how its inputs are obtained, and the only input with any real ambiguity is σ. Here we present a straightforward approach to its estimation based on the security's historical price series.

Since volatility is an unstable attribute of a stock, by convention it is viewed as unreliable to go more than 180 days into the past for the choice of historical period. Furthermore, since we are trying to estimate the μ, σ of a continuously compounded return, the interval of measurement should be, in principle, as small as possible. For most practical applications, daily data is the best we can obtain.

The procedure is as follows:

i. Select the number of chosen historical observations and index them $i = 0, 1, 2, \ldots, n$ with observation 0 most distant into the past and observation n most recent. This gives us $n + 1$ price observations. From this we will obtain n daily return observations.

ii. Compute the equivalent continuously compounded ROR on the underlying asset over the time intervals implied by the selection of the data (i.e., if we choose to use daily data we compute the continuously compounded daily rate):

$$r_i = \ln\left(\frac{S_i}{S_{i-1}}\right)$$

This is the equivalent continuously compounded ROR from the end of period $i - 1$ to the end of period i.

Why is this the correct calculation? Suppose $S_i = 110, S_{i-1} = 100$; we want that continuously compounded return x such that

$$S_{i-1}e^x = S_i \text{ or } 100e^x = 110$$
$$e^x = (^{110}\!/_{100})$$
$$x = \ln(^{110}\!/_{100}) = .0953.$$

This is the continuously compounded rate that will increase the price from $100 to $110.

iii. Compute the sample mean

$$\hat{\mu} = \frac{1}{n}\left(\sum_{i=1}^{n} r_1\right)$$

Remark: If the time intervals are all adjacent; in other words, if we have not omitted any observations, then

$$\mu = \frac{1}{n}\sum_{i=1}^{n} r_i$$

$$= \frac{1}{n}\left[\ln\left(\frac{S_1}{S_0}\right) + \ldots + \ln\left(\frac{S_n}{S_{n-1}}\right)\right]$$

$$= \frac{1}{n}\left[\ln\left(\frac{S_1}{S_0}\frac{S_2}{S_1}\cdots\frac{S_n}{S_{n-1}}\right)\right]$$

$$= \frac{1}{n}\ln\left(\frac{S_n}{S_0}\right)$$

Note that if we omit some calendar observations (perhaps due to, *say,* merger rumors at the time that are no longer relevant), this shortcut fails.

iv. Estimate σ

$$\hat{\sigma} = \sqrt{\frac{1}{n-1}\left(\sum_{i=1}^{n}(r_i - \hat{\mu})^2\right)}, \text{ or}$$

$$\hat{\sigma} = \sqrt{\frac{1}{n-1}\sum_{i=1}^{n}r_i^2 - \frac{1}{n(n-1)}\left(\sum_{i=1}^{n}r_i\right)^2}$$

Example: Consider the daily data presented in Table A8-2.

In this case $\hat{\mu} = \frac{1}{4}\ln(26.50/26) = \frac{1}{4}\ln(1.0192308) = .004762$. Using this formula,

$$\sum_{i=1}^{4} r_i^2 = (.0190482)^2 + (-.009479)^2$$
$$+ (.0094787)^2 = .0005472$$

$$\left(\sum_{i=1}^{4} r_i\right)^2 = (.0190482 - .009479 + .0094787)^2$$

$$= (.01905)^2 = .0003628$$

$$\hat{\sigma} = \sqrt{\frac{1}{3}(.005472) - \frac{1}{12}(.003628)}$$

$$= \sqrt{.0001809 - .0000302}$$

$$= \sqrt{.0001507} = .0123$$

$$\hat{\sigma}^2 = (.0123)^2 = .00001507$$

v. Annualize the estimate of σ. We will assume 250 trading days per year. Our estimate for the continuously compounded annual return is thus:

$$\hat{\sigma}_{annual}^2 = 250(\underbrace{.0001507}_{\hat{\sigma}_{daily}^2}) = .0377$$

Remark: Why do we do this? Why can we multiply our estimate by 250 to scale things up? We can do this because of the geometric Brownian motion assumption that returns are independently distributed. This is detailed as follows.

TABLE A8-2   A Data Set of Daily Price Data and the Implied Returns

Period	Closing Price	$\ln\left(\dfrac{S_i}{S_{i-1}}\right)$
$i = 0$	$26.00	$r_1 = \ln\left(\dfrac{26.50}{26}\right) = .0190482$
$i = 1$	$26.50	$r_2 = \ln\left(\dfrac{26.25}{26.50}\right) = -.009479$
$i = 2$	$26.25	$r_3 = \ln\left(\dfrac{26.25}{26.25}\right) = 0$
$i = 3$	$26.25	
$i = 4$	$26.50	$r_4 = \ln\left(\dfrac{26.50}{26.25}\right) = .0094787$

Our objective: an estimate for $\mathrm{Var}(\ln(S_{T=1\mathrm{yr}}/S_0))$ given 250 trading days,

$$\mathrm{Var}\left(\ln\left(\frac{S_{T=1\mathrm{yr}}}{S_0}\right)\right) = \mathrm{Var}\left(\ln\left(\frac{S_{\mathrm{day}}}{S_0} = 250\right)\right)$$

$$= \mathrm{var}\left(\ln\left(\frac{S_{\mathrm{day}\,1}}{S_0} \cdot \frac{S_{\mathrm{day}\,2}}{S_{\mathrm{day}\,1}} \cdots \frac{S_{\mathrm{day}\,250}}{S_{\mathrm{day}\,249}}\right)\right)$$

$$= \mathrm{var}\left(\ln\left(\frac{S_{\mathrm{day}\,1}}{S_0}\right) + \ln\left(\frac{S_{\mathrm{day}\,2}}{S_{\mathrm{day}\,1}}\right)\right.$$

$$\left. + \cdots + \ln\left(\frac{S_{\mathrm{day}\,250}}{S_{\mathrm{day}\,249}}\right)\right)$$

$$= \mathrm{var}\left(\ln\left(\frac{S_{\mathrm{day}\,1}}{S_0}\right)\right) + \mathrm{var}\left(\ln\left(\frac{S_{\mathrm{day}\,2}}{S_{\mathrm{day}\,1}}\right)\right)$$

$$+ \cdots + \mathrm{var}\left(\ln\left(\frac{S_{\mathrm{day}\,250}}{S_{249}}\right)\right)$$

The latter is true because returns are uncorrelated from day to day under the geometric Brownian motion assumption.

Furthermore, the daily return distribution is presumed to be the same for every day, and hence the daily variance is the same for every day under geometric Brownian motion.

Thus, $\mathrm{Var}\left(\ln\left(\frac{S_{T=1\mathrm{yr}}}{S_0}\right)\right) = 250\sigma_{\mathrm{daily}}^2$.

We have obtained an estimate for $\sigma_{\mathrm{daily}}^2$, which we will write as $\hat{\sigma}_{\mathrm{daily}}^2$. To convert this to an annual variance, we must multiply by 250.

Thus $\hat{\sigma}_{\mathrm{annual}}^2 = 250\hat{\sigma}_{\mathrm{daily}}^2 = .0377$, as noted.

If a weekly $\hat{\sigma}^2$ were obtained, it would be multiplied by 52.

A8.4   THE BLACK-SCHOLES FORMULA FOR AN INDEX

Recall that the Black-Scholes formula assumed that the underlying stock did not pay any dividends, and if this is not the case an adjustment must be made. A natural way to consider adapting the Black-Scholes formula to the dividend situation is to replace the underlying asset's price S in the formula by $S - PV(EDIVs)$, where $PV(EDIVs)$ is the present value, relative to $t = 0$, the date at which the calculation is being undertaken, of all dividends expected to be paid over the time to the option's expiration. In cases where the dividend is highly uncertain, this calculation could be problematic. We want to make this adjustment because the payment of a dividend reduces the underlying stock's value by the amount of the dividend, and thus reduces the value (ceteris paribus) of the option written on it. Options are not *dividend protected*, as it is said.

For an index, such as the S&P 500, the dividend yield on the index portfolio can be viewed as continuous, and the steady payment of this dividend will have a continuous tendency to reduce the index value. Let D denote the dividend yield on the index. In a manner exactly analogous to the single stock dividend treatment, the corresponding Black-Scholes formula is

$$C = Se^{-dT}N(d_1) - Ee^{-r_f T}N(d_2)$$

where $d_1 = \dfrac{\ln(S/E) + (r_f - D + (\sigma^2/2))T}{\sigma\sqrt{T}}$

$$d_2 = d_1 - \sigma\sqrt{T}.$$

CHAPTER 9

THE MARTINGALE MEASURE
IN DISCRETE TIME, PART I

9.1 INTRODUCTION

Valuing risky cash flows or, equivalently, pricing risky assets is at the heart of financial theory. The more traditional approach to this problem proposes to price an asset as the appropriately discounted sum of its expected future cash flows and the two pricing models discussed so far are naturally cast in this mold. The logic is straightforward: To price an asset equal to the present value of its expected future cash flows discounted at a particular rate is to price the asset in a manner such that, at its present value price, it is expected to earn that discount rate. The appropriate rate, in turn, must be the analyst's estimate of the rate of return on other financial assets that represent title to cash flows similar in risk and timing to that of the asset in question. This strategy has the consequence of pricing the asset to pay the prevailing competitive rate for its risk class.

Such a procedure is naturally imprecise. Not only are there difficulties involved in reliably forecasting future cash flows, but it is also difficult, in principle, to identify other securities that represent title to cash flows of a risk similar to the original asset's cash flow risk, or to forecast their expected future rates of return. This is where asset pricing models such as the CAPM enter the picture.[1] The CAPM tells us that of all the characteristics we might have to consider in assessing whether one asset's cash flows were similar in risk to another's, only one matters: the asset's systematic risk as measured by its beta. The CAPM thus suggests that finding similar assets is not difficult: Select an asset with the same estimated β as the one we want to value. Furthermore, the SML gives a simple method for forecasting future expected rates of return, but the CAPM cannot be considered the last word. Strictly speaking it applies only to one-period cash flows or perpetuities and it relies on the large assumption of homogenous expectations. There are distributional assumptions as well.

The Arrow-Debreu pricing theory reviewed in Chapter 8 proposes to price an asset by valuing the portfolio of state claims with the same state-by-state future payoff pattern. Here the challenging discounting procedure is performed state-of-nature by state-of-nature with the price of the relevant Arrow-Debreu security providing the

---

[1]The APT to be discussed in Chapter 12 is often used for the same purpose.

equilibrium discount factor. This method has its own complications: Arrow-Debreu securities are not usually traded so that their prices must somehow be recovered from the prices of other assets, and markets may not be complete implying that some Arrow-Debreu prices cannot be recovered and thus some cash flows cannot be priced. One approach, consisting of computing Arrow-Debreu prices outright, would require knowing the endowments and preferences of all the market participants, a tall order indeed! Another is to identify states of the world with ranges of the market portfolio and state claims with specific portfolios of options written on it. If these options are not traded, however, we need to rely on option pricing formulas to value the Arrow-Debreu securities and ultimately the risky cash flows. These formulas are only as robust as their underlying assumptions. Note as well that they are based on the same preference-free arbitrage principles as those emphasized in the present chapter.

There is another approach to the pricing problem, one that we have used on and off. It consists in altering the *numerator* of the pricing equations (the sum of expected cash flows) so that it is permissible to discount at the risk-free rate. This approach is based on the concept of certainty equivalent, which we discussed in Chapter 3. The idea is simple: If we replace each element of the future cash flow by its CE, it is clearly permissible to discount at the risk-free rate. It turns out that this approach, which we shall illustrate in the next chapter, raises exactly the same set of issues as the more common one: An asset pricing model is required to tell us what risk premium it is appropriate to deduct from the expected cash flow to obtain its CE. Again the CAPM helps solve this problem:[2] The risk premium is then defined as the product of the beta of the corresponding cash flow and the equilibrium risk premium, the expected excess return of the market portfolio (over the risk-free return). We describe this procedure in Appendix 9.1.

The theory of risk-neutral valuation reviewed in the present chapter proposes a fourth possible way to tackle the valuation problem.[3] Rather than modify the denominator—the discount factor—to take account of the risky nature of a cash flow to be valued, or the numerator, by transforming the expected cash flows into their certainty equivalent, risk-neutral valuation simply corrects the probabilities with respect to which the expectations of the future cash flows is taken, in such a way that discounting at the risk-free rate is legitimate. It is thus a procedure by which an asset valuation problem is transformed into one in which the asset's expected cash flow, computed now with respect to a new set of risk-neutral probabilities, can be discounted at the risk-free rate. The risk-neutral valuation methodology thus places an arbitrary valuation problem into a context in which all fairly priced assets earn the risk-free rate.

More importantly, however, the Martingale pricing theory or, equivalently, the theory of risk-neutral valuation is founded on preference-free pure arbitrage principles. That is, it is free of the structural assumptions on preferences, expectations, and endowments that make the CAPM so questionable and the Arrow-Debreu theory so hard to implement. In this respect, the present chapter illustrates how far one can go in pricing financial assets while abstracting from the usual structural assumptions.

Risk-neutral probability distributions naturally assume a variety of forms, depending on the choice of setting. We first illustrate them in the context of a well-understood,

---

[2]Or, similarly, the APT.
[3]The theory of risk-neutral valuation was first developed by Harrison and Kreps (1979). Pliska (1997) provides a very nice review in discrete time. The present chapter is based on his presentation.

finite time Arrow-Debreu complete markets economy. This is not the context in which the idea is most useful, but it is the one from which the basic intuition can be most easily understood.

9.2 THE SETTING AND THE INTUITION

Our setting for these preliminary discussions is the particularly simple one with which we are now long familiar. There are two dates, $t=0$ and $t=1$. At date $t=1$, any one of $j=1,2,\ldots,J$ possible states of nature can be realized; denote the jth state by θ_j and its objective probability by π_j. We assume $\pi_j > 0$ for all θ_j.

Securities are competitively traded in this economy. There is a risk-free security that pays a fixed return r_f; its period t price is denoted by $q^b(t)$. By convention, we customarily assume $q^b(0)=1$, and its price at date 1 is $q^b(1)\equiv q^b(\theta_j,1)=(1+r_f)$, for all states θ_j. Since the date 1 price of the security is $(1+r_f)$ in any state, we can as well drop the first argument in the pricing function indicating the state in which the security is valued.[4]

Also traded are $i=1,2,\ldots,N$ fundamental risky securities, which we think of as stocks. The period $t=0$ price of the ith such security is represented as $q_i^e(0)$. In period $t=1$ its contingent payoff, given that state θ_j is realized, is given by $q_i^e(\theta_j,1)$. It is also assumed that investors may hold any linear combination of the fundamental risk-free and risky securities. No assumption is made, however, regarding the number of securities that may be linearly independent vis-à-vis the number of states of nature: The securities market may or may not be complete. Neither is there any mention of agents' preferences. Otherwise the setting is standard Arrow-Debreu. Let **S** denote the set of all fundamental securities, the stocks and the bond, and linear combinations thereof.

For this setting, the existence of a set of risk-neutral probabilities or, in more customary usage, a risk-neutral probability measure, effectively means the existence of a set of state probabilities, $\pi_j^{RN} > 0, j=1,2,\ldots,J$ such that for each and every fundamental security $i, i=1,2,\ldots,N$

$$q_i^e(0) = \frac{1}{(1+r_f)} E_{\pi^{RN}}(q_i^e(\theta,1)) = \frac{1}{(1+r_f)}\sum_{j=1}^{J}\pi_j^{RN}q_i^e(\theta_j,1) \qquad (9.1)$$

(the analogous relationship automatically holds for the risk-free security).

To gain some intuition as to what might be necessary, at a minimum, to guarantee the existence of such probabilities, first observe that in our setting the π_j^{RN} represent strictly positive numbers that must satisfy a large system of equations of the form

$$q_i^e(0) = \pi_1^{RN}\left(\frac{q_i^e(\theta_1,1)}{1+r_f}\right) + \ldots + \pi_J^{RN}\left(\frac{q_i^e(\theta_J,1)}{1+r_f}\right), i=1,2,\ldots,N, \qquad (9.2)$$

together with the requirement that $\pi_j^{RN} > 0$ for all j and $\sum_{j=1}^{J}\pi_j^{RN}=1$.

---

[4]In this chapter, it will be useful for the clarity of exposition to alter some of our previous notational conventions. One of the reasons is that we will want, symmetrically for all assets, to distinguish between their price at date 0 and their price at date 1 under any given state θ_j.

Such a system most certainly will not have a solution if there exist two fundamental securities, s and k, with the same $t = 0$ price, $q_s^e(0) = q_k^e(0)$, for which one of them, say k, pays as much as s in every state, and strictly more in at least one state; in other words,

$$q_k^e(\theta_j, 1) \geq q_s^e(\theta_j, 1) \text{ for all } j, \text{ and } q_k^e(\theta_{\hat{j}}, 1) > q_s^e(\theta_{\hat{j}}, 1) \qquad (9.3)$$

for at least one $j = \hat{j}$. Equations (9.2) corresponding to securities s and k would, for any set $\{\pi_j^{RN}: j = 1, 2, \ldots, N\}$ have the same left-hand sides, yet different right-hand sides, implying no solution to the system. But two such securities cannot themselves be consistently priced because, together, they constitute an *arbitrage opportunity:* Short one unit of security s, long one unit of security k and pocket the difference $q_k^e(\theta_{\hat{j}}, 1) - q_s^e(\theta_{\hat{j}}, 1) > 0$ if state $\hat{j}$ occurs; replicate the transaction many times over. These remarks suggest, therefore, that the existence of a risk-neutral measure is, in some intimate way, related to the absence of arbitrage opportunities in the financial markets. This is, in fact, the case, but first some notation, definitions, and examples are in order.

9.3 NOTATION, DEFINITIONS, AND BASIC RESULTS

Consider a portfolio, P, composed of n_P^b risk-free bonds and n_P^i units of risky security i, $i = 1, 2, \ldots, N$. No restrictions will be placed n_P^b, n_P^i: Short sales are permitted; they can, therefore, take negative values, and fractional share holdings are acceptable. The value of this portfolio at $t = 0$, $V_P(0)$, is given by

$$V_P(0) = n_P^b q^b(0) + \sum_{i=1}^{N} n_P^i q_i^e(0), \qquad (9.4)$$

while its value at $t = 1$, given that state θ_j is realized, is

$$V_P(\theta_j, 1) = n_P^b q^b(1) + \sum_{i=1}^{N} n_P^i q_i^e(\theta_j, 1). \qquad (9.5)$$

With this notation we are now in a position to define our basic concepts.

Definition 9.1:
A portfolio P in $\boldsymbol{S}$ constitutes an arbitrage opportunity provided the following conditions are satisfied:

(i) $V_P(0) = 0$,
(ii) $V_P(\theta_j, 1) \geq 0$, for all $j \in \{1, 2, \ldots, J\}$,
(iii) $V_P(\theta_{\hat{j}}, 1) > 0$, for at least one $\hat{j} \in \{1, 2, \ldots, J\}$.   (9.6)

This is the standard sense of an arbitrage opportunity: With no initial investment and no possible losses (thus no risk), a profit can be made in at least one state. Our second crucial definition is Definition 9.2.

> **Definition 9.2:**
> A probability measure $\{\pi_j^{RN}\}_{j=1}^J$ defined on the set of states $\{\theta_j, j = 1, 2, \ldots, J\}$ is said to be a risk-neutral probability measure if
>
> (i) $\pi_j^{RN} > 0$, for all $j = 1, 2, \ldots, J$, and
>
> (ii) $q_i^e(0) = E_{\pi^{RN}}\left\{\dfrac{q_i^e(\theta, 1)}{1 + r_f}\right\}$ for all fundamental securities $i = 1, 2, \ldots, N$ in $\mathcal{S}$. $\qquad$ **(9.7)**

Both elements of this definition are crucial. Not only must each individual security be priced equal to the present value of its expected payoff, the latter computed using the risk-neutral probabilities (and thus it must also be true of portfolios of them), but these probabilities must also be strictly positive. To find them, if they exist, it is necessary only to solve the system of equations implied by Equation 9.7(ii) of the risk-neutral probability definition. Consider the Examples 9.1 through 9.4.

Example 9.1:
There are two periods and two fundamental securities, a stock and a bond, with prices and payoffs presented in Table 9-1.

TABLE 9-1 Fundamental Securities for Example 9.1			
Period t = 0 Prices	**Period t = 1 Payoffs**		
		θ_1	θ_2
$q^b(0)$: 1	$q^b(1)$:	1.1	1.1
$q^e(0)$: 4	$q^e(\theta_j, 1)$:	3	7

By the definition of a risk-neutral probability measure, it must be the case that simultaneously

$$4 = \pi_1^{RN}\left(\frac{3}{1.1}\right) + \pi_2^{RN}\left(\frac{7}{1.1}\right)$$
$$1 = \pi_1^{RN} + \pi_2^{RN}$$

Solving this little system of equations, we obtain $\pi_1^{RN} = .65$, $\pi_2^{RN} = .35$. For future reference note that the fundamental securities in this example define a complete set of financial markets for this economy, and that there are clearly no arbitrage opportunities among them.

Example 9.2:
Consider next an analogous economy with three possible states of nature, and three securities, as found in Table 9-2. The relevant system of equations is now

$$2 = \pi_1^{RN}\left(\frac{3}{1.1}\right) + \pi_2^{RN}\left(\frac{2}{1.1}\right) + \pi_3^{RN}\left(\frac{1}{1.1}\right)$$
$$3 = \pi_1^{RN}\left(\frac{1}{1.1}\right) + \pi_2^{RN}\left(\frac{4}{1.1}\right) + \pi_3^{RN}\left(\frac{6}{1.1}\right)$$
$$1 = \pi_1^{RN} + \pi_2^{RN} + \pi_3^{RN}$$

TABLE 9-2 Fundamental Securities for Example 9.2				
Period $t = 0$ Prices	**Period $t = 1$ Payoffs**			
		θ_1	θ_2	θ_3
$q^b(0)$: 1	$q^b(1)$:	1.1	1.1	1.1
$q_1^e(0)$: 2	$q_1^e(\theta_j, 1)$:	3	2	1
$q_2^e(0)$: 3	$q_2^e(\theta_j, 1)$:	1	4	6

The solution to this set of equations,

$$\pi_1^{RN} = .3, \qquad \pi_2^{RN} = .6, \qquad \pi_3^{RN} = .1,$$

satisfies the requirements of a risk-neutral measure. By inspection we again observe that this financial market is complete, and that there are no arbitrage opportunities among the three securities.

Example 9.3:

To see what happens when the financial markets are incomplete, consider the securities in Table 9-3.

TABLE 9-3 Fundamental Securities for Example 9.3				
Period $t = 0$ Prices	**Period $t = 1$ Payoffs**			
		θ_1	θ_2	θ_3
$q^b(0)$: 1	$q^b(1)$:	1.1	1.1	1.1
$q^e(0)$: 2	$q^e(\theta_j, 1)$:	1	2	3

For this example the relevant system is

$$2 = \pi_1^{RN}\left(\frac{1}{1.1}\right) + \pi_2^{RN}\left(\frac{2}{1.1}\right) + \pi_3^{RN}\left(\frac{3}{1.1}\right)$$
$$1 = \pi_1^{RN} + \pi_2^{RN} + \pi_3^{RN}$$

Because this system is under-determined, there will be many solutions. Without loss of generality, first solve for π_2^{RN} and π_3^{RN} in terms of π_1^{RN}:

$$2.2 - \pi_1^{RN} = 2\pi_2^{RN} + 3\pi_3^{RN}$$
$$1 - \pi_1^{RN} = \pi_2^{RN} + \pi_3^{RN},$$

which yields the solution $\pi_3^{RN} = .2 + \pi_1^{RN}$, and $\pi_2^{RN} = .8 - 2\pi_1^{RN}$.

In order for a triple $(\pi_1^{RN}, \pi_2^{RN}, \pi_3^{RN})$ to simultaneously solve this system of equations, while also satisfying the strict positivity requirement of risk-neutral probabilities, the following inequalities must hold:

$$\pi_1^{RN} > 0$$
$$\pi_2^{RN} = .8 - 2\pi_1^{RN} > 0$$
$$\pi_3^{RN} = .2 + \pi_1^{RN} > 0$$

By the second inequality $\pi_1^{RN} < .4$, and by the third $\pi_1^{RN} > -.2$. In order that all probabilities be strictly positive, it must, therefore, be the case that

$$0 < \pi_1^{RN} < .4,$$

with π_2^{RN} and π_3^{RN} given by the indicated equalities.

In an incomplete market, therefore, there appear to be many risk-neutral probability sets: Any triple $(\pi_1^{RN}, \pi_2^{RN}, \pi_3^{RN})$ where

$$\{\pi_1^{RN}, \pi_2^{RN}, \pi_3^{RN}\} \in \{(\lambda, .8 - 2\lambda, .2 + \lambda): 0 < \lambda < .4\}$$

serves as a risk-neutral probability measure for this economy.

Example 9.4:

Lastly, we may as well see what happens if the set of fundamental securities contains an arbitrage opportunity (see Table 9-4).

TABLE 9-4 Fundamental Securities for Example 9.4			
Period t = 0 Prices	*Period t = 1 Payoffs*		
		θ_1	θ_2	θ_3
$q^b(0)$: 1	$q^b(1)$:	1.1	1.1	1.1
$q_1^e(0)$: 2	$q_1^e(\theta_j, 1)$:	2	3	1
$q_2^e(0)$: 2.5	$q_2^e(\theta_j, 1)$:	4	5	3

Any attempt to solve the system of equations defining the risk-neutral probabilities fails in this case. There is no solution. Notice also the implicit arbitrage opportunity: risky security 2 dominates a portfolio of one unit of the risk-free security and one unit of risky security 1, yet it costs less.

It is also possible to have a solution in the presence of arbitrage. In this case, however, at least one of the solution probabilities will be zero, disqualifying the set for the risk-neutral designation.

Together with our original intuition, these examples suggest that arbitrage opportunities are incompatible with the existence of a risk-neutral probability measure. This is the substance of the first main result.

Proposition 9.1:

Consider the two-period setting described earlier in this chapter. Then there exists a risk-neutral probability measure on **S**, if and only if there are no arbitrage opportunities among the fundamental securities.

Proposition 9.1 tells us that, provided the condition of the absence of arbitrage opportunities characterizes financial markets, our ambition to use distorted, risk-neutral probabilities to compute expected cash flows and discount at the risk-free rate has some legitimacy! Note, however, that the proposition admits the possibility that there may be many such measures, as in Example 9.3.

Proposition 9.1 also provides us, in principle, with a method for testing whether a set of fundamental securities contains an arbitrage opportunity: If the system of Equation (9.7.ii) has no solution probability vector where all the terms are strictly positive, an arbitrage opportunity is present. Unless we are highly confident of the actual states of nature and the payoffs to the various fundamental securities in those states, however, this observation is of limited use. But even for a very large number of securities it is easy to check computationally.

Although we have calculated the risk-neutral probabilities with respect to the prices and payoffs of the fundamental securities only, the analogous relationship must hold for arbitrary portfolios in S—all linear combinations of the fundamental securities—in the absence of arbitrage opportunities. This result is formalized in Proposition 9.2.

Proposition 9.2:

Suppose the set of securities S is free of arbitrage opportunities. Then for any portfolio $\hat{P}$ in S

$$V_{\hat{P}}(0) = \frac{1}{(1 + r_f)} E_{\pi^{RN}} \tilde{V}_{\hat{P}}(\theta, 1), \tag{9.8}$$

for any risk-neutral probability measure π^{RN} on S.

Proof:

Let $\hat{P}$ be an arbitrary portfolio in S, and let it be composed of $n_{\hat{P}}^b$ bonds and $n_{\hat{P}}^i$ shares of fundamental risky asset i. In the absence of arbitrage, $\hat{P}$ must be priced equal to the value of its constituent securities, in other words,

$$V_{\hat{P}}(0) = n_{\hat{P}}^b q^b(0) + \sum_{i=1}^{N} n_{\hat{P}}^i q_i^e(0)$$

$$= n_{\hat{P}}^b E_{\pi^{RN}}\left(\frac{q^b(1)}{1 + r_f}\right) + \sum_{i=1}^{N} n_{\hat{P}}^i E_{\pi^{RN}}\left(\frac{\tilde{q}_i^e(\theta, 1)}{1 + r_f}\right),$$

for any risk neutral probability measure π^{RN},

$$= E_{\pi^{RN}}\left\{\frac{n_{\hat{P}}^b q^b(1) + \sum_{i=1}^{N} n_{\hat{P}}^i \tilde{q}_i^e(\theta, 1)}{1 + r_f}\right\}$$

$$= \frac{1}{(1 + r_f)} E_{\pi^{RN}}(\tilde{V}_{\hat{P}}(\theta, 1)).$$

Proposition 9.2 is merely a formalization of the obvious fact that if every security in the portfolio is priced equal to the present value, discounted at r_f, of its expected payoffs computed with respect to the risk-neutral probabilities, the same must be true of the portfolio itself. This follows from the linearity of the expectations operator and the fact that the portfolio is valued as the sum total of its constituent securities, which must be the case in the absence of arbitrage opportunities.

A multiplicity of risk-neutral measures on S does not compromise this conclusion in any way, because each of them assigns the same value to the fundamental securities and thus to the portfolio itself via Equation (9.8). For completeness, we note that a form of a converse to Proposition 9.2 is also valid.

> **Proposition 9.3:**
> Consider an arbitrary period $t = 1$ payoff $\tilde{x}(\theta, 1)$ and let M represent the set of all risk-neutral probability measures on the set $\mathbf{S}$. Assume $\mathbf{S}$ contains no arbitrage opportunities. If $(1/(1 + r_f))E_{\pi^{RN}}\tilde{x}(\theta, 1) = (1/(1 + r_f))E_{\tilde{\pi}^{RN}}\tilde{x}(\theta, 1)$ for any $\pi^{RN}, \tilde{\pi}^{RN} \in M$, then there exists a portfolio in $\mathbf{S}$ with the same $t = 1$ payoff as $\tilde{x}(\theta, 1)$.

It would be good to be able to dispense with the complications attendant to multiple risk-neutral probability measures on $\mathbf{S}$. When this is possible is the subject of Section 9.4.

9.4 UNIQUENESS

Examples 9.1 and 9.2 both possessed unique risk-neutral probability measures. They were also complete markets models. This illustrates an important general proposition.

> **Proposition 9.4:**
> Consider a set of securities $\mathbf{S}$ without arbitrage opportunities. Then $\mathbf{S}$ is complete if and only if there exists exactly one risk-neutral probability measure.
>
> **Proof:**
> Let us prove one side of the proposition, as it is particularly revealing. Suppose $\mathbf{S}$ is complete and there were two risk-neutral probability measures $\{\pi_j^{RN}: j = 1, 2, \ldots, J\}$ and $\{\tilde{\pi}_j^{RN}: j = 1, 2, \ldots, J\}$. Then there must be at least one state $\hat{j}$ for which $\pi_{\hat{j}}^{RN} \neq \tilde{\pi}_{\hat{j}}^{RN}$. Since the market is complete, one must be able to construct a portfolio P in $\mathbf{S}$ such that
>
> $$V_P(0) > 0, \text{ and } \begin{cases} V_P(\theta_j, 1) = 0 & j \neq \hat{j} \\ V_P(\theta_j, 1) = 1 & j = \hat{j} \end{cases}.$$
>
> This is simply the statement of the existence of an Arrow-Debreu security associated with $\theta_{\hat{j}}$.
> But then $\{\pi_j^{RN}: j = 1, 2, \ldots, J\}$ and $\{\tilde{\pi}_j^{RN}: j = 1, 2, \ldots, J\}$ cannot both be risk-neutral measures as, by Proposition 9.2,
>
> $$V_P(0) = \frac{1}{(1 + r_f)} E_{\pi^{RN}}\tilde{V}_P(\theta, 1) = \frac{\pi_{\hat{j}}^{RN}}{(1 + r_f)} \neq \frac{\tilde{\pi}_j^{RN}}{(1 + r_f)}$$
> $$= \frac{1}{(1 + r_f)} E_{\tilde{\pi}^{RN}}\tilde{V}_P(\theta, 1)$$
> $$= V_P(0), \text{ a contradiction.}$$
>
> Thus, there cannot be more than one risk-neutral probability measure in a complete market economy.

(continued)

Proposition 9.4: (*continued*)

We omit a formal proof of the other side of the proposition. Informally, if the market is not complete, then the fundamental securities do not span the space. Hence, the system of Equations (9.7ii) contains more unknowns than equations, yet they are all linearly independent (no arbitrage). There must be a multiplicity of solutions and hence a multiplicity of risk-neutral probability measures.

Concealed in the proof of Proposition 9.4 is an important observation: The price of an Arrow-Debreu security that pays 1 unit of payoff if event θ_j is realized and nothing otherwise must be $\pi_j^{RN}/(1 + r_f)$ the present value of the corresponding risk-neutral probability. In general,

$$q_j(0) = \frac{\pi_j^{RN}}{(1 + r_f)}$$

where $q_j(0)$ is the $t = 0$ price of a state claim paying 1 if and only if state θ_j realized. Provided the financial market is complete, risk-neutral valuation is nothing more than valuing an uncertain payoff in terms of the value of a replicating portfolio of Arrow-Debreu claims. Notice, however, that we thus identify the all-important Arrow-Debreu prices without having to impose any of the economic structure of Chapter 7; in particular, knowledge of the agents' preferences is not required. This approach can be likened to describing the Arrow-Debreu pricing theory from the perspective of Proposition 7.2, without any of the structure imposed in the first 5 sections of Chapter 7. It is possible, and less restrictive, to limit our inquiry to extracting Arrow-Debreu prices from the prices of a (complete) set of complex securities and proceed from there to price arbitrary cash flows. In the absence of further structure, nothing can be said, however, on the determinants of Arrow-Debreu prices (or risk-neutral probabilities).

Let us illustrate with the data of our second example. There we identified the unique risk-neutral measure to be:

$$\pi_1^{RN} = .3, \qquad \pi_2^{RN} = .6, \qquad \pi_3^{RN} = .1,$$

Together with $r_f = .1$, these values imply that the Arrow-Debreu security prices must be

$$q_0(1) = \frac{.3}{1.1} = .27; \qquad q_0(2) = \frac{.6}{1.1} = .55; \qquad q_0(3) = \frac{.1}{1.1} = .09.$$

Conversely, given a set of Arrow-Debreu claims with strictly positive prices, we can generate the corresponding risk-neutral probabilities and the risk-free rate. As noted in earlier chapters, the period zero price of a risk-free security (one that pays one unit of the numeraire in every date $t = 1$ state) in this setting is given by

$$p_{r_f} = \sum_{j=1}^{J} q_j(0), \text{ and thus}$$

$$(1 + r_f) = \frac{1}{p_{r_f}} = \frac{1}{\sum_{j=1}^{J} q_j(0)}$$

We define the risk-neutral probabilities $\{\pi^{RN}(\theta)\}$ according to

$$\pi_j^{RN} = \frac{q_j(0)}{\sum_{j=1}^{J} q_j(0)} \tag{9.9}$$

Clearly $\pi_j^{RN} > 0$ for each state j (since $q_j(0) > 0$ for every state) and, by construction $\sum_{j=1}^{J} \pi_j^{RN} = 1$. As a result, the set $\{\pi_j^{RN}\}$ qualifies as a risk-neutral probability measure.

Referring now to the example developed in Section 7.3, let us recall that we had found a complete set of Arrow-Debreu prices to be $q_0(1) = .24$; $q_0(2) = .3$; this means, in turn, that the unique risk-neutral measure for the economy there described is

$$\pi_1^{RN} = \frac{.24}{.54} = .444, \qquad \pi_2^{RN} = \frac{.3}{.54} = .556.$$

For complete markets we see that the relationship between strictly positively priced state claims and the risk-neutral probability measure is indeed an intimate one: each implies the other. Since, in the absence of arbitrage possibilities, there can exist only one set of state claims prices, and thus only one risk-neutral probability measure, Proposition 9.4 is reconfirmed.

9.5 INCOMPLETENESS

What about the case in which S is an incomplete set of securities? By Proposition 9.4 there will be a multiplicity of risk-neutral probabilities, but these will all give the same valuation to elements of S (Proposition 9.2). Consider, however, a $t = 1$ bounded state-contingent payoff vector $\tilde{x}(\theta, 1)$ that does not coincide with the payoff to any portfolio in S. By Proposition 9.4, different risk-neutral probability measures will assign different values to this payoff: essentially, its price is not well defined. It is possible, however, to establish *arbitrage bounds* on the value of this claim. For any risk-neutral probability π^{RN}, defined on S, consider the following quantities:

$$H_x = \inf\left\{ E_{\pi^{RN}}\left[\frac{\tilde{V}_P(\theta, 1)}{1 + r_f}\right] : V_P(\theta_j, 1) \geq x(\theta_j, 1) \text{ for all } j = 1, 2, \ldots, J \text{ and } P \in S \right\} \tag{9.10}$$

$$L_x = \sup\left\{ E_{\pi^{RN}}\left[\frac{\tilde{V}_P(\theta, 1)}{1 + r_f}\right] : V_P(\theta_j, 1) \leq x(\theta_j, 1) \text{ for all } j = 1, 2, \ldots, J \text{ and } P \in S \right\}. \tag{9.11}$$

In these evaluations we don't care what risk-neutral measure is used because any one of them gives identical valuations for all portfolios in S. Since, for some γ, $\gamma q^b(1) > x(\theta_j, 1)$, for all j, H_x is bounded above by $\gamma q^b(0)$, and hence is well defined (an analogous comment applies to L_x). The claim is that the no arbitrage price of x, $q^x(0)$ lies in the range

$$L_x \leq q^x(0) \leq H_x$$

To see why this must be so, suppose that $q^x(0) > H_x$ and let P^* be any portfolio in S for which

$q^x(0) > V_{P*}(0) > H_x$, and

$$V_{P*}(\theta_j, 1) \geq x(\theta_j, 1), \text{ for all } \theta_j, j = 1, 2, \ldots, J. \tag{9.12}$$

We know that such a $P*$ exists because the set

$$S_x = \{P: P \in S, V_P(\theta_j, 1) \geq x(\theta_j, 1), \text{ for all } \ldots, j = 1, 2, \ldots, J\}$$

is closed. Hence there is a $\hat{P} \in S_x$ such that $E_{\pi^{RN}}\tilde{V}_{\hat{P}}(\theta, 1) = H_x$. By the continuity of the expectations operator, we can find a $\lambda > 1$ such that $\lambda\hat{P} \in S_x$ and[5]

$$q^x(0) > \frac{1}{1 + r_f} E_{\pi^{RN}}\tilde{V}_{\lambda\hat{P}}(\theta, 1) = \lambda \frac{1}{1 + r_f} E_{\pi^{RN}}\tilde{V}_{\hat{P}}(\theta, 1) = \lambda H_x > H_x.$$

Since $\lambda > 1$, for all j, $V_{\lambda\hat{P}}(\theta_j, 1) > V_{\hat{P}}(\theta_j, 1) \geq x(\theta_j, 1)$; let $P* = \lambda\hat{P}$. Now the arbitrage argument: Sell the security with title to the cash flow $x(\theta_j, 1)$, and buy the portfolio $P*$. At time $t = 0$, you receive $q^x(0) - V_{P*}(0) > 0$, while at time $t = 1$ the cash flow from the portfolio, by Equation (9.12), fully covers the obligation under the short sale in every state; in other words, there is an arbitrage opportunity. An analogous argument demonstrates that $L_x \leq q^x(0)$.

In some cases it is readily possible to solve for these bounds.

Example 9.5:
Revisit, for example, our earlier Example 9.3, and consider the payoff.

	θ_1	θ_2	θ_3
$x(\hat{\theta}_j, 1)$:	0	0	1

This security is most surely not in the span of the securities (1.1, 1.1, 1.1) and (1, 2, 3), a fact that can be confirmed by observing that the system of equations implied by equaling

$$(0, 0, 1) = a(1.1, 1.1, 1.1) + b(1, 2, 3),$$

in other words, the system:

$$0 = 1.1a + b$$
$$0 = 1.1a + 2b$$
$$1 = 1.1a + 3b$$

has no solution. But any portfolio in S can be expressed as a linear combination of (1.1, 1.1, 1.1) and (1, 2, 3) and thus must be of the form

$$a(1.1, 1.1, 1.1) + b(1, 2, 3) = (a(1.1) + b, a(1.1) + 2b, a(1.1) + 3b)$$

for some a, b real numbers.
We also know that in computing H_x, L_x, any risk-neutral measure can be employed. Recall that we had identified the solution of Example 9.3 to be

$$(\pi_1^{RN}, \pi_2^{RN}, \pi_3^{RN}) \in \{(\lambda, .8 - 2\lambda, .2 + \lambda): 0 < \lambda < .4\}$$

Without loss of generality, choose $\lambda = .2$; thus

$$(\pi_1^{RN}, \pi_2^{RN}, \pi_3^{RN}) = (.2, .4, .4).$$

---

[5]By $\lambda\hat{P}$ we mean a portfolio with constituent bonds and stocks in the proportions $(\lambda n_p^b, \lambda n_p^b)$.

For any choice of a, b (thereby defining a $\tilde{V}_P(\theta; 1)$)

$$E_{\pi^{RN}}\left[\frac{\tilde{V}_P(\theta, 1)}{(1 + r_f)}\right] = \frac{.2\{(1.1)a + b\} + .4\{(1.1)a + 2b\} + .4\{(1.1)a + 3b\}}{1.1}$$

$$= \frac{(1.1)a + (2.2)b}{1.1} = a + 2b.$$

Thus,

$$H_x = \inf_{a,b \in R} \{(a + 2b): a(1.1) + b \geq 0, a(1.1) + 2b \geq 0, \text{ and } a(1.1) + 3b \geq 1\}$$

Similarly,

$$L_x = \sup_{a,b \in R} \{(a + 2b): a(1.1) + b \leq 0, a(1.1) + 2b \leq 0, \text{ and } a(1.1) + 3b \leq 1\}$$

Because the respective sets of admissible pairs are closed in R^2, we can replace inf and sup by, respectively, min and max.
Solving for H_x, L_x thus amounts to solving small linear programs. The solutions, obtained via MATLAB are detailed in Table 9-5.

TABLE 9-5	Solutions for H_x and L_x	
	H_x	L_x
a*	−.4545	−1.8182
b*	.5	1
H_x	.5455	
L_x		.1818

The value of the security (state claim), we may conclude, lies in the interval (.1818, .5455).

Before turning to the applications there is one additional point of clarification.

9.6   EQUILIBRIUM AND NO ARBITRAGE CONDITION

Thus far we have made no reference to financial equilibrium, in the sense discussed in earlier chapters. Clearly equilibrium implies no arbitrage opportunities: The presence of an arbitrage opportunity will induce investors to assume arbitrarily large short and long positions, which is inconsistent with the existence of equilibrium. The converse is also clearly not true. It could well be, in some specific market, that supply exceeds demand or conversely, without this situation opening up an arbitrage opportunity in the strict sense understood in this chapter. In what follows the attempt is made to convey the sense of risk-neutral valuation as an equilibrium phenomena.

To illustrate, let us return to the first example in Chapter 7. The basic data of that Arrow-Debreu equilibrium is provided in Table 9-6. The $t = 0$ corresponding equilibrium state prices are $q_1(0) = .24$ and $q_2(0) = .30$. In this case the risk-neutral probabilities are

$$\pi_1^{RN} = \frac{.24}{.54}, \text{ and } \pi_2^{RN} = \frac{.30}{.54}.$$

TABLE 9-6   The Exchange Economy of Section 7.3—Endowments and Preferences

	Endowments			*Preferences*
	t = 0	*t = 1*		
Agent 1	10	1	2	$U^1(c_0, c_1) = \frac{1}{2}c_0^1 + .9(\frac{1}{3}\ln(c_1^1 + \frac{2}{3}\ln(c_2^1))$
Agent 2	5	4	6	$U^2(c_0, c_1) = \frac{1}{2}c_0^2 + .9(\frac{1}{3}\ln(c_1^2 + \frac{2}{3}\ln(c_2^2))$

Suppose a stock were traded where $q^e(\theta_1, 1) = 1$, and $q^e(\theta_2, 1) = 3$. By risk-neutral valuation (or equivalently, using Arrow-Debreu prices), its period $t = 0$ price must be

$$q^e(0) = .54\left[\frac{.24}{.54}(1) + \frac{.30}{.54}(3)\right] = 1.14;$$

the price of the risk-free security is $q^b(1) = .54$.

Verifying this calculation is a bit tricky because, in the original equilibrium, this stock, in particular, was not traded. Introducing such assets requires us to decide what the original endowments must be, that is, who owns what in period 0. We cannot just add the stock arbitrarily, as the wealth levels of the agents would change as a result and, in general, this would alter the state prices, risk-neutral probabilities, and all subsequent valuations. The solution of this problem is to compute the equilibrium for a similar economy in which the two agents have the same preferences and in which the only traded assets are this stock and a bond. Furthermore, the initial endowments of these instruments must be such as to guarantee the same period $t = 0$ and $t = 1$ net endowment allocations as in the first equilibrium.

Let $\hat{n}_e^i, \hat{n}_b^i$ denote, respectively, the initial endowments of the equity and debt securities of agent $i, i = 1, 2$. The equivalence noted previously is accomplished as outlined in Table 9-7 (see Appendix 9.2).

A straightforward computation of the equilibrium prices yields the same $q^e(0) = 1.14$, and $q^b(1) = .54$ as predicted by risk-neutral valuation.

We conclude this section with one additional remark. Suppose one of the two agents were risk neutral; without loss of generality let this be agent 1. Under the original endowment scheme, his problem becomes:

$$\max(10 + 1q_1(0) + 2q_2(0) - c_1^1q_1(0) - c_2^1q_2(0)) + .9(\frac{1}{3}c_1^1 + \frac{2}{3}c_2^1)$$
$$\text{s.t. } c_1^1q_1(0) + c_2^1q_2(0) \leq 10 + q_1(0) + 2q_2(0).$$

TABLE 9-7   Initial Holdings of Equity and Debt Achieving Equivalence with Arrow-Debreu Equilibrium Endowments

	t = 0		
	Consumption	$\hat{n}_e^i$	$\hat{n}_b^i$
Agent 1	10	½	½
Agent 2	5	1	3

The first order conditions are

$$c_1^1: q_1(0) = \tfrac{1}{3} \cdot 0.9$$
$$c_2^1: q_2(0) = \tfrac{2}{3} \cdot 0.9$$

from which it follows that $\pi_1^{RN} = (\tfrac{1}{3} 0.9)/0.9 = \tfrac{1}{3}$ while $\pi_2^{RN} = (\tfrac{2}{3} 0.9)/0.9 = \tfrac{2}{3}$, that is, in equilibrium, the risk-neutral probabilities coincide with the true probabilities. This is the source of the term *risk-neutral probabilities:* If at least one agent is risk neutral, the risk-neutral probabilities and the true probabilities coincide.

We conclude from this example that risk-neutral valuation holds in equilibrium, as it must because equilibrium implies no arbitrage. The risk-neutral probabilities thus obtained, however, are to be uniquely identified with that equilibrium, and it is meaningful to use them only for valuing securities that are elements of the participants' original endowments.

9.7 APPLICATION: MAXIMIZING THE EXPECTED UTILITY OF TERMINAL WEALTH

9.7.1 PORTFOLIO INVESTMENT AND RISK-NEUTRAL PROBABILITIES

Risk-neutral probabilities are intimately related to the *basis* or the set of fundamental securities in an economy. Under no arbitrage, given the prices of fundamental securities, we obtain a risk-neutral probability measure, and vice versa. This raises the possibility that it may be possible to formulate any problem in wealth allocation, for example the classic consumption-savings problem, in the setting of risk-neutral valuation. In this section we consider a number of these connections.

The simplest portfolio allocation problem with which we have dealt involves an investor choosing a portfolio so as to maximize the expected utility of his period $t = 1$ (terminal) wealth (we retain, without loss of generality, the two-period framework). In our current notation, this problem takes the form: choose portfolio P, among all feasible portfolios, (i.e., P must be composed of securities in $\boldsymbol{S}$ and the date-0 value of this portfolio (its acquisition price) cannot exceed initial wealth) so as to maximize expected utility of terminal wealth, which corresponds to the date-1 value of P:

$$\max_{\{n_P^b, n_P^i, i = 1,2,\ldots,N\}} EU(\tilde{V}_P(\theta, 1))$$
$$\text{s.t. } V_P(0) = V_0, P \in \boldsymbol{S}, \tag{9.13}$$

where V_0 is the investor's initial wealth, $U(\ )$ is his period utility function, assumed to have the standard properties, and n_P^b, n_P^i are the positions (not proportions, but units of indicated assets) in the risk-free asset and the risky asset $i = 1, 2, \ldots, N$, respectively, defining portfolio P. It is not obvious that there should be a relationship between the solvability of this problem and the existence of a risk-neutral measure, but this is the case.

Proposition 9.5:
If Equation (9.13) has a solution, then there are no arbitrage opportunities in $\boldsymbol{S}$. Hence there exists a risk-neutral measure on $\boldsymbol{S}$.

(continued)

Proposition 9.5 (*continued*)

Proof:

The idea is that an arbitrage opportunity is a costless way to endlessly improve upon the (presumed) optimum. So no optimum can exist. More formally, we prove the proposition by contradiction. Let $\hat{P} \in S$ be a solution to Equation (9.13), and let $\hat{P}$ have the structure $\{n_{\hat{P}}^b, n_{\hat{P}}^i: i = 1, 2, \ldots, N\}$. Assume also that there exists an arbitrage opportunity, in other words, a portfolio $\tilde{P}$, with structure $\{n_{\tilde{P}}^b, n_{\tilde{P}}^i: i = 1, 2, \ldots, N\}$, such that $V_{\tilde{P}}(0) = 0$ and $E\tilde{V}_{\tilde{P}}(\theta, 1) > 0$. Consider the portfolio $P*$ with structure

$$\{n_{P*}^b, n_{P*}^i: i = 1, 2, \ldots, N\}$$
$$n_{P*}^b = n_{\hat{P}}^b + n_{\tilde{P}}^b \text{ and } n_{P*}^i = n_{\hat{P}}^i + n_{\tilde{P}}^i, i = 1, 2, \ldots, N$$

$P*$ is still feasible for the agent and it provides strictly more wealth in at least one state. Since $U(\ )$ is strictly increasing,

$$EU(\tilde{V}_{P*}(\theta, 1)) > EU(V_{\hat{P}}(\theta, 1)).$$

This contradicts $\hat{P}$ as a solution to Equation (9.13). We conclude that there cannot exist any arbitrage opportunities and thus, by Proposition 9.1, a risk-neutral probability measure on S must exist.

Proposition 9.5 informs us that arbitrage opportunities are incompatible with an optimal allocation—the allocation can always be improved upon by incorporating units of the arbitrage portfolio. More can be said. The solution to the agents' problem can, in fact, be used to identify the risk-neutral probabilities. To see this, let us first rewrite the objective function in Equation (9.13) as follows:

$$\max_{\{n_P^i: i=1,2,\ldots,N\}} EU\left((1 + r_f)\left\{V_0 - \sum_{i=1}^{N} n_P^i q_i^e(0)\right\} + \sum_{i=1}^{N} n_P^i \tilde{q}_i^e(\theta, 1)\right)$$

$$= \max_{\{n_P^i: i=1,2,\ldots,N\}} \sum_{j=1}^{J} \pi_j U\left((1 + r_f)\left\{V_0 + \sum_{i=1}^{N} n_P^i \frac{q_i^e(\theta_j, 1)}{1 + r_f} - \sum_{i=1}^{N} n_P^i q_i^e(0)\right\}\right)$$

$$= \max_{\{n_P^i: i=1,2,\ldots,N\}} \sum_{j=1}^{J} \pi_j U\left((1 + r_f)\left\{V_0 + \sum_{i=1}^{N} n_P^i \left(\frac{q_i^e(\theta_j, 1)}{1 + r_f} - q_i^e(0)\right)\right\}\right) \quad \textbf{(9.14)}$$

The necessary and sufficient first-order conditions for this problem are of the form:

$$0 = \sum_{j=1}^{J} \pi_j U_1\left((1 + r_f)\left\{V_0 + \sum_{i=1}^{N} n_P^i \left(\frac{q_i^e(\theta_j, 1)}{1 + r_f} - q_i^e(0)\right)\right\}\right)$$

$$\times (1 + r_f)\left[\frac{q_i^e(\theta_j, 1)}{1 + r_f} - q_i^e(0)\right] \quad \textbf{(9.15)}$$

Note that the quantity $\pi_j U_1(V_P(\theta_j, 1))(1 + r_f)$ is strictly positive because $\pi_j > 0$ and $U(\ )$ is strictly increasing. If we normalize these quantities we can convert them into probabilities. Let us define

$$\check{\pi}_j = \frac{\pi_j U_1(V_P(\theta_j, 1))(1 + r_f)}{\sum\limits_{j=1}^{J} \pi_j U_1(V_P(\theta_j, 1))(1 + r_f)} = \frac{\pi_j U_1(V_P(\theta_j, 1))}{\sum\limits_{j=1}^{J} \pi_j U_1(V_P(\theta_j, 1))}, j = 1, 2, \ldots, J.$$

Since $\check{\pi}_j > 0$, $j = 1, 2, \ldots, J$, $\sum_{j=1}^{J} \check{\pi}_j = 1$, and, by (9.15)

$$q_i^e(0) = \sum_{j=1}^{J} \check{\pi}_j \frac{q_i^e(\theta_j, 1)}{1 + r_f};$$

these three properties establish the set $\{\check{\pi}_j \colon j = 1, 2, \ldots, N\}$ as a set of risk-neutral probabilities.

We have just proved one half of the following proposition:

Proposition 9.6:

Let $\{n_{P*}^b, n_{P*}^i \colon i = 1, 2, \ldots, N\}$ be the solution to the optimal portfolio problem (9.13). Then the set $\{\pi_j^* \colon j = 1, 2, \ldots, J\}$, defined by

$$\pi_j^* = \frac{\pi_j U_1(V_{P*}(\theta_j, 1))}{\displaystyle\sum_{j=1}^{J} \pi_j U_1(V_{P*}(\theta_j, 1))}, \tag{9.16}$$

constitutes a risk-neutral probability measure on $\mathbf{S}$. Conversely, if there exists a risk-neutral probability measure $\{\pi_j^{RN} \colon j = 1, 2, \ldots, J\}$ on $\mathbf{S}$, there must exist a concave, strictly increasing, differentiable utility function $U(\ )$ and an initial wealth V_0 for which Equation (9.13) has a solution.

Proof:

We have proved the first part. The proof of the less important *converse* proposition is relegated to Appendix 9.3.

9.7.2 SOLVING THE PORTFOLIO PROBLEM

Now we can turn to solving Equation (9.13). Since there is as much information in the risk-neutral probabilities as in the security prices, it should be possible to fashion a solution to Equation (9.13) using that latter construct. Here we will choose to restrict our attention to the case in which the financial markets are complete.

In this case there exists exactly one risk-neutral measure, which we denote by $\{\pi_j^{RN} \colon j = 1, 2, \ldots, N\}$. Since the solution to Equation (9.13) will be a portfolio in $\mathbf{S}$ that maximizes the date $t = 1$ expected utility of wealth, the solution procedure can be decomposed into a two-step process:

Step 1: Solve $\qquad\qquad \max EU(\tilde{x}(\theta, 1))$

$$\text{s.t. } E_{\pi^{RN}}\left(\frac{\tilde{x}(\theta, 1)}{1 + r_f}\right) = V_0 \tag{9.17}$$

The solution to this problem identifies the feasible uncertain payoff that maximizes the agent's expected utility. But why is the constraint a perfect summary of feasibility? The constraint makes sense first because, under complete markets, every uncertain payoff lies in $\mathbf{S}$. Furthermore, in the absence of arbitrage opportunities, every payoff is valued at the present value of its expected payoff computed using the unique risk-neutral probability measure. The essence of the budget constraint is that a feasible payoff be affordable: that its price equals V_0, the agent's initial wealth.

Step 2: Find the portfolio P in S such that $V_P(\theta_j, 1) = x(\theta_j, 1), j = 1, 2 \ldots, J$.

In step 2 we simply find the precise portfolio allocations of fundamental securities that give rise to the optimal uncertain payoff identified in step 1. The theory is all in step 1; in fact, we have used all of our major results thus far to write the constraint in the indicated form.

Now let us work out a problem, first abstractly and then by a numerical example. Equation (9.17) of step 1 can be written as

$$\max E_\pi U(\tilde{x}(\theta, 1)) - \lambda \left[E_{\pi^{RN}} \left(\frac{\tilde{x}(\theta, 1)}{1 + r_f} \right) - V_0 \right], \qquad (9.18)$$

where λ denotes the Lagrange multiplier and where we have made explicit the probability distributions with respect to which each of the expectations is being taken.

Equation (9.18) can be rewritten as

$$\max_x \sum_{j=1}^{J} \pi_j \left[U(x(\theta_j, 1)) - \lambda \frac{\pi_j^{RN}}{\pi_j} \frac{x(\theta_j, 1)}{(1 + r_f)} \right] - \lambda V_0. \qquad (9.19)$$

The necessary first-order conditions, one equation for each state θ_j, are thus

$$U_1(x(\theta_j, 1)) = \frac{\lambda \pi_j^{RN}}{\pi_j(1 + r_f)}, j = 1, 2, \ldots, J \qquad (9.20)$$

from which the optimal asset payoffs may be obtained as per

$$x(\theta_j, 1) = U_1^{-1} \left(\frac{\lambda \pi_j^{RN}}{\pi_j(1 + r_f)} \right), j = 1, 2, \ldots, J \qquad (9.21)$$

with U_1^{-1} representing the inverse of the MU function.

The Lagrange multiplier λ is the remaining unknown. It must satisfy the budget constraint when Equation (9.21) is substituted for the solution; that is, λ must satisfy

$$E_{\pi^{RN}} \left(\frac{1}{(1 + r_f)} U_1^{-1} \left(\frac{\lambda \pi_j^{RN}}{\pi_j(1 + r_f)} \right) \right) = V_0. \qquad (9.22)$$

A value for λ that satisfies Equation (9.22) may not exist. For all the standard utility functions that we have dealt with, $U(x) = \ln x$ or $x^{1-\gamma}/1 - \gamma$ or $e^{-\nu x}$, however, it can be shown that such a λ will exist. Let $\hat{\lambda}$ solve Equation (9.22); the optimal feasible contingent payoff is thus given by

$$x(\theta_j, 1) = U_1^{-1} \left(\frac{\hat{\lambda} \pi_j^{RN}}{\pi_j(1 + r_f)} \right) \text{ (from Equation (9.21)).} \qquad (9.23)$$

Given this payoff, step 2 involves finding the portfolio of fundamental securities that will give rise to it. This is accomplished by solving the customary system of linear equations.

9.7.3 A NUMERICAL EXAMPLE

Now, a numerical example: Let us choose a utility function from the familiar CRRA class, $U(x) = x^{1-\gamma}/1 - \gamma$, and consider the market structure of Example 9.2: Markets are complete and the unique risk-neutral probability measure is as noted.

Since $U_1(x) = x^{-\gamma}$, $U_1^{-1}(y) = y^{-1/\gamma}$, Equation (9.21) reduces to

$$x(\theta_j, 1) = \left(\frac{\lambda \pi_j^{RN}}{\pi_j(1 + r_f)} \right)^{-1/\gamma} \tag{9.24}$$

from which follows the counterpart to Equation (9.22):

$$\sum_{j=1}^{J} \pi_j^{RN} \left(\frac{1}{(1 + r_f)} \left(\frac{\lambda \pi_j^{RN}}{\pi_j(1 + r_f)} \right)^{-1/\gamma} \right) = V_0.$$

Isolating λ gives

$$\hat{\lambda} = \left\{ \sum_{j=1}^{J} \pi_j^{RN} \left(\frac{1}{(1 + r_f)} \left(\frac{\pi_j^{RN}}{\pi_j(1 + r_f)} \right)^{-1/\gamma} \right) \right\}^{\gamma} V_0^{-\gamma}. \tag{9.25}$$

Let us consider some numbers: Assume $\gamma = 3$, $V_0 = 10$, and that (π_1, π_2, π_3), the true probability distribution, takes on the value ($\frac{1}{3}$, $\frac{1}{3}$, $\frac{1}{3}$). Refer to Example 9.2 where the risk-neutral probability distribution was found to be $(\pi_1^{RN}, \pi_2^{RN}, \pi_3^{RN}) = (.3, .6, .1)$. Accordingly, from (9.25)

$$\hat{\lambda} = 10^{-3} \left\{ .3 \left(\frac{1}{(1.1)} \left(\frac{.3}{(\frac{1}{3})(1.1)} \right)^{-1/3} \right) + .6 \left(\frac{1}{(1.1)} \left(\frac{.6}{(\frac{1}{3})(1.1)} \right)^{-1/3} \right) \right.$$

$$\left. + .1 \left(\frac{1}{(1.1)} \left(\frac{.1}{(\frac{1}{3})(1.1)} \right)^{-1/3} \right) \right\}^3$$

$$\hat{\lambda} = \left(\frac{1}{1000} \right) \{.2916 + .4629 + .14018\}^3 = .0007161$$

The distribution of the state-contingent payoffs follows from (9.24):

$$x(\theta_j, 1) = \left(\frac{.0007161 \pi_j^{RN}}{\pi_j(1 + r_f)} \right)^{-1/\gamma} = \begin{cases} 11.951 & j = 1 \\ 9.485 & j = 2 \\ 17.236 & j = 3 \end{cases} \tag{9.26}$$

The final step is to convert this payoff to a portfolio structure via the identification:

$$(11.951, 9.485, 17.236) = n_P^b(1.1, 1.1, 1.1) + n_P^1(3, 2, 1) + n_P^2(1, 4, 6) \text{ or}$$
$$11.951 = 1.1n_P^b + 3n_P^1 + n_P^2$$
$$9.485 = 1.1n_P^b + 2n_P^1 + 4n_P^2$$
$$17.236 = 1.1n_P^b + n_P^1 + bn_P^2$$

The solution to this system of equations is

$$n_P^b = 97.08 \qquad \text{(invest a lot in the risk-free asset)}$$
$$n_P^1 = -28.192 \quad \text{(short the first stock)}$$
$$n_P^2 = -10.225 \quad \text{(also short the second stock)}$$

Lastly, we confirm that this portfolio is feasible:

Cost of portfolio $= 97.08 + 2(-28.192) + 3(-10.225) = 10 = V_0$, the agent's initial wealth, as required.

Note the computational simplicity of this method: We need only solve a linear system of equations. Using more standard methods would result in a system of three non-linear equations to solve. Analogous methods are also available to provide bounds in the case of market incompleteness.

9.8 CONCLUSIONS

Under the procedure of risk-neutral valuation, we construct a new probability distribution—the risk-neutral probabilities—under which all assets may be valued at their expected payoff discounted at the risk-free rate. More formally it would be said that we undertake a *transformation of measure* by which all assets are then expected to earn the risk-free rate. The key to our ability to find such a measure is that the financial markets exhibit no arbitrage opportunities.

Our setting was the standard Arrow-Debreu two-period equilibrium and we observed the intimate relationship between the risk-neutral probabilities and the relative prices of state claims. Here the practical applicability of the idea is limited. Applying these ideas to the real world would, after all, require a denumeration of all future states of nature and the contingent payoffs to all securities in order to compute the relevant risk-neutral probabilities, something for which there would be no general agreement.

Even so, this particular way of approaching the optimal portfolio problem was shown to be a source of useful insights. In more restrictive settings, it is also practically powerful and, in Chapter 12, will be seen to lie behind all modern derivatives pricing.

References

Harrison, M., and D. Kreps, "Martingales and Multi-Period Securities Market," *Journal of Economic Theory* 20 (1979): 381–408.

Pliska, S. R., *Introduction to Mathematical Finance: Discrete Time Models*, Malden, Mass.: Basil Blackwell, 1997.

A P P E N D I X   9 . 1

CAPM-Based Certainty Equivalents

In this appendix, we develop the CAPM-based formula, which allows for risk-free discounting by transforming period-by-period cash flows into their market certainty equivalents. In the case of a one-period cash flow, this is accomplished as follows: For any (one period) asset j,

$$E\tilde{r}_j = r_f + \beta_j[E\tilde{R}_M - r_f],$$

where $\tilde{r}_j = (C\tilde{F}_j^1/P_0) - 1$ and P_0 is the to-be-estimated current value of the cash flow. Substituting this expression into SML yields,

$$E\left(\frac{C\tilde{F}_j^1}{P_0} - 1\right)$$
$$= r_f + \frac{\text{cov}\left(\dfrac{C\tilde{F}_j^1}{P_0} - 1, \tilde{R}_M\right)}{\sigma_M^2}[E\tilde{R}_M - r_f]$$

$$\frac{C\tilde{F}_j^1}{P_0} - 1 = r_f + \frac{1}{P_0}\text{cov}(C\tilde{F}_j^1, \tilde{R}_M)\left[\frac{E\tilde{R}_M - r_f}{\sigma_M^2}\right].$$

Solving for P_0 yields

$$P_0 = \frac{EC\tilde{F}_j^1 - \text{cov}(C\tilde{F}_j^1, \tilde{R}_M)\left[\dfrac{E\tilde{R}_M - r_f}{\sigma_M^2}\right]}{1 + r_f}.$$

A P P E N D I X   9 . 2

Finding the Stock and Bond Economy That Is Directly Analogous to the Arrow-Debreu Economy in Which Only State Claims Are Traded

The text is summarized in Table A9-1.

We wish to price the stock and bond with the payoff structures in Table A9-2.

In order for the economy in which the stock and bond are traded to be equivalent to the Arrow-Debreu economy where state claims are traded, we need the former to imply the same effective endowment structure. This is accomplished as follows:

Agent 1: Let his endowments of the stock and bond be denoted by $\hat{z}_1^e$ and $\hat{z}_1^b$, then,

In state θ_1: $\hat{z}_1^b + \hat{z}_1^e = 1$
In state θ_2: $\hat{z}_1^b + 3\hat{z}_1^e = 2$
Solution: $\hat{z}_1^e = \hat{z}_1^b = \frac{1}{2}$ (half a share and half a bond).

Agent 2: Let his endowments of the stock and bond be denoted by $\hat{z}_2^e$ and $\hat{z}_2^b$, then,

In state θ_2: $\hat{z}_1^b + \hat{z}_2^e = 4$
In state θ_2: $3\hat{z}_2^b + \hat{z}_2^e = 6$
Solution: $\hat{z}_2^e = 1, \hat{z}_2^b = 3$

With these endowments the decision problems of the agent become:

Agent 1:

$$\max_{z_1^e, z_1^b} \tfrac{1}{2}(10 + \tfrac{1}{2}q^e + \tfrac{1}{2}q^b - z_1^e q^e - z_1^b q^b)$$
$$+ .9(\tfrac{1}{3}\ln(z_1^e + z_1^b) + \tfrac{2}{3}\ln(3z_1^e + z_1^b)$$

Agent 2:

$$\max_{z_2^e, z_2^b} \tfrac{1}{2}(5 + q^e + 3q^b - z_2^e q^e - z_2^b q^b)$$
$$+ .9(\tfrac{1}{3}\ln(z_2^e + z_2^b) + \tfrac{2}{3}\ln(3z_2^e + z_2^b))$$

The FOCs are

$$z_1^e: \ \tfrac{1}{2}q^e = .9\left(\frac{1}{3}\left(\frac{1}{z_1^e + z_1^b}\right) + \frac{2}{3}\left(\frac{1}{3z_1^e + z_1^b}\right)(3)\right)$$

$$z_1^b: \ \tfrac{1}{2}q^b = .9\left(\frac{1}{3}\left(\frac{1}{z_1^e + z_1^b}\right) + \frac{2}{3}\left(\frac{1}{3z_1^e + z_1^b}\right)\right)$$

$$z_2^e: \ \tfrac{1}{2}q^e = .9\left(\frac{1}{3}\left(\frac{1}{z_2^e + z_2^b}\right) + \frac{2}{3}\left(\frac{1}{3z_2^e + z_2^b}\right)(3)\right)$$

$$z_2^b: \ \tfrac{1}{2}q^b = .9\left(\frac{1}{3}\left(\frac{1}{z_2^e + z_2^b}\right) + \frac{2}{3}\left(\frac{1}{3z_2^e + z_2^b}\right)(1)\right)$$

Since these securities span the space and since the period 1 and period 2 endowments are

TABLE A9-1 The Arrow-Debreu Economy			
	Endowments		*Preferences*
	$t = 0$	$t = 1$	
		θ_1	θ_2	
Agent 1	10	1	2	$\frac{1}{2}c_0^1 + .9(\frac{1}{3}\ln(c_1^1) + \frac{2}{3}\ln(c_2^1))$
Agent 2	5	4	6	$\frac{1}{2}c_0^2 + .9(\frac{1}{3}\ln(c_1^2) + \frac{2}{3}\ln(c_2^2))$

TABLE A9-2	Payoff Structures	
_t = 0_	_t = 1_	
	θ_1	θ_2
$-q^e(0)$	1	3
$-q^b(0)$	1	1

the same, the real consumption allocations must be the same as in the Arrow-Debreu economy:

$$c_1^1 = c_1^2 = 2.5$$
$$c_2^1 = c_2^2 = 4$$

Thus,

$$q^e = 2(.9)\left\{\frac{1}{3}\left(\frac{1}{2.5}\right) + \frac{2}{3}\left(\frac{1}{4}\right)3\right\} = 1.14$$

$$q^b = 2(.9)\left\{\frac{1}{3}\left(\frac{1}{2.5}\right) + \frac{2}{3}\left(\frac{1}{4}\right)\right\} = .54,$$

as computed previously.

To compute the corresponding security holding, observe that:

Agent 1:

$$\begin{aligned} z_1^e + z_1^b &= 2.5 \\ 3z_1^e + z_1^b &= 4 \end{aligned} \Rightarrow \begin{aligned} z_1^e &= .75 \\ z_1^b &= 1.75 \end{aligned}$$

Agent 2: (same holdings)

$$z_2^e = .75$$
$$z_2^b = 1.75$$

Supply must equal demand in equilibrium:

$$\hat{z}_1^e + \hat{z}_2^e = \tfrac{1}{2} + 1 = 1.5 = z_1^e + z_2^e$$
$$\hat{z}_1^b + \hat{z}_2^b = \tfrac{1}{2} + 3 = 3.5 = z_1^b + z_2^b$$

The period zero consumptions are identical to the earlier calculation as well.

Proof of the Second Part of Proposition 9.6

Define $\hat{U}(x, \theta_j) = x\{\pi_j^{RN}/\pi_j(1 + r_f)\}$, where $\{\pi_j: j = 1, 2, \ldots, J\}$ are the true objective state probabilities. This is a state-dependent utility function that is linear in wealth. We will show that for this function, Equation (9.13), indeed, has a solution. Consider an arbitrary allocation of wealth to the various fundamental assets $\{n_p^i: j = 1, 2, \ldots, J\}$ and let P denote that portfolio. Fix the wealth at any level V_0, arbitrary. We next compute the expected utility associated with this portfolio, taking advantage of representation (9.14):

$$E\hat{U}(\tilde{V}_p(\theta, 1))$$

$$= E\hat{U}\left\{(1 + r_f)\left[V_0 + \sum_{i=1}^{N} n_p^i\right.\right.$$

$$\times \left.\left(\frac{\tilde{q}_i^e(\theta, 1)}{(1 + r_f)} - q_i^e(0)\right)\right]\}$$

$$= \sum_{j=1}^{J} \pi_j(1 + r_f)\left\{V_0 + \sum_{i=1}^{N} n_p^i\right.$$

$$\times \left.\left(\frac{q_i^e(\theta_j, 1)}{(1 + r_f)} - q_i^e(0)\right)\right\}\frac{\pi_j^{RN}}{\pi_j(1 + r_f)}$$

$$= \sum_{j=1}^{J} \pi_j^{RN}\left\{V_0 + \sum_{i=1}^{N} n_p^i\left(\frac{q_i^e(\theta_j, 1)}{(1 + r_f)} - q_i^e(0)\right)\right\}$$

$$= \sum_{j=1}^{J} \pi_j^{RN} V_0 + \sum_{j=1}^{J} \pi_j^{RN} \sum_{i=1}^{N} n_p^i$$

$$\times \left(\frac{q_i^e(\theta_j, 1)}{(1 + r_f)} - q_i^e(0)\right)$$

$$= V_0 + \sum_{i=1}^{N} n_p^i\left(\sum_{j=1}^{J} \pi_j^{RN}\left(\frac{q_i^e(\theta_j, 1)}{(1 + r_f)} - q_i^e(0)\right)\right)$$

$$= V_0.$$

In other words, with this utility function, every trading strategy has the same value. Thus problem (9.13) has, trivially, a solution.

CHAPTER 10

THE CONSUMPTION CAPITAL ASSET PRICING MODEL (CCAPM)

10.1   INTRODUCTION

So far, our asset pricing models have been either one-period models, such as the CAPM, or multiperiod but static, such as the Arrow-Debreu model. In the latter case, even if a large number of future periods is assumed, all decisions including security trades take place at date zero. It is in that sense that the Arrow-Debreu model is static. Reality is different, however. Assets are traded every period, as new information becomes available, and decisions are made sequentially, one period at a time, all the while keeping in mind the fact that today's decisions impact tomorrow's opportunities. Our objective in this chapter is to capture these dynamic features and price assets in such an environment.

Besides adding an important dimension of realism, another advantage of a dynamic setup is to make it possible to draw the link between the financial markets and the real side of the economy. Again, strictly speaking, this can be accomplished within an Arrow-Debreu economy. The main issues, however, require a richer dynamic context where real production decisions are not made once and for all at the beginning of time, but progressively, as time evolves. Building a model in which we can completely understand how real events impact the financial side of the economy in the spirit of fundamental financial analysis is beyond the scope of the present chapter. The model discussed here, however, opens up interesting possibilities in this regard, which current research is attempting to exploit. We will point out possible directions as we go along.

10.2   THE REPRESENTATIVE AGENT HYPOTHESIS AND ITS NOTION OF EQUILIBRIUM

10.2.1   AN INFINITELY LIVED REPRESENTATIVE AGENT

To accomplish these goals in a model of complete generality (in other words, with many different agents and firms) and in a way that asset prices can be tractably computed is beyond the present capability of economic science. As an alternative, we will make life simpler by postulating many *identical* infinitely lived consumers. This allows us to examine the decisions of a representative, stand-in consumer and explore their implications for asset pricing. In particular, we will assume that agents act to maximize the expected present value of discounted utility of consumption over their entire, infinite, lifetimes:

$$\max E\left(\sum_{t=0}^{\infty} \delta^t U(\tilde{c}_t)\right),$$

where δ is the discount factor and $U(\ )$ the period utility function where $U'(\ ) > 0$, $U''(\ ) < 0$. This construct is the natural generalization to the case of infinite lifetimes of the preferences considered in our earlier two-period example. Its use can be justified by the following considerations.

First, if we model the economy as ending at some terminal date T (as opposed to assuming an infinite horizon), then the agent's investment behavior will reflect this fact. In the last period of his life, in particular, he will stop saving, liquidate his portfolio, and consume its entire value. There is no real-world counterpart for this action as the real economy continues forever. Assuming an infinite horizon eliminates these terminal date complications. Second, it can be shown, under fairly general conditions, that an infinitely lived agent setup is formally equivalent to one in which agents live only a finite number of periods themselves, provided they derive utility from the utility of their descendants (a bequest motive). This argument is detailed in Barro (1974).

Restrictive as it may seem, the identical agents assumption can be justified by the fact that, in a competitive equilibrium with complete securities markets, there is an especially intuitive sense of a representative agent: one whose utility function is a weighted average of the utilities of the various agents in the economy. In Box 10-1 we detail the precise way in which one can construct such a representative individual and we discuss some of the issues at stake.

BOX 10-1

Constructing a Representative Agent

In order to illustrate the issue, let us return to the two-period ($t = 0, 1$) Arrow-Debreu economy considered earlier. In that economy, each agent k, $k = 1, 2, \ldots, K$, solves:

$$\max U^k(c_0^k) + \delta \sum_{\theta=1}^{N} \pi_\theta U^k(c_\theta^k)$$

$$\text{s.t. } c_0^k + \sum_{\theta=1}^{N} q_\theta c_\theta^k \le e_0^k + \sum_{\theta=1}^{N} q_\theta e_\theta^k$$

where the price of period 0 endowment is normalized to 1, and the endowments of a typical agent k are described by the vector

$$\begin{pmatrix} e_0^k \\ e_1^k \\ \vdots \\ e_N^k \end{pmatrix}.$$

In equilibrium, not only are the allocations optimal, but at the prevailing prices, supply equals demand in every market:

$$\sum_{k=0}^{K} c_0^k = \sum_{k=1}^{K} e_0^k, \text{ and}$$

$$\sum_{k=1}^{K} c_{\theta_j}^k = \sum_{k=1}^{K} e_j^k, \text{ for every state } \theta_j.$$

(continued)

BOX 10-1 (*continued*)

We know this competitive equilibrium allocation is Pareto optimal: No one can be made better off without making someone else worse off. One important implication of this property for our problem is that there exists some set of weights $(\lambda_1, \ldots, \lambda_K)$, which in general will depend on the initial endowments, such that the solution to the following problem gives an allocation that is identical to the equilibrium allocation:

$$\max \sum_{k=1}^{K} \lambda_k \left\{ U^k(c_0^k) + \delta^k \sum_{\theta=1}^{N} \pi_\theta U^k(c_\theta^k) \right\}$$

$$\text{s.t. } \sum_{k=1}^{K} c_0^k = \sum_{k=1}^{K} e_0^k$$

$$\text{and, for each } \theta: \sum_{k=1}^{K} c_\theta^k = \sum_{k=1}^{K} e_\theta^k;$$

$$\sum_{k=1}^{K} \lambda_k = 1; \lambda_k \geq 0 \text{ for all } k.$$

This maximization is meant to represent the problem of a benevolent central planner attempting to allocate the aggregate resources of the economy so as to maximize the weighted sum of the utilities of the individual agents. This result is suggestive of the form the representative agent's preference ordering, defined over aggregate consumption, can take (the representative agent is denoted by the superscript A):

$$U^A(c_0^A, c_\theta^A) = U_0^A(c_0^A) + \sum_{\theta=1}^{N} \pi_\theta U^A(c_\theta^A),$$

where,

$$U_0^A(c_0^A) = \sum_{k=1}^{K} \lambda_k U_0^k(c_0^k) \text{ with}$$

$$\sum_{k=1}^{K} c_0^k = \sum_{k=1}^{K} e_0^k \equiv c_0^A$$

$$U^A(c_\theta^A) = \sum_{k=1}^{K} \delta^k \lambda_k U^k(c_\theta^k) \text{ with}$$

$$\sum_{k=1}^{K} c_\theta^k = \sum_{k=1}^{K} e_\theta^k \equiv c_\theta^A, \text{ for each state } \theta,$$

where c_0^k, c_θ^k solve the initial problem.

In this case, the aggregate utility function directly takes into account the distribution of consumption across agents. This setup generalizes to as many periods as we like and, with

certain modifications, to an infinite horizon. It is an intuitive sense of a representative agent as one who constitutes a weighted average of all the economy's participants.

A conceptual problem with this discussion resides in the fact that, in general, the weights $\{\lambda_1, \lambda_2, \ldots, \lambda_K\}$ will depend on the initial endowments: Loosely speaking, the agent with more wealth gets a bigger λ weight. It can be shown, however, that the utility function, constructed as previously shown, will, in addition, be independent of the initial endowment distribution if two further conditions are satisfied:

1. the discount factor of every agent is the same (i.e., all agents δ's are the same).
2. agents' period preferences are of either of the two following forms:

$$U^k(c) = \frac{\gamma}{\gamma - 1}(\alpha^k + \gamma c)^{1-(1/\gamma)} \quad \text{or}$$

$$U^k(c) = -e^{-\alpha^k c}.$$

If either of these two conditions are satisfied, that is, by and large, if the agents' preferences can be represented by either a CRRA or a CARA utility function, then there exists a representative agent economy for which the equilibrium Arrow-Debreu prices are the same as they are for the K agent economy, and for which

$$U^A(c) = g(c)H(\lambda_1, \ldots, \lambda_K)$$

where

$$g_1(c) > 0, g_{11}(c) < 0.$$

In this case, the weights do not affect preferences because they appear in the form of a multiplicative scalar.

Let us repeat that, even if the individual agent preferences do not take either of the two forms previously listed, there will still be a representative agent whose preferences are the weighted average of the individual agent preferences. Unlike the prior case, however, this ordering will then depend on the initial endowments [see Constantinides (1982)].

10.2.2   ON THE CONCEPT OF A "NO-TRADE" EQUILIBRIUM

In a representative agent economy we must, of necessity, use a somewhat specialized notion of equilibrium—a *no-trade equilibrium*. If, indeed, for a particular model specification, some security is in positive net supply, the equilibrium price will be the price at which the representative agent is willing to hold that amount—the total supply—of the security. In other specifications we will price securities that do not explicitly appear—securities that are said to be in zero net supply. The prototype of the latter is an IOU type of contract: In a one agent economy, the total net supply of IOUs must, of course, be zero. In this case, if at some price the representative agent wants to supply (sell) the security, since there is no one to demand it, supply exceeds demand. Conversely, if at some price the representative agent wants to buy the security (and thus no one wants to supply it), demand exceeds supply. Financial markets are thus in equilibrium, if and only if, at the prevailing price, supply equals demand and both are simultaneously zero. In all cases, the equilibrium price is that price at which the representative agent wishes to hold exactly the amount of the security present in the economy. Therefore, the essential question being asked is: What prices must securities assume so that the amount the representative agent *must* hold (for all markets to clear) exactly equals what he *wants* to hold. At these prices, further trade is not utility enhancing. In a more conventional multi-agent economy, an identical state of affairs is verified post-trade. The representative agent class of models is not appropriate, of course, for the analysis of some issues in finance; for example, issues linked with the volume of trade cannot be studied since, in a representative agent model, trading volume is, by construction, equal to zero.

10.3   AN EXCHANGE (ENDOWMENT) ECONOMY

10.3.1   THE MODEL

This economy will be directly analogous to the Arrow-Debreu exchange economies considered earlier: production is in the background and abstracted away. It is, however, an economy that admits recursive trading, resulting from investment decisions made over time, period after period (as opposed to being made once and for all at date 0).

There is one, perfectly divisible, *share* which we can think of as representing the market portfolio of the CAPM (later we shall relax this assumption). Ownership of this share entitles the owner to all the economy's output (in this economy, all firms are publicly traded). Output is viewed as arising exogenously, and as being stochastically variable through time, although in a stationary fashion. This is the promised, although still remote, link with the real side of the economy. And we will indeed use macroeconomic data to calibrate the model in the forthcoming sections. At this point, we can think of the output process as being governed by a large-number-of-states version of the three-state probability transition matrix found in Table 10-1.

TABLE 10-1	Three-State Probability Transition Matrix		

		Output in Period $t+1$		
		Y^1	Y^2	Y^3

$$
\text{Output in Period } t \quad
\begin{matrix} Y^1 \\ Y^2 \\ Y^3 \end{matrix}
\begin{bmatrix} \pi_{11} & \pi_{12} & \pi_{13} \\ \pi_{21} & \pi_{22} & \pi_{23} \\ \pi_{31} & \pi_{32} & \pi_{33} \end{bmatrix} = T
$$

where $\pi_{ij} = \text{Prob}(Y_{t+1} = Y^j \,|\, Y_t = Y^i)$ for any t. That is, there are a given number of output states, levels of output that can be achieved at any given date, and the probabilities of transiting from one output state to another are given and constant. The stationarity hypothesis embedded in this formulation may, at first sight, appear extraordinarily restrictive. The output levels defining the states may, however, be normalized variables, for instance to allow for a constant rate of growth. Alternatively, the states could themselves be defined in terms of growth rates of output rather than output levels. See Appendix 10.1 for an application.

If we adopt a continuous-state version of this perspective, the output process can be similarly described by a probability transition *function*

$$G(Y_{t+1}|Y_t) = \text{Prob}(Y_{t+1} \le Y^j \,|\, Y_t = Y^i).$$

We can imagine the security as representing ownership of a fruit tree where the (perishable) output (the quantity of fruit produced by the tree—the dividend) varies from year to year. This interpretation is often referred to as the *Lucas fruit tree* economy in tribute to 1996 Nobel prize winner, R. E. Lucas Jr., who, in his 1978 article, first developed the CCAPM. The power of the approach, however, resides in the fact that any mechanism delivering a stochastic process on aggregate output, such as a full macroeconomic equilibrium model, can be grafted on the CCAPM. This opens up the way to an in-depth analysis of the rich relationships between the real and the financial sides of an economy.

This will be a *rational expectations economy*. By this expression we mean that the representative agent's expectations will be on average correct, and in particular will exhibit no systematic bias. In effect we are assuming, in line with a very large literature (and with most of what we have done implicitly so far), that the representative agent knows both the general structure of the economy and the exact output distribution as summarized by the matrix T. One possible justification is that this economy has been functioning for a long enough time to allow the agent to learn the probability process governing output and to understand the environment in which he operates. Accumulating such knowledge is clearly in his own interest if he wishes to maximize his expected utility.

The agent buys and sells securities (fractions of the single, perfectly divisible share) and consumes dividends. The security purchases solve:

$$\max_{\{z_t\}} E\left(\sum_{t=0}^{\infty} \delta^t U(\tilde{c}_t) \right)$$

$$\left. \begin{array}{l} \text{s.t. } c_t + p_t z_{t+1} \le z_t Y_t + p_t z_t \\ \qquad z_t \le 1 \end{array} \right\}, \forall t$$

where p_t is the period t real price of the security in terms of consumption[1] (the price of consumption is 1) and z_t is the agent's beginning-of-period t holdings of the security. Holding a fraction z_t of the security entitles the agent to the corresponding fraction of the distributed dividend, which in an exchange economy without investment, equals total available output. The expectations operator applies across all possible values of Y feasible at each date t with the probabilities provided by the matrix T.

Let us assume the representative agent's period utility function is strictly concave with $\lim_{c_t \to 0} U_1(c_t) = \infty$. Making this latter assumption insures that it is never optimal for the agent to select a zero consumption level. It thus normally insures an interior solution to the relevant maximization problem. The necessary and sufficient condition for the solution to this problem is then given by: For all t, z_{t+1} solves:

$$U_1(c_t)p_t = \delta E_t\{U_1(\tilde{c}_{t+1})(\tilde{p}_{t+1} + \tilde{Y}_{t+1})\} \qquad (10.1)$$

where $c_t = (p_t z_t + z_t Y_t - p_t z_{t+1})$. Note that the expectations operator applies across possible output state levels; if we make explicit the functional dependence on the output state variables, Equation (10.1) can be written (assuming Y^i is the current state):

$$U_1(c_t(Y^i))p_t(Y^i) = \delta \sum_j U_1(c_{t+1}(\tilde{Y}^j))(p_{t+1}(\tilde{Y}^j) + \tilde{Y}^j)\pi_{ij}$$

In Equation (10.1), $U_1(c_t)p_t$ is the utility loss in period t associated with the purchase of an additional unit of the security, while $\delta U_1(\tilde{c}_{t+1})$ is the marginal utility of an additional unit of consumption in period $t+1$ and $(\tilde{p}_{t+1} + \tilde{Y}_{t+1})$ is the extra consumption (income) in period $t+1$ from selling the additional unit of the security after collecting the dividend entitlement. The RHS is thus the expected discounted gain in utility associated with buying the extra unit of the security. The agent is in equilibrium (utility maximizing) at the prevailing price p_t if the loss in utility today, which he would incur by buying one more unit of the security $(U_1(c_t)p_t)$, is exactly offset by (equals) the expected gain in utility tomorrow $(\delta E_t\{U_1[\tilde{c}_{t+1}][\tilde{p}_{t+1} + \tilde{Y}_{t+1}]\})$, which the ownership of that additional security will provide. If this equality is not satisfied, the agent will try either to increase or to decrease his holdings of securities,[2]

For the entire economy to be in equilibrium, it must, therefore, be true that:

(i) $z_t = z_{t+1} = z_{t+2} = \ldots \equiv 1$, in other words, the representative agent owns the entire security;

(ii) $c_t = Y_t$, that is, ownership of the entire security entitles the agent to all the economy's output and,

(iii) $U_1(c_t)p_t = \delta E_t\{U_1(\tilde{c}_{t+1})(\tilde{p}_{t+1} + \tilde{Y}_{t+1})\}$, or, the agents' holdings of the security are optimal given the prevailing prices. Substituting (ii) into (iii) informs us that the equilibrium price must satisfy:

$$U_1(Y_t)p_t = \delta E_t\{U_1(\tilde{Y}_{t+1})(\tilde{p}_{t+1} + \tilde{Y}_{t+1})\} \qquad (10.2)$$

---

[1] In the notation of the previous chapter: $p = q^e$.
[2] In equilibrium, however, this is not possible and the price will have to adjust until the equality in Equation (10.1) is satisfied.

If there were many firms in this economy—say J firms, with firm $j, j = 1, 2, \ldots, J$— producing the (exogenous) output $\tilde{Y}_{j,t}$, then the same equation would be satisfied for each firm's stock price, $p_{j,t}$, that is,

$$p_{j,t} U_1(c_t) = \delta E_t\{[U_1(\tilde{c}_{t+1})][\tilde{p}_{j,t+1} + \tilde{Y}_{j,t+1}]\} \tag{10.3}$$

where $c_t = \sum_{j=1}^{j} Y_{j,t}$ in equilibrium.

Equations (10.2) and (10.3) are the fundamental equations of the consumption-based capital asset pricing model.[3]

A recursive substitution of Equation (10.2) into itself yields[4]

$$p_t = E_t \sum_{\tau=1}^{\infty} \delta^{\tau} \left[\frac{U_1(\tilde{c}_{t+\tau})}{U_1(c_t)} \tilde{Y}_{t+\tau} \right], \tag{10.4}$$

establishing the stock price as the sum of all expected discounted future dividends. Equation (10.4) resembles the standard discounting formula of elementary finance, but for the important observation that discounting takes place using the inter-temporal marginal rates of substitution defined on the consumption sequence of the representative agent. If the utility function displays risk neutrality and the marginal utility is constant ($U_{11} = 0$), Equation (10.4) reduces to

$$p_t = E_t \sum_{\tau=1}^{\infty} \delta^{\tau} [\tilde{Y}_{t+\tau}] = E_t \sum_{\tau=1}^{\infty} \left[\frac{\tilde{Y}_{t+\tau}}{(1 + r_f)^{\tau}} \right], \tag{10.5}$$

which states that the stock price is the sum of expected future dividends discounted at the (constant) risk-free rate. The intuitive link between the discount factor and the risk-free rate leading to the second inequality in Equation (10.5) will be formally established in Equation (10.7). The difference between Equations (10.4) and (10.5) is the necessity, in a world of risk aversion, of discounting the flow of expected dividends at a rate higher than the risk-free rate, so as to include a risk premium. The question as to the appropriate risk premium constitutes the central issue in financial theory. Equation (10.4) proposes a definite, if not fully operational (due to the difficulty in measuring marginal rates of substitution), answer.

BOX 10-2

Calculating the Equilibrium Price Function

Equation (10.2) implicitly defines the equilibrium price series. Can it be solved directly to produce the actual equilibrium prices $\{p(Y^i): i = 1, 2, \ldots, N\}$? The answer is posi-

(continued)

---

[3]The fact that the representative agent's consumption stream—via his MRS—is critical for asset pricing is true for all versions of this model, including ones with nontrivial production settings. More general versions of this model may not, however, display an identity between consumption and dividends. This will be the case, for example, if there is wage income to the agent.

[4]That is, update Equation (10.2) with p_{t+1} on the left-hand side and p_{t+2} in the RHS and substitute the resulting RHS (which now contains a term in p_{t+2}) into the original Equation (10.2); repeat for p_{t+2}, p_{t+3}, and so on, regroup terms and extrapolate.

BOX 10-2 (*continued*)

tive. First, we must specify parameter values and functional forms. In particular, we need to select values for δ and for the various output levels Y^i, to specify the probability transition matrix T and the form of the representative agent's period utility function (a CRRA function of the form $U(c) = c^{1-\gamma}/(1-\gamma)$ is a natural choice). We may then proceed as follows. Solve for the $\{p(Y^i) : i = 1, 2, \ldots, N\}$ as the solution to a system of linear equations. Notice that Equation (10.2) can be written as the following system of linear equations (one for each of the N possible current states Y^i):

$$U_1(Y^1)p(Y^1) = \delta \sum_{j=1}^{N} \pi_{1j} U_1(Y^j) Y^j$$

$$+ \delta \sum_{j=1}^{N} \pi_{1j} U_1(Y^j) p(Y^j)$$

$$\vdots \qquad \vdots \qquad \vdots$$

$$\vdots \qquad \vdots \qquad \vdots$$

$$U_1(Y^N)p(Y^N) = \delta \sum_{j=1}^{N} \pi_{Nj} U_1(Y^j) Y^j$$

$$+ \delta \sum_{j=1}^{N} \pi_{Nj} U_1(Y^j) p(Y^j)$$

with unknowns $p(Y^1), p(Y^2), \ldots, p(Y^N)$. Notice that for each of these equations, the first term on the right-hand side is simply a number while the second term is a linear combination of the $p(Y^i)$'s. Barring a very unusual output process, this system will have a solution: one price for each Y^i, that is, the equilibrium price function.

   Let us illustrate: Suppose $U(c) = \ln(c)$, $\delta = .96$, and $(Y^1, Y^2, Y^3) = (1.5, 1, .5)$—an exaggeration of *boom, normal, and depression* times. The transition matrix is taken to be as

found in Table 10-2. The equilibrium conditions just listed then read:

$$Y^1\colon \tfrac{2}{3}p(1.5) = .96 + .96\{\tfrac{1}{3}p(1.5) + \tfrac{1}{4}p(1) + \tfrac{1}{2}p(.5)\}$$

$$Y^2\colon \quad p(1) = .96 + .96\{\tfrac{1}{6}p(1.5) + \tfrac{1}{2}p(1) + \tfrac{1}{2}p(.5)\}$$

$$Y^3\colon \quad 2p(.5) = .96 + .96\{\tfrac{1}{6}p(1.5) + \tfrac{1}{4}p(1) + 1p(.5)\}$$

$$Y^1\colon \quad 0 = .96 - .347p(1.5) + .24p(1) + .48p(.5)$$

$$\text{or, } Y^2\colon \quad 0 = .96 + .16p(1.5) - .52p(1) + .48p(.5)$$

$$Y^3\colon \quad 0 = .96 + .16p(1.5) + .24p(1) - 1.04p(.5)$$

(i)–(ii) yields: $p(1.5) = \dfrac{.76}{.507}p(1)$

$$= 1.5p(1)$$

(ii)–(iii) gives: $p(.5) = \dfrac{.76}{1.52}p(1)$

$$= \tfrac{1}{2}p(1)$$

substituting (iv) and (v) into Equation (i) to solve for $p(1)$ yields

$$p(1) = 23.70;$$
$$p(1.5) = 35.55 \text{ and } p(.5) = 11.85 \text{ follow.}$$

TABLE 10-2
Transition Matrix

	1.5	1	.5
1.5	.5	.25	.25
1	.25	.5	.25
.5	.25	.25	.5

10.3.2 INTERPRETING THE EXCHANGE EQUILIBRIUM

To bring about a closer correspondence with traditional asset pricing formulae we must first relate the asset prices derived previously with rates of return. In particular, we will want to understand, in this model context, what determines the amount by which the risky asset's expected return exceeds that of a risk-free asset. This basic question is also the one for which the standard CAPM provides such a simple, elegant, answer $(E\tilde{r}_j - r_f = \beta_j(E\tilde{r}_M - r_f))$. Define the period t to $t+1$ return for security j as

$$1 + r_{j,t+1} = \frac{P_{j,t+1} + Y_{j,t+1}}{P_{j,t}}$$

Then Equation (10.3) may be rewritten as:

$$1 = \delta E_t \left\{ \frac{U_1(\tilde{c}_{t+1})}{U_1(c_t)} (1 + \tilde{r}_{j,t+1}) \right\} \tag{10.6}$$

Let q_t^b denote the price in period t of a one-period riskless discount bond in zero net supply, which pays one unit of consumption (income) in every state in the next period. By reasoning analogous to that presented previously,

$$q_t^b U_1(c_t) = \delta E_t \{ U_1(\tilde{c}_{t+1}) 1 \}$$

The price q_t^b is the equilibrium price at which the agent desires to hold zero units of the security, and thus supply equals demand. This is so because if he were to buy one unit of this security at a price q_t^b, the loss in utility today would exactly offset the gain in expected utility tomorrow. The representative agent is, therefore, content to hold zero units of the security.

Since the risk-free rate over the period from date t to $t+1$, denoted $r_{f,t+1}$, is defined by $q_t^b(1 + r_{f,t+1}) = 1$, we have

$$\frac{1}{1 + r_{f,t+1}} = q_t^b = \delta E_t \left\{ \frac{U_1(\tilde{c}_{t+1})}{U_1(c_t)} \right\}, \tag{10.7}$$

which formally establishes the link between the discount rate and the risk-free rate of return we have used in Equation (10.5) under the risk neutrality hypothesis. Note that in the latter case $(U_{11} = 0)$, Equation (10.7) implies that the risk-free rate must be a constant.

Now we will combine Equations (10.6) and (10.7). Since, for any two random variables $\tilde{x}, \tilde{y}, E(\tilde{x} \cdot \tilde{y}) = E(\tilde{x}) \cdot E(\tilde{y}) + \text{cov}(\tilde{x} \cdot \tilde{y})$, we can rewrite Equation (10.6) in the form

$$1 = \delta E_t \left\{ \frac{U_1(\tilde{c}_{t+1})}{U_1(c_t)} \right\} E_t \{ 1 + \tilde{r}_{j,t+1} \} + \delta \, \text{cov}_t \left\{ \frac{U_1(\tilde{c}_{t+1})}{U_1(c_t)}, \tilde{r}_{j,t+1} \right\} \tag{10.8}$$

Let us denote $E_t \{ 1 + \tilde{r}_{j,t+1} \} = 1 + \bar{r}_{j,t+1}$. Then substituting Equation (10.7) into Equation (10.8) gives

$$1 = \frac{1 + \bar{r}_{j,t+1}}{1 + r_{f,t+1}} + \delta \, \text{cov}_t \left(\frac{U_1(\tilde{c}_{t+1})}{U_1(c_t)}, \tilde{r}_{j,t+1} \right), \text{ or, rearranging,}$$

$$\frac{1 + \bar{r}_{j,t+1}}{1 + r_{f,t+1}} = 1 - \delta \, \text{cov}_t \left(\frac{U_1(\tilde{c}_{t+1})}{U_1(c_t)}, \tilde{r}_{j,t+1} \right), \text{ or}$$

$$\bar{r}_{j,t+1} - r_{f,t+1} = -\delta(1 + r_{f,t+1})\text{cov}_t\left(\frac{U_1(\tilde{c}_{t+1})}{U_1(c_t)}, \tilde{r}_{j,t+1}\right). \tag{10.9}$$

Equation (10.9) is the central relationship of the consumption CAPM and we must consider its implications. The LHS of Equation (10.9) is the risk-premium on security j. Equation (10.9) tells us that the risk premium will be large when $\text{cov}_t(U_1(\tilde{c}_{t+1})/U_1(c_t), \tilde{r}_{j,t+1})$ is large and negative, that is, for those securities paying high returns when consumption is high (and thus when $U_1(c_{t+1})$ is low), and low returns when consumption is low (and $U_1(c_t)$ is high). These securities are not very desirable for consumption risk reduction (consumption smoothing): They pay high returns when we don't need them (consumption is high anyway) and low returns when we would need them (consumption is low). Since they are not desirable, they have a low price and high expected returns relative to the risk-free security.

The CAPM tells us that a security is relatively undesirable and thus commands a high return when it covaries positively with the market portfolio, that is, when its return is high precisely in those circumstances when the return on the market portfolio is also high, and conversely. The consumption CAPM is not in contradiction with this basic idea but it adds some further degree of precision. From the viewpoint of smoothing *consumption* and risk diversification, an asset is desirable if it has a high return when consumption is low and vice versa.

When the portfolio and asset pricing problem is placed in its proper multiperiod context, the notion of utility of end of period wealth (our paradigm of Chapters 4 to 6) is no longer relevant and we have to go back to the more fundamental formulation in terms of the utility derived from consumption: $U(c_t)$. But then it becomes clear that the possibility of expressing the objective as maximizing the utility of end-of-period wealth in the two dates/one period setting has, in some sense, lured us down a false trail: In a fundamental sense, the key to an asset's value is its covariation with the marginal utility of consumption, not with the marginal utility of wealth.

Equation (10.9) has the unappealing feature that the risk premium is defined, in part, in terms of the marginal utility of consumption, which is not observable. To eliminate this feature, we shall make the following approximation.

Let $U(c_t) = ac_t - (b/2)c_t^2$ (i.e., a quadratic utility function or a truncated Taylor series expansion of a general $U(.)$) where $a > 0, b > 0$, and the usual restrictions apply on the range of consumption. It follows that $U_1(c_t) = a - bc_t$; substituting this into Equation (10.9) gives

$$\bar{r}_{j,t+1} - r_{f,t+1} = -\delta(1 + r_{f,t+1})\text{cov}_t\left(\tilde{r}_{j,t+1}, \frac{a - b\tilde{c}_{t+1}}{a - bc_t}\right)$$

$$= -\delta(1 + r_{f,t+1})\frac{1}{a - bc_t}\text{cov}_t(\tilde{r}_{j,t+1}, \tilde{c}_{t+1})(-b), \text{ or}$$

$$\bar{r}_{j,t+1} - r_{f,t+1} = \frac{\delta b(1 + r_{f,t+1})}{a - bc_t}\text{cov}_t(\tilde{r}_{j,t+1}, \tilde{c}_{t+1}) \tag{10.10}$$

Equation (10.10) makes this point easier to grasp: since the term in front of the covariance expression is necessarily positive, if next-period consumption covaries in a large positive way with $r_{j,t+1}$, then the risk premium on j will be high.

10.3.3 THE FORMAL CONSUMPTION CAPM

As a final step in our construction, let us denote the portfolio most highly correlated with consumption by the index $j = c$, and its expected rate of return for the period from t to $t + 1$ by $\bar{r}_{c,t+1}$.

Equation (10.10) applies as well to this security so we have

$$\bar{r}_{c,t+1} - r_{f,t+1} = \left[\frac{\delta b(1 + r_{f,t+1})}{a - bc_t}\right] \text{cov}_t(\tilde{r}_{c,t+1}, \tilde{c}_{t+1}) \tag{10.11}$$

Dividing Equation (10.10) by (10.11) and thus eliminating the term $[\delta b(1 + r_{f,t+1})/a - bc_t]$, one obtains

$$\frac{\bar{r}_{j,t+1} - r_{f,t+1}}{\bar{r}_{c,t+1} - r_{f,t+1}} = \frac{\text{cov}_t(\tilde{r}_{j,t+1}, \tilde{c}_{t+1})}{\text{cov}_t(\tilde{r}_{c,t+1}, \tilde{c}_{t+1})}, \text{ or}$$

$$\frac{\bar{r}_{j,t+1} - r_{f,t+1}}{\bar{r}_{c,t+1} - r_{f,t+1}} = \frac{\dfrac{\text{cov}_t(\tilde{r}_{j,t+1}, \tilde{c}_{t+1})}{\text{var}(\tilde{c}_{t+1})}}{\dfrac{\text{cov}_t(\tilde{r}_{c,t+1}, \tilde{c}_{t+1})}{\text{var}(\tilde{c}_{t+1})}}, \text{ or}$$

$$\bar{r}_{j,t+1} - r_{f,t+1} = \frac{\beta_{j,c_t}}{\beta_{c,c_t}}[\bar{r}_{c,t+1} - r_{f,t+1}] \tag{10.12}$$

for $\beta_{j,c_t} = \text{cov}_t(\tilde{r}_{j,t+1}, \tilde{c}_{t+1})/\text{Var}(\tilde{c}_{t+1})$, the consumption-$\beta$ of asset j, and $\text{cov}_t(\tilde{r}_{c,t+1}, \tilde{c}_{t+1})/\text{Var}(\tilde{c}_{t+1})$, the consumption-$\beta$ of portfolio c. This equation defines the consumption CAPM.

If it is possible to construct a portfolio c such that $\beta_{c,c_t} = 1$ one gets the direct analogue to the CAPM, with $\bar{r}_{c,t+1}$ replacing the expected return on the market and β_{j,c_t} the relevant beta:

$$\bar{r}_{j,t+1} - r_{f,t+1} = \beta_{j,c_t}(\bar{r}_{c,t+1} - r_{f,t+1}) \tag{10.13}$$

10.4 PRICING ARROW-DEBREU STATE-CONTINGENT CLAIMS WITH THE CCAPM

Chapter 7 dwelled on the notion of an Arrow-Debreu state claim as the basic building block for all asset pricing and it is interesting to understand what form these securities and their prices assume in the Consumption CAPM setting. Our treatment will be very general and will accommodate more complex settings where the state is characterized by more than one variable.

Whatever model we happen to use, let s_t denote the state in period t. In the prior sections s_t coincided with the period t output, Y_t.

Given that we are in state s in period t, what is the price of an Arrow-Debreu security that pays one unit of consumption if and only if state s' occurs in period $t + 1$? We consider two cases.

1. Let the number of possible states be finite; denote the Arrow-Debreu price as

$$q(s_{t+1} = s'; s_t = s)$$

with the ' superscript referring to the value taken by the random state variable in the next period. Since this security is assumed to be in zero net supply,[5] it must satisfy, in equilibrium,

$$U_1(c(s))q(s_{t+1} = s'; s_t = s) = \delta U_1(c(s'))\text{prob}(s_{t+1} = s'; s_t = s), \text{ or}$$

$$q(s_{t+1} = s'; s_t = s) = \delta \frac{U_1(c(s'))}{U_1(c(s))} \text{prob}(s_{t+1} = s'; s_t = s).$$

As a consequence of our maintained stationarity hypothesis, the same price occurs when the economy is in state s and the claim pays one unit of consumption in the next period if and only if state s' occurs, whatever the current time period t. We may thus drop the time subscript and write $q(s'; s) = \delta \frac{U_1(c(s'))}{U_1(c(s))} \text{prob}(s'; s) = \delta \frac{U_1(c(s'))}{U_1(c(s))} \pi_{ss'}$, in the notation of our transition matrix representation.

2. For a continuum of possible states, the analogous expression is

$$q(s'; s) = \delta \frac{U_1(c(s'))}{U_1(c(s))} f(s'; s)$$

where $f(s'; s)$ is the conditional density function on s_{t+1} given s, evaluated at s'.

Note that *under risk neutrality,* we have a reconfirmation of our earlier identification of Arrow-Debreu prices as being proportional to the relevant state probabilities, with the proportionality factor corresponding to the time discount coefficient:

$$q(s'; s) = \delta f(s'; s) = \delta \pi_{ss'}.$$

These prices are for one-period state-contingent claims; what about N-period claims? They would be priced *exactly analogously:*

$$q^N(s_{t+N} = s'; s_t = s) = \delta^N \frac{U_1(c(s'))}{U_1(c(s))} \text{prob}(s_{t+N} = s'; s_t = s).$$

The price of an N-period risk-free discount bound q_t^{bN}, given state s, is thus given by

$$q_t^{bN}(s) = \delta^N \sum_{s'} \frac{U_1(c(s'))}{U_1(c(s))} \text{prob}(s_{t+N} = s'; s_t = s) \qquad (10.14)$$

or, in the continuum of states notation,

$$q_t^{bN}(s) = \delta^N \int_{s'} \frac{U_1(c(s'))}{U_1(c(s))} f_N(s'; s) ds' = E_s \left\{ \delta^N \frac{U_1(c_{t+N}(s'))}{U_1(c(s))} \right\},$$

where the expectation is taken over all possible states s' conditional on the current state being s.[6]

Now let us review Equation (10.4) in the light of the expressions we have just derived.

$$p_t = E_t \sum_{\tau=1}^{\infty} \delta^\tau \left[\frac{U_1(c_{t+\tau})}{U_1(c_t)} Y_{t+\tau} \right]$$

---

[5]And thus its introduction does not alter the structure of the economy described previously.
[6]The corresponding transition probabilities are given by the Nth power of the matrix **T**.

$$= \sum_{\tau=1}^{\infty} \sum_{s'} \delta^{\tau} \left[\frac{U_1(c_{t+\tau}(s'))}{U_1(c_t)} Y_{t+\tau}(s') \right] \text{prob}(s_{t+\tau} = s'; s_t = s),$$

$$= \sum_{\tau} \sum_{s'} q^{\tau}(s', s) Y_{t+\tau}(s')$$

What this development tells us is that taking the appropriately discounted (at the intertemporal MRS) sum of expected future dividends is simply valuing the stream of future dividends at the appropriate Arrow-Debreu prices [compare with Equation (7.4)]! The fact that there are no restrictions in the present context in extracting the prices of Arrow-Debreu contingent claims is indicative of the fact that this economy is one of complete markets.[7] Of course, in the spirit of Chapters 7 and 8, we can use these Arrow-Debreu prices to value all other securities.

Applying the same substitution to Equation (10.4) as employed to obtain Equation (10.8) yields:

$$p_t = \sum_{\tau=1}^{\infty} \delta^{\tau} \left\{ E_t \left[\frac{U_1(\tilde{c}_{t+\tau})}{U_1(c_1)} \right] E_t[\tilde{Y}_{t+\tau}] + \text{cov}\left(\frac{U_1(\tilde{c}_{t+\tau})}{U_1(c_t)}, \tilde{Y}_{t+\tau} \right) \right\}$$

$$= \sum_{\tau=1}^{\infty} \delta^{\tau} \left\{ E_t \left[\frac{U_1(\tilde{c}_{t+\tau})}{U_1(c_t)} \right] E_t[\tilde{Y}_{t+\tau}] \left(1 + \frac{\text{cov}\left(\frac{U_1(\tilde{c}_{t+\tau})}{U_1(c_t)}, \tilde{Y}_{t+\tau} \right)}{E_t \left[\frac{U_1(\tilde{c}_{t+\tau})}{U_1(c_t)} \right] E_t[\tilde{Y}_{t+\tau}]} \right) \right\},$$

where the expectations operator applies across all possible values of the state output variable, with probabilities given by the matrix T raised to the relevant power given that the current state is s_t.

Using the expression for the price of a risk-free discount bond of τ periods to maturity derived earlier and the fact that $(1 + r_{f,t+\tau})^{\tau} \cdot q_t^{b\tau} = 1$, we can rewrite this expression as:

$$p_t = \sum_{\tau=1}^{\infty} \frac{\left\{ E_t[Y_{t+\tau}] \left\{ 1 + \frac{\text{cov}(U_1(\tilde{c}_{t+\tau}), \tilde{Y}_{t+\tau})}{E_t[U_1(\tilde{c}_{t+\tau})]E_t[\tilde{Y}_{t+\tau}]} \right\} \right\}}{(1 + r_{f,t+\tau})^{\tau}}. \tag{10.15}$$

The quantity being discounted (at the risk-free rate applicable to the relevant period) in the present value term is the equilibrium certainty equivalent of the real cash flow generated by the asset. This is the analogue for the CCAPM of the CAPM expression derived in Appendix 9.1.

If the cash flows exhibit no stochastic variation (i.e., they are risk free), then Equation (10.15) reduces to

$$p_t = \sum_{\tau=1}^{\infty} \frac{Y_{t+\tau}}{(1 + r_{f,t+\tau})^{\tau}}.$$

This is exactly the same relationship that we derived earlier in Chapter 5 where we discounted risk-free cash flows at the term structure of interest rates. If, on the other hand,

---

[7]This result, which is not trivial (we have an infinity of states of nature and only one asset—the equity), is the result of the twin assumptions of rational expectations and agents' homogeneity.

the cash flows are risky, yet investors are risk neutral (constant marginal utility of consumption), Equation (10.15) becomes

$$p_t = \sum_{\tau=1}^{\infty} \frac{E[\tilde{Y}_{t+\tau}]}{(1 + r_{f,t+\tau})^{\tau}} , \qquad (10.16)$$

which is identical to Equation (10.5) once we recall that, from Equation (10.7), the risk-free rate must be constant under risk neutrality.

Equation (10.15) is fully in harmony with the intuition of Section 10.3: if the representative agent's consumption is highly positively correlated with the security's real cash flows, the certainty equivalent values of these cash flows will be smaller than their expected values (viz., $\text{cov}(U_1(c_{t+\tau}), Y_{t+\tau}) < 0$). This is so because such a security is not very useful for hedging the agent's future consumption risk. As a result it will have a low price and a high expected return. In fact, its price will be less than what it would be in an economy of risk-neutral agents [Equation (10.16)]. The opposite is true if the security's cash flows are negatively correlated with the agent's consumption.

10.5   TESTING THE CONSUMPTION CAPM: THE EQUITY PREMIUM PUZZLE

In the rest of this chapter we discuss the empirical validity of the CCAPM. We do this here (and not with the CAPM and other pricing models seen so far) because a set of simple and robust empirical observations has been put forward that falsifies this model in an unusually strong way. This forces us to question its underlying hypotheses and, a fortiori, those underlying some of the less-sophisticated models seen before. Thus, in this instance, the recourse to sophisticated econometrics for drawing significant lessons about our approach to modeling financial markets is superfluous.

A few key empirical observations regarding financial returns in U.S. markets are summarized in Table 10-3, which shows that over a long period of observation the average ex-post return on a diversified portfolio of U.S. stocks (the market portfolio, as approximated in the United States by the S&P 500) has been close to 7 percent (in real

TABLE 10-3 Properties of U.S. Real Asset Returns Annualized Data		
	U.S. Economy	
	(a)	*(b)*
r	6.98	16.54
r_f	.80	5.67
$r - r_f$	6.18	16.67

(a) annualized mean values in percent.

(b) Annualized standard deviation in percent.

Source: Data from R. Mehra and E. C. Prescott, "The Equity Premium: A Puzzle," *Journal of Monetary Economics,* 15 (1985): 145–161.

terms, net of inflation) while the real return on one-year T-bills (taken to represent the return on the risk-free asset) has averaged less than 1 percent. These twin observations make up for an equity risk premium of 6.2 percent. This observation is robust in the sense that it has applied in the United States for a very long period, and in several other important countries as well. Its meaning is not totally undisputed, however. Goetzmann and Jorion (1999), in particular, argue that the high return premium obtained for holding U.S. equities is the exception rather than the rule.[8]

Here we will take the 6 percent equity premium at face value, as has the huge literature that followed the uncovering of the *equity premium puzzle* by Mehra and Prescott (1985). The puzzle is this: Mehra and Prescott argue that the CCAPM is completely unable, once reasonable parameter values are inserted in the model, to replicate such a high observed equity premium.

Let us illustrate their reasoning. According to the consumption CAPM, the only factors determining the characteristics of security returns are the representative agent's utility function, his subjective discount factor, and the process on consumption (which equals output or dividends in the exchange economy equilibrium). Consider the utility function first. It is natural in light of Chapter 2 to assume the agent's period utility function displays CRRA; thus let us set

$$U(c) = \frac{c^{1-\gamma}}{1 - \gamma}.$$

Empirical studies associated with this model have placed γ in the range of $(1, 2)$. A convenient consequence of this utility specification is that the inter-temporal marginal rate of substitution can be written as in Equation (10.17).

$$\frac{U_1(c_{t+1})}{U_1(c_t)} = \left(\frac{c_{t+1}}{c_t} \right)^{-\gamma}. \tag{10.17}$$

The second major ingredient is the consumption process. In our version of the model, consumption is a stationary process: It does not grow through time. In reality, however, consumption *is* growing through time. In a growing economy, the analogous notion to the variability of consumption is variability in the growth rate of consumption.

Let $x_{t+1} = c_{t+1}/c_t$, denote per capita consumption growth, and assume, for illustration that x_t is independently and identically lognormally distributed through time. For the period 1889 through 1978, the U.S. economy aggregate consumption has been growing at an average rate of 1.83 percent annually with a standard deviation of 3.57 percent, and a slightly negative measure of autocorrelation $(-.14)$ [cf. Mehra and Prescott (1985)].

---

[8]Using shorter, mostly postwar, data, premia close or even higher than the U.S. equity premium are obtained for France, Germany, the Netherlands, Sweden, Switzerland, and the United Kingdom [see, e.g., Campbell (1998)]. Goetzmann and Jorion (1999) however argue that such data samples do not correct for crashes and period of market interruptions, often associated with WW II, and thus are not immune from a survivorship bias. To correct for such a bias, they assemble long data series for all markets that existed during the twentieth century. They find that the United States has had "by far the highest uninterrupted real rate of appreciation of all countries, at about 5 percent annually. For other countries, the median appreciation rate is about 1.5 percent."

The remaining item is the agent's subjective discount factor δ: What value should it assume? Time impatience requires, of course, that $\delta < 1$, but this is insufficiently precise. One logical route to its estimation is as follows: Roughly speaking, the equity in the CCAPM economy represents a claim to the aggregate income from the underlying economy's entire capital stock. We have just seen that, in the United States, equity claims to private capital flows average a 7 percent annual real return, while debt claims average 1 percent.[9] Furthermore, the economy-wide debt-to-equity rates are not very different from 1. These facts together suggest an overall average real annual return to capital of about 4 percent.

If there were no uncertainty in the model, and if the constant growth rate of consumption were to equal its long-run historical average (1.0183), the asset pricing Equation (10.6) would reduce to

$$1 = \delta E_t \left(\frac{\tilde{c}_{t+1}}{c_t} \right)^{-\gamma} R_{t+1} = \delta(\bar{x})^{-\gamma} \bar{R},$$

where R_{t+1} is the gross rate of return on equity and the upper bars denote historical averages.[10] For $\gamma = 1$, $\bar{x} = 1.0183$, and $\bar{R} = 1.04$, we can solve for the implied δ to obtain $\delta \cong 0.97$. Since we have used an annual estimate for $\bar{x}$, the resulting δ must be viewed as an annual or yearly subjective discount factor; on a quarterly basis it corresponds to $\delta \cong 0.99$. If, on the other hand, we want to assume $\gamma = 2$, the previous equation solves for $\delta = .99$ on an annual basis, yielding a quarterly δ even closer to 1. This reasoning demonstrates that assuming higher rates of risk aversion would be incompatible with maintaining the hypothesis of a time discount factor less than 1. While technically, in the case of positive consumption growth, we could entertain the possibility of a negative rate of time preference, and thus of a discount factor larger than 1, we rule it out on grounds of plausibility.

At the root of this difficulty is the low return on the risk-free asset (1 percent), which will haunt us in other ways. As we know, highly risk-averse individuals want to smooth consumption over time, meaning they want to transfer consumption from good times to bad times. When consumption is growing predictably, the good times lie in the future. Agents want to borrow now against their future income. In a representative agent model, this is hard to reconcile with a low rate on borrowing: everyone is on the same side of the market, a fact that inevitably forces a higher rate. This problem calls for an independent explanation for the abnormally low average risk-free rate [e.g., in terms of the liquidity advantage of short-term government debt as in Bansal and Coleman (1996)] or the acceptance of the possibility of a negative rate of time preference so that future consumption is given more weight than present consumption. We will not follow either of these routes here, but rather will, in the course of the present exercise, limit the rate of risk aversion to a maximal value of 2.

---

[9]Strictly speaking, there are the returns to publicly traded debt and equity claims. If private capital earns substantially different returns, however, capital is being inefficiently allocated; we assume this is not the case.

[10]Time average and expected values should coincide in a stationary model, provided the time series is of sufficient length.

With these added assumptions we can manipulate the fundamental asset pricing Equation (10.5) to yield two equations that can be used indirectly to test the model. The key step in the reasoning is to demonstrate that, in the context of these assumptions, the equity price formula takes the form

$$p_t = v Y_t$$

where v is a constant coefficient. That is, the stock price at date t is proportional to the dividend paid at date t.[11] To confirm this statement, we use a standard trick consisting of guessing that this is the form taken by the equilibrium pricing function and then verifying that this guess is indeed borne out by the structure of the model. Under the $p_t = v Y_t$ hypothesis, Equation (10.1) becomes:

$$v Y_t = \delta E_t \left\{ (v \tilde{Y}_{t+1} + \tilde{Y}_{t+1}) \frac{U_1(\tilde{c}_{t+1})}{U_1(c_t)} \right\}.$$

Using Equation (10.17) and dropping the conditional expectations operator, since x is independently and identically distributed through time (its mean is independent of time), this equation can be rewritten as

$$v = \delta E \left\{ (v + 1) \frac{\tilde{Y}_{t+1}}{Y_t} \tilde{x}_{t+1}^{-\gamma} \right\}.$$

The market clearing condition implies that $Y_{t+1}/Y_t = x_{t+1}$, thus

$$v = \frac{\delta E\{\tilde{x}_{t+1}^{1-\gamma}\}}{1 - \delta E\{\tilde{x}_{t+1}^{1-\gamma}\}}.$$

This is indeed a constant and our initial guess is thus confirmed!

Taking advantage of the validated pricing hypothesis, the equity return can be written as:

$$R_{t+1} \equiv 1 + r_{t+1} = \frac{p_{t+1} + Y_{t+1}}{p_t} = \frac{v + 1}{v} \frac{Y_{t+1}}{Y_t}.$$

Taking expectations we obtain:

$$E_t(\tilde{R}_{t+1}) = E(\tilde{R}_{t+1}) = \frac{v + 1}{v} E(\tilde{x}_{t+1}) = \frac{E(\tilde{x}_{t+1})}{\delta E\{\tilde{x}_{t+1}^{1-\gamma}\}}.$$

The risk-free rate is [Equation (10.6)]:

$$R_{f,t+1} \equiv \frac{1}{q_t^b} = \left[\delta E_t \left\{ \frac{U_1(\tilde{c}_{t+1})}{U_1(c_t)} \right\} \right]^{-1} = \frac{1}{\delta} \frac{1}{E\{\tilde{x}_{t+1}^{-\gamma}\}}, \qquad \textbf{(10.18)}$$

which is seen to be constant under our current hypotheses.

Taking advantage of the lognormality hypothesis, the ratio of the two preceding equations can be expressed as (see Appendix 10.1 for details)

$$\frac{E(\tilde{R}_{t+1})}{R_f} = \frac{E\{\tilde{x}_{t+1}\} E\{\tilde{x}_{t+1}^{-\gamma}\}}{E\{\tilde{x}_{t+1}^{1-\gamma}\}} = \exp[\gamma \sigma_x^2],$$

---

[11]Note that this property holds true as well for the example developed in Box 10-2 as Equations (iv) and (v) attest.

where σ_x^2 is the variance of $\ln x$. Taking logs, we finally obtain:

$$\ln(ER) - \ln(R_f) = \gamma\sigma_x^2. \tag{10.19}$$

Now, we are in a position to confront the model with the data. Let us start with Equation (10.19). Feeding in the return characteristics of the U.S. economy and solving for γ, we obtain (see Appendix 10.2 for the computation of σ_x^2),

$$\frac{\ln(ER) - \ln(ER_f)}{\sigma_x^2} = \frac{1.0698 - 1.008}{.00123} = 50.24 = \gamma.$$

Alternatively, if we assume $\gamma = 2$ and multiply by σ_x^2 as per Equation (10.19), one obtains an equity premium of

$$2(.00123) = .002 = (\ln(ER) - \ln(ER_f)) \cong ER - ER_f \tag{10.20}$$

In either case, this reasoning identifies a major discrepancy between model prediction and reality. The observed equity premium can only be explained by assuming an extremely high coefficient of relative risk aversion (50), one that is completely at variance with independent estimates. An agent with risk aversion of this level would be too fearful to take a bath (many accidents involve falling in a bathtub), or to cross the street. On the other hand, insisting on a more reasonable coefficient of risk aversion of two leads to predicting a minuscule premium of 0.2 percent, much below the 6.2 percent that has been historically observed over long periods.

Similarly, it is shown in Appendix 10.2 that $E\{x_t^{-\gamma}\} = .97$ for $\gamma = 2$; Equation (10.18) and the observed value for R_f (1.008) then implies that δ should equal be larger than 1 (1.02). This problem was to be anticipated from our discussion of the calibration of δ, which was based on reasoning similar to that underlying Equation (10.18). Here the problem is compounded by the fact that we are using an even lower risk-free rate (.8 percent) rather than the steady-state rate of return on capital of 4 percent used in the former reasoning. In the present context, this difficulty in calibrating δ or, equivalently, in explaining the low rate of return on the risk-free asset has been dubbed the *risk-free rate puzzle* by Weil (1989). As said previously, we read this result as calling for a specific explanation for the observed low return on the risk-free asset, one that the CCAPM is not designed to provide.

10.6   TESTING THE CONSUMPTION CAPM: HANSEN-JAGANNATHAN BOUNDS

Another, parallel, perspective on the puzzle is provided by the Hansen-Jagannathan (1991) bound. The idea is very similar to our prior test and the end result is the same. The underlying reasoning, however, postpones as long as possible making specific modeling assumptions. It is thus more general than a test of a specific version of the CCAPM. The bound proposed by Hansen and Jagannathan potentially applies to other asset pricing formulations. It similarly leads to a falsification of the standard CCAPM.

The reasoning goes as follows: For all homogeneous agent economies, the fundamental equilibrium asset pricing Equation (10.1) can be expressed as

$$p(s_t) = E_t[m_{t+1}(\tilde{s}_{t+1})X_{t+1}(\tilde{s}_{t+1}); s_t], \tag{10.21}$$

where s_t is the state today (it may be today's output in the context of a simple exchange economy or it may be something more elaborate as in the case of a production economy), $X_{t+1}(\tilde{s}_{t+1})$ is the total return in the next period (e.g., in the case of an exchange economy this equals $\tilde{p}_{t+1} + Y_{t+1}$) and $m_{t+1}(\tilde{s}_{t+1})$ is the *equilibrium pricing kernel,* also known as the *stochastic discount factor:*

$$m_{t+1}(\tilde{s}_{t+1}) = \frac{\delta U_1(c_{t+1}(\tilde{s}_{t+1}))}{U_1(c_t)}.$$

As before $U_1(\ )$ is the marginal utility of the representative agent and c_t is his equilibrium consumption. Equation (10.21) is thus the general statement that the price of an asset today must equal the expectation of its total payout tomorrow multiplied by the appropriate pricing kernel. For notational simplicity, let us suppress the state dependence, leaving it as understood, and write Equation (10.21) as

$$p_t = E_t[\tilde{m}_{t+1}\tilde{X}_{t+1}]. \tag{10.22}$$

This is equivalent to

$$1 = E_t[\tilde{m}_{t+1}\tilde{R}_{t+1}],$$

where $\tilde{R}_{t+1}$ is the gross return on ownership of the asset. Since Equation (10.22) holds for each state s_t, it also holds unconditionally for any period; we thus can also write

$$1 = E[\tilde{m}\tilde{R}]$$

where E denotes the unconditional expectation. For any two assets i and j (to be viewed shortly as the return on the market portfolio and the risk-free return, respectively) it must, therefore, be the case that

$$E[\tilde{m}(\tilde{R}_i - \tilde{R}_j)] = 0, \text{ or}$$
$$E[\tilde{m}\tilde{R}_{i-j}] = 0,$$

where, again for notational convenience, we substitute $\tilde{R}_{i-j}$ for $\tilde{R}_i - \tilde{R}_j$. This latter expression furthermore implies the following series of relationships:

$$E\tilde{m}E\tilde{R}_{i-j} + \text{cov}(\tilde{m}, \tilde{R}_{i-j}) = 0, \text{ or}$$
$$E\tilde{m}E\tilde{R}_{i-j} + \rho(\tilde{m}, \tilde{R}_{i-j})\sigma_m\sigma_{R_{i-j}} = 0, \text{ or}$$
$$\frac{E\tilde{R}_{i-j}}{\sigma_{R_{i-j}}} + \rho(\tilde{m}, \tilde{R}_{i-j})\frac{\sigma_m}{E\tilde{m}} = 0, \text{ or}$$
$$\frac{E\tilde{R}_{i-j}}{\sigma_{R_{i-j}}} = -\rho(\tilde{m}, \tilde{R}_{i-j})\frac{\sigma_m}{E\tilde{m}}. \tag{10.23}$$

It follows from Equation (10.23) and the fact that a correlation is never larger than 1 that

$$\frac{\sigma_m}{E\tilde{m}} > \frac{|E\tilde{R}_{i-j}|}{\sigma_{R_{i-j}}}. \tag{10.24}$$

The inequality in expression (10.24) is referred to as the Hansen-Jagannathan lower bound on the pricing kernel. If, as noted earlier, we designate asset i as the market portfolio and asset j as the risk-free return, then the data from Table 10-3 and Equation (10.24) together imply (for the U.S. economy):

$$\frac{\sigma_m}{E\tilde{m}} > \frac{|E(\tilde{r}_M - r_f)|}{\sigma_{r_M - r_f}} = \frac{.062}{.167} = .37.$$

Let us check whether this bound is satisfied for our model. From Equation (10.17) $\tilde{m}(\tilde{c}_{t+1}, c_t) = \delta(x_t)^{-\gamma}$, which we have computed (Appendix 10.2) to yield

$$E\tilde{m} = \delta \exp(-\gamma\mu_x + \tfrac{1}{2}\gamma^2\sigma_x^2) = .99(.967945) = .96 \text{ for } \gamma = 2.$$

In fact, Equation (10.18) reminds us that Em is simply the expected value of the price of a one-period risk-free discount bound, which cannot be very far away from 1. This implies that for the Hansen-Jagannathan bound to be satisfied, the standard deviation of the pricing kernel cannot be much lower than .3; given the information we have on x_t, it is a short step to estimate this parameter numerically under the assumption of log-normality. When we do this (see Appendix 10.2), we obtain an estimate for $\sigma_m = .002$, which is an order of magnitude lower than what is required for Equation (10.24) to be satisfied. The message is that it is very difficult to get the equilibrium $\sigma_m/E\tilde{m}$ to be anywhere near the required level. In a homogeneous agent, complete market model with standard preferences, where the variation in equilibrium consumption matches the data, consumption is just too smooth and the marginal utility of consumption does not vary sufficiently to satisfy the bound implied by the data (unless the curvature of the utility function—the degree of risk aversion—is assumed to be astronomically high, an assumption which, as we have seen, raises problems of its own).

10.7   SOME EXTENSIONS

10.7.1   REVIEWING THE DIAGNOSIS

Our first dynamic general equilibrium model thus fails when confronted with actual data. Let us review the source of this failure. Recall our original pricing Equation (10.9), specialized for a single asset, the market portfolio:

$$\bar{r}_{M,t+1} - r_{f,t+1} = -\delta(1 + r_{f,t+1})\text{cov}\left(\frac{U_1(\tilde{c}_{t+1})}{U_1(c_t)}, \tilde{r}_{M,t+1}\right)$$

$$= -\delta(1 + r_{f,t+1})\rho\left(\frac{U_1(\tilde{c}_{t+1})}{U_1(c_t)}, \tilde{r}_{M,t+1}\right)\sigma\left(\frac{U_1(\tilde{c}_{t+1})}{U_1(c_t)}\right)\sigma(\tilde{r}_{M,t+1})$$

$$= -(1 + r_{f,t+1})\rho(\tilde{m}_t, \tilde{r}_{M,t+1})\sigma(\tilde{m}_t)\sigma(\tilde{r}_{M,t+1})$$

Written in this way, it is clear that the equity premium depends upon the standard deviation of the MRS (or, equivalently, the stochastic discount factor), the standard deviation of the return on the market portfolio, and the correlation between these quantities. For the United States, and most other industrial countries, the problem with a model in which pricing and return relationships depend so much on consumption (and thus MRS) variation, is that average per capita consumption does not vary much at all. If this model is to have any hope of matching the data, we must modify it in a way that will increase the standard deviation of the relevant MRS, or the variability of the dividend being priced (and thus the $\sigma(r_{M,t+1})$). We do not have complete freedom over this latter quantity as it must be matched to the data as well.

10.7.2 THE CCAPM WITH EPSTEIN-ZIN UTILITY

At this stage it is interesting to inquire whether, in addition to its intellectual appeal on grounds of generality, Epstein and Zin's (1989) separation of time and risk preferences might contribute a solution to the equity premium puzzle, and more generally, alter our vision of the CCAPM and its message.

Let us start by looking specifically at the equity premium puzzle. It will facilitate our discussion to repeat Equations (4.9.i) and (4.9.ii) defining the Epstein-Zin preference representation (refer to Chapter 4 for a discussion and for the log case):

$$U(c_t, CE_{t+1}) = [(1 - \kappa)c_t^\rho + \kappa CE_{t+1}^\rho]^{1/\rho}, 0 \neq \rho < 1, \text{ with} \quad (4.9\text{i})$$
$$[CE(\tilde{U}_{t+1})]^{1-\gamma} = E_t(\tilde{U}_{t+1})^{1-\gamma}, 1 \neq \gamma > 0, \text{ or} \quad (4.9\text{ii})$$

Weil (1989) uses these preferences in a setting otherwise identical to that of Mehra and Prescott (1985). Asset prices and returns are computed similarly. What he finds, however, is that this greater generality does not resolve the *risk premium puzzle,* but rather tends to underscore what we have already introduced as the *risk-free rate puzzle.*

The Epstein-Zin (1989, 1991) preference representation does not innovate along the risk dimension, with the parameter γ alone capturing risk aversion, in a manner very similar to the standard case. It is, therefore, not surprising that Weil (1989) finds that only if this parameter is fixed at implausibly high levels ($\gamma \approx 45$) can a properly calibrated model replicate the premium—the Mehra and Prescott (1985) result revisited. With respect to time preferences, if ρ is calibrated to respect empirical studies, then the model also predicts a risk-free rate that is much too high. The reason for this is the same as the one outlined at the end of Section 10.5: Separately calibrating the inter-temporal substitution parameter ρ tends to strengthen the assumption that the representative agent is highly desirous of a smooth inter-temporal consumption stream. With consumption growing on average at 1.8 percent per year, the agent must be offered a very high risk-free rate in order to be induced to save more and thus making his consumption tomorrow even more in excess of what it is today (less smoothing).

While Epstein and Zin preferences do not help in solving the equity premium puzzle, it is interesting to study a version of the CCAPM with these generalized preferences. The idea is that the incorporation of separate time and risk preferences may enhance the ability of that class of models to explain the general pattern of security returns. The setting is once again a Lucas (1978) style economy with N assets, with the return on the equilibrium portfolio of all assets representing the return on the market portfolio. Using an elaborate dynamic programming argument, Epstein and Zin (1989, 1991) derive an asset pricing equation of the form

$$E_t \left\{ \left[\delta \left(\frac{\tilde{c}_{t+1}}{c_t} \right)^{\rho-1} \right]^{\gamma/\rho} \left[\frac{1}{1 + \tilde{r}_{M,t+1}} \right]^{1-(\gamma/\rho)} (1 + \tilde{r}_{j,t+1}) \right\} \equiv 1, \qquad \textbf{(10.25)}$$

where $\tilde{r}_{M,t}$ denotes the period t return on the market portfolio, and r_t^j the period t return on some asset in it. Note that when time and risk preferences coincide ($\gamma = \rho$), Equation (10.25) reduces to the pricing equation of the standard time-separable CCAPM case.

The pricing kernel itself is of the form

$$\left[\delta \left(\frac{\tilde{c}_{t+1}}{c_t} \right)^{\rho-1} \right]^{\gamma/\rho} \left[\frac{1}{1 + \tilde{r}_{M,t+1}} \right]^{1-(\gamma/\rho)}, \qquad \textbf{(10.26)}$$

which is a geometric average (with weights γ/ρ and $1 - (\gamma/\rho)$ respectively) of the pricing kernel of the standard CCAPM, $[\delta(\tilde{c}_{t+1}/c_t)^{\rho-1}]$, and the pricing kernel for the log ($\rho = 0$) case $[1/(1 + \tilde{r}_{M,t+1})]$.

Epstein and Zin (1991) next consider a linear approximation to the geometric average in Equation (10.26),

$$\frac{\gamma}{\rho}\left[\delta\left(\frac{\tilde{c}_{t+1}}{c_t}\right)^{\rho-1}\right] + \left(1 - \frac{\gamma}{\rho}\right)\left[\frac{1}{1 + \tilde{r}_{M,t+1}}\right]. \tag{10.27}$$

Substituting Equation (10.27) into Equation (10.25) gives

$$E_t\left\{\left[\frac{\gamma}{\rho}\left[\delta\left(\frac{\tilde{c}_{t+1}}{c_t}\right)^{\rho-1}\right] + \left(1 - \frac{\gamma}{\rho}\right)\left[\frac{1}{1 + \tilde{r}_{M,t+1}}\right]\right](1 + \tilde{r}_{j,t+1})\right\} \approx 1, \text{ or} \tag{10.28}$$

$$\frac{\gamma}{\rho}E_t\left\{\delta\left(\frac{c_{t+1}}{c_t}\right)^{\rho-1}(1 + \tilde{r}_{j,t+1})\right\} + \left(1 - \frac{\gamma}{\rho}\right)E_t\left\{\left(\frac{1}{1 + \tilde{r}_{M,t+1}}\right)(1 + \tilde{r}_{j,t+1})\right\} \approx 1. \tag{10.29}$$

Equation (10.29) is revealing. As we noted earlier, the standard CAPM relates the (essential, non-diversifiable) risk of an asset to the covariance of its returns with M, while the CCAPM relates its riskiness to the covariance of its returns with the growth rate of consumption (via the IMRS). With separate time and risk preferences, Equation (10.29) suggests that both covariances matter for an asset's return pattern.[12] But why are these effects both present separately and individually? The covariance of an asset's return with M captures its atemporal, non-diversifiable risk. The covariance of its returns with the growth rate of consumptions fundamentally captures its risk across successive time periods. When risk and time preferences are separated, it is not entirely surprising that both sources of risk should be individually present.

This relationship is more strikingly apparent if we assume joint lognormality and heteroskedasticity in consumption and asset returns; Campbell et al. (1997) then express Equation (10.29) in a form whereby the risk premium on asset i satisfies:

$$E_t(\tilde{r}_{i,t+1}) - r_{f,t+1} + \frac{\sigma_i^2}{2} = \kappa\frac{\sigma_{ic}}{\psi} + (1 - \kappa)\sigma_{iM}, \tag{10.30}$$

where $\kappa = (1 - \gamma)/\rho, \psi = 1/(1 - \rho), \sigma_{ic} = \text{cov}(\tilde{r}_{i,t}, \tilde{c}_t/c_{t-1})$ and $\sigma_{iM} = \text{cov}(\tilde{r}_{i,t}, \tilde{r}_{M,t})$. Both sources of risk are clearly present.

10.7.3   HABIT FORMATION

In the narrower perspective of solving the equity premium puzzle, probably the most successful modification of the standard setup has been to admit utility functions that exhibit higher rates of risk aversion at the margin, and thus can translate small variations in consumption into a large variability of the MRS. One way to achieve this objective without being confronted with the risk-free rate puzzle—which is exacerbated if we simply decide to postulate a higher γ—is to admit some form of *habit formation*. This is the notion that the agent's utility today is determined not by her absolute consumption level, but rather by the relative position of her current consumption vis-à-vis what can be viewed as a *stock of habit,* summarizing either her past consumption history (with

---

[12]To see this recall that for two random variables $\tilde{x}$ and $\tilde{y}$, $E(\tilde{x}\tilde{y}) = E(\tilde{x})E(\tilde{y}) + \text{cov}(\tilde{x}, \tilde{y})$, and employ this substitution in both terms on the left-hand side of Equation (10.29).

more or less weight placed on distant or old consumption levels) or the history of aggregate consumption (summarizing in a sense the consumption habits of her neighbors; a "keeping up with the Joneses" effect). This modeling perspective thus takes the view that utility of consumption is primarily dependent on (affected by) departures from prior consumption history, either one's own or that of a social reference group; departures from what we have been accustomed to consuming; or what we may have been led to consider fair consumption. This concept is open to a variety of different specifications, with diverse implications for behavior and asset pricing. The interested reader is invited to consult Campbell and Cochrane (1999) for a review. Here we will be content to illustrate briefly the underlying working principle. To that end, we specify the representative agent's period preference ordering to be of the form

$$U(c_t, c_{t-1}) \equiv \frac{(c_t - \chi c_{t-1})^{1-\gamma}}{1 - \gamma},$$

where $\chi \leq 1$ is a parameter. In an extreme case, $\chi = 1$, the period utility depends only upon the deviation of current period t consumption from the prior period's consumption. As we noted earlier, actual data indicates that per capita consumption for the United States and most other developed countries is very smooth. This implies that $(c_t - c_{t-1})$ is likely to be very small most of the time. For this specification, the agent's effective (marginal) relative risk aversion reduces to $R_R(c_t) = \gamma/(1 - (c_{t-1}/c_t))$; with $c_t \approx c_{t-1}$, the effective $R_R(c)$ will thus be very high, even with a low γ, and the representative agent will appear as though he is very risk averse. This opens the possibility for a very high return on the risky asset. With a careful choice of the habit specification, the risk-free asset pricing equation will not be materially affected and the risk-free rate puzzle will be avoided [see Constantinides (1990) and Campbell and Cochrane (1999)].

We find this development interesting not only because of its implications for pricing assets in an exchange economy. It also suggests a more general reevaluation of the standard utility framework discussed in Chapter 2. It may, however, lead to questioning some of the basic tenets of our financial knowledge: It would hardly be satisfactory to solve a puzzle by assuming habit formation and high effective rates of risk aversion and ignore this behavioral assumption when attending to other problems tackled by financial theory. In fact, a confirmed habit formation utility specification would, for the same reasons, have significant implications for macroeconomics as well (as modern macroeconomics builds on the same theoretical principles as the CCAPM of this section). It is not clear, however, that high effective rates of risk aversion are consistent with our current understanding of short-run macroeconomic fluctuations. This discussion suggests that it is worthwhile to explore alternative potential solutions to the puzzle, all the while attempting to understand better the connections between the real and the financial sides of the economy.

10.7.4 DISTINGUISHING STOCKHOLDERS FROM NON-STOCKHOLDERS

In this spirit, another approach to addressing the outstanding financial puzzles starts by recognizing that only a small fraction of the population holds substantial financial assets, stocks in particular. This fact implies that only the variability of the consumption stream of the stockholding class should matter for pricing risky assets. There are reasons to believe that the consumption patterns of this class of the population are both more variable and more highly correlated with stock returns than average per capita consumption.[13] Observing, furthermore, that wages are very stable and that the aggregate wage share is countercyclical (that is, proportionately larger in bad times when aggregate income is relatively low), it is not unreasonable to assume that firms, and thus their owners, the shareholders, insure workers against income fluctuations associated with the business cycle. If this is a significant feature of the real world, it should have implications for asset pricing as we presently demonstrate.

Before trying to incorporate such a feature into a CCAPM-type model, it is useful first to recall the notion of risk sharing. Consider the problem of allocating an uncertain income (consumption) stream between two agents so as to maximize overall utility. Assume, furthermore, that these income shares are not fixed across all states, but can be allocated on a state-by-state basis. This task can be summarized by the allocation problem

$$\max_{c_1(\theta),c_2(\theta)} U(c_1(\tilde{\theta})) + \mu V(c_2(\tilde{\theta}))$$
$$\text{s.t. } c_1(\tilde{\theta}) + c_2(\tilde{\theta}) \le Y(\tilde{\theta}),$$

where $U(\ )$, $V(\ )$ are, respectively, the two agents' utility functions, $c_1(\tilde{\theta})$ and $c_2(\tilde{\theta})$ their respective income assignments, $Y(\tilde{\theta})$ the economy-wide state-dependent aggregate income stream, and μ their relative weight.

The necessary and sufficient first-order condition for this problem is

$$U_1(c_1(\tilde{\theta})) = \mu V_1(c_2(\tilde{\theta})). \tag{10.31}$$

Equation (10.31) states that the ratio of the marginal utilities of the two agents should be constant. We have seen it before as Equation (7.3) of Chapter 7. As we saw there, it can be interpreted as an optimal risk sharing condition in the sense that it implicitly assigns more of the income risk to the less risk-averse agent. To see this, take the extreme case where one of the agents, say the one with utility function $V(\ )$ is risk neutral—indifferent to risk. According to Equation (10.31) it will then be optimal for the other agent's income stream to be constant across all states: He will be perfectly insured. Agent $V(\ )$ will thus absorb all the risk (in exchange for a higher average income share).

To understand the potential place of these ideas in the consumption CAPM setting, let $V(\ )$ now denote the period utility function of the representative shareholder, and $U(\ )$ the period utility function of the representative worker who is assumed not to hold any financial assets and who consequently consumes his wage w_t. As before, let Y_t be the uncertain (exogenously given) output. The investment problem of the shareholders—the maximization problem with which we started this chapter—now becomes

$$\max_{\{z_t\}} E\left(\sum_{t=0}^{\infty} \delta^t V(\tilde{c}_t) \right)$$
$$\text{s.t., } \forall t,$$
$$c_t + p_t z_{t+1} \le z_t d_t + p_t z_t$$
$$d_t = Y_t - w_t$$

[13]Mankiw and Zeldes (1991) attempt, successfully, to confirm this conjecture. They indeed find that shareholder consumption is 2.5 times as variable as non-shareholder consumption. Data problems, however, preclude taking their results as more than indicative.

$$U_1(w_t) = \mu V_1(d_t),$$
$$z_t \leq 1$$

Here we simply introduce a distinction between the output of the tree, Y_t, and the dividends paid to its owners, d_t, on the plausible grounds that people (workers) need to be paid to take care of the trees and collect the fruits. This payment is w_t. Moreover, we introduce the idea that the wage bill may incorporate a risk insurance component, which we formalize by assuming that the variability of wage payments is determined by an optimal risk sharing rule equivalent to Equation (10.31). One key parameter is the income share parameter, μ, which may be interpreted as reflecting the relative bargaining strengths of the two groups. Indeed, a larger μ gives more income to the worker.

Assets in this economy are priced as before with Equation (10.1) becoming

$$V_1(c_t)p_t = \delta E_t\{V_1(\tilde{c}_{t+1})(\tilde{p}_{t+1} + \tilde{d}_{t+1})\}. \tag{10.32}$$

While the differences between Equations (10.1) and (10.32) may appear purely notational, their importance cannot be overstated. First, the pricing kernel derived from Equation (10.32) will build on the firm owners' MRS, defined over shareholder consumption (dividend) growth rather than the growth in average per capita consumption. Moreover, the definition of dividends as output minus a stabilized stream of wage payments opens up the possibility that the flow of payments to which firm owners are entitled is effectively much more variable, not only than consumption but than output as well. Therein lies a concept of leverage, one that has been dubbed *operating leverage,* similar to the familiar notion of financial leverage. In the same way that bondholders come first, and are entitled to a fixed, noncontingent interest payment, workers also have priority claims to the income stream of the firm and macroeconomic data on the cyclical behavior of the wage share confirm that wage payments are more stable than aggregate income.

We have explored the potential of these ideas in recent research work (Danthine and Donaldson, 1999) to which the reader is referred for details, and find that this class of models can generate significantly increased equity premia. When we add an extra notion of distributional risk associated with the possibility that μ varies stochastically, in a way that permits better accounting of the observed behavior of the wage share over the medium run, the premium approaches 6 percent.

10.8 CONCLUSIONS

The two modifications discussed in the previous section are far from representing the breadth and depth of the research that has been stimulated by the provocative result presented in Mehra and Prescott (1985). For a broader and more synthetic perspective, we refer the reader to the excellent recent survey of Kocherlakota (1996).

The material covered in this chapter contains recent developments illustrating some of the most important directions taken by modern financial theory. Much work remains to be done, as the latest sections indicate, and this is indeed a fertile area for current research. At this juncture, one may be led to the view that structural asset pricing theory, based on rigorous dynamic general equilibrium models, provides limited operational support in our quest for understanding financial market phenomena. While the search goes on, this state of affairs nevertheless explains the popularity of less encompassing approaches based on the concept of arbitrage (as reviewed in Chapters 9, 11, and 12).

References

Bansal, R., and W. J. Coleman, "A Monetary Explanation of the Equity Premium, Term Premium and Risk-Free Rates Puzzles," *Journal of Political Economy*, 104 (1996): 1135–1171.

Barro, R. J., "Are Government Bonds Net Wealth?" *Journal of Political Economy*, 82 (1974): 1095–1117.

Campbell, J. Y., "Asset Prices, Consumption, and the Business Cycle," NBER Working paper 6485, March 1998, forthcoming in the *Handbook of Macroeconomics*, Amsterdam: North Holland.

Campbell, J. Y., and J. H. Cochrane, "By Force of Habit: A Consumption-Based Explanation of Aggregate Stock Market Behavior," *Journal of Political Economy*, 107 (1999), 205–251.

Campbell, J., Lo, A., and A. C. MacKinlay, *The Econometrics of Financial Markets*, Princeton, N.J.: Princeton University Press, 1997.

Constantinides, G. M., "Intertemporal Asset Pricing with Heterogeneous Consumers and without Demand Aggregation," *Journal of Business*, 55 (1982): 253–267.

Constantinides, G. M., "Habit Formation: A Resolution of the Equity Premium Puzzle," *Journal of Political Economy*, 98 (1990): 519–543.

Danthine, J. P., and J. B. Donaldson (1999), "Labor Relations and Asset Returns," University of Lausanne and Columbia University. Mimeographed.

Epstein, L., and S. Zin, "Substitution, Risk Aversion, and the Temporal Behavior of Consumption and Asset Returns: A Theoretical Framework," *Econometrica*, 57 (1989): 937–969.

Epstein, L., and S. Zin, "Substitution, Risk Aversion, and the Temporal Behavior of Consumption and Asset Returns: An Empirical Analysis," *Journal of Political Economy*, 99 (1991): 263–286.

Goetzman, W., and P. Jorion, "A Century of Global Stock Markets," *Journal of Finance*, 55 (1999): 953–980.

Hansen, L., and R. Jagannathan, "Implications of Security Market Data for Models of Dynamic Economies," *Journal of Political Economy*, 99 (1991): 225–262.

Kocherlakota, N., "The Equity Premium: It's Still a Puzzle," *Journal of Economic Literature*, 34 (1996): 42–71.

Lucas, R. E., "Asset Pricing in an Exchange Economy," *Econometrica*, 46 (1978): 1429–1445.

Mankiw, G., and S. Zeldes, "The Consumption of Stockholders and Non-Stockholders," *Journal of Financial Economics*, 29 (1991): 97–112.

Mehra, R., and E. C. Prescott, "The Equity Premium: A Puzzle," *Journal of Monetary Economics*, 15 (1985): 145–161.

Weil, P. W., "The Equity Premium Puzzle and the Risk-Free Rate Puzzle," *Journal of Monetary Economics*, 24 (1989): 401–421.

A P P E N D I X   1 0 . 1

Solving the CCAPM with Growth

Assume also that there is a finite set of possible growth rates $\{x_1, \ldots, x_N\}$ whose realizations are governed by a Markov process with transition matrix T and entries π_{ij}. Then, for whatever x_i is realized in period $t+1$,

$$d_{t+1} = x_{t+1}Y_t = x_{t+1}c_t = x_ic_t.$$

Under the usual utility specification, $U(c) = c^{1-\gamma}/1 - \gamma$, the basic asset pricing equation reduces to

$$c_t^{-\gamma}p(Y_t, x_i) = \delta \sum_{j=1}^{N} \pi_{ij}(x_jc_t)^{-\gamma}$$
$$\times [c_tx_j + p(x_jY_t, x_j)], \text{ or}$$
$$p(Y_t, x_i) = \delta \sum_{j=1}^{N} \pi_{ij}\left(\frac{x_jc_t}{c_t}\right)^{-\gamma}[c_tx_j + p(x_jY_t, x_j)],$$

So we see that the MRS is determined exclusively by the consumption growth rate.

The essential insight of Mehra and Prescott (1985) was to observe that a solution to this linear system has the form

$$p(Y_t, x_i) = p(c_t, x_i) = v_ic_t$$

for a set of constants $\{v_1, \ldots, v_N\}$, each identified with the corresponding growth rate.

With this functional form, the asset pricing equation reduces to

$$v_ic_t = \delta \sum_{j=1}^{N} \pi_{ij}(x_j)^{-\gamma}[x_jc_t + v_jx_jc_t], \text{ or}$$
$$v_i = \delta \sum_{j=1}^{N} \pi_{ij}(x_j)^{1-\gamma}[1 + v_j]. \quad \textbf{(A10.1)}$$

This is again a system of linear equations in the N unknowns $\{v_1, \ldots, v_N\}$. Provided the growth rates are not too large (so that the agent's utility is not unbounded), a solution exists—a set of $\{v_1^*, \ldots, v_N^*\}$ that solves the system of Equations (A10.1).

Thus, for any state $(Y, x_j) = (c, x_j)$, the equilibrium equity asset price is

$$p(Y, x_j) = v_j^*Y.$$

If we suppose the current state is (Y, x_i) while next period it is (x_jY, x_j), then the one-period return earned by the equity security over this period is

$$r_{ij} = \frac{p(x_jY, x_j) + x_jY - p(Y, x_i)}{p(Y, x_i)}$$
$$= \frac{v_j^*x_jY + x_jY - v_i^*Y}{v_i^*Y}$$
$$= \frac{x_j(v_j^* + 1)}{v_i^*} - 1,$$

and the mean or expected return, conditional on state i is

$$r_i = \sum_{j=1}^{N} \pi_{ij}r_{ij},$$

The unconditional equity return is thus given by

$$Er = \sum_{j=1}^{N} \hat{\pi}_jr_j,$$

where $\hat{\pi}_j$ are the long-run stationary probabilities of each state.

The risk-free security is analogously priced as:

$$p^{rf}(c, x_i) = \delta \sum_{j=1}^{N} \pi_{ij}(x_j)^{-\gamma}, \text{ etc.}$$

A P P E N D I X   1 0 . 2

Some Properties of the Lognormal Distribution

Definition A10.1:
A variable x is said to follow a lognormal distribution if $\ln x$ is normally distributed.

Suppose $\ln x \sim N(\mu_x, \sigma_x^2)$. If this is the case,

$$E(x) = \exp\{\mu_x + \tfrac{1}{2}\sigma_x^2\}$$
$$E(x^a) = \exp\{a\mu_x + \tfrac{1}{2}a^2\sigma_x^2\}$$
$$\mathrm{var}(x) = \exp\{2\mu_x + \sigma_x^2\}(\exp\sigma_x^2 - 1)$$

Suppose further that x and y are two variables that are independently and identically lognormally distributed; then we also have

$$E(x^a y^b) = \exp\{a\mu_x + b\mu_y$$
$$+ \tfrac{1}{2}(a^2\sigma_x^2 + b^2\sigma_y^2) + 2\rho ab\sigma_x\sigma_y\}$$

where ρ is the correlation coefficient between $\ln x$ and $\ln y$.

Applications to consumption growth: x_t is lognormally distributed, that is, $\ln x_t \sim N(\mu_x, \sigma_x^2)$.

We know that $E(x_t) = 1.0183$ and $\mathrm{var}(x_t) = (.0357)^2$. To identify (μ_x, σ_x^2), we need to find solutions of

$$1.0183 = \exp\{\mu_x + \tfrac{1}{2}\sigma_x^2\}$$
$$(.0357)^2 = \exp\{2\mu_x + \sigma_x^2\}(\exp\sigma_x^2 - 1)$$

Substituting the first equation squared into the second [by virtue of the fact that $[\exp(y)]^2 = \exp(2y)$] and solving for σ_x^2, one obtains

$$\sigma_x^2 = .00123.$$

Substituting this value in the equation for μ_x, one solves for

$$\mu_x = .01752.$$

We can directly use these values to solve Equation (10.18):

$$E\{x_t^{-\gamma}\} = \exp\{-\gamma\mu_x + \tfrac{1}{2}\gamma^2\sigma_x^2\}$$
$$= \exp\{-.03258\} = .967945,$$

thus $\delta = 1.024$.

Focusing now on the numerator of Equation (10.18), one has:

$$\exp\{\mu_x + \tfrac{1}{2}\sigma_x^2\}\exp\{-\gamma\mu_x + \tfrac{1}{2}\gamma^2\sigma_x^2\},$$

while the denominator is

$$\exp\{(1 - \gamma)\mu_x + \tfrac{1}{2}(1 - \gamma)^2\sigma_x^2\}.$$

It remains to recall that $\exp(a)\exp(b)/\exp(c) = \exp(a + b - c)$ to obtain Equation (10.19).

Another application: Estimating the standard deviation of the pricing kernel $m_t = x_t^{-\gamma}$ where consumption growth x_t is lognormally distributed. Given that Em_t is as derived in Section 10.6, one estimates $\sigma^2(m_t) \cong \frac{1}{k}\{\sum_{i=1}^{k}[\delta(x_i)^{-\gamma} - Em_t]^2\}$, for $\ln x_i$ drawn from $N(.01752; .00123)$ and k sufficiently large (say $k = 10{,}000$). For $\gamma = 2$, one obtains $\sigma^2(m_t) = (.00234)^2$, which yields $\sigma_m/E\tilde{m} \cong .00234/.9559 = .00245$.

CHAPTER 11

THE MARTINGALE MEASURE IN DISCRETE TIME, PART II

11.1 INTRODUCTION

We return to the notion of risk-neutral valuation, which we now extend to settings with many time periods. This will be accomplished in two very different ways. First, we extend the concept to the CCAPM setting. Recall that this is a discrete time, general equilibrium framework: Preferences and endowment processes must be specified and no-trade prices computed. We will demonstrate that, here as well, assets may be priced equal to the present value, discounted at the risk-free rate of interest, of their expected payoffs when expectations are computed using the set of risk-neutral probabilities. We would expect this to be possible: The CCAPM is an equilibrium model (hence there are no arbitrage opportunities and a set of risk-neutral probabilities must exist) with complete markets (hence this set is unique).

Second, we extend the idea to the partial equilibrium setting of equity derivatives (e.g., equity options) valuations. The key to derivatives pricing is to have an accurate model of the underlying price process. We hypothesize such a process (it is not derived from underlying fundamentals—preferences, endowments etc.; rather, it is a pure statistical model), and demonstrate that, in the presence of *local* market completeness and *local* no arbitrage situations, there exists a transformation of measure by which all derivatives written on that asset may be priced equal to the present value, discounted at the risk-free rate, of their expected payoffs computed using this transformed measure.[1] The Black-Scholes formula, for example, may be derived in this way.

11.2 DISCRETE TIME INFINITE HORIZON ECONOMIES: A CCAPM SETTING

As in Chapter 10, time now evolves according to $t = 0, 1, \ldots, T, T+1, \ldots$. We retain the context of a single good endowment economy and presume the existence of a com-

---

[1]By *local* we mean that valuation is considered only in the context of the derivative, the underlying asset (a stock), and a risk-free bond.

plete markets Arrow-Debreu financial structure. In period t, any one of N_t possible states, indexed by θ_t, may be realized.

We will assume that a period t event is characterized by two quantities:

(i) the actually occurring period t event as characterized by θ_t,

(ii) the unique history of events $(\theta_1, \theta_2, \ldots, \theta_{t-1})$ that precedes it.

Requirement (ii), in particular, suggests an evolution of uncertainty similar to that of a tree structure in which the branches never join (two events always have distinct prior histories). While this is stronger than CCAPM, it will allow us to avoid certain notational ambiguities; subsequently, assumption (ii) will be dropped. We are interested more in the idea than in any broad application, so generality is not an important consideration.

Let $\pi(\theta_t, \theta_{t+1})$ represent the probability of state θ_{t+1} being realized in period $t+1$, given that θ_t is realized in period t. The financial market is assumed to be complete in the following sense: At every date t, and for every state θ_t, there exists a short-term contingent claim that pays one unit of consumption if state θ_{t+1} is realized in period $t+1$ (and nothing otherwise). We denote the period t, state θ_t price of such a claim by $q(\theta_t, \theta_{t+1})$.

Arrow-Debreu long-term claims (relative to $t=0$) are not formally traded in this economy. Nevertheless, they can be synthetically created by dynamically trading short-term claims. (In general, more trading can substitute for fewer claims). To illustrate, let $q(\theta_0, \theta_{t+1})$ represent the period $t=0$ price of a claim to one unit of the numeraire, if and only if event θ_{t+1} is realized in period $t+1$. It must be the case that

$$q(\theta_0, \theta_{t+1}) = \prod_{s=0}^{t} q(\theta_s, \theta_{s+1}), \tag{11.1}$$

where $(\theta_0, \ldots, \theta_t)$ is the unique prior history of θ_{t+1}. By the uniqueness of the path to θ_{t+1}, $q(\theta_0, \theta_{t+1})$ is well defined. By no-arbitrage arguments, if the long-term Arrow-Debreu security were also traded, its price would conform to Equation (11.1). Arrow-Debreu securities can thus be effectively created via dynamic (recursive) trading, and the resulting financial market structure is said to be dynamically complete.[2] By analogy, the price in period t, state θ_t, of a security that pays one unit of consumption if state θ_{t+J} is observed in period $t+J$, $q(\theta_t, \theta_{t+J})$, is given by

$$q(\theta_t, \theta_{t+J}) = \prod_{s=t}^{t+J-1} q(\theta_s, \theta_{s+1}).$$

It is understood that θ_{t+J} is feasible from θ_t, that is, given that we are in state θ_t in period t, there is some positive claims probability for the economy to find itself in state θ_{t+J} in period $t+J$; otherwise the claims price must be zero.

Since our current objective is to develop risk-neutral pricing representations, a natural next step is to define risk-free bond prices and associated risk-free rates. Given the current date state is (θ_t, t), the price, $q^b(\theta_t, t)$, of a risk-free one-period (short-term) bond is given by (no arbitrage)

$$q^b(\theta_t, t) = \sum_{\theta_{t+1}=\theta_1}^{\theta_{N_{t+1}}} q(\theta_t, \theta_{t+1}); \tag{11.2}$$

---

[2]This fact suggests that financial markets may need to be "very incomplete" if incompleteness per se is to have a substantial effect on equilibrium asset prices and, for example, have a chance to resolve some of the puzzles uncovered in Chapter 10. See Telmer (1993).

Note here that the summation sign applies across all N_{t+1} future states of nature. The corresponding risk-free rate must satisfy

$$(1 + r_f(\theta_t)) = \{q^b(\theta_t, t + 1)\}^{-1}.$$

Pricing a k period risk-free bond is similar:

$$q^b(\theta_t, t + k) = \sum_{\theta_{t+k}=1}^{\theta_{N_{t+k}}} q(\theta_t, \theta_{t+k}). \tag{11.3}$$

The final notion is that of an *accumulation factor*, denoted by $g(\theta_t, \theta_{t+k})$, and defined for a specific path $(\theta_t, \theta_{t+1}, \ldots, \theta_{t+k})$ as follows:

$$g(\theta_t, \theta_{t+k}) = \prod_{s=t}^{t+k-1} q^b(\theta_s, s + 1). \tag{11.4}$$

The idea being captured by the accumulation factor is this: An investor who invests one unit of consumption in short-term risk-free bonds from date t to $t+k$, continually rolling over his investment, will accumulate $[g(\theta_t, \theta_{t+k})]^{-1}$ units of consumption by date $t + k$, if events $\theta_{t+1}, \ldots, \theta_{t+k}$ are realized. Alternatively,

$$[g(\theta_t, \theta_{t+k})]^{-1} = \prod_{s=0}^{k-1} (1 + r_f(\theta_{t+s})). \tag{11.5}$$

Note that from the perspective of date t, state θ_t, the factor $[g(\theta_t, \theta_{t+k})]^{-1}$ is an uncertain quantity as the actual state realizations in the succeeding time periods are not known at period t. From the $t = 0$ perspective, $[g(\theta_t, \theta_{t+k})]^{-1}$ is in the spirit of a (conditional) forward rate.

Let us illustrate with the two-date forward accumulation factor. We take the perspective of the investor investing one unit of the numeraire in a short-term risk-free bond from date t to $t+2$. His first investment is certain since the current state θ_t is known and it returns $(1 + r_f(\theta_t))$. At date $t + 1$, this sum will be invested again in a one-period risk-free bond with return $(1 + r_f(\theta_{t+1}))$ contracted at $t + 1$ and received at $t + 2$. From the perspective of date t, this is indeed an uncertain quantity. The compounded return on the investment is: $(1 + r_f(\theta_t)) (1 + r_f(\theta_{t+1}))$. This is the inverse of the accumulation factor $g(\theta_t, \theta_{t+1})$ as spelled out in Equation (11.5).

Let us next translate these ideas directly into the CCAPM settings.

11.3 RISK-NEUTRAL PRICING IN THE CCAPM

We make two additional assumptions in order to restrict our current setting to the context of the CCAPM.

A11.1: There is one agent in the economy with time-separable VNM preferences represented by

$$\mathcal{U}(\tilde{c}) = E_0 \left(\sum_{t=0}^{\infty} U(\tilde{c}_t, t) \right),$$

where $\{U(\cdot, t)\}$ is a family of strictly increasing, concave, differentiable period utility functions, with $\tilde{c}_t = c(\theta_t)$ is the uncertain period t consumption, and E_0 the expectations operator conditional on date $t = 0$ information.

This treatment of the agent's preferences is quite general. For example, $U(c_t, t)$ could be of the form $\delta^t U(c_t)$ as in earlier chapters. Alternatively, the period utility function could itself be changing through time in deterministic fashion, or some type of habit formation could be postulated. In all cases, it is understood that the set of feasible consumption sequences will be such that the sum exists (is finite).

A11.2: Output in this economy, $\tilde{Y}_t = Y(\tilde{\theta}_t)$ is exogenously given, and, by construction, represents the consumer's income. In equilibrium it represents his consumption as well.

Recall that equilibrium-contingent claims prices in the CCAPM economy are no-trade prices, supporting the consumption sequences $\{\tilde{c}_t\}$ in the sense that at these prices, the representative agent does not want to purchase any claims; that is, at the prevailing contingent-claims prices his existing consumption sequence is optimal. The loss in period t utility experienced by purchasing a contingent claim $q(\theta_t, \theta_{t+1})$ is exactly equal to the resultant increase in expected utility in period $t + 1$. There is no benefit to further trade. More formally,

$$U_1(c(\theta_t), t)q(\theta_t, \theta_{t+1}) = \pi(\theta_t, \theta_{t+1})U_1(c(\theta_{t+1}), t + 1), \text{ or}$$

$$q(\theta_t, \theta_{t+1}) = \pi(\theta_t, \theta_{t+1})\left\{\frac{U_1(c(\theta_{t+1}), t + 1)}{U_1(c(\theta_t), t)}\right\}. \qquad \textbf{(11.6)}$$

Equation (11.6) corresponds to Equation (7.1) of Chapter 7. State probabilities and inter-temporal marginal rates of substitution appear once again as the determinants of equilibrium Arrow-Debreu prices. Note that the more general utility specification adopted in this chapter does not permit bringing out explicitly the element of time discounting embedded in the inter-temporal marginal rates of substitution. A short-term risk-free bond is thus priced according to

$$q^b(\theta_t, t + 1) = \sum_{\theta_{t+1}=1}^{N_t} q(\theta_t, \theta_{t+1}) = \frac{1}{U_1(c(\theta_t), t)} E_t\{U_1(c(\tilde{\theta}_{t+1}), t + 1)\}. \qquad \textbf{(11.7)}$$

Risk-neutral valuation is in the spirit of discounting at the risk-free rate. Accordingly, we may ask: At what probabilities must we compute the expected payoff to a security in order to obtain its price by discounting that payoff at the risk-free rate? But which risk-free rates are we speaking about? In a multiperiod context, there are two possibilities and the alternative we choose will govern the precise form of the probabilities themselves.

The spirit of the dilemma is portrayed in Figure 11-1, which illustrates the case of a $t = 3$ period cash flow.

FIGURE 11-1   Two Possibilities of Discounting a $t = 3$ Period Cash Flow

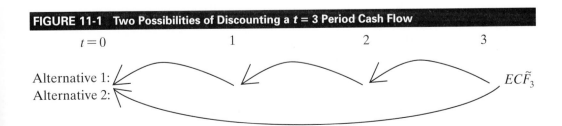

Under the first alternative, the cash flow is discounted at a series of consecutive short (one-period) rates, while in the second we discount back at the term structure of multiperiod discount bonds. These methods provide the same price, although the form of the risk-neutral probabilities will differ substantially. Here we offer a discussion of alternative 1; alternative 2 is considered in Appendix 11.1.

Since the one-period state claims are the simplest securities, we will first ask what the risk-neutral probabilities must be in order that they be priced equal to the present value of their expected payoff, discounted at the risk-free rate.[3] As before, let these numbers be denoted by $\pi^{RN}(\theta_t, \theta_{t+1})$. They are defined by:

$$q(\theta_t, \theta_{t+1}) = \pi(\theta_t, \theta_{t+1})\left\{\frac{U_1(c(\theta_{t+1}), t+1)}{U_1(c(\theta_t), t)}\right\} = q^b(\theta_t, t+1)[\pi^{RN}(\theta_t, \theta_{t+1})].$$

The second equality reiterates the tight relationship found in Chapter 9 between Arrow-Debreu prices and risk-neutral probabilities. Substituting Equation (11.7) for $q^b(\theta_t, t+1)$ and rearranging terms, one obtains:

$$\pi^{RN}(\theta_t, \theta_{t+1}) = \pi(\theta_t, \theta_{t+1})\left\{\frac{U_1(c(\theta_{t+1}), t+1)}{U_1(c(\theta_t), t)}\right\}\frac{U_1(c(\theta_t), t)}{E_t\{U_1(c(\tilde{\theta}_{t+1}), t+1)\}}$$

$$= \pi(\theta_t, \theta_{t+1})\left\{\frac{U_1(c(\theta_{t+1}), t+1)}{E_t U_1(c(\tilde{\theta}_{t+1}), t+1)}\right\}. \tag{11.8}$$

Since $U(\ldots, t)$ is assumed to be strictly increasing, $U_1 > 0$ and $\pi^{RN}(\theta_t, \theta_{t+1}) > 0$ (without loss of generality we may assume $\pi(\theta_t, \theta_{t+1}) > 0$). Furthermore, by construction, $\sum_{\theta_{t+1}}^N \pi^{RN}(\theta_t, \theta_{t+1}) = 1$. The set $\{\pi^{RN}(\theta_t, \theta_{t+1})\}$ thus defines a set of conditional (on θ_t) risk-neutral transition probabilities. As in our earlier more general setting, if the representative agent is risk neutral, $U_1(c(\theta_t), t) \equiv$ constant for all t, and $\pi^{RN}(\theta_t, \theta_{t+1})$ coincides with $\pi(\theta_t, \theta_{t+1})$, the true probability. Using these transition probabilities, expected future consumption flows may be discounted at the intervening risk-free rates. Notice how the risk-neutral probabilities are related to the true probabilities: They represent the true probabilities scaled up or down by the relative consumption scarcities in the different states. For example, if, for some state θ_{t+1}, the representative agent's consumption is usually low, his marginal utility of consumption in that state will be much higher than average marginal utility and thus

$$\pi^{RN}(\theta_t, \theta_{t+1}) = \pi(\theta_t, \theta_{t+1})\left\{\frac{U_1(c(\theta_{t+1}), t+1)}{E_t U_1(c(\theta_{t+1}), t+1)}\right\} > \pi(\theta_t, \theta_{t+1}).$$

The opposite will be true if a state has a relative abundance of consumption. When we compute expected payoffs to assets using risk-neutral probabilities we are thus implicitly taking into account both the (no-trade) relative equilibrium scarcities (prices) of their payoffs and their objective relative scarcities. This allows discounting at the risk-free rate: No further risk adjustment need be made to the discount rate as all such adjustments have been implicitly undertaken in the expected payoff calculation.

To gain a better understanding of this notion let us go through a few examples.

---

[3]Recall that since all securities can be expressed as portfolios of state claims, we can use the state claims alone to construct the risk-neutral probabilities.

Example 11.1

Denote a stock's associated dividend stream by $\{d(\tilde{\theta}_t)\}$. Under the basic state-claim valuation perspective (Chapter 7, Section 7.6), its ex-dividend price at date t, given that θ_t has been realized, is:

$$q^e(\theta_t, t) = \sum_{s=t+1}^{\infty} \sum_{j=1}^{N_s} q(\theta_t, \theta_s(j)) d(\theta_s(j)), \tag{11.9}$$

or, with a recursive representation,

$$q^e(\theta_t, t) = \sum_{\theta_{t+1}} q(\theta_t, \theta_{t+1})\{q^e(\theta_{t+1}, t+1) + d(\theta_{t+1})\} \tag{11.10}$$

Equation (11.10) may also be expressed as

$$q^e(\theta_t, t) = q^b(\theta_t, t+1) E_t^{RN}\{q^e(\tilde{\theta}_{t+1}, t+1) + d(\tilde{\theta}_{t+1})\}, \tag{11.11}$$

where E_t^{RN} denotes the expectation taken with respect to the relevant risk-neutral transition probabilities; equivalently,

$$q^e(\theta_t, t) = \frac{1}{1 + r_f(\theta_t)} E_t^{RN}\{q^e(\tilde{\theta}_{t+1}, t+1) + d(\tilde{\theta}_{t+1})\},$$

Returning again to the present value expression, Equation (11.9), we have

$$q^e(\theta_t, t) = \sum_{s=t+1}^{\infty} E_t^{RN}\{g(\theta_t, \tilde{\theta}_s) d(\tilde{\theta}_s)\} = \sum_{s=t+1}^{\infty} E_t^{RN}\left\{\frac{d(\tilde{\theta}_s)}{\prod_{j=0}^{s-1}(1 + r_f(\tilde{\theta}_{t+j}))}\right\}. \tag{11.12}$$

What does Equation (11.12) mean? Any state $\hat{\theta}_s$ in period $s \geq t+1$ has a unique sequence of states preceding it. The product of the risk-neutral transition probabilities associated with the states along the path defines the (conditional) risk-neutral probability of $\hat{\theta}_s$ itself. The product of this probability and the payment as $d(\hat{\theta}_s)$ is then discounted at the associated accumulation factor—the present value factor corresponding to the risk-free rates identified with the succession of states preceding $\hat{\theta}_s$. For each $s \geq t+1$, the expectation represents the sum of all these terms, one for each θ_s feasible from θ_t.

Since the notational intensity tends to obscure what is basically a very straightforward idea, let us turn to a small numerical example.

Example 11.2

Let us value a two-period equity security, where $U(c_t, t) \equiv U(c_t) = \ln c_t$ for the representative agent (no discounting). The evolution of uncertainty is given by Figure 11-2 where

$$\pi(\theta_0, \theta_{1,1}) = .6 \qquad \pi(\theta_{1,1}, \theta_{2,1}) = .3$$
$$\pi(\theta_0, \theta_{1,2}) = .4 \qquad \pi(\theta_{1,1}, \theta_{2,2}) = .7$$
$$\pi(\theta_{1,2}, \theta_{2,3}) = .6$$
$$\pi(\theta_{1,2}, \theta_{2,4}) = .4$$

The consumption at each node, which equals the dividend, is represented as the quantity in parenthesis ( ). To valuate this asset risk neutrally, we consider three stages.

1. Compute the (conditional) risk-neutral probabilities at each node:

$$\pi^{RN}(\theta_0, \theta_{1,1}) = \pi(\theta_0, \theta_{1,1})\left\{\frac{U_1(c(\theta_{1,1}))}{E_0\{U_1(c(\tilde{\theta}_1))\}}\right\} = \frac{\frac{1}{5}}{(.6(\frac{1}{5}) + .4(\frac{1}{3}))} = .4737$$

$$\pi^{RN}(\theta_0, \theta_{1,2}) = 1 - \pi^{RN}(\theta_0, \theta_{1,1}) = .5263$$

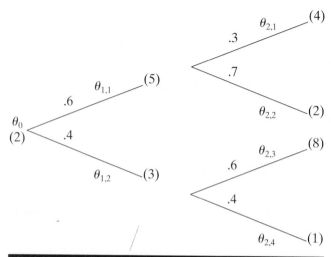

FIGURE 11-2 The Structure of Security Payoffs—Two Periods—Two States at Each Node

$$\pi^{RN}(\theta_{1,1}, \theta_{2,1}) = \pi(\theta_{1,1}, \theta_{2,1}) \left\{ \frac{\frac{1}{4}}{(.3(\frac{1}{4}) + .7(\frac{1}{2}))} \right\} = .1765$$

$$\pi^{RN}(\theta_{1,1}, \theta_{2,2}) = 1 - \pi^{RN}(\theta_{1,1}, \theta_{2,1}) = .8235$$

$$\pi^{RN}(\theta_{1,2}, \theta_{2,3}) = .1579$$

$$\pi^{RN}(\theta_{1,2}, \theta_{2,4}) = \pi(\theta_{1,2}, \theta_{2,4}) \left\{ \frac{1}{(.6(\frac{1}{8}) + .4(1))} \right\} = .8421$$

2. Compute the conditional bond prices.

$$q^b(\theta_0, 1) = \frac{1}{U_1(c_0)} E_0\{U_1(c_1(\tilde{\theta}))\} = \frac{1}{(\frac{1}{2})}\{.6(\frac{1}{5}) + .4(\frac{1}{3})\} = .5066$$

$$q^b(\theta_{1,1}, 2) = \frac{1}{(\frac{1}{5})}\{.3(\frac{1}{4}) + .7(\frac{1}{2})\} = 2.125$$

$$q^b(\theta_{1,2}, 2) = \frac{1}{(\frac{1}{3})}\{.6(\frac{1}{8}) + .4(\frac{1}{1})\} = 1.425$$

3. Value the asset.

$$q^e(\theta_0, 0) = \sum_{s=1}^{2} E_0^{RN}\{g(\theta_0, \tilde{\theta}_s)d(\tilde{\theta}_s)\}$$

$$= q^b(\theta_0, 1)\{\pi^{RN}(\theta_0, \theta_{1,1})(5) + \pi^{RN}(\theta_0, \theta_{1,2})(3)\}$$
$$+ q^b(\theta_0, 1)q^b(\theta_{1,1}, 2)\{\pi^{RN}(\theta_0, \theta_{1,1})\pi^{RN}(\theta_{1,1}, \theta_{2,1})(4)$$
$$+ \pi^{RN}(\theta_0, \theta_{1,1})\pi^{RN}(\theta_{1,1}, \theta_{2,2})(2)\} + q^b(\theta_0, 1)q^b(\theta_{1,2}, 2)$$
$$\times \{\pi^{RN}(\theta_0, \theta_{1,2})\pi^{RN}(\theta_{1,2}, \theta_{2,3})(8) + \pi^{RN}(\theta_0, \theta_{1,2})\pi^{RN}(\theta_{1,2}, \theta_{2,4})(1)\} = 4.00$$

At a practical level this appears to be a messy calculation at best, but it is not obvious how we might compute the no-trade equilibrium asset prices more easily. The Lucas tree methodologies, for example, do not apply here as the setting is not infinitely recursive. This leaves us to solve for the equilibrium prices by working back through the tree and solving for the no-trade prices at each node. It is not clear that this will be any less involved.

Sometimes, however, the risk-neutral valuation procedure does allow for a very suc-
cinct, convenient representation of specific asset prices or price interrelationship. A
case in point is that of a long-term discount bond.

Example 11.3
To price at time t, state θ_t, a long-term discount bond maturing in date $t + k$, observe
that the corresponding dividend $d_{t+k}(\theta_{t+k}) \equiv 1$ for every θ_{t+k} feasible from state θ_t.
Applying Equation (11.12) yields

$$q^b(\theta_t, t + k) = E_t^{RN} g(\theta_t, \tilde{\theta}_{t+k}), \text{ or}$$

$$\frac{1}{(1 + r(\theta_t, t + k))^k} = E_t^{RN}\left\{\frac{1}{\prod_{s=t}^{t+k-1}(1 + r(\theta_s, s + 1))}\right\}. \tag{11.13}$$

Equation (11.13), in either of its incarnations, informs us that the long term rate is the
expectation of the short rates taken with respect to the risk-neutral transition probabilities. This is generally not true if the expectation is taken with the ordinary or
true probabilities.

At this point we draw this formal discussion to a close. We now have an idea what
risk-neutral valuation might mean in a CCAPM context. Appendix 11.1 briefly discusses
the second valuation procedure and illustrates it with the pricing of call and put options.

We thus see that the notion of risk-neutral valuation carries over easily to a
CCAPM context. This is not surprising: The key to the existence of a set of risk-neutral
probabilities is the presence of a complete set of securities markets, which is the case
with the CCAPM. In fact, the somewhat weaker notion of dynamic completeness was
sufficient.

We next turn our attention to equity derivatives pricing. The setting is much more
specialized and not one of general equilibrium (though not inconsistent with it). One
instance of this specialization is that the underlying stock's price is presumed to follow
a specialized stochastic process. The term structure is also presumed to be flat. These
assumptions, taken together, are sufficient to generate the existence of a unique risk-
neutral probability measure, which can be used to value any derivative security written
on the stock. That these probabilities are uniquely identified with the specific underlying stock has led us to dub them *local*.

11.4   THE BINOMIAL MODEL OF DERIVATIVES VALUATION

Under the binomial abstraction we imagine a many-period world in which, at every
date-state node only a stock and a bond are traded. With only two securities to trade,
dynamic completeness requires that at each node there be only two possible succeeding states. For simplicity, we will also assume that the stock pays no dividend, in other
words, that $d(\tilde{\theta}_t) \equiv 0$ for all $t \leq T$. Lastly, in order to avoid any ambiguity in the risk-free
discount factors, it is customary to require that the risk-free rate be constant across all
dates and states. We formalize these assumptions as follows:
   A11.3: The risk-free rate is constant;

$$q^b(\theta_t, t + 1) = \frac{1}{1 + r_f} \quad \text{for all } t \leq T.$$

A11.4: The stock pays no dividends: $d(\tilde{\theta}_t) \equiv 0$ for all $t \le T$.

A11.5: The rate of return to stock ownership follows an i.i.d. process of the form:

$$q^e(\theta_{t+1}, t+1) = \begin{cases} uq^e(\theta_t, t), \text{ with probability } \pi \\ dq^e(\theta_t, t), \text{ with probability } 1 - \pi, \end{cases}$$

where u (up) and d (down) represent gross rates of return. In order to preclude the existence of an arbitrage opportunity it must be the case that

$$u > R_f > d,$$

where, in this context, $R_f = 1 + r_f$.

There are effectively only two possible future states in this model ($\theta_t \in \{\theta_1, \theta_2\}$ where θ_1 is identified with u and θ_2 identified with d) and thus the evolution of the stock's price can be represented by a simple tree structure as seen in Figure 11-3.

Why such a simple setting should be of use is not presently clear, but an explanation will be forthcoming in due course.

In this context, the risk-neutral probabilities can be easily computed from Equation (11.11) specialized to accommodate $d(\theta_t) \equiv 0$:

$$q^e(\theta_t, t) = q^b(\theta_t, t+1)E_t^{RN}\{q^e(\tilde{\theta}_{t+1}, t+1)\}$$
$$= q^b(\theta_t, t+1)\{\pi^{RN}uq^e(\theta_t, t) + (1 - \pi^{RN})dq^e(\theta_t, t)\}. \quad \textbf{(11.14)}$$

This implies

$$R_f = \pi^{RN}u + (1 - \pi^{RN})d,$$

or

$$\pi^{RN} = \frac{R_f - d}{u - d}. \quad \textbf{(11.15)}$$

The power of this simple context is made clear when comparing Equation (11.15) with Equation (11.8). Here risk-neutral probabilities can be expressed without refer-

FIGURE 11-3   A Binomial Tree Structure

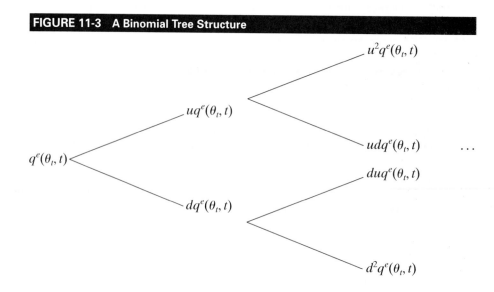

ence to marginal rates of substitution, that is, to agents' preferences.[4] This provides an immense simplification, which all derivative pricing will exploit in one way or another. Of course the same is true for one-period Arrow-Debreu securities since they are priced equal to the present value of their respective risk-neutral probabilities:

$$q(\theta_t, \theta_{t+1} = u) = \left(\frac{1}{R_f}\right)\left(\frac{R_f - d}{u - d}\right), \text{ and}$$

$$q(\theta_t, \theta_{t+1} = d) = \left(\frac{1}{R_f}\right)\left(1 - \frac{R_f - d}{u - d}\right).$$

Furthermore, since the risk-free rate is assumed constant in every period, the price of a claim to one unit of the numeraire to be received $T - t > 1$ periods from now if state θ_T is realized is given by

$$q(\theta_t, \theta_T) = \frac{1}{(1 + r_f(\theta_t, T))^{T-t}} \sum_{\{\theta_t, \dots, \theta_{T-1}\} \in \Omega} \prod_{s=t}^{T-1} \pi^{RN}(\theta_s, \theta_{s+1}),$$

where Ω represents the set of all time paths $\{\theta_t, \theta_{t+1}, \dots, \theta_{T-1}\}$ leading to θ_T. In the binomial setting this becomes

$$q(\theta_t, \theta_T) = \frac{1}{(R_f)^{T-t}} \binom{T - t}{s} (\pi^{RN})^s (1 - \pi^{RN})^{T-t-s}, \qquad \text{(11.16)}$$

where s is the number of intervening periods in which the u state is observed on any path from θ_t to θ_T. Note that although there will be many possible paths to the same state θ_T, all will face the same number of u and d intervening states, respectively. To illustrate the simplicity of this setting we again consider several examples.

Example 11.4
 A European call option revisited: Let the option expire at $T > t$; the price of a European call with exercise price E, given the current date-state (θ_t, t), is

$$C_{\mathcal{E}}(\theta_t, t) = \left(\frac{1}{R_f}\right)^{T-t} E_t^{RN}(\max\{q^e(\theta_T, T) - E, 0\})$$

$$= \left(\frac{1}{R_f}\right)^{T-t} \sum_{s=0}^{T-t} \binom{T - t}{s} (\pi^{RN})^s (1 - \pi^{RN})^{T-t-s} (\max\{q^e(\theta_t, t) u^s d^{T-t-s} - E, 0\})$$

The expression $\binom{T - t}{s}$ represents the number of ways s successes (u moves) can

occur in $T - t$ trials. A standard result states $\binom{T - t}{s} = \dfrac{(T - t)!}{s!(T - t - s)!}$. The expla-

nation is as follows. Any possible period T price of the underlying stock will be identified with a unique number of u and d realizations. Suppose, for example, that $s_1 u$ realizations are required. There are then $\binom{T - t}{s_1}$ possible paths, each of which

has exactly $s_1 u$ and $T - t - s_1 d$ states, leading to the pre-specified period T price. Each path has the common risk-neutral probability $(\pi^{RN})^{s_1} (1 - \pi^{RN})^{T-t-s_1}$. As an example, suppose $T - t = 3$, and the particular final price is the result of 2 up-moves and 1 down-move. Then, there are $3 = 3!/2!1! = 3 \times 2 \times 1/(2 \times 1)(1)$ possible paths leading to that final state: *uud, udu,* and *duu.*

---

[4]Notice that the risk-neutral probability distribution is i.i.d. as well.

When taking the expectation we sum over all possible values of $s \leq T - t$, thus weighting each possible option payoff by the risk-neutral probability of attaining it. Define the quantity $\hat{s}$ as the minimum number of intervening up states necessary for the underlying asset, the stock, to achieve a price in excess of E. The prior expression can then be simplified to:

$$C_{\mathcal{E}}(\theta_t, t) = \frac{1}{(R_f)^{T-t}} \sum_{s=\hat{s}}^{T-t} \binom{T-t}{s} (\pi^{RN})^s (1 - \pi^{RN})^{T-t-s} [q^e(\theta_t, t) u^s d^{T-t-s} - E], \text{ or} \quad \textbf{(11.17)}$$

$$C_{\mathcal{E}}(\theta_t, t) = \frac{1}{(R_f)^{T-t}} \left\{ \sum_{s=\hat{s}}^{T-t} \binom{T-t}{s} (\pi^{RN})^s (1 - \pi^{RN})^{T-t-s} q^e(\theta_t, t) \right.$$

$$\left. - \sum_{s=\hat{s}}^{T-t} \binom{T-t}{s} (\pi^{RN})^s (1 - \pi^{RN})^{T-t-s} E \right\} \quad \textbf{(11.18)}$$

The first term within the braces of Equation (11.18) is the risk-neutral expected value at expiration of the acquired asset if the option is exercised, while the second term is the risk-neutral expected cost of acquiring it. The difference is the risk-neutral expected value of the call's payoff (value) at expiration.[5] To value the call today, this quantity is then put on a present value basis by discounting at the risk-free rate R_f. This same valuation can also be obtained by working backward, recursively, through the tree. Since markets are complete, in the absence of arbitrage opportunities any asset—the call included—is priced equal to its expected value in the succeeding time period discounted at R_f. This implies

$$C_{\mathcal{E}}(\theta_t, t) = q^b(\theta_t, t) E^{RN} C_{\mathcal{E}}(\tilde{\theta}_{t+1}, t + 1). \quad \textbf{(11.19)}$$

Let us next illustrate how this fact may be used to compute the call's value in a simple three-period example.

Example 11.5

Let $u = 1.1$, $d = 1/u = .91$, $q^e(\theta_t, t) = \$50$, $E = \$53$, $R_f = 1.05$, $T - t = 3$.

$$\pi^{RN} = \frac{R_f - d}{u - d} = \frac{1.05 - .91}{1.1 - .91} = .70$$

The numbers in parenthesis in Figure 11-4 are the recursive values of the call, working backward in the manner of Equation (11.19). These are obtained as follows:

$$C_{\mathcal{E}}(u^3, t + 3) = \frac{1}{1.05} \{.70(12.55) + .30(2)\} = 8.94$$

$$C_{\mathcal{E}}(u^2 d, t + 2) = \frac{1}{1.05} \{.70(2) + .30(0)\} = 1.33$$

$$C_{\mathcal{E}}(u, t + 1) = \frac{1}{1.05} \{.70(8.94) + .30(1.33)\} = 6.34$$

$$C_{\mathcal{E}}(d, t + 1) = \frac{1}{1.05} \{.70(1.33) + .30(0)\} = .89$$

$$C_{\mathcal{E}}(\theta_t, t) = \frac{1}{1.05} \{.70(6.34) + .30(.89)\} = 4.49$$

---

[5] Recall that there is no actual transfer of the security. Rather, this difference $q^e(\theta_T, T) - E$ represents the amount of money the writer (seller) of the call must transfer to the buyer at the expiration date if the option is exercised.

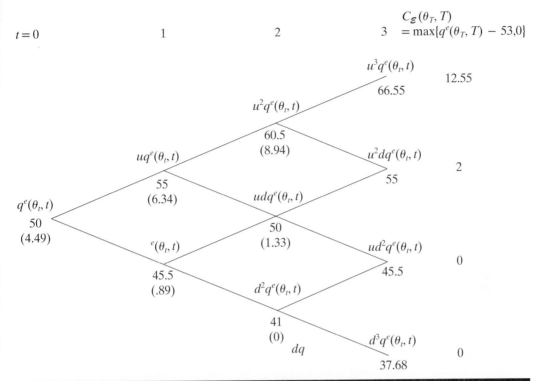

FIGURE 11-4   The Binomial Tree of Example 11.5

For a simple call, its payoff at expiration is dependent only upon the value of the underlying asset (relative to E) at that time, irrespective of its price history. For example, the value of the call when $q^e(\theta_T, T) = 55$ is the same if the price history is (50, 55, 50, 55) or (50, 45.5, 50, 55).

For other derivatives, however, this is not the case; they are *path dependent*. An Asian (path-dependent) option is a case in point. Nevertheless, the same valuation methods apply: Its expected payoff is computed using the risk-neutral probabilities, discounted at the risk-free rate.

TABLE 11-1   Payoff Pattern—Asian Option

t	$T + 1$	$t + 2$	$\ldots$	$T - 1$	T
0	0	0		0	$\max\{q^e_{\text{AVG}}(\theta_T, T) - E, 0\}$

Example 11.6

A path dependent option: We consider an Asian call option for which the payoff pattern assumes the form outlined in Table 11-1.

where $q^{\text{AVG}}_e(\theta_T, T)$ is the average price of the stock along the path from $q^e(\theta_t, t)$ to, and including, $q^e(\theta_T, T)$. We may express the period t value of such an option as

$$C_A(\theta_t, t) = \frac{1}{(R_f)^{T-t}} E_t^{RN}\{\max\{q^e_{\text{AVG}}(\theta_T, T) - E, 0\}$$

$$= \frac{1}{(R_f)^{T-t}} \sum_{s=0}^{T-t} \binom{T-t}{s} (\pi^{RN})^s (1 - \pi^{RN})^{T-t-s} (\max\{q^e_{AVG}(\theta_T, T) - E, 0\})$$

A simple numerical example with $T - t = 2$ follows. Let $q^e(\theta_t, t) = 100$, $E = 100$, $u = 1.05$, $d = 1/u = .95$, and $R_f = 1.005$. The corresponding risk-neutral probabilities are

$$\pi^{RN} = \frac{R_f - d}{u - d} = \frac{1.005 - .95}{1.05 - .95} = .55; \ 1 - \pi^{RN} = .45$$

With two periods remaining, the possible evolutions of the stock's price and corresponding option payoffs are those found in Figure 11-5. Thus,

$$C_A(\theta_t, t) = \frac{1}{(1.005)^2} \{(.55)^2(5.083) + (.55)(.45)(1.67)\}$$
$$= \$1.932$$

Note that we may as well work backward, recursively, in the price/payoff tree as shown in Figure 11-6

$$\text{where} \quad C_A(\theta_{t+1} = u, t+1) = 3.53 = \frac{1}{(1.005)} \{.55(5.083) + .45(1.67)\}, \text{ and}$$

$$C_A(\theta_t, t) = \frac{1}{(1.005)} \{.55(3.53) + .45(0)\} = \$1.932.$$

A number of fairly detailed comments are presently in order. Note that with a path-dependent option it is not possible to apply, naively, a variation on Equation (11.18). Unlike with straightforward calls, the value of this type of option is not the same for all paths leading to the same final-period asset price.

Who might be interested to purchase such an option? For one thing, they have payoff patterns similar in spirit to an ordinary call, but are generally less expensive

FIGURE 11-5 Evolution of the Stock's Price and the Asian Option Payoffs

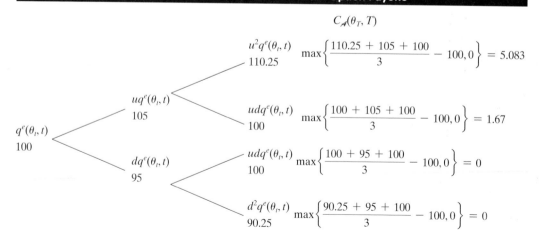

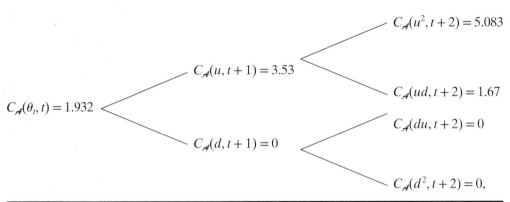

$$C_A(u^2, t+2) = 5.083$$

$$C_A(u, t+1) = 3.53$$

$$C_A(ud, t+2) = 1.67$$

$$C_A(\theta_t, t) = 1.932$$

$$C_A(du, t+2) = 0$$

$$C_A(d, t+1) = 0$$

$$C_A(d^2, t+2) = 0,$$

FIGURE 11-6   Computing Recursively the Value of the Asian Option

(there is less upward potential in the average than in the price itself). This feature has contributed to the usefulness of path-dependent options in foreign exchange trading. Consider a firm that needs to provide a stream of payments (say, perhaps, for factory construction) in a foreign currency. It would want protection against a rise in the value of the foreign currency relative to its own, because such a rise would increase the cost of the payment stream in terms of the firm's own currency. Since many payments are to be made, what is of concern is the average price of the foreign currency rather than its price at any specific date. By purchasing the correct number of Asian calls on the foreign currency, the firm can create a payment for itself if, on average, the foreign currency's value exceeds the strike price—the level above which the firm would like to be insured. By analogous reasoning, if the firm wished to protect the average value of a stream of payments it was receiving in a foreign currency, the purchase of Asian puts would be one alternative.

We do not want to lose sight of the fact that risk-neutral valuation is a direct consequence of the dynamic completeness (at each node there are two possible future states and two securities available for trade) and the no-arbitrage assumption, a connection that is especially apparent in the binomial setting. Consider a call option with expiration one period from the present. Over this period the stock's price behavior and the corresponding payoffs to the call option are as found in Figure 11-7.

FIGURE 11-7   A Call Option One Period to Expiration and the Underlying Stock's Price

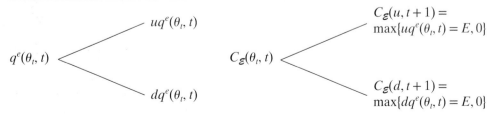

$$uq^e(\theta_t, t)$$

$$C_\varepsilon(u, t+1) = \max\{uq^e(\theta_t, t) = E, 0\}$$

$$q^e(\theta_t, t)$$

$$C_\varepsilon(\theta_t, t)$$

$$dq^e(\theta_t, t)$$

$$C_\varepsilon(d, t+1) = \max\{dq^e(\theta_t, t) = E, 0\}$$

By the assumed dynamic completeness we know that the payoff to the option can be replicated on a state-by-state basis by a position in the stock and the bond. Let this position be characterized by a portfolio of Δ shares and a bond investment of value B (for simplicity of notation we suppress the dependence of these latter quantities on the current state and date). Replication requires

$$uq^e(\theta_t, t)\Delta + R_f B = C_{\mathcal{E}}(u, t + 1), \text{ and}$$
$$dq^e(\theta_t, t)\Delta + R_f B = C_{\mathcal{E}}(d, t + 1)$$

from which follows

$$\Delta = \frac{C_{\mathcal{E}}(u, t + 1) - C_{\mathcal{E}}(d, t + 1)}{(u - d)q^e(\theta_t, t)}, \text{ and}$$

$$B = \frac{uC_{\mathcal{E}}(d, t + 1) - dC_{\mathcal{E}}(u, t + 1)}{(u - d)R_f}.$$

By the no arbitrage assumption:

$$
\begin{aligned}
C_{\mathcal{E}}(\theta_t, t) &= \Delta q^e(\theta_t, t) + B \\
&= \left\{ \frac{C_{\mathcal{E}}(u, t + 1) - C_{\mathcal{E}}(d, t + 1)}{(u - d)q^e(\theta_t, t)} q^e(\theta_t, t) \right. \\
&\quad \left. + \frac{uC_{\mathcal{E}}(d, t + 1) - dC_{\mathcal{E}}(u, t + 1)}{(u - d)R_f} \right\} \\
&= \left(\frac{1}{R_f}\right) \left\{ \left(\frac{R_f - d}{u - d}\right) C_{\mathcal{E}}(u, t + 1) + \left(\frac{u - R_f}{u - d}\right) C_{\mathcal{E}}(d, t + 1) \right\} \\
&= \left(\frac{1}{R_f}\right) \{\pi^{RN} C_{\mathcal{E}}(u, t + 1) + (1 - \pi^{RN}) C_{\mathcal{E}}(d, t + 1)\},
\end{aligned}
$$

which is just a specialized case of Equation (11.18).

Valuing an option (or other derivative) using risk-neutral valuation is thus equivalent to pricing its replicating portfolio of stock and debt. Working backward in the tree corresponds to recomputing the portfolio of stock and debt that replicates the derivative's payoffs at each of the succeeding nodes. In the earlier example of the Asian option, the value 3.53 at the intermediate u node represents the value of the portfolio of stocks and bonds necessary to replicate the option's values in the second-period nodes leading from it (5.083 in the u state, 1.67 in the d state).

Let us see how the replicated portfolio evolves in the case of the Asian option written on a stock.

$$\Delta_u = \frac{C_A(u^2, t + 2) - C_A(ud, t + 2)}{(u - d)q^e(\theta_t, t)} = \frac{5.083 - 1.67}{(1.05 - .95)(105)} = .325$$

$$B_u = \frac{uC_A(ud, t + 2) - dC_A(u^2, t + 2)}{(u - d)R_f} = \frac{(1.05)(1.67) - (.95)(5.083)}{(1.05 - .95)(1.005)} = -30.60$$

$$\Delta_d = 0$$
$$B_d = 0 \quad \text{(all branches leading from the "}d\text{" node result in zero option value)}$$

$$\Delta = \frac{C_A(u, t + 1) - C_A(d, t + 1)}{(u - d)q^e(\theta_t, t)} = \frac{3.53 - 0}{(1.05 - .95)(100)} = .353$$

$$B = \frac{uC_A(d, t + 1) - dC_A(u, t + 1)}{(u - d)R_f} = \frac{(1.05)(0) - (.95)(3.53)}{(1.05 - .95)(1.005)} = -33.33$$

We interpret these numbers as follows. In order to replicate the value of the Asian option, irrespective of whether the underlying stock's price rises to $105 or falls to $95.20, it is necessary to construct a portfolio composed of a loan of $33.33 at R_f in conjunction with a long position of .353 share. The net cost is

$$.353(100) - 33.33 = \$1.97,$$

the cost of the Asian call, except for rounding errors. To express this idea slightly differently, if you want to replicate, at each node, the value of the Asian option, borrow $33.33 (at R_f) and, together with your own capital contribution of $1.97, take this money and purchase .353 share of the underlying stock.

As the underlying stock's value evolves through time, this portfolio's value will evolve so that at any node it matches exactly the call's value. At the first u node, for example, the portfolio will be worth $3.53. Together with a loan of $30.60, this latter sum will allow the purchase of .325 share, with no additional capital contribution required. Once assembled, the portfolio is entirely self-financing, no additional capital need be added and none may be withdrawn (until expiration).

This discussion suggests that Asian call options represent a levered position in the underlying stock. To see this, note that at the initial node the replicating portfolio consists of a $1.97 equity contribution by the purchaser in conjunction with a loan of $30.60. This implies a debt/equity ratio of $30.60/1.97 $\cong$ 15.5! For the analogous straight call, with the same exercise price as the Asian call and the same underlying price process, the analogous quantities are, respectively, $3.07 and $54.47, giving a debt/equity ratio of approximately 18. Call-related securities are thus attractive instruments for speculation! For a relatively small cash outlay, a stock's entire upward potential (within a limited span of time) can be purchased.

Under this pricing perspective there are no arbitrage opportunities within the universe of the underlying asset, the bond, or any derivative asset written on the underlying asset. We were reminded of this fact in the prior discussion! The price of the call at all times equals the value of the replicating portfolio. It does not, however, preclude the existence of such opportunities among different stocks or among derivatives written on different stocks.

These discussions make apparent the fact that binomial risk-neutral valuation views derivative securities, and call options in particular, as redundant assets, redundant in the sense that their payoffs can be replicated with a portfolio of preexisting securities. The presence or absence of these derivatives is deemed not to affect the price of the underlying asset (the stock) on which they are written. This is in direct contrast to our earlier motivation for the existence of options: their desirable property in assisting in the completion of the market. In principle, the introduction of an option has the potential of changing all asset values if it makes the market more complete.

This issue has been examined fairly extensively in the literature. From a theoretical perspective, Detemple and Selden (1991) construct a mean variance example where there is one risky asset, one risk-free asset, and an incomplete market. There the introduction of a call option is shown to increase the equilibrium price of the risky asset. In light of our earlier discussions, this is not entirely surprising: The introduction of the option enhances opportunities for risk sharing, thereby increasing demand and consequently the price of the risky asset. This result can be shown not to be fully applicable to all contexts, however. On the empirical side, Detemple and Jorion (1990) examine a large sample of options introductions over the period 1973 to 1986 and find that, on average, the underlying stock's price rises 3 percent as a result and its volatility diminishes.

11.5 CONTINUOUS TIME: AN INTRODUCTION TO THE BLACK-SCHOLES FORMULA

While the binomial model presents a transparent application of risk-neutral valuation, it is not clear that it represents the accurate description of the price evolution of any known security. We deal with this issue presently.

Fat tails aside, there is ample evidence to suggest that stock prices may be modeled as being lognormally distributed; more formally,

$$\ln q^e(\theta_T, T) \sim N(\ln q^e(\theta_t, t) + \mu(T - t), \sigma\sqrt{T - t}),$$

where μ and σ denote, respectively, the mean and standard deviation of the continuously compounded rate of return over the reference period, typically one year (recall Appendix to Chapter 8 where these quantities were estimated). Regarding t as the present time, this expression describes the distribution of stock prices at some time T in the future given the current price $q^e(\theta_t, t)$. The length of the time horizon $T - t$ is measured in years.

The key result is this: properly parameterized, the distribution of final prices generated by the binomial distribution can arbitrarily well approximate the prior lognormal distribution when the number of branches becomes very large. More precisely, we may imagine a binomial model in which we divide the period $T - t$ into n subintervals of equal length $\Delta t(n) = (T - t)/n$. If we adjust u, d, p (the true probability of a u price move) and R_f appropriately, then as $n \to \infty$, the distribution of period T prices generated by the binomial model will converge in probability to the hypothesized lognormal distribution. The adjustment requires that

$$u(n) = e^{\sigma\sqrt{\Delta t(n)}}, \quad d(n) = \frac{1}{u(n)}, \quad p = \frac{e^{\mu\Delta t(n)} - d(n)}{u(n) - d(n)}, \text{ and}$$

$$R_f(n) = (R_f)^{1/n} \tag{11.20}$$

For this identification, the binomial valuation formula for a call option, Equation (11.18), converges to the Black-Scholes formula for a European call option written on a non-dividend paying stock:

$$C_g(\theta_t, t) = q^e(\theta_t, T)N(d_1) - Ee^{-\hat{r}_f(T-t)}N(d_2) \tag{11.21}$$

where $N(\ )$ is the cumulative normal probability distribution function,

$$\hat{r}_f = \ln(R_f)$$

$$d_1 = \frac{\ln\left(\dfrac{q_e(\theta_t, t)}{E}\right) + (T - t)\left(\hat{r}_f + \dfrac{\sigma^2}{2}\right)}{\sigma\sqrt{T - t}}$$

$$d_2 = d_1 - \sigma\sqrt{T - t}$$

Cox and Rubinstein (1985) provide a detailed development and proof of this equivalence, but we can see the rudiments of its origin in Equation (11.18), which we now present, modified to make apparent its dependence on the number of subintervals n:

$$C_{\mathcal{E}}(\theta_t, t; n) = \frac{1}{(R_f(n))^n}\left\{ \sum_{s=a(n)}^{n} \binom{n}{s} (\pi(n)^{RN})^s (1 - \pi(n)^{RN})^{n-s} q^e(\theta_t, t)\right.$$
$$\left. - \sum_{s=a(n)}^{n} \binom{n}{s} (\pi(n)^{RN})^s (1 - \pi(n)^{RN})^{n-s} E\right\} \qquad \textbf{(11.22)}$$

where

$$\pi(n)^{RN} = \frac{R_f(n) - d(n)}{u(n) - d(n)}.$$

Rearranging terms yields

$$C_{\mathcal{E}}(\theta_t, t; n) = q^e(\theta_t, t) \sum_{s=a}^{n} \binom{n}{s}\left(\frac{\pi(n)^{RN}}{R_f(n)}\right)^s \left(\frac{1 - \pi(n)^{RN}}{R_f(n)}\right)^{n-s}$$
$$- E\left(\frac{1}{R_f(n)}\right)^n \sum_{s=a}^{n} \binom{n}{s} (\pi(n)^{RN})^s (1 - \pi(n)^{RN})^{n-s}, \qquad \textbf{(11.23)}$$

which is of the general form

$$C_{\mathcal{E}}(\theta_t, t; n) = q_e(\theta_t, t) \times \text{Probability} - (\text{present value factor}) \times E \times \text{Probability},$$

as per the Black-Scholes formula. Since, at each step of the limiting process (i.e., for each n, as $n \mapsto \infty$), the call valuation formula is fundamentally an expression of risk-neutral valuation, the same must be true of its limit. As such, the Black-Scholes formula represents the first hint at the translation of risk-neutral methods to the case of continuous time.

Let us conclude this section with a few more observations. The first concerns the relationship of the Black-Scholes formula to the replicating portfolio idea. Since at each step of the limiting process the call's value is identical to that of the replicating portfolio, this notion must carry over to the continuous time setting. This is indeed the case: in a context when investors may continuously and costlessly adjust the composition of the replicating portfolio, the initial position to assume (at time t) is one of $N(d_1)$ shares, financed in part by a risk-free loan of $Ee^{-R_f T}N(d_2)$. The net cost of assembling the portfolio is the Black-Scholes value of the call.

Notice also that neither the mean return on the underlying asset nor the true probabilities explicitly enter anywhere in the discussion.[6] None of this is surprising. The short explanation is simply that risk-neutral valuation abandons the true probabilities in favor of the risk-neutral ones and, in doing so, all assets are determined to earn the risk-free rate. The underlying assets' mean return still matters, but it is now R_f. More intuitively, risk-neutral valuation is essentially no-arbitrage pricing. In a world with full information and without transaction costs, investors will eliminate all arbitrage opportunities irrespective of their objective likelihood or of the mean returns of the assets involved.

It is sometimes remarked that to purchase a call option is to buy volatility, and we need to understand what this expression is intended to convey. Returning to the binomial approximation [in conjunction with Equation (11.18)], we observe first that a larger σ implies the possibility of a higher underlying asset price at expiration, with the attendant

---

[6]They are implicitly present in the equilibrium price of the underlying asset.

higher call payoff. More formally, σ is the only statistical characteristic of the underlying stock's rate of return process to appear in the Black-Scholes formula. Given r_f, E, and $q^e(\theta_t, t)$, there is a unique identification between the call's value and σ. For this reason, estimates of an asset's volatility are frequently obtained from its corresponding call price by inverting the Black-Scholes formula. This is referred to as an *implied volatility estimate*.

The use of risk-neutral methods for the valuation of options is probably the area in which asset pricing theory has made the most progress. Indeed, Scholes and Merton were awarded the Nobel Prize for their work (Fischer Black had died). So much progress has, in fact, been made that the finance profession has largely turned away from conceptual issues in derivatives valuation to focus on the development of fast computer valuation algorithms that mimic the risk-neutral methods. This, in turn, has allowed the use of derivatives, especially for hedging purposes, to increase so enormously over the past 20 years.

For a more detailed discussion of the continuous time setting and applications of risk-neutral valuation in that context, the reader is referred to Appendix 11.2.

11.6 DYBVIG'S EVALUATION OF DYNAMIC TRADING STRATEGIES

Let us next turn to a final application of these methods: the evaluation of dynamic trading strategies. To do so, we retain the partial equilibrium setting of the binomial model, but invite agents to have preferences over the various outcomes. Note that under the pure pricing perspective of Section 11.4, preferences were irrelevant. All investors would agree on the prices of call and put options (and all other derivatives) regardless of their degrees of risk aversion, or their subjective beliefs as to the true probability of an up or down state. This is simply a reflection of the fact that any rational investor, whether highly risk averse or risk neutral, will seek to profit by an arbitrage opportunity, whatever the likelihood, and that in equilibrium, assets should thus be priced so that such opportunities are absent. In this section our goal is different, and preferences will have a role to play. We return to assumption A11.1.

Consider the optimal consumption problem of an agent who takes security prices as given and who seeks to maximize the present value of time-separable utility (A11.1). His optimal consumption plan solves

$$\max E_0\left(\sum_{t=0}^{\infty} U(\tilde{c}_t, t) \right)$$

$$\text{s.t.} \sum_{t=0}^{\infty} \sum_{s \in N_t} q(\theta_0, \theta_t(s))c(\theta_t(s)) \leq Y_0, \tag{11.24}$$

where Y_0 is his initial period 0 wealth and $q(\theta_0, \theta_t(s))$ is the period $t = 0$ price of an Arrow-Debreu security paying one unit of the numeraire if state s is observed at time $t > 0$. Assuming a finite number of states and expanding the expectations operator to make explicit the state probabilities, the Lagrangian for this problem is

$$\mathcal{L}(\ ) = \sum_{t=0}^{\infty} \sum_{s=1}^{N_t} \pi(\theta_0, \theta_t(s))U(c(\theta_t(s), t)) + \lambda\left(Y_0 - \sum_{t=0}^{\infty} \sum_{s=1}^{N_t} q(\theta_0, \theta_t(s))c(\theta_t(s)) \right),$$

where $\pi(\theta_0, \theta_t(s))$ is the conditional probability of state s occurring, at time t and λ the Lagrange multiplier.

The first order condition is

$$U_1(c(\theta_t(s)), t)\pi(\theta_0, \theta_t(s)) = \lambda q(\theta_0, \theta_t(s)).$$

By the concavity of $U(\ )$, if $\theta_t(1)$ and $\theta_t(2)$ are two states, then

$$\frac{q(\theta_0, \theta_t(1))}{\pi(\theta_0, \theta_t(1))} > \frac{q(\theta_0, \theta_t(2))}{\pi(\theta_0, \theta_t(2))}, \text{ if and only if } c(\theta_t(1), t) < c(\theta_t(2), t). \quad \textbf{(11.25)}$$

It follows that if

$$\frac{q(\theta_0, \theta_t(1))}{\pi(\theta_0, \theta_t(1))} = \frac{q(\theta_0, \theta_t(2))}{\pi(\theta_0, \theta_t(2))}, \text{ then } c(\theta_t(1)) = c(\theta_t(2)).$$

The $q(\theta_0, \theta_t(s))/\pi(\theta_0, \theta_t(s))$ ratio measures the relative scarcity of consumption in state $\theta_t(s)$: A high ratio in some state suggests that the price of consumption is very high relative to the likelihood of that state being observed. This suggests that consumption is scarce in the high $q(\theta_0, \theta_t(s))/\pi(\theta_0, \theta_t(s))$ states. A rational agent will consume less in these states and more in the relatively cheaper ones, as Equation (11.25) suggests.

This observation is, in fact, quite general as Proposition 11.1 demonstrates.

Proposition 11.1 [Dybvig (1988)]:
Consider the consumption allocation problem described by Equation (11.24). For any rational investor for which $U_{11}(c_t, t) < 0$, his optimal consumption plan is a decreasing function of $q(\theta_0, \theta_t(s))/\pi(\theta_0, \theta_t(s))$. Furthermore, for any consumption plan with this monotonicity property, there exists a rational investor with concave period utility function $U(c_t, t)$ for which the consumption plan is optimal in the sense of solving Equation (11.24).

Dybvig (1988) illustrates the power of this result most effectively in the binomial context where the price-to-probability ratio assumes an especially simple form. Note that in the binomial model the state at time t is completely characterized by the number of up states, u, preceding it. Consider a state $\theta_t(s)$ where s denotes the number of preceding up states. The true conditional probability of $\theta_t(s)$ is

$$\pi(\theta_0, \theta_t(s)) = \pi^s(1 - \pi)^{t-s},$$

while the corresponding state claim has price

$$q(\theta_0, \theta_t(s)) = (R_f)^{-t}(\pi^{RN})^s(1 - \pi^{RN})^{t-s}.$$

The price/probability ratio thus assumes the form

$$\frac{q(\theta_0, \theta_t(s))}{\pi(\theta_0, \theta_t(s))} = (R_f)^{-t}\left(\frac{\pi^{RN}}{\pi}\right)^s\left(\frac{1 - \pi^{RN}}{1 - \pi}\right)^{t-s} = (R_f)^{-t}\left(\frac{\pi^{RN}(1 - \pi)}{(1 - \pi^{RN})\pi}\right)^s\left(\frac{1 - \pi^{RN}}{1 - \pi}\right)^t.$$

We now specialize the binomial process by further requiring the condition in assumption A11.6.

A11.6: $\pi u + (1 - \pi)d > R_f$, in other words, the expected return on the stock exceeds the risk-free rate.

Assumption A11.6 implies that

$$\pi > \frac{R_f - d}{u - d} = \pi^{RN},$$

$$\text{so that } \frac{\pi^{RN}(1 - \pi)}{(1 - \pi^{RN})\pi} < 1,$$

for any time t, and the price probability ratio $q(\theta_0, \theta_t(s))/\pi(\theta_0, \theta_t(s))$ is a decreasing function of the number of preceding up moves, s. By Proposition 11.1 the period t level of optimal, planned consumption across states $\theta_t(s)$ is thus an *increasing function of the number of up moves, s, preceding it.*

Let us now specialize our agent's preferences to assume that he is only concerned with his consumption at some terminal date T, at which time he consumes his wealth. Equation (11.24) easily specializes to this case:

$$\max \sum_{s=1}^{N_t} \pi(\theta_0, \theta_T(s))U(c(\theta_T(s)))$$

$$\text{s.t. } \sum_{s=1}^{N_t} q(\theta_0, \theta_T(s))c(\theta_T(s)) \leq Y_0. \tag{11.26}$$

In effect, we set $U(c_t, t) \equiv 0$ for $t \leq T$.

Remember also that a stock, from the perspective of an agent who is concerned only with terminal wealth, can be viewed as a portfolio of period t state claims. The results of Proposition 11.1 thus apply to this security as well.

Dybvig (1988) shows how these latter observations can be used to assess the optimality of many commonly used trading strategies. The context of his discussion is illustrated with the example in Figure 11-8, where the investor is presumed to consume his wealth at the end of the trading period.

For this particular setup, $\pi^{RN} = \frac{1}{3}$. He considers the following frequently cited equity trading strategies:

1. Technical analysis: buy the stock and sell it after an up move; buy it back after a down move; invest at R_f (zero in this example) when out of the market. But under this strategy

$$c_4(\theta_t(s)|uuuu) = \$32, \text{ yet}$$
$$c_4(\theta_t(s)|udud) = \$48; \text{ in other words,}$$

the investor consumes more in the state with the fewer preceding up moves, which violates the optimality condition. This cannot be an optimal strategy.
2. Stop-loss strategy: buy and hold the stock, sell only if the price drops to $8, and stay out of the market. Consider, again, two possible evolutions of the stock's price:

$$c_4(\theta_t(s)|duuu) = \$8$$
$$c_4(\theta_t(s)|udud) = \$16.$$

Once again, consumption is not an increasing function of the number of up states under this trading strategy, which must, therefore, be suboptimal.

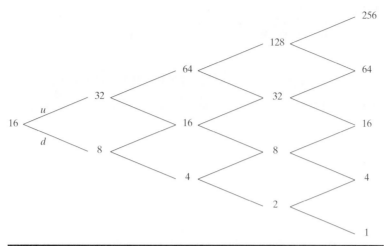

FIGURE 11-8   Binomial Evolution of a Stock's Price Over Four Periods

11.7   CONCLUSIONS

We have extended the notion of risk-neutral valuation to two important contexts: the dynamic setting of the general equilibrium consumption CAPM, and the partial equilibrium binomial model. The return on our investment is particularly apparent in the latter framework. The reasons are clear: In the binomial context, which provides the conceptual foundations for an important part of continuous time finance, the risk-neutral probabilities can be identified independently from agents' preferences. Knowledge of the relevant inter-temporal marginal rates of substitution, in particular, is superfluous. This is the huge dividend of the twin modeling choices of binomial framework and arbitrage pricing. It has paved the way for routine pricing of complex derivative-based financial products and for their attendant use in a wide range of modern financial contracts.

References

Cox, J., and M. Rubinstein, *Option Markets*, Upper Saddle River, N.J.: Prentice Hall, 1985.

Detemple, J., and P. Jorion, "Option Listing and Stock Returns: An Empirical Analysis," *Journal of Banking and Finance*, 14 (1990): 781–801.

Detemple, J., and L. Selden, "A General Equilibrium Analysis of Option and Stock Market Interactions," *International Economic Review*, 32 (1991): 279–303.

Dybvig, P. H., "Inefficient Dynamic Portfolio Strategies or How to Throw Away a Million Dollars in the Stock Market," *The Review of Financial Studies*, 1 (1988): 67–88.

Mehra, R., and R. Sah, "Mood Fluctuations, Projection Bias, and Volatility of Equity Prices," mimeo, University of California–Santa Barbara, Department of Economics, 2001.

Telmer, C., "Asset Pricing Puzzles and Incomplete Markets," *Journal of Finance*, 48 (1993): 1803–1832.

For an excellent text that deals with continuous time from an applications perspective, see Luenberger, D., *Investments*, New York: Oxford University Press, 1998.

For an excellent text with a more detailed description of continuous time processes, see Dumas, B., and B. Allaz, *Financial Securities*, London: Chapman and Hall, 1996.

A P P E N D I X   1 1 . 1

Risk-Neutral Valuation When Discounting at the Term Structure

STRUCTURE OF MULTIPERIOD DISCOUNT BOND

Here we seek a valuation formula where we discount not at the succession of one-period rates, but at the term structure. This necessitates a different set of risk-neutral probabilities with respect to which the expectation is taken.

Define the k period, time adjusted risk-neutral transition probabilities as:

$$\hat{\pi}^{RN}(\theta_t, \theta_{t+k}) = \left\{ \frac{\pi^{RN}(\theta_t, \theta_{t+k}) g(\theta_t, \theta_{t+k})}{q^b(\theta_t, \theta_{t+k})} \right\},$$

where $\pi^{RN}(\theta_t, \theta_{t+k}) = \prod_{s=t}^{t+k-1} \pi^{RN}(\theta_s, \theta_{s+1})$, and $\{\theta_t, \dots, \theta_{t+k-1}\}$ is the path of states preceding θ_{t+k}. Clearly, the $\hat{\pi}^{RN}()$ are positive since $\pi^{RN}() \geq 0, g(\theta_t, \theta_{t+k}) > 0$ and $q^b(\theta_t, \theta_{t+k}) > 0$. Furthermore, by Equation (11.13),

$$\sum_{\theta_{t+k}} \hat{\pi}^{RN}(\theta_t, \theta_{t+k})$$

$$= \left(\frac{1}{q^b(\theta_t, \theta_{t+k})} \right) \sum_{\theta_{t+k}} \pi^{RN}(\theta_t, \theta_{t+k}) g(\theta_t, \theta_{t+k})$$

$$= \frac{q^b(\theta_t, \theta_{t+k})}{q^b(\theta_t, \theta_{t+k})} = 1.$$

Let us now use this approach to price European call and put options. A European call op-

tion contract represents the right (but not the obligation) to buy some underlying asset at some prespecified price (referred to as the exercise or strike price) at some prespecified future date (date of contract expiration). Since such a contract represents a right, its payoff is as shown in Table A11-1, where T represents the time of expiration and E the exercise price.

Let $C_{\mathcal{E}}(\theta_t, t)$ denote the period t, state θ_t price of the call option. Clearly,

$$C_{\mathcal{E}}(\theta_t, t)$$
$$= E_t^{RN}\{g(\theta_t, \tilde{\theta}_T)(\max\{q^e(\tilde{\theta}_T, T) - E, 0\})\}$$
$$= q^b(\theta_t, T)\hat{E}_t^{RN}\{\max\{q^e(\tilde{\theta}_T, T) - E, 0\}\},$$

where $\hat{E}_t^{RN}$ denotes the expectations operator corresponding to the $\{\hat{\pi}^{RN}\}$.

A European put option is similarly priced according to

$$P_{\mathcal{E}}(\theta_t, t)$$
$$= E_t^{RN}\{g(\theta_t, \tilde{\theta}_T)(\max\{q^e(\tilde{\theta}_T, T) - E, 0\})\}$$
$$= q^b(\theta_t, T)\hat{E}_t^{RN}\{\max\{q^e(\tilde{\theta}_T, T) - E, 0\}\}$$

TABLE A11-1 Payoff Pattern—European Call Option

t	$t+1$	$t+2$	$\dots$	$T-1$	T
0	0	0		0	$\max\{q^e(\theta_T, T) - E, 0\}$

APPENDIX   11.2

An Intuitive Overview of Continuous Time Finance

A11.2.1   INTRODUCTION

If we think of stock prices as arising from the equilibration of traders' demands and supplies, then the binomial model is implicitly one in which security trading occurs at discrete time intervals, however short, and this is, in fact, factually what actually happens. It will be mathematically convenient, however, to abstract from this intuitive setting and hypothesize that trading takes place "continuously." This is consistent with the notion of continuous compounding. But it is not fully realistic: It implies that an uncountable number of individual transactions may transpire in any interval of time, however small, which is physically impossible.

Continuous time finance is principally concerned with techniques for the pricing of derivative securities under the fiction of continuous trading. These techniques frequently allow closed-form pricing solutions to be obtained—at the cost of working in a context that is less intuitive than discrete time. In this appendix we hope to convey some idea as to how this is done.

We will need first to develop a continuous time model of a stock's price evolution through time. Such a model must respect the statistical regularities that are known to characterize, empirically, equity returns:

1. Stock prices are lognormally distributed as per Equation (11.18), which means that returns (continuously compounded) are normally distributed.
2. For short time horizons, stock returns are independently and identically distributed over nonoverlapping time intervals.

After we have faithfully represented these equity regularities in a continuous time setting, we will move on to a consideration of derivatives pricing. In doing so we aim to give some idea how the principles of risk-neutral valuation carry over to this specialized setting. The discussion aims at intuition; no attempt is made to be mathematically complete.

In all cases this intuition has its origins in the discrete time context. This leads to a discussion of random walks.

A11.2.2   RANDOM WALKS AND BROWNIAN MOTION

Consider a time horizon composed of N adjacent time intervals each of duration Δt, and indexed successively by $t_0, t_1, t_2, \ldots, t_N$; that is,

$$t_i - t_{i-1} = \Delta t, i = 1, 2, \ldots, N.$$

We define a discrete time stochastic process, $\tilde{x}$, on this succession of time indices by

$$x(t_0) = 0$$
$$\tilde{x}(t_{j+1}) = x(t_j) + \tilde{\varepsilon}(t_j)\sqrt{\Delta t},$$
$$j = 0, 1, 2, \ldots, N - 1,$$

where, for all j, $\tilde{\varepsilon}(t_j) \sim N(0, 1)$. It is further assumed that the random factors $\tilde{\varepsilon}(t_j)$ are independent of one another which implies

$$E(\tilde{\varepsilon}(t_j)\,\tilde{\varepsilon}(t_i)) = 0, i \neq j.$$

This is a particular example of a random walk, particular in the sense that the uncertain disturbance term follows a specific distribution.[7]

---

[7]A very simple random walk is of the form $\tilde{x}(t_{j+1}) = x(t_j) + \tilde{n}(t_j)$, where for all $j = 0, 1, 2 \ldots$

$$\tilde{n}(t_j) = \begin{cases} +1, \text{ if a coin is flipped and heads appears} \\ -1, \text{ if a coin is flipped and tails appears.} \end{cases}$$

We are interested in understanding the behavior of a random walk over extended time periods. More precisely, we want to characterize the statistical properties of the incremental difference

$$x(t_k) - x(t_j) \text{ for any } j < k.$$

Clearly,

$$\tilde{x}(t_k) - x(t_j) = \sum_{i=j}^{k-1} \tilde{\varepsilon}(t_i) \sqrt{\Delta t}.$$

Since the random disturbances $\tilde{\varepsilon}(t_i)$ all have mean zero,

$$E(\tilde{x}(t_k) - x(t_j)) = 0.$$

Furthermore,

$$
\begin{aligned}
\text{var}(\tilde{x}(t_k) - x(t_j)) &= E\left(\sum_{i=j}^{k-1} \tilde{\varepsilon}(t_i) \sqrt{\Delta t} \right)^2 \\
&= E\left(\sum_{i=j}^{k-1} [\tilde{\varepsilon}(t_i)]^2 \Delta t \right) \\
&\quad \text{(by independence)} \\
&= \sum_{i=j}^{k-1} (1)\Delta t = (k-j)\Delta t,
\end{aligned}
$$

since $E[\tilde{\varepsilon}(t_i)]^2 = 1$.

If we identify

$$x_{t_j} = \ln q_{t_j}^e,$$

where $q_{t_j}^e$ is the price of the stock at time t_j, then this simple random walk model becomes a candidate for our model of stock price evolution beginning from $t = 0$: At each node t_j, the logarithm of the stock's price is distributed normally, with mean $\ln q_{t_0}^e$ and variance $j\Delta t$.

Since the discrete time random walk is so respectful of the empirical realities of stock prices, it is natural to seek its counterpart for "continuous time." This is referred to as a *Brownian Motion* (or a *Wiener process*), and it represents the limit of the discrete time random walk as we pass to continuous time; that is, as $\Delta t \mapsto 0$. It is represented symbolically by

$$dz = \tilde{\varepsilon}(t) \sqrt{dt},$$

where $\tilde{\varepsilon}(t) \sim N(0, 1)$, and for any times t, t' where $t \neq t'$, and $\tilde{\varepsilon}(t)$, $\tilde{\varepsilon}(t')$ are independent. We used the word *symbolically* not only because the term dz does not represent a differential in the terminology of ordinary calculus, but because we make no attempt here to describe how such a limit is taken. Following what is commonplace notation in the literature we don't write a ~ over z even though it represents a random quantity.

More formally, a stochastic process $z(t)$ defined on $[0, T]$ is a Brownian motion provided the following three properties are satisfied:

1. for any $t_1 < t_2$, $z(t_2) - z(t_1)$ is normally distributed with mean zero and variance $t_2 - t_1$;
2. for any $0 \leq t_1 < t_2 \leq t_3 < t_4$, $z(t_4) - z(t_3)$ is statistically independent of $z(t_2) - z(t_1)$; and
3. $z(t_0) \equiv 0$ with probability one.

A Brownian motion is a very unusual stochastic process, and we can only give a hint about what is actually transpiring as it evolves. Three of its properties are considered:

1. First, a Brownian motion is a continuous process. If we were able to trace out a sample path $z(t)$ of a Brownian motion, we would not see any jumps.[8]
2. However, the sample path is not at all *smooth* and is, in fact, as "jagged as can be," which we formalize by saying that it is nowhere differentiable. A function must be essentially smooth if it is to be differentiable. That is, if we magnify a segment of its time path sufficiently, it will appear approximately linear. This *smoothness* is totally absent in a Brownian motion.
3. Lastly, a Brownian motion is of *unbounded variation*. This is perhaps the least intuitive of its properties. This conveys the idea that if we could take one of those mileage wheels that are drawn along a route on a map to assess the overall distance (each revolution of the wheel corresponding to a fixed number of kilometers) and apply it to

---

At each time interval $x(t_j)$ either increases or diminishes by one depending on the outcome of the coin toss. Suppose we think of $x(t_0) \equiv 0$ as representing the center of the sidewalk where an intoxicated person staggers one step to the right or to the left of the center in a manner that is consistent with independent coin flips (heads implies to the right). This example is the source of the term *random walk*.

[8]At times such as the announcement of a take-over bid, stock prices exhibit jumps. We will not consider such *jump processes*, although considerable current research effort is being devoted to studying them, and to the pricing of derivatives written on them.

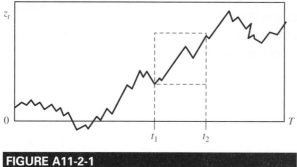

FIGURE A11-2-1

the sample path of a Brownian motion, no matter how small the time interval, the mileage wheel would record an *infinite distance* (if it ever got to the end of the path!).

One way of visualizing such a process is to imagine a rough sketch of a particular sample path where we connect its position at a sequence of discrete time intervals by straight lines. Figure A11-2-1 proposes one such path.

Suppose that we were next to enlarge the segment between time intervals t_1 and t_2. We would find something on the order of Figure A11-2-2.

Continue this process of taking a segment, enlarging it, taking another subsegment of that segment, enlarging it, etc. (in Figure A11-2-2 we would next enlarge the segment from t_3 to t_4). Under a typical differentiable function of bounded variation, we would eventually be enlarging such a small segment that it would appear

as a straight line. With a Brownian motion, however, this will never happen. No matter how much we enlarge even a segment that corresponds to an arbitrarily short time interval, the same "sawtooth" pattern will appear, and there will be many, many "teeth."

A Brownian motion represents a special case of a continuous process with independent increments. For such processes the standard deviation per unit of time becomes unbounded as the time interval becomes small:

$$\lim_{\Delta t \to 0} \frac{\sigma \sqrt{\Delta t}}{\Delta t} = \lim_{\Delta t \to 0} \frac{\sigma}{\sqrt{\Delta t}} = \infty.$$

No matter how small the time period, proportionately, a **lot** of variation remains. This constitutes our abstraction of a random walk to a context of continuous trading.[9]

FIGURE A11-2-2

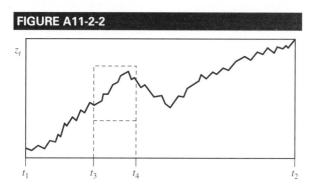

---

[9]The name Brownian motion comes from a nineteenth-century physicist named Brown, who studied the behavior of dust particles floating on the surface of water. Under a microscope, dust particles are seen to move randomly about in a manner similar to the sawtooth pattern shown except that the motion can be in any 360° direction. The interpretation of the phenomena is that the dust particles experience the effect of random collisions by water molecules.

A11.2.3 MORE GENERAL CONTINUOUS TIME PROCESSES

A Brownian motion will be the principal building block of our description of the continuous time evolution of a stock's price—it will be the *engine* or *source* of the uncertainty. To it is often added a deterministic component intended to capture the "average" behavior through time of the process. Together we have something of the form

$$dx(t) = adt + b\tilde{\varepsilon}(t)\sqrt{dt}$$
$$= adt + bdz, \quad \text{(A11.2.1)}$$

where the first component is the deterministic one and a is referred to as the drift term.

This is an example of a generalized Brownian motion or, to use more common terminology, a generalized Wiener process. If there were no uncertainty, $x(t)$ would evolve deterministically: if we integrate

$$dx(t) = adt, \text{ we obtain}$$
$$x(t) = x(0) + at.$$

The solution to Equation (A11.2.1) is thus of the form

$$x(t) = x(0) + at + bz(t), \quad \text{(A11.2.2)}$$

where the properties of $z(t)$ were articulated earlier (recall conditions 1, 2, and 3 of the definition). These imply that:

$$E(x(t)) = x(0) + at,$$
$$\text{var}(x(t)) = b^2t, \text{ and}$$
$$\text{s.d. } (x(t)) = b\sqrt{t}.$$

Equation (A11.2.2) may be further generalized to allow the coefficients to depend upon the time and the current level of the process:

$$dx(t) = a(x(t), t)dt + b(x(t), t)dz. \quad \text{(A11.2.3)}$$

In this latter form, it is referred to as an Ito process after one of the earliest and most important developers of this field (see Section A11.2.5.1). An important issue in the literature—but one we will ignore—is to determine the conditions on $a(x(t), t)$ and $b(x(t), t)$ in order for Equation (A11.2.3) to have a solution. Equations (A11.2.1)

and (A11.2.3) are generically referred to as *stochastic differential equations*.

Given this background, we now return to the original objective of modeling the behavior of a stock's price process.

A11.2.4 A CONTINUOUS-TIME MODEL OF STOCK PRICE BEHAVIOR

Let us now restrict our attention only to those stocks that do not pay dividends, so that stock returns are exclusively determined by price changes (we will maintain this assumption throughout the Appendix). Our basic discrete time model formulation is:

$$\ln q^e(t + \Delta t) - \ln q^e(t)$$
$$= \mu\Delta t + \sigma\tilde{\varepsilon}\sqrt{\Delta t}. \quad \text{(A11.2.4)}$$

Notice that the stochastic process is imposed on differences in the logarithm of the stock's price. Equation (A11.2.4) thus asserts that the continuously compounded return to the stock's ownership over the time period t to $t + \Delta t$ is distributed normally with mean $\mu\Delta t$ and variance $\sigma^2\Delta t$.

This is clearly a lognormal model:

$$\ln(q^e(t + \Delta t)) \sim N(\ln q^e(t) + \mu\Delta t, \sigma\sqrt{\Delta t}).$$

It is a more general formulation than a pure random walk as it admits the possibility that the mean increase in the logarithm of the price is positive. The continuous time analogue of Equation (A11.2.4) is

$$d\ln q^e(t) = \mu dt + \sigma dz. \quad \text{(A11.2.5)}$$

Following Equation (A11.2.2), it has the solution

$$\ln q^e(t) = \ln q^e(0) + \mu t + \sigma z(t), \quad \text{(A11.2.6)}$$

where

$$E \ln q^e(t) = \ln q^e(0) + \mu t, \text{ and}$$
$$\text{var } q^e(t) = \sigma^2 t.$$

Since the $\ln q^e(t)$ on average grows linearly with t (so that, on average, $q^e(t)$ will grow exponentially), Equations (A11.2.5) and (A11.2.6) are, together, referred to as a geometric Brownian motion (GBM). It is clearly a lognormal process: $\ln q^e(t) \sim N(\ln q^e(0) + \mu t, \sigma\sqrt{t})$, and the parameters μ and σ can be estimated exactly as was illustrated in the Appendix to Chapter 8 with the maintained assumption that time is measured in years.

While Equation (A11.2.6) is a complete description of the evolution of the logarithm of a stock's price, we are rather interested in the evolution of the price itself. Passing from a continuous time process on $\ln q^e(t)$ to one on $q^e(t)$ is not a trivial matter, however, and we need some additional background to make the conversion correctly. This is considered in the next few paragraphs.

The essence of lognormality is the idea that if a random variable $\tilde{y}$ is distributed normally, then the random variable $\tilde{w} = e^{\tilde{y}}$ is distributed lognormally. Suppose, in particular, that $\tilde{y} \sim N(\mu_y, \sigma_y)$. A natural first question is: How are μ_w and σ_w related to μ_y and σ_y when $\tilde{w} = e^{\tilde{y}}$? We first note that

$$\mu_w \neq e^{\mu_y}, \text{ and } \sigma_w \neq e^{\sigma_y}.$$

Rather, it can be shown (tedious calculation) that

$$\mu_w = e^{\mu_y + \frac{1}{2}\sigma_y^2} \qquad \text{(A11.2.7)}$$

and

$$\sigma_w = e^{\mu_y + \frac{1}{2}\sigma_y^2}(e^{\sigma_y^2} - 1)^{1/2}. \qquad \text{(A11.2.8)}$$

These formulae are not obvious, but we can at least shed some light on Equation (11.2.7): Why should the variance of y have an impact on the mean of $\tilde{w}$? To see why this is so, let us remind ourselves of the shape of the lognormal distribution, as found in Figure A11-2-3.

Suppose there is an increase in variance. Since this distribution is pinched off to the left at zero, a higher variance of y can only imply (within the same class of distributions) that probability is principally shifted to higher values of $\tilde{w}$. But this will have the simultaneous effect of increasing the mean of $\tilde{w}$. The variance of y and the mean of w cannot be specified independently. The mean and standard deviation of the lognormal variable $\tilde{w}$ are thus each related to both the mean and variance of $\tilde{y}$ as per the relationships in Equations (A11.2.7) and (A11.2.8).

These results allow us to express the mean and standard deviation of $q^e(t)$ (by analogy, $\tilde{w}$) in relation to $\ln q^e(t) + \mu t$ and $\sigma^2 t$ (by analogy, the mean and variance of $\tilde{y}$) via Equations (A11.2.5) and (A11.2.6):

$$Eq^e(t) = e^{\ln q^e(0) + \mu t + \frac{1}{2}\sigma^2 t}$$
$$= q^e(0)e^{\mu t + \frac{1}{2}\sigma^2 t} \qquad \text{(A11.2.9)}$$
$$\text{s.d. } q^e(t) = e^{\ln q^e(0) + \mu t + \frac{1}{2}\sigma^2 t}(e^{\sigma^2 t} - 1)^{1/2}$$
$$= q^e(0)e^{\mu t + \frac{1}{2}\sigma^2 t}(e^{\sigma^2 t} - 1)^{1/2}. \text{ (A11.2.10)}$$

We are now in a position, at least at an intuitive level, to pass from a stochastic differential equation describing the behavior of $\ln q^e(t)$ to one that governs the behavior of $q^e(t)$. If $\ln q^e(t)$ is governed by Equation (A11.2.5), then

$$\frac{dq^e(t)}{q^e(t)} = (\mu + \frac{1}{2}\sigma^2)dt + \sigma dz(t) \quad \text{(A11.2.11)}$$

where $dq^e(t)/q^e(t)$ can be interpreted as the instantaneous (stochastic) rate of price change. Rewriting Equation (A11.2.11) slightly differently yields

$$dq^e(t) = (\mu + \frac{1}{2}\sigma^2)q^e(t)dt$$
$$+ \sigma q^e(t)dz(t) \qquad \text{(A11.2.12)}$$

which informs us that the stochastic differential equation governing the stock's price represents an Ito process since the coefficients of dt and $dz(t)$ are both time dependent (and stochastic).

FIGURE A11-2-3

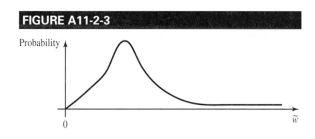

We would also expect that if $q^e(t)$ were governed by

$$dq^e(t) = \mu q^e(t)dt + \sigma q^e(t)dz(t), \text{ then} \quad \textbf{(A11.2.13)}$$

$$d\ln q^e(t) = (\mu - \tfrac{1}{2}\sigma^2)dt + \sigma dz(t). \quad \textbf{(A11.2.14)}$$

Equations (A11.2.13) and (A11.2.14) are fundamental to what follows.

A11.2.5   SIMULATION AND CALL PRICING

A11.2.5.1   ITO PROCESSES

Ito processes and their constituents, most especially the Brownian motion, are difficult to grasp at this abstract level and it will assist our intuition to describe how we might simulate a discrete time approximation to them.

Suppose we have estimated $\hat{\mu}$ and $\hat{\sigma}$ for a stock's price process as per the appendix to Chapter 8. Recall that these estimates are derived from daily price data properly scaled up to reflect the fact that in this literature it is customary to measure time in years. We have two potential stochastic differential equations to guide us—Equations (A11.2.13) and (11.2.14)—and each has a discrete time approximate counterpart.

(i) Discrete Time Counterpart to Equation (A11.2.13)

If we approximate the stochastic differential $dq^e(t)$ by the change in the stock's price over a short interval of time Δt we have,

$$q^e(t + \Delta t) - q^e(t)$$
$$= \hat{\mu}q^e(t)\Delta t + \hat{\sigma}q^e(t)\tilde{\varepsilon}(t)\sqrt{\Delta t}, \text{ or}$$
$$q^e(t + \Delta t) = q^e(t)[1 + \hat{\mu}\Delta t + \hat{\sigma}\tilde{\varepsilon}(t)\sqrt{\Delta t}].$$
$$\textbf{(A11.2.15)}$$

There is a problem with this representation, however, because for any $q^e(t)$, the price in the next period, $q^e(t + \Delta t)$, is normally distributed (recall that $\tilde{\varepsilon}(t) \sim N(0, 1)$) rather than lognormal as a correct match to the data requires. In particular, there is the unfortunate possibility that the price could go negative, although for small time intervals Δt, this is exceedingly unlikely.

(ii) Discrete Time Counterpart to Equation (A11.2.14)

Approximating $d\ln q^e(t)$ by successive log values of the price over small time intervals Δt yields

$$\ln q^e(t + \Delta t) - \ln q^e(t)$$
$$= (\hat{\mu} - \tfrac{1}{2}\hat{\sigma}^2)\Delta t + \hat{\sigma}\tilde{\varepsilon}(t)\sqrt{\Delta t}, \text{ or}$$
$$\ln q^e(t + \Delta t)$$
$$= \ln q^e(t) + (\hat{\mu} - \tfrac{1}{2}\hat{\sigma}^2)\Delta t + \hat{\sigma}\tilde{\varepsilon}\sqrt{\Delta t}.$$
$$\textbf{(A11.2.16)}$$

Here it is the logarithm of the price in period $t + \Delta t$ that is normally distributed, as required, and for this reason we'll limit ourselves to Equation (A11.2.16) and its successors. For simulation purposes, it is convenient to express Equation (A11.2.16) as

$$q^e(t + \Delta t) = q^e(t)e^{(\hat{\mu}-\tfrac{1}{2}\hat{\sigma}^2)\Delta t+\hat{\sigma}\tilde{\varepsilon}(t)\sqrt{\Delta t}}. \quad \textbf{(A11.2.17)}$$

It is easy to generate a possible sample path of price realizations for Equation (A11.2.17). First select an interval of time Δt, and the number of successive time periods of interest (this will be the length of the sample path), say N. Using a random number generator, next generate N successive draws from the standard normal distribution. By construction, these draws are independent and thus successive rates of return $(q^e(t + \Delta t)/q^e(t) - 1)$ will be statistically independent of one another. Let this series of N draws be represented by $\{\varepsilon_j\}_{j=1}^N$. The corresponding sample path (or "time series") of prices is thus created as per Equations (A11.2.18).

$$q^e(t_{j+1}) = q^e(t_j)e^{(\hat{\mu}-\tfrac{1}{2}\hat{\sigma}^2)\Delta t+\hat{\sigma}\varepsilon_j\sqrt{\Delta t}}, \quad \textbf{(A11.2.18)}$$

where $t_{j+1} = t_j + \Delta t$. This is not the price path we would use for derivatives pricing, however.

A11.2.5.2   BINOMIAL MODEL

Under the binomial model, call valuation is undertaken in a context where the probabilities have been changed in such a way that all assets, including the underlying stock, earn the risk-free rate. The simulation-based counterpart to this transformation is to replace $\hat{\mu}$ by $\ln(1 + r_f)$ in Equations (A11.2.17) and (A11.2.18):

$$q^e(t + \Delta t) = q^e(t)e^{(\ln(1+r_f)-\tfrac{1}{2}\hat{\sigma}^2)\Delta t+\sigma\tilde{\varepsilon}(t)\sqrt{\Delta t}},$$
$$\textbf{(A11.2.19)}$$

where r_f is the one-year risk-free rate (not continuously compounded) and $\ln(1 + r_f)$ is its continuously compounded counterpart.

How would we proceed to price a call in this simulation context? Since the value of the call at expiration is exclusively determined by the value of the underlying asset at that time, we first need a representative number of possible risk-neutral prices for the underlying asset at expiration. The entire risk neutral sample path—as per Equation (A11.2.18)—is not required. By representative we mean enough prices so that their collective distribution is approximately lognormal. Suppose it was resolved to create J sample prices (to be even reasonably accurate, $J \geq 1000$) at expiration, T years from now. Given random draws $\{\varepsilon_k\}_{k=1}^J$ from $N(0, 1)$, the corresponding underlying stock price realizations are $\{q_k^e(T)\}_{k=1}^J$ as given by

$$q_k^e(T) = q^e(0)e^{(\ln(1+r_f)-\frac{1}{2}\hat{\sigma}^2)T+\sigma\tilde{\varepsilon}_k\sqrt{T}}. \quad \text{(A11.2.20)}$$

For each of these prices, the corresponding call value at expiration is

$$C_k^T = \max\{0, q_k^e(T) - E\}, k = 1, 2, \ldots, J.$$

The average expected payoff across all these possibilities is

$$C_{\text{Avg}}^T = \frac{1}{J}\sum_{k=1}^J C_k^T.$$

Since under risk-neutral valuation the expected payoff of any derivative asset in the span of the underlying stock and a risk-free bond is discounted back at the risk-free rate, our estimate of the call's value today (when the stock's price is $q^e(0)$) is

$$C^0 = e^{-\ln(1+r_f)T}C_{\text{Avg}}^T. \quad \text{(A11.2.21)}$$

In the case of an Asian option or some other path-dependent option, a large number of sample paths would need to be generated since the exercise price of the option (and thus its value at expiration) is dependent upon the entire sample path of underlying asset prices leading to it.

Monte Carlo simulation, as the previous method is called, is not the only pricing technique where the underlying idea is related to the notion of risk-neutral valuation. There are ways that stochastic differential equations can be solved directly.

11.2.6 SOLVING STOCHASTIC DIFFERENTIAL EQUATIONS: A FIRST APPROACH

Monte Carlo simulation employs the notion of risk-neutral valuation but it does not, of course, provide closed-form solutions for derivatives prices, such as the Black-Scholes formula in the case of calls.[10] How are such closed-form expressions obtained? In what follows we provide a nontechnical outline of the first of two available methods. The context will once again be call valuation (no dividends).

The idea is to obtain a partial differential equation whose solution, given the appropriate boundary condition, is the price of the call. This approach is due to Black and Scholes (1973) and, in a more general context, Merton (1973). The latter author's arguments will guide our discussion here.

In the same spirit as the replicating portfolio approach mentioned in Section 11.4, Merton (1973) noticed that the payoff to a call can be represented in continuous time by a portfolio of the underlying stock and a risk-free bond whose quantities are continuously adjusted. Given the stochastic differential equation that governs the stock's price [Equation (11.2.13)] and another non-stochastic differential equation governing the bond's price evolution, it becomes possible to construct the stochastic differential equation governing the value of the replicating portfolio. This latter transformation is accomplished via an important theorem referred to in the literature as Ito's lemma. Using results from the stochastic calculus, this expression can be shown to imply that the value of the replicating portfolio must satisfy an ordinary partial differential equation. Together with the appropriate boundary condition (e.g., that $C(T) = \max\{q^e(T) - E, 0\}$), this partial differential equation has a known solution—the Black-Scholes formula.

In what follows we begin with a brief overview of this first approach. This is accomplished in three steps.

---

[10]The estimate obtained using a Monte Carlo simulation will very likely closely approximate the Black-Scholes value to a high degree of precision, however, if the number of simulated underlying stock prices is large ($\geq 10,000$) and the parameters $r_f, E, \sigma,$ and T are identical.

A11.2.6.1 THE BEHAVIOR OF STOCHASTIC DIFFERENTIALS

In order to motivate what follows, we need to get a better idea of what the object $dz(t)$ means. It is clearly a random variable of some sort. We first explore its moments. Formally, $dz(t)$ is

$$\lim_{\Delta t \to 0} z(t + \Delta t) - z(t), \quad \textbf{(A11.2.22)}$$

where we will not attempt to be precise as to how the limit is taken. We are reminded, however, that

$E[z(t + \Delta t) - z(t)] = 0$, and
$var[z(t + \Delta t) - z(t)] = (\sqrt{\Delta t})^2 = \Delta t$, for all Δt.

It is not entirely surprising, therefore, that

$$E(dz(t)) \equiv \lim_{\Delta t \to 0} E[z(t + \Delta t) - z(t)] = 0, \text{ and}$$
$$\textbf{(A11.2.23)}$$
$$var(dz(t)) \equiv \lim_{\Delta t \to 0} E[(z(t + \Delta t) - z(t))^2] = dt.$$
$$\textbf{(A11.2.24)}$$

The object $dz(t)$ may thus be viewed as denoting an infinitesimal random variable with zero mean and variance dt (very small, but we are in a world of infinitesimals).

There are several other useful relationships:

$$E(dz(t)dz(t)) \equiv var(dz(t)) = dt \quad \textbf{(A11.2.25)}$$
$$var(dz(t)dz(t))$$
$$= \lim_{\Delta t \to 0} E[(z(t + \Delta t) - z(t))^4 - (\Delta t)^2]$$
$$\approx 0 \quad \textbf{(A11.2.26)}$$
$$E(dz(t)dt) = \lim_{\Delta t \to 0} E[(z(t + \Delta t) - z(t))\Delta t] = 0$$
$$\textbf{(A11.2.27)}$$
$$var(dz(t)dt)$$
$$= \lim_{\Delta t \to 0} E[(z(t + \Delta t) - z(t))^2(\Delta t)^2] \approx 0$$
$$\textbf{(A11.2.28)}$$

Equations (A11.2.28) and (A11.2.26) imply, respectively, that Equations (11.2.25) and (11.2.27) are not only satisfied in expectation but with equality. Equation (A11.2.25) is, in particular, quite surprising, as it argues that the square of a Brownian motion random process is effectively deterministic.

These results are frequently summarized by Table A11-2.

TABLE A11-2

	dz	dt
dz	dt	0
dt	0	0

where $(dt)^2$ is negligible in the sense that it is very much smaller than dt and we may treat it as zero.

The power of these results is apparent if we explore their implications for the computation of a quantity such as $(dq^e(t))^2$:

$$(dq^e(t))^2 = (\mu dt + \sigma dz(t))^2$$
$$= \mu^2(dt)^2 + 2\mu\sigma dt dz(t) + \sigma^2(dz(t))^2$$
$$= \sigma^2 dt,$$

since, by the results in Table A11.2 $(dt)(dt) = 0$ and $dt dz(t) = 0$.

The object $dq^e(t)$ thus behaves in the manner of a random walk in that its variance is proportional to the length of the time interval.

We will use these results in the context of Ito's lemma.

A11.2.6.2 ITO'S LEMMA

A statement of this fundamental result is outlined as follows.

Theorem A11.2.1 (Ito's Lemma):
Consider an Ito process $dx(t)$ of form $dx(t) = a(x(t), t)dt + b(x(t), t)dz(t)$, where $dz(t)$ is a Brownian motion, and consider a process $y(t) = F(x(t), t)$. Under quite general conditions $y(t)$ satisfies the stochastic differential equation

$$dy(t) = \frac{\partial F}{\partial x} dx(t) + \frac{\partial F}{\partial t} dt + \frac{1}{2} \frac{\partial^2 F}{\partial x^2} (dx(t))^2. \quad \textbf{(A11.2.29)}$$

The presence of the right-most term (which would be absent in a standard differential equation) is due to the unique properties of a stochastic differential equation. Taking advantage of the results in Table A11-2, let us specialize Equation (A11.2.29) to the standard Ito process where, for notational simplicity, we suppress the dependence of coefficients $a(\ )$ and $b(\ )$ on $x(t)$ and t:

$$dy(t) = \frac{\partial F}{\partial x}(adt + bdz(t)) + \frac{\partial F}{\partial t}dt$$
$$+ \frac{1}{2}\frac{\partial^2 F}{\partial x^2}(adt + bdz(t))^2$$
$$= \frac{\partial F}{\partial x}adt + \frac{\partial F}{\partial x}bdz(t) + \frac{\partial F}{\partial t}dt$$
$$+ \frac{1}{2}\frac{\partial^2 F}{\partial x^2}(a^2(dt)^2 + abdtdz(t) + b^2(dz(t))^2)$$

Note that $(dt)^2 = 0$, $dtdz(t) = 0$, and $(dz(t))^2 = dt$.

Making these substitutions and collecting terms gives

$$dy(t) = \left(\frac{\partial F}{\partial x}a + \frac{\partial F}{\partial t} + \frac{1}{2}\frac{\partial^2 F}{\partial x^2}b^2\right)dt + \frac{\partial F}{\partial x}bdz(t).$$
$$\textbf{(A11.2.30)}$$

As a simple application, let us take as given

$$dq^e(t) = \mu q^e(t)dt + \sigma q^e(t)dz(t),$$

and try to derive the relationship for $d \ln q^e(t)$. Here we have $a(q^e(t), t) \equiv \mu q^e(t)$,
$$b(q^e(t), t) \equiv \sigma q^e(t), \text{ and}$$
$$\frac{\partial F}{\partial q^e(t)} = \frac{1}{q^e(t)}, \text{ and } \frac{\partial^2 F}{\partial q^e(t)^2} = -\frac{1}{q^e(t)^2}.$$
Lastly $\frac{\partial F(\ )}{\partial t} = 0$.

Substituting these results into Equation (A11.2.30) yields

$$d \ln q^e(t) = \left[\frac{1}{q^e(t)}\mu q^e(t) + 0\right.$$
$$+ \frac{1}{2}(-1)\left(\frac{1}{q^e(t)}\right)^2(\sigma q^e(t))^2\Big]dt$$
$$+ \frac{1}{q^e(t)}\sigma q^e(t)dz(t)$$
$$= (\mu - \tfrac{1}{2}\sigma^2)dt + \sigma dz(t),$$

as was observed earlier.
This is the background.

A11.2.6.3 THE BLACK-SCHOLES FORMULA

Merton (1973) requires four assumptions:

1. There are no market imperfections (perfect competition), transactions costs, taxes, short sales constraints, or any other impediment to the continuous trading of securities.
2. There is unlimited riskless borrowing and lending at the constant risk-free rate. If q^b is the period t price of a discount bond, then q^b is governed by the differential equation

$$dq^b(t) = r_f q^b(t)dt, \text{ or}$$
$$q^b(t) = q^b(0)e^{r_f t};$$

3. The underlying stock's price dynamics is given by a geometric Brownian motion of the form

$$dq^e(t) = \mu q^e(t)dt + \sigma q^e(t)dz(t),$$
$$q^e(0) > 0;$$

4. There are no arbitrage opportunities across the financial markets in which the call, the underlying stock, or the discount bond are traded.

Attention is restricted to call pricing formulae, which are functions only of the stock's price currently and the time (so, e.g., the possibility of past stock price dependence is ignored); that is,

$$C = C(q^e(t), t).$$

By a straightforward application of Ito's lemma, the call's price dynamics must be given by

$$dC = \left[\mu q^e(t)\frac{\partial C}{\partial q^e(t)} + \frac{\partial C}{\partial t} + \frac{\sigma^2}{2}\frac{\partial^2 C}{\partial q^e(t)^2}\right]dt$$
$$+ \sigma q^e(t)\frac{\partial C}{\partial q^e(t)}dz(t)$$

which is of limited help since the form of $C(q^e(t), t)$ is precisely what is not known. The partials with respect to $q^e(t)$ and t of $C(q^e(t), t)$ must be somehow circumvented.

Following the replicating portfolio approach, Merton (1973) defines the value of the call in terms of the self-financing, continuously adjustable portfolio P composed of $\Delta(q^e(t), t)$ shares and $N(q^e(t), t)$ risk-free discount bonds:

$$V(q^e(t), t) = \Delta(q^e(t), t)q^e(t) + N(q^e(t), t)q^b(t).$$
$$\textbf{(A11.2.31)}$$

By a straightforward application of Ito's lemma once again, the value of the portfolio must evolve according to (suppressing functional dependence in order to reduce the burdensome notation):

$$dV = \Delta dq^e + Ndq^b + d\Delta q^e$$
$$+ dNq^b + (d\Delta)dq^e \quad \textbf{(A11.2.32)}$$

Since $V(\ )$ is assumed to be self-financing, any change in its value can only be due to changes in the values of the constituent assets and not in the numbers of them. Thus it must be that

$$dV = \Delta dq^e + Ndq^b, \quad \textbf{(A11.2.33)}$$

which implies that the remaining terms in Equation (A11.2.32) are identically zero:

$$d\Delta q^e + dNq^b + (d\Delta)dq^e \equiv 0. \quad \textbf{(A11.2.34)}$$

But both $\Delta(\ )$ and $N(\ )$ are functions of $q^e(t)$ and t and thus Ito's lemma can be applied to represent their evolution in terms of $dz(t)$ and dt. Using the relationships of Table (A11-2) and collecting terms, both those preceding $dz(t)$ and those preceding dt must individually be zero.

Together these relationships imply that the value of the portfolio must satisfy partial differential:

$$\tfrac{1}{2}\sigma^2(q^e)^2 V_{q^eq^e} + r_f q_e V_{q^e} + V_t = r_f V, \quad \textbf{(A11.2.35)}$$

which can be shown to have as its solution the Black-Scholes formula when coupled with the terminal condition $V(q^e(T), T) = \max[0, q^e(T) - E]$.

A11.2.7 A SECOND APPROACH: MARTINGALE METHODS

This method originated in the work of Harrison and Kreps (1979). It is popular as a methodology because it frequently allows for simpler computations than in the PDE approach. The underlying mathematics, however, are very complex and beyond the scope of this book. In order to convey a sense of what is going on, we present a brief heuristic argument that relies on the binomial abstraction.

Recall that in the binomial model, we undertook our pricing in a tree context where the underlying asset's price process had been modified. In particular, the true probabilities of the up and down states were replaced by the corresponding risk-neutral probabilities. All assets (including the underlying stock) displayed an expected return equal to the risk-free rate in the transformed setting.

Under geometric Brownian motion, the underlying price process is represented by an Ito stochastic differential equation of the form

$$dq^e(t) = \mu q^e(t)dt + \sigma q^e(t)dz(t) \quad \textbf{(A11.2.36)}$$

In order to transform this price process into a risk-neutral setting, two changes must be made.

1. The expression μ defines the mean return and it must be replaced by r_f. Only with this substitution will the mean return on the underlying stock become r_f. Note that r_f denotes the corresponding continuously compounded risk-free rate.

2. The standard Brownian motion process must be modified. In particular, we replace dz by dz^*, where the two processes are related via the transformation:

$$dz^* = dz + (\mu - r_f)/\sigma.$$

The transformed price process is thus

$$dq^e(t) = r_f q^e(t)dt + \sigma q^e(t)dz^*(t). \quad \textbf{(A11.2.37)}$$

By Equation (A11.2.14) the corresponding process on $\ln q^e(t)$ is

$$d\ln q^e(t) = (r_f - \tfrac{1}{2}\sigma^2)dt + \sigma dz^*(t) \quad \textbf{(A11.2.38)}$$

Let T denote the expiration date of a simple European call option. In the same spirit as the binomial model, the price of a call must be the present value of its expected payoff at expiration under the transformed process.

Equation (A11.2.38) informs us that in the transformed economy,

$$\ln\left(\frac{q^e(T)}{q^e(0)}\right) \sim N((r_f - (\tfrac{1}{2})\sigma^2)T, \sigma^2 T).$$
$$\textbf{(A11.2.39)}$$

Since

$$\text{Prob}_{\substack{\text{transformed}\\\text{economy}}}(q^e(t) \geq E)$$
$$= \text{Prob}_{\substack{\text{transformed}\\\text{economy}}}(\ln q^e(t) \geq \ln E),$$

we can compute the call's value using the probability density implied by Equation (A11.2.39):

$$C = e^{-r_f T} \int_{\ln E}^{\infty} (e^s - E) f(s) ds,$$

where $f(s)$ is the probability density on the ln of the stock's price.

This becomes

$$C = e^{-r_f T} \left(\frac{1}{\sqrt{2\pi\sigma^2 T}} \right) \int_{\ln E}^{\infty} (e^s - E)$$

$$\times\ e^{-[s - \ln q^e(0) - r_f T + (\sigma^2 T/2)]^2 / 2\sigma^2 T} ds \quad \textbf{(A11.2.40)}$$

which, when the integration is performed, yields the Black-Scholes Formula.

A11.2.8   APPLICATIONS

We make reference to a number of applications that have been considered earlier in the text.

A11.2.8.1   THE CONSUMPTION-SAVINGS PROBLEM

This is a classic economic problem and we considered it fairly thoroughly in Chapter 4. Without the requisite math background, there is not a lot we can say about the continuous time analogue other than to set up the problem, but even that first step will be helpful.

Suppose the risky portfolio (M) is governed by the following price process:

$$dq^M(t) = q^M(t)[\mu_M dt + \sigma_M dz(t)],$$

$q^M(0)$ given, and the risk-free asset by

$$dq^B(t) = r_f q^B(t) dt, q^B(0) \text{ given.}$$

If an investor has initial wealth $Y(0)$, and chooses to invest the proportion $w(t)$ (possibly continuously varying) in the risky portfolio, then his wealth $Y(t)$ will evolve according to

$$dY(t) = Y(t)[w(t)(\mu_M - r_f) + r_f] dt$$
$$+\ Y(t)[w(t)\sigma dz(t)] - c(t) dt, \quad \textbf{(A11.2.41)}$$

where $c(t)$ is his consumption path. With objective function

$$\max_{c(t), w(t)} E \int_0^T e^{-\gamma t} U(c(t)) dt \quad \textbf{(A11.2.42a)}$$

the investor's problem is one of maximizing Equation (A11.2.42a) subject to Equation (A11.2.41) and initial conditions on wealth and the constraint that $Y(t) \geq 0$ for all t.

A classic result allows us to transform this problem into one that can be solved much more easily:

$$\max_{c(t), w(t)} E \int_0^T e^{-\gamma t} U(c(t)) dt$$

$$\text{s.t. } PV_0(c(t)) = E^* \int_0^T e^{-r_f t} c(t) dt \leq Y(0)$$
$$\textbf{(A11.2.42b)}$$

where E^* is the transformed risk-neutral measure under which the growth rate of the risky portfolio is r_f.

In what we have presented so far, all the notation is directly analogous to that of Chapter 4: $U(\ )$ is the investor's utility of (instantaneous) consumption, γ his (instantaneous) discount rate, and T his time horizon.

A11.2.8.2   AN APPLICATION TO PORTFOLIO ANALYSIS

Here we hope to give a hint of how to extend the portfolio analysis of Chapters 5 and 6 to a setting where trading is (hypothetically) continuous and individual security returns follow geometric Brownian motions.

Let there be $i = 1, 2, \ldots, N$ equity securities, each of whose return is governed by the process in Equation (A11.2.43).

$$\frac{dq_i^e(t)}{q_i^e(t)} = \mu_i dt + \sigma_i dz_i(t) \quad \textbf{(A11.2.43)}$$

where $\sigma > 0$. These processes may also be correlated with one another in a manner that we can represent precisely. Conducting a portfolio analysis in this setting has been found to have two principal advantages. First, it provides new insights concerning the implications of diversification for long-run portfolio returns and, second, it allows for an easier solution to certain classes of problems. We will note these advantages with the implicit understanding that the derived portfolio rules must be viewed as guides for practical applications. Literally interpreted they will imply, for example, continuous portfolio rebalancing—at an unbounded total expense, if the cost of doing each rebalancing is positive—which is absurd. In practice one would rather employ them weekly or perhaps daily.

The stated objective is to maximize the expected rate of appreciation of a portfolio's value, or equivalently, to maximize its expected terminal value, which is the terminal wealth of the investor who owns it. Most portfolio managers would be familiar with this goal.

To get an idea of what this simplest criterion implies, and to make it more plausible in our setting, we first consider the discrete time equivalent (and, by implication) the discrete time approximation to GBM.

DIGRESSION TO DISCRETE TIME

Suppose a CRRA investor has initial wealth $Y(0)$ at time $t = 0$ and is considering investing in any or all of a set of stocks whose returns are iid. Since the rate of expected appreciation of the portfolio is its expected rate of return, and since the return distributions of the available assets are iid, the investor's optional portfolio proportions will be invariant to the level of his wealth, and the distribution of his portfolio's returns will itself be iid. At the conclusion of his planning horizon, T periods from the present, the investor's wealth will be

$$Y_T = Y_0 \prod_{s=1}^{T} \tilde{R}_s^P, \qquad \textbf{(A11.2.44)}$$

where $\tilde{R}_s^P$ denotes the (*iid*) gross portfolio return in period s. It follows that

$$\ln\left(\frac{Y_T}{Y_0}\right) = \sum_{s=1}^{T} \ln \tilde{R}_s^P, \text{ and}$$

$$\ln\left(\frac{Y_T}{Y_0}\right)^{1/T} = \left(\frac{1}{T}\right) \sum_{s=1}^{T} \ln \tilde{R}_s^P. \quad \textbf{(A11.2.45)}$$

Note that whenever we introduce the ln we effectively assume continuous compounding within the time period. As the number of periods in the time horizon grows without bound, $T \mapsto \infty$, by the Law of Large Numbers,

$$\left(\frac{Y_T}{Y_0}\right)^{1/T} \mapsto e^{E \ln \tilde{R}^P}, \text{ or} \quad \textbf{(A11.2.46)}$$

$$Y_T \mapsto Y_0 e^{TE \ln \tilde{R}^P} \qquad \textbf{(A11.2.47)}$$

Consider an investor with a many-period time horizon who wishes to maximize her expected terminal wealth under continuous compounding. The relationship in Equation (A11.2.47) informs her that

1. it is sufficient, under the aforementioned assumptions, for her to choose portfolio proportions that maximize $E \ln \tilde{R}^P$, the expected logarithm of the one-period return, and
2. by doing so the average growth rate of her wealth will approach a deterministic limit.

Before returning to the continuous time setting, let us present a brief classic example, one in which an investor must decide what fractions of his wealth to assign to a highly risky stock and to a risk-free asset (actually, the risk-free asset is equivalent to keeping money in a shoebox under the bed). For an amount Y_0 invested in either asset, the respective returns are found in Figure A11-2-4.

Let w represent the proportion in the stock, and notice that the expected gross return to either asset under continuous compounding is *zero:*

Stock: $E \ln R^e = \frac{1}{2} \ln(2) + \frac{1}{2} \ln(\frac{1}{2}) = 0$
Shoebox: $E \ln R^{sb} = \frac{1}{2} \ln(1) + \frac{1}{2} \ln(1) = 0.$

With each asset paying the same expected return, and the stock being wildly risky, at first appearance the shoebox would seem the way to go. But according to Equation (A11.2.47) the investor ought to allocate his wealth between the two assets so as to maximize the expected ln of the portfolio's one-period gross return:

$$\max E \ln \tilde{R}^P = \max_{w}\{\frac{1}{2} \ln(2w + (1 - w)) + \frac{1}{2} \ln(\frac{1}{2}w + (1 - w))\}.$$

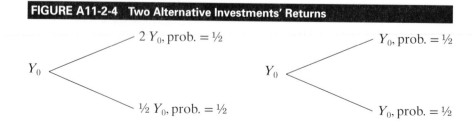

FIGURE A11-2-4   Two Alternative Investments' Returns

Y_0 ⟨ $2Y_0$, prob. = $\frac{1}{2}$ / $\frac{1}{2}Y_0$, prob. = $\frac{1}{2}$

Y_0 ⟨ Y_0, prob. = $\frac{1}{2}$ / Y_0, prob. = $\frac{1}{2}$

A straightforward application of the calculus yields $w = \frac{3}{4}$, with consequent portfolio returns in each state as shown in Figure A11-2-5.

As a result, $E \ln \tilde{R}^P = 0.0448$ with an effective risk-free period return (for a very long time horizon) of 4.5% ($e^{0.448} = 1.045$).

This result is surprising and the intuition is not obvious. Briefly, the optimal proportions of $w = \frac{3}{4}$ and $1 - w = \frac{1}{4}$ reflect the fact that by always keeping a fixed fraction of wealth in the risk-free asset, the worst wealth trajectories can be avoided. By frequent trading, although each asset has an expected return of zero, the indicated combination will yield an expected return that is strictly positive, and over a long time horizon, effectively riskless. Once again, frequent trading expands market opportunities.

RETURN TO CONTINUOUS TIME

The previous setup applies directly to a continuous time setting as all of the fundamental assumptions are satisfied. In particular, there are a very large number of periods (an uncountable number, in fact) and the returns to the various securities are iid through time. Let us make the added generalization that the individual asset returns are correlated through their Brownian motion components. By an application of Ito's lemma, we may write

$$\text{cov}(dz_i, dz_j) = E(dz_i(t)dz_j(t)) = \sigma_{ij}dt,$$

where σ_{ij} denotes the (i, j) entry of the (instantaneous) variance-covariance matrix.

As has been our custom, denote the portfolio's proportions for the N assets by $w_1, \ldots, w_N$ and let the superscript P denote the portfolio itself. As in earlier chapters, the process on the portfolio's instantaneous rate of return, $(dY^P(t))/(Y^P(t))$ will be the weighted average of the instantaneous constituent asset returns [as given in Equation (A11.2.43):

$$\frac{dY^P(t)}{Y^P(t)} = \sum_{i=1}^{N} w_i \frac{dq_i^e(t)}{q_i^e(t)} = \sum_{i=1}^{N} w_i(\mu_i dt + dz_i(t))$$

$$= \left(\sum_{i=1}^{N} w_i \mu_i\right) dt + \sum_{i=1}^{N} w_i dz_i(t), \quad \textbf{(A11.2.48)}$$

where the variance of the stochastic term is given by

$$E\left(\sum_{i=1}^{N} w_i dz_i(t)\right)^2$$

$$= E\left\{\left(\sum_{i=1}^{N} w_i dz_i(t)\right)\left(\sum_{j=1}^{N} w_j dz_j(t)\right)\right\}$$

$$= \left(\sum_{i=1}^{N}\sum_{j=1}^{N} w_i w_j \sigma_{ij}\right) dt$$

Equation (A11.2.48) describes the process on the portfolio's rate of return and we see that it implies that the portfolio's value, at any future time horizon T will be lognormally distributed; furthermore, an uncountable infinity of periods will have passed. By analogy (and formally) our discrete time reflections suggest that an investor should, in this context, also choose portfolio proportion so as to maximize the mean growth rate, v_P, of the portfolio as given by

$$E\left\{\ln \frac{Y^P(t)}{Y(0)}\right\} = T v_P$$

Since the portfolio's value itself follows a Brownian motion (with drift $\sum_{i=1}^{N} w_i \mu_i$ and disturbance $\sum_{i=1}^{N} w_i dz_i$),

$$E\left[\ln \frac{Y^P(t)}{Y(0)}\right] = \left(\sum_{i=1}^{N} w_i \mu_i\right) T$$

$$- \frac{1}{2}\left(\sum_{i=1}^{N}\sum_{j=1}^{N} w_i w_j \sigma_{ij}\right) T, \text{ and thus} \quad \textbf{(A11.2.49)}$$

$$v_P = \left(\frac{1}{T}\right) E\left[\ln \frac{Y^P(t)}{Y(0)}\right] = \sum_{i=1}^{N} w_i \mu_i$$

$$- \frac{1}{2}\sum_{i=1}^{N}\sum_{j=1}^{N} w_i w_j \sigma_{ij}, \quad \textbf{(A11.2.50)}$$

FIGURE A11-2-5 Optimal Portfolio Returns in Each State

$\ln(1 + w) = \ln(1.75) = 0.5596, \text{prob.} = \frac{1}{2}$

$\ln(1 - \frac{1}{2}\ln w) = \ln(0.625) = -0.47, \text{prob.} = \frac{1}{2}.$

The investor should choose portfolio proportions to maximize this latter quantity.

Without belaboring this development much further, it behooves us to recognize the message implicit in Equation (A11.2.50). This can be accomplished most straightforwardly in the context of an equally weighted portfolio where each of the N assets is distributed independently of one another ($\sigma_{ij} = 0$ for $i \neq j$), and all have the same mean and variance ($(\mu_i, \sigma_i) = (\mu, \sigma)$ $i = 1, 2, \ldots, N$.

In this case Equation (A11.2.50) reduces to

$$v_P = \mu - \left(\frac{1}{2N}\right)\sigma^2, \quad \textbf{(A11.2.51)}$$

with the direct implication that the more identical stocks the investor adds to the portfolio the higher the mean instantaneous return. In this sense it is useful to search for many similarly volatile stocks whose returns are independent of one another: by combining them in a portfolio where we continually (frequently) rebalance to maintain equal proportions, not only will portfolio variance decline ($(1/2N)\sigma^2$), as in the discrete time case, but the mean return will also rise (which is *not* the case in discrete time!).

A11.2.8.3 THE CONSUMPTION CAPM IN CONTINUOUS TIME

Our final application concerns the consumption CAPM of Chapter 10, and the question we address is this: What is the equilibrium asset price behavior in a Mehra-Prescott asset pricing context when the growth rate in consumption follows a GBM? Specializing preferences to be of the customary form $U(c) = (c^{1-\gamma}/1 - \gamma)$, pricing relationship (10.4) reduces to:

$$P_t = E_t\left\{Y_t \sum_{j=1}^{\infty} \beta^j x_{t+j}^{1-\gamma}\right\}$$
$$= Y_t \sum_{j=1}^{\infty} \beta^j E_t\{x_{t+j}^{1-\gamma}\},$$

where x_{t+j} is the growth rate in output (equivalently, consumption in the Mehra-Prescott economy) from period j to period $j + 1$.

We hypothesize that the growth rate x follows a GBM of the form

$$dx = \mu x \, dt + \sigma x \, dz,$$

where we interpret x_{t+j} as the discrete time realization of $x(t)$ at time $t + j$.

One result from statistics is needed. Suppose $\tilde{w}$ is lognormally distributed which we write $\tilde{w} \sim L(\xi, \eta)$ where $\xi = E \ln \tilde{w}$ and $\eta^2 = \text{var} \ln \tilde{w}$. Then for any real number q,

$$E\{\tilde{w}^q\} = e^{q\xi + \frac{1}{2}q^2\eta^2}.$$

By the process on the growth rate just assumed, $x(t) \sim L((\mu - \frac{1}{2}\sigma^2)t, \sigma\sqrt{t})$ so that at time $t + j, x_{t+j} \sim L((\mu - \frac{1}{2}\sigma^2)j, \sigma\sqrt{j})$. By this result,

$$E_t\{x_{t+j}^{1-\gamma}\} = e^{(1-\gamma)(\mu - \frac{1}{2}\sigma^2)j + \frac{1}{2}(1-\gamma)^2\sigma^2 j}$$
$$= e^{(1-\gamma)(\mu - \frac{1}{2}\gamma\sigma^2)j},$$

and thus,

$$P_t = Y_t \sum_{j=1}^{\infty} \beta^j e^{(1-\gamma)(\mu - \frac{1}{2}\gamma\sigma^2)j}$$
$$= Y_t \sum_{j=1}^{\infty} (\beta e^{(1-\gamma)(\mu - \frac{1}{2}\gamma\sigma^2)})^j,$$

which is well defined (the sum has a finite value) if $\beta e^{(1-\gamma)(\mu - \frac{1}{2}\gamma\sigma^2)} < 1$, which we will assume to be the case. Then

$$P_t = Y_t \frac{\beta e^{(1-\gamma)(\mu - \frac{1}{2}\gamma\sigma^2)}}{1 + \beta e^{(1-\gamma)(\frac{1}{2}\gamma\sigma^2)}}.$$

This is an illustration of the fact that working in continuous time often allows convenient closed form solutions.

Our remarks are taken from Mehra and Sah (2001).

A11.2.9 FINAL COMMENTS

There is much more to be said. There are many more extensions of CCAPM style models to a continuous time setting. Another issue is the sense in which a continuous time price process [e.g., Equation (A11.2.13)] can be viewed as an equilibrium price process in the sense of that concept as presented in this book. This remains a focus of research.

Continuous time is clearly different from discrete time, but does its use (as a derivatives pricing tool) enrich our economic understanding of the larger financial and macroeconomics reality? That is not clear.

CHAPTER 12

THE ARBITRAGE PRICING
THEORY

12.1   INTRODUCTION

We have made a first attempt (Chapters 9 and 11) at asset pricing from an arbitrage perspective, that is, without specifying a complete equilibrium structure. Here we try again
from a different, more empirically based angle. Let us first collect a few thoughts as to
the differences between an arbitrage approach and equilibrium modeling.

In the context of general equilibrium theory, we make hypotheses about agents—
consumers, producers, investors; in particular, we start with some form of rationality hypothesis leading to the specification of maximization problems under constraints. We
also make hypotheses about markets: Typically we assume that supply equals demand
in all markets under consideration.

We have repeatedly used the fact that at general equilibrium with fully informed
optimizing agents, there can be no arbitrage opportunities; in other words, no possibilities to make money risklessly at zero cost. An arbitrage opportunity implies that at least
one agent can reach a higher level of utility without violating his/her budget constraint
(since there is no extra cost).

In particular, our assertion that one can price any asset (income stream) from the
knowledge of Arrow-Debreu prices relied implicitly on a no-arbitrage hypothesis: With
a complete set of Arrow-Debreu securities, it is possible to replicate any given income
stream and hence the value of a given income stream, the price paid on the market for
the corresponding asset, cannot be different from the value of the replicating portfolio
of Arrow-Debreu securities. Otherwise an arbitrageur could make arbitrarily large
profits by selling short large quantities of the more expensive of the two and buying the
cheapest in equivalent amount. Such an arbitrage would have zero cost and be riskless.

While general equilibrium implies the no-arbitrage condition, it is more restrictive
in the sense of imposing a heavier structure on modeling. The reverse implication is *not*
true: No arbitrage opportunities[1]—the fact that all arbitrage opportunities have been

---

[1]An arbitrage portfolio is a self-financing (zero net-investment) portfolio. An arbitrage opportunity exists if
an arbitrage portfolio exists that yields non-negative cash flows in all states of nature and positive cash
flows in some states (Chapter 9).

exploited—does not imply that a general equilibrium in all markets has been obtained. Nevertheless, or precisely for that reason, it is interesting to see how far one can go in exploiting the less restrictive hypothesis that no arbitrage opportunities are left unexploited.

The underlying logic of the APT to be reviewed in this chapter is, in a sense, very similar to the fundamental logic of the Arrow-Debreu model and it is very much in the spirit of a complete market structure. It distinguishes itself in two major ways: First it replaces the underlying structure based on fundamental securities defined as paying exclusively in a given state of nature with other fundamental securities exclusively remunerating some form of risk taking. More precisely, the APT abandons the analytically powerful, but empirically cumbersome, concept of states of nature as the basis for the definition of its primitive securities. It also replaces it with the hypothesis that there exists a (stable) set of factors that are essential and exhaustive determinants of all asset returns. The primitive security will then be defined as a security whose risk is exclusively determined by its association with one specific risk factor and totally immune from association with any other factors. The other difference is that the prices of the fundamental securities are not derived from primitives—supply and demand, themselves resulting from agents' endowments and preferences—but will be deduced empirically from observed asset returns without attempting to explain them. Once the price of each fundamental security has been inferred from observed return distributions, the usual arbitrage argument applied to complex securities will be made.[2]

12.2 FACTOR MODELS

The main building block of the APT is a factor model, also known as a return-generating process. As discussed previously, this is the structure that is to replace the concept of states of nature. The motivation has been evoked before: States of nature are analytically convincing and powerful objects. In practice, however, they are difficult to work with and, moreover, often not verifiable, implying that contracts cannot necessarily be written contingent on a specific state of nature. We discussed these shortcomings of the Arrow-Debreu pricing theory in Chapter 8. The temptation is thus irresistible to attack the asset pricing problem from the opposite angle and build the concept of primitive securities on an empirically more operational notion, abstracting from its potential theoretical credentials. This structure is what factor models are for.

The simplest conceivable factor model is a one-factor market model, usually labeled the *Market Model,* which asserts that ex-post returns on individual assets can be entirely ascribed either to their own specific stochastic components or to their common association in a single factor, which in the CAPM world would naturally be selected as the return on the market portfolio. This simple factor model can be summarized by the following equation (or process):[3]

$$\tilde{r}_j = \alpha_j + \beta_j \tilde{r}_M + \tilde{\varepsilon}_j, \tag{12.1}$$

with $E\tilde{\varepsilon}_j = 0$, $\text{cov}(\tilde{r}_M, \tilde{\varepsilon}_j) = 0$, $\forall j$, and $\text{cov}(\tilde{\varepsilon}_j, \tilde{\varepsilon}_k) = 0$, $\forall j \neq k$.

---

[2]The arbitrage pricing theory was first developed by Ross (1976), and substantially interpreted by Huberman (1982) and Conner (1984) among others. For a presentation emphasizing practical applications, see Burmeister et al. (1994).

[3]Factors are frequently measured as deviations from their mean. When this is the case, α_j becomes an estimate of the mean return on asset j.

This model states that there are three components in individual returns: (1) an asset-specific constant α_j; (2) a common influence, in this case the unique factor—the return on the market—which affects all assets in varying degrees, with β_j measuring the sensitivity of asset j's return to fluctuations in the market return; and (3) an asset-specific stochastic term $\tilde{\varepsilon}_j$ summarizing all other stochastic components of $\tilde{r}_j$ unique to asset j.

Equation (12.1) has no *bite* (such an equation can always be written) until one adds the hypothesis $\text{cov}(\tilde{\varepsilon}_j, \tilde{\varepsilon}_k) = 0$, $j \neq k$, which signifies that *all* return characteristics common to different assets are subsumed in their link with the market return. If this were empirically verified, the CAPM would be the undisputed end point of asset pricing. At an empirical level, one may say that it is quite unlikely that a single factor model will suffice.[4] But the strength of the APT is that it is agnostic as to the number of underlying factors (and their identity). As we increase the number of factors, hoping that this will not require a number too large to be operational, a generalization of Equation (12.1) becomes more and more plausible. But let us for the moment maintain the hypothesis of one common factor for pedagogical purposes.

12.2.1   ABOUT THE MARKET MODEL

Besides serving as a potential basis for the APT, the Market Model, despite all its weaknesses, is also of interest on two grounds. First, it produces estimates for the β's that play a central role in the CAPM. Note, however, that estimating β's from past data alone is useful only to the extent that some degree of stationarity in the relationship between asset returns and the return on the market is present. Empirical observations suggest a fair amount of stationarity is plausible at the level of portfolios, but not of individual assets. On the other hand, estimating the β's does not require all the assumptions of the Market Model; in particular, a violation of the $\text{cov}(\tilde{\varepsilon}_i, \tilde{\varepsilon}_j) = 0$, $i \neq j$, hypothesis is not damaging.

The second source of interest in the Market Model, crucially dependent on this latter hypothesis, is that it permits economizing on the computation of the matrix of variances and covariances of asset returns at the heart of the MPT. Indeed, under the Market Model hypothesis, one can write (you are invited to prove these statements):

$$\sigma_j^2 = \beta_j^2 \sigma_M^2 + \sigma_{\varepsilon_j}^2 \qquad \forall j$$
$$\sigma_{ij} = \beta_i \beta_j \sigma_M^2$$

This effectively means that the information requirements for the implementation of MPT can be substantially weakened. Suppose there are N risky assets under consideration. In that case the computation of the efficient frontier requires knowledge of N expected returns, N variances, and $(N^2 - N)/2$ covariance terms (N^2 is the total number of entries in the matrix of variances and covariances, take away the N variance/diagonal terms and divide by 2 since $\sigma_{ij} = \sigma_{ji}, \forall i, j$).

Working via the Market Model, on the other hand, requires estimating Equation (12.1) for the N risky returns producing estimations for the $N\beta_j$'s and the $N\sigma_{\varepsilon_j}^2$ and estimating the variance of the market return, that is, $2N + 1$ information items.

---

[4]Recall the difficulty in constructing the empirical counterpart of M.

12.3   THE APT: STATEMENT AND PROOF

12.3.1   A QUASI-COMPLETE MARKET HYPOTHESIS

To a return-generating process such as the Market Model, the APT superposes a second major hypothesis that is akin to assuming that the markets are quasi-complete. What is needed is the existence of a *rich* market structure with a large number of assets with different characteristics and a minimum number of trading restrictions. This market structure, in particular, makes it possible to form a portfolio P with the following three properties:

Property 1: P has zero cost; in other words, it requires no investment. This is the first requirement of an arbitrage portfolio.

Let us denote x_i as the *value* of the position in the ith asset in portfolio P. Portfolio P is then fully described by the vector $x' = (x_1, x_2, \ldots, x_N)$ and the zero cost condition becomes

$$\sum_{i=1}^{N} x_i = 0 = x^T \cdot \mathbf{1}.$$

With $\mathbf{1}$ the (column) vector of 1's. (Positive positions in some assets must be financed by short sales of others.)

Property 2: P has zero sensitivity (zero beta) to the common factor:[5]

$$\sum_{i}^{N} x_i \beta_i = 0 = x^T \cdot \beta.$$

Property 3: P is a well-diversified portfolio. The specific risk of P is (almost) totally eliminated:

$$\sum_{i=1}^{N} x_i^2 \sigma_{\varepsilon_i}^2 \cong 0.$$

The APT builds on the assumed existence of such a portfolio, which requires a rich market structure.

12.3.2   STATEMENT AND PROOF OF THE APT

The APT relationship is the direct consequence of the factor structure hypothesis, the existence of a portfolio P satisfying these conditions, and the no-arbitrage assumption. Given that returns have the structure of Equation (12.1), Properties 2 and 3 imply that P is essentially riskless. The fact that P has zero cost (Property 1) then entails that an arbitrage opportunity will exist unless:

$$\bar{r}_p = 0 = x^T \cdot \bar{r} \tag{12.2}$$

The APT theorem states, as a consequence of this succession of statements, that there must exist scalars λ_0, λ_1, such that:

$$\bar{r} = \lambda_0 \cdot \mathbf{1} + \lambda_1 \beta, \text{ or}$$
$$\bar{r}_i = \lambda_0 + \lambda_1 \beta_i \quad \text{for all assets } i. \tag{12.3}$$

This is the main equation of the APT.

---

[5]Remember that the beta of a portfolio is the weighted sum of the betas of the assets in the portfolio.

Equation (12.2) and Properties 1 and 2 are statements about 4 vectors: x, β, **1**, and $\bar{r}$. Property 1 states that x is orthogonal to **1**. Property 2 asserts that x is orthogonal to β.

Together these statements imply a geometric configuration that we can easily visualize if we fix the number of risky assets at $N = 2$, which implies that all vectors have dimension 2. This is illustrated in Figure 12-1.

Equation (12.2)—no arbitrage—implies that x and $\bar{r}$ are orthogonal. But this means that the vector $\bar{r}$ must lie in the plane formed by **1** and β, or, that $\bar{r}$ can be written as a linear combination of 1 and β, as Equation (12.3) asserts.

More generally, one can deduce from the triplet $\sum_i^N x_i = \sum_i^N x_i \beta_i = \sum_i^N x_i \bar{r}_i = 0$ that there exist scalars λ_0, λ_1, such that:

$$\bar{r}_i = \lambda_0 + \lambda_1 \beta_i \quad \text{for all assets } i. \tag{12.3}$$

This is a consequence of the orthonormal projection of the vector $\bar{r}_i$ into the subspace spanned by the other two.

12.3.3 MEANING OF λ_0 AND λ_1

Suppose that there exists a risk-free asset or, alternatively, that the sufficiently rich market structure hypothesis permits constructing a fully diversified portfolio with zero-sensitivity to the common factor (but positive investment). Then

$$\bar{r}_f = r_f = \lambda_0.$$

That is, λ_0 is the return on the risk-free asset or the risk-free portfolio.

Now let us compose a portfolio Q with unitary sensitivity to the common factor $\beta = 1$. Then applying the APT relation, one gets:

$$\bar{r}_Q = r_f + \lambda_1 \cdot 1$$

Thus, $\lambda_1 = \bar{r}_Q - r_f$, the excess-return on the pure-factor portfolio Q. It is now possible to write:

$$\bar{r}_i = r_f + \beta_i(\bar{r}_Q - r_f). \tag{12.4}$$

If, as we have assumed, the unique common factor is the return on the market portfolio, in which case $Q = M$ and $\tilde{r}_Q \equiv \tilde{r}_M$, then Equation (12.4) is simply the CAPM equation:

$$\bar{r}_i = r_f + \beta_i(\bar{r}_M - r_f).$$

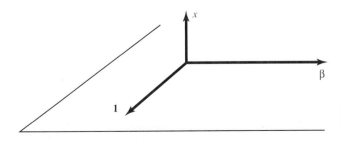

FIGURE 12-1 Geometric Representation: x orthogonal to 1 and β

12.4   MULTIFACTOR MODELS AND THE APT

The APT approach is generalizable to any number of factors. It does not, however, provide any clue as to what these factors should be, or any particular indication as to how they should be selected. This is both its strength and its weakness. Suppose we can agree on a two-factor model:

$$\tilde{r}_j = a_j + b_{j1}\tilde{F}_1 + b_{j2}\tilde{F}_2 + \tilde{e}_j \tag{12.5}$$

with $E\tilde{e}_j = 0$, $\mathrm{cov}(\tilde{F}_1, \tilde{e}_j) = \mathrm{cov}(\tilde{F}_2, \tilde{e}_j) = 0$, $\forall j$, and $\mathrm{cov}(\tilde{e}_j, \tilde{e}_k) = 0$, $\forall j \neq k$.

As was the case for Equation (12.1), Equation (12.5) implies that one cannot reject, empirically, the hypothesis that the ex-post return on an asset j has two stochastic components: specific ($\tilde{e}_j$) and systematic ($b_{j1}\tilde{F}_1 + b_{j2}\tilde{F}_2$). What is new is that the systematic component is not viewed as the result of a single common factor influencing all assets. Common or systematic risks may now be traced to two fundamental factors affecting, in varying degrees, the returns on all individual assets (and thus on portfolios as well). Without loss of generality we may assume that these factors are uncorrelated.

As before, an expression such as Equation (12.5) is useful only to the extent that it describes a relationship that is relatively stable over time. The two factors F_1 and F_2 must really summarize *all* that is common in individual asset returns.

What could these fundamental factors be? In an important article, Chen, Roll, and Ross (1986) propose that the systematic forces influencing returns must be those affecting discount factors and expected cash flows. They then isolate a set of candidates such as industrial production, expected and unexpected inflation, measures of the risk premium and the term structure, and even oil prices. At the end, they conclude that the most significant determinants of asset returns are industrial production (affecting cash flow expectations), changes in the risk premium measured as the spread between the yields of low- and high-risk corporate bonds (witnessing changes in the market risk appetite), and twists in the yield curve, as measured by the spread between short- and long-term interest rates (representing movements in the market rate of impatience). Measures of unanticipated inflation and changes in expected inflation also play a (less important) role.

Let us follow, in a simplified way, Chen, Roll, and Ross's lead and decide that our two factors are industrial production (F_1) and changes in the risk premium (F_2). How would we go about implementing the APT? First we have to measure our two factors. Let $IP(t)$ denote the rate of industrial production in month t; then $MP(t) = \log IP(t) - \log IP(t-1)$ is the monthly growth rate of IP. This is our first explanatory variable.

To measure changes in the risk premium, let us define

$$UPR(t) = \text{``Baa and under'' bond portfolio return}(t) - LGB(t)$$

where $LGB(t)$ is the return on a portfolio of long-term government bonds. With these definitions we can rewrite Equation (12.5) as

$$\tilde{r}_{jt} = a_j + b_{j1}MP(t) + b_{j2}UPR(t) + \tilde{e}_j$$

The b_{jk}, $k = 1, 2$, are often called *factor loadings*. They can be estimated directly by multivariate regression or, alternatively, one could construct *pure factor portfolios*—well-diversified portfolios mimicking the underlying factors—and compute their correlation with asset j. The pure factor portfolio P_1 would be a portfolio with $b_{P,1} = 1$, $b_{P,2}$

and $\sigma_{e_{P,1}} = 0$; portfolio P_1 would be defined similarly to track the stochastic behavior of $UPR(t)$. Let us go on hypothesizing (wrongly according to Chen, Roll, and Ross) that this two-factor model satisfies the necessary assumptions ($\text{cov}(\tilde{e}_i, \tilde{e}_j) = 0 \; \forall \; i \neq j$) and further assume the existence of a risk-free portfolio P_f with zero sensitivity to either of our two factors and zero specific risk. Then the APT states that there exist scalars $\lambda_0, \lambda_1, \lambda_2$ such that:

$$\bar{r}_j = \lambda_0 + \lambda_1 b_{j1} + \lambda_2 b_{j2}.$$

That is, the expected return on an arbitrary asset j is perfectly and completely described by a linear function of asset j's factor loadings b_{j1}, b_{j2}. This can appropriately be viewed as a (two-factor) generalization of the SML.

Furthermore the coefficients of the linear function are:

$$\lambda_0 = r_f$$
$$\lambda_1 = \bar{r}_{P_1} - r_f$$
$$\lambda_2 = \bar{r}_{P_2} - r_f$$

where P_1 and P_2 are our pure factor portfolios.

The APT agrees with the CAPM that the risk premium on an asset, $\bar{r}_j - \lambda_0$, is not a function of its specific or diversifiable risk. It potentially disagrees with the CAPM in the identification of the systematic risk. The APT decomposes the systematic risk into elements of risk associated with a particular asset's sensitivity to a few fundamental common factors.

Note the parallelism with the Arrow-Debreu pricing approach. In both contexts, every individual asset or portfolio can be viewed as a complex security, or a combination of primitive securities: Arrow-Debreu securities in one case, the pure factor portfolios in the other. Once the prices of the primitive securities are known, it is a simple step to compose replicating portfolios and, by a no-arbitrage argument, price complex securities and arbitrary cash flows. The difference, of course, resides in the identification of the primitive security. While the Arrow-Debreu approach sticks to the conceptually clear notion of states of nature, the APT takes the position that there exist a few common and stable sources of risk and that they can be empirically identified. Once the corresponding risk premia are identified, by observing the market-determined premia on the primitive securities—(the portfolios with unit sensitivity to a particular factor and zero sensitivity to all others)—the pricing machinery can be put to work.

Let us illustrate. In our two-factor example, a security j with, say, $b_{j1} = 0.8$ and $b_{j2} = 0.4$ is like a portfolio with proportions of 0.8 of the pure portfolio P_1, 0.4 of pure portfolio P_2, and consequently proportion -0.2 in the riskless asset. By our usual (no-arbitrage) argument, the expected rate of return on that security must be:

$$\bar{r}_j = -0.2r_f + 0.8\bar{r}_{P_1} + 0.4\bar{r}_{P_2}$$
$$= -0.2r_f + 0.8r_f + 0.4r_f + 0.8(\bar{r}_{P_1} - r_f) + 0.4(\bar{r}_{P_2} - r_f)$$
$$= r_f + 0.8(\bar{r}_{P_1} - r_f) + 0.4(\bar{r}_{P_2} - r_f)$$
$$= \lambda_0 + b_{j1}\lambda_1 + b_{j2}\lambda_2$$

The APT equation can thus be seen as the immediate consequence of the linkage between pure factor portfolios and complex securities in an arbitrage-free context. The reasoning is directly analogous to our derivation of the value additivity theorem in

Chapter 7 and leads to a similar result: Diversifiable risk is not priced in a complete (or quasi-complete) markets world.

While potentially more general, the APT does not necessarily contradict the CAPM. That is, it may simply provide another, more disaggregated, way of writing the expected return premium associated with systematic risk, and thus represent a decomposition of the latter in terms of its fundamental elements. Clearly the two theories have the same implications if (keeping with our two-factor model, the generalization is trivial):

$$\beta_j(\bar{r}_M - r_f) = b_{j1}(\bar{r}_{P_1} - r_f) + b_{j2}(\bar{r}_{P_2} - r_f) \tag{12.6}$$

Let β_{P_1} be the (market) beta of the pure portfolio P_1 and similarly for β_{P_2}. Then if the CAPM is valid, not only is the LHS of Equation (12.6) the expected risk premium on asset j, but we also have:

$$\bar{r}_{P_1} - r_f = \beta_{P_1}(\bar{r}_M - r_f)$$
$$\bar{r}_{P_2} - r_f = \beta_{P_2}(\bar{r}_M - r_f)$$

Thus the APT expected risk premium may be written as:

$$b_{j1}[\beta_{P_1}(\bar{r}_M - r_f)] + b_{j2}[\beta_{P_2}(\bar{r}_M - r_f)] = (b_{j1}\beta_{P_1} + b_{j2}\beta_{P_2})(\bar{r}_M - r_f)$$

which is the CAPM equation provided:

$$\beta_j = b_{j1}\beta_{P_1} + b_{j2}\beta_{P_2}$$

In other words, CAPM and APT have identical implications if the sensitivity of an arbitrary asset j with the market portfolio fully summarizes its relationship with the two underlying common factors. In that case, the CAPM is another, more synthetic, way of writing the APT.

In reality, of course, there are reasons to think that the APT with an arbitrary number of factors will always do at least as well in identifying the sources of systematic risk as the CAPM. And indeed Chen, Roll, and Ross observe that their five factors *cover* the market return in the sense that adding the return on the market to their preselected five factors does not help in explaining expected returns on individual assets.

12.5 ADVANTAGE OF THE APT FOR STOCK OR PORTFOLIO SELECTION

The APT helps to identify the sources of systematic risk, or to split systematic risk into its fundamental components. It can thus serve as a tool for helping the portfolio manager modulate his risk exposure. For example, studies show that, among U.S. stocks, the stocks of chemical companies are much more sensitive to short-term inflation risk than stocks of electrical companies. This would be compatible with both having the same exposure to variations in the market return (same beta). Such information can be useful in at least two ways. When managing the portfolio of an economic agent whose natural position is sensitive to short-term inflation risk, chemical stocks may be less attractive than electricals, all other things equal (even though they may both have the same market beta). Second, conditional expectations, or accurate predictions, on short-term inflation may be easier to achieve than predictions of the market return. Such a refining of the information requirements needed to take aggressive positions can, in that context, be of great use.

12.6   CONCLUSIONS

We have now completed our review of asset pricing theories. At this stage it may be useful to draw a final distinction between the equilibrium theories covered in Chapters 6, 7, and 10 and the theories based on arbitrage such as the Martingale pricing theory and the APT. Equilibrium theories aim at providing a complete theory of value on the basis of *primitives*: preferences, technology, and market structure. They are inevitably *heavier,* but their weight is proportional to their ambition. By contrast, arbitrage-based theories can only provide a relative theory of value. With what may be viewed as a minimum of assumptions, they

- offer bounds on option values as a function of the price of the underlying asset, the stochastic behavior of the latter being taken as given (and unexplained);
- permit estimating the value of arbitrary cash flows or securities using risk-neutral measures extracted from the market prices of a set of fundamental securities, or in the same vein, using Arrow-Debreu prices extracted from a complete set of prices for complex securities;
- explain expected returns on any asset or cash flow stream once the price of risk associated with pure factor portfolios has been estimated from market data on the basis of a postulated return-generating process.

Arbitrage-based theories currently have the upper hand in practitioners' circles where their popularity far outstrips the degree of acceptance of equilibrium theories. This, possibly temporary, state of affairs may be interpreted as a measure of our ignorance and the need to restrain our ambitions as a result.

References

Burmeister, E., R. Roll, and S. A. Ross, "A Practitioner's Guide to Arbitrage Pricing Theory," in *A Practitioner's Guide to Factor Models*, Charlottesville, Va.: Research Foundation of the Institute of Chartered Financial Analysts, 1994.

Chen, N. F., R. Roll, and S. A. Ross, "Economic Forces and the Stock Market," *Journal of Business*, 59(3), (1986): 383–404.

Connor, G., "A Unified Beta Pricing Theory," *Journal of Economic Theory*, 34(1), (1984): 13–31.

Huberman, G., "A Simple Approach to Arbitrage Pricing," *Journal of Economic Theory*, 28 (1982): 183–191.

Ross, S. A., "The Arbitrage Pricing Theory," *Journal of Economic Theory*, 1 (1976): 341–360.

CHAPTER 13

FINANCIAL STRUCTURE AND FIRM VALUATION IN INCOMPLETE MARKETS

13.1   INTRODUCTION

We have so far motivated the creation of financial markets by the fundamental need of individuals to transfer income across states of nature and across time periods. In Chapter 7 (Section 7.5), we initiated a discussion of the possibility of market failure in financial innovation. There we raised the possibility that coordination problems in the sharing of the benefits and the costs of setting up a new market could result in the failure of a Pareto-improving market to materialize. In reality, however, the bulk of traded securities are issued by firms with the view of raising capital for investment purposes, rather than by private individuals. It is thus legitimate to explore the incentives for security issuance taking the viewpoint of the corporate sector. This is what we do in this chapter. Doing so involves touching upon a set of fairly broad and not fully understood topics. One of them is the issue of *security design*. This term refers to the various forms financial contracts can take (and to their properties) in the context of managing the relationship between a firm and its managers on the one hand and financiers and owners on the other. We will not touch on these incentive issues here but will first focus on the following two questions.

13.1.1   WHAT SECURITIES SHOULD A FIRM ISSUE IF THE VALUE OF THE FIRM IS TO BE MAXIMIZED?

This question is, of course, central to standard financial theory and is usually resolved under the heading *Modigliani-Miller* (MM) *Theorem* (1958). The MM Theorem tells us that if markets are complete, the financial decisions of the firm are irrelevant: In particular, absent any tax considerations, whether the firm is financed by debt or equity has no impact on its valuation. Here we go one step further and rephrase the question in a context where markets are incomplete and a firm's financing decision modifies the set of available securities. In such a world, the financing decisions of the firm are important for individuals as they may affect the possibilities offered to them for transferring income across states. In this context is it still the case that the firm's financing decisions are irrelevant for its valuation? If not, can we be sure that the interests of the firm's owners as regards the firm's financing decisions coincide with the interests of society at large?

In a second step, we cast the same *security design* issue in the context of inter-temporal investment that can be loosely connected with the finance and growth issues touched upon in Chapter 1. Specifically, we raise the following complementary question.

13.1.2 WHAT SECURITIES SHOULD A FIRM ISSUE IF IT IS TO GROW AS RAPIDLY AS POSSIBLE?

We first discuss the connection between the supply of savings and the financial market structure and then consider the problem of a firm wishing to raise capital from the market. The questions suggested by 13.1.1 are relevant: Is the financial structure relevant for a firm's ability to obtain funds to finance its investments? If so, are the interests of the firm aligned with those of society?

13.2 FINANCIAL STRUCTURE AND FIRM VALUATION

Our discussion will be phrased in the context of the following simple example. We assume the existence of a unique firm owned by an entrepreneur who wishes only to consume at date $t = 0$; for this entrepreneur, $U'(c_0) > 0$. The assumption of a single entrepreneur circumvents the problem of *shareholder unanimity:* If markets are incomplete, the firm's objective does not need to be maximization of market value. This is because, if markets are incomplete, agents cannot reallocate income across all dates and states as they may wish: By definition, there are missing markets. But then they may well have differing preferred payment patterns by the firm—over time and across states—depending on the specificities of their own endowments. One shareholder, for example, may prefer investment project A because it implies the firm will flourish and pay high dividends in future circumstances where he himself would otherwise have a low income. Another shareholder would prefer the firm to undertake some other investment project or to pay higher current dividends because her personal circumstances are different. Furthermore, there may be no markets where the two shareholders could insure one another.

The firm's financial structure consists of a finite set of claims against the firm's period 1 output. These securities are assumed to exhaust the returns to the firm in each state of nature. Since the entrepreneur wishes to consume only in period 0, yet his firm creates consumption goods only in period 1, he will want to sell claims against period 1 output in exchange for consumption in period 0.

The other agents in our economy are agents 1 and 2 of the standard Arrow-Debreu setting of Chapter 7 and we retain the same general assumptions:

1. There are two dates: 0, 1.
2. At date 1, N possible states of nature, indexed $\theta = 1, 2, \ldots, N$, with probabilities π_θ, may be realized. In fact, for nearly all that we wish to illustrate $N = 2$ is sufficient.
3. There is one consumption good.
4. Besides the entrepreneur, there are two consumers, indexed $k = 1, 2$, with preferences given by

$$U_0^k(c_0^k) + \delta^k \sum_{\theta=1}^{N} \pi_\theta U^k(c_\theta^k) = \alpha c_0^k + E \ln c_\theta^k$$

and endowments e_0^k, $(e_\theta^k)_{\theta=1,2,\dots,N}$. We interpret c_θ^k, to be the consumption of agent k if state θ should occur, and c_0^k his period zero consumption. Agents' period utility functions are all assumed to be concave, α is the constant period 1 marginal utility, which, for the moment, we will specify to be 0.1, and the discount factor is unity (there is no time discounting). The endowment matrix for the two agents is assumed to be as shown in Table 13-1.

TABLE 13-1 Endowment Matrix			
	Date t = 0	*Date t = 1*	
		State θ = 1	*State θ = 2*
Agent $k = 1$	4	1	5
Agent $k = 2$	4	5	1

Each state has probability ½ (equally likely) and consumption in period 0 cannot be stored and carried over into period 1. Keeping matters as simple as possible, let us further assume the returns to the firm are the same in each state of nature, as seen in Table 13-2.

TABLE 13-2 Returns at Date $t = 1$		
	θ = 1	*θ = 2*
Firm	2	2

There are at least two different financial structures that could be written against this output vector:

$$F_1 = \{(2,2)\} \text{—pure equity;}[1]$$
$$F_2 = \{(2,0),(0,2)\} \text{—Arrow-Debreu securities.}[2]$$

From our discussion in Chapter 7, we expect financial structure F_2 to be more desirable to agents 1 and 2, as it better allows them to effect income (consumption) stabilization: F_2 amounts to a complete market structure with the two required Arrow-Debreu securities. Let us compute the value of the firm (what the claims to its output could be sold for) under both financial structures. Note that the existence of either set of securities affords an opportunity to shift consumption between periods. This situation is fundamentally different, in this way, from the pure reallocation examples in the pure exchange economies of Chapter 7.

13.2.1 FINANCIAL STRUCTURE F1

Let p denote the price (in terms of date 0 consumption) of the equity security $\{(2,2)\}$ and let z_1, z_2 respectively, be the quantities demanded by agents 1 and 2. In equilibrium,

---

[1] Equity is risk-free here. This is the somewhat unfortunate consequence of our symmetry assumption (same output in the two date $t = 1$ states). The reader may want to check that our message carries over with a state $\theta = 2$ output of 3.

[2] Of course, we could have assumed, equivalently, that the firm issues two units of the two conceivable *pure* Arrow-Debreu securities, ($\{(1,0),(0,1)\}$).

$z_1 + z_2 = 1$ since there is one unit of equity issued; holding z units of equity entitles the owner to a dividend of $2z$ both in state 1 and in state 2.

Agent 1 solves: $\max (.1)(4 - pz_1) + \frac{1}{2}[\ln(1 + 2z_1) + \ln(5 + 2z_1)]$.
$$pz_1 \leq 4$$

Agent 2 solves: $\max (.1)(4 - pz_2) + \frac{1}{2}[\ln(5 + 2z_2) + \ln(1 + 2z_2)]$.
$$pz_2 \leq 4$$

Assuming an interior solution, the FOCs for agents 1 and 2 are, respectively,

$$z_1: \quad \left(\frac{1}{10}\right)p = \frac{1}{2}\left[\frac{2}{1 + 2z_1}\right] + \frac{1}{2}\left[\frac{2}{5 + 2z_1}\right]$$

$$\frac{p}{10} = \left[\frac{1}{1 + 2z_1} + \frac{1}{5 + 2z_1}\right]$$

$$z_2: \qquad \frac{p}{10} = \left[\frac{1}{5 + 2z_2} + \frac{1}{1 + 2z_2}\right]$$

Clearly $z_1 = z_2 = \frac{1}{2}$, and $\frac{p}{10} = [\frac{1}{(1+1)} + \frac{1}{(5+1)}] = [\frac{1}{2} + \frac{1}{6}] = \frac{2}{3}$ or $p = \frac{20}{3}$. Thus, $V_{F_1} = p = \frac{20}{3} = 6\frac{2}{3}$, and the resulting equilibrium allocation is displayed in Table 13-3.

TABLE 13-3   Equilibrium Allocation

	$t = 0$	$t = 1$	
		θ_1	θ_2
Agent 1	$4 - 3\frac{1}{3}$	$1 + 1$	$5 + 1$
Agent 2	$4 - 3\frac{1}{3}$	$5 + 1$	$1 + 1$

Agents are thus willing to pay a large proportion of their period 1 consumption in order to increase period 2 consumption. On balance, agents (except the entrepreneur) wish to shift income from the present (when MU $= \alpha = 0.1$) to the future and now there is a device by which they may do so.

Since markets are incomplete in this example, the competitive equilibrium need not be Pareto optimal. That is the case here. There is no way to equate the ratios of the two agents' marginal utilities across the two states: In state 1, the MU ratio is $\frac{1}{2}/\frac{1}{6} = 3$ while it is $\frac{1}{6}/\frac{1}{2} = \frac{1}{3}$ in state 2. A transfer of one unit of consumption from agent 2 to agent 1 in state 1 in exchange for one unit of consumption in the other direction in state 2 would obviously be Pareto improving. Such a transfer cannot, however, be effected with the limited set of financial instruments available. This is the reality of incomplete markets.

Note that our economy is one of three agents: agents 1 and 2, and the original firm owner. The equilibrium allocation under F_1 is not a Pareto optimum because a redistribution of wealth between agents 1 and 2 could be effected making them both better off in ex ante expected utility terms while not reducing the utility of the firm owner (which is, presumably, directly proportional to the price he receives for the firm). In particular the allocation that dominates the one achieved under F_1 is shown in Table 13-4.

13.2.2   FINANCIAL STRUCTURE F₂

This is a complete Arrow-Debreu financial structure. It will be notationally clearer here if we deviate from our usual notation and denote the securities as $X = (2, 0)$, $W = (0, 2)$ with prices q_X, q_W respectively (q_X thus corresponds to the price of two units of the state-1

TABLE 13-4	A Pareto-Superior Allocation		
	$t = 0$	$t = 1$	
		θ_1	θ_2
Agent 1	⅔	4	4
Agent 2	⅔	4	4
Owner	6⅔	0	0

Arrow-Debreu security while q_W is the price of two units of the state-2 Arrow-Debreu security), and quantities $z_X^1, z_X^2, z_W^1, z_W^2$. The problems confronting the agents are as follows.

Agent 1 solves: $\max(\frac{1}{10})(4 - q_X z_X^1 - q_W z_W^1) + [\frac{1}{2} \ln(1 + 2z_X^1) + \frac{1}{2} \ln(5 + 2z_W^1)]$
$q_X z_X^1 + q_W z_W^1 \le 4$

Agent 2 solves: $\max(\frac{1}{10})(4 - q_X z_X^2 - q_W z_W^2) + [\frac{1}{2} \ln(5 + 2z_X^2) + \frac{1}{2} \ln(5 + 2z_W^2)]$
$q_X z_X^2 + q_W z_W^2 \le 4$

The FOCs are:

Agent 1: $\begin{cases} \text{(i)} \; \dfrac{1}{10} q_X = \dfrac{1}{2}\left(\dfrac{1}{1 + 2z_X^1}\right)2 \\[3mm] \text{(ii)} \; \dfrac{1}{10} q_W = \dfrac{1}{2}\left(\dfrac{1}{5 + 2z_W^1}\right)2 \end{cases}$

Agent 2: $\begin{cases} \text{(iii)} \; \dfrac{1}{10} q_X = \dfrac{1}{2}\left(\dfrac{1}{5 + 2z_X^2}\right)2 \\[3mm] \text{(iv)} \; \dfrac{1}{10} q_W = \dfrac{1}{2}\left(\dfrac{1}{1 + 2z_W^2}\right)2. \end{cases}$

By equation (i): $\dfrac{1}{10} q_X = \dfrac{1}{1 + 2z_X^1} \Rightarrow 1 + 2z_X^1 = \dfrac{10}{q_X} \Rightarrow z_X^1 = \dfrac{5}{q_X} - \dfrac{1}{2}.$

By equation (iii): $\dfrac{1}{10} q_X = \dfrac{1}{5 + 2z_X^2} \Rightarrow 5 + 2z_X^2 = \dfrac{10}{q_X} \Rightarrow z_X^2 = \dfrac{5}{q_X} - \dfrac{5}{2}.$

With one security of each type issued:

$$z_X^1 + z_X^2 = 1 \; (z_X^1 \ge 0; z_X^2 \ge 0)$$

$$\dfrac{5}{q_X} - \dfrac{1}{2} + \dfrac{5}{q_X} - \dfrac{5}{2} = 1 \Rightarrow \dfrac{10}{q_X} = 4 \Rightarrow q_X = \frac{10}{4}.$$

Similarly, $q_W = \frac{10}{4}$ (by symmetry) and $V_F = q_X + q_W = \frac{10}{4} + \frac{10}{4} = \frac{20}{4} = 5.$

So we see that $\mathbf{V_F}$ *has declined* from 6⅔ in the F_1 case to 5. Let us further examine this result. Consider the allocations implied by the complete financial structure:

$$z_X^1 = \dfrac{5}{q_X} - \dfrac{1}{2} = \dfrac{5}{5/2} - \dfrac{1}{2} = 2 - \frac{1}{2} = 1\frac{1}{2}$$

$$z_X^2 = \dfrac{5}{P_X} - \dfrac{5}{2} = \dfrac{5}{5/2} - \dfrac{5}{2} = 2 - \frac{5}{2} = -\frac{1}{2}$$

$z_W^1 = -\frac{1}{2}, z_W^2 = 1\frac{1}{2}$ by symmetry $\left(\begin{array}{l}(z_X^1, z_W^1) = (1\frac{1}{2}, -\frac{1}{2}) \\ (z_X^2, z_W^2) = (-\frac{1}{2}, 1\frac{1}{2})\end{array}\right).$

Thus, agent 1 wants to short sell security 2 while agent 2 wants to short sell security 1. Of course, in the case of financial structure F_1 (2, 2), there was no possibility of short selling since, in equilibrium, every agent must have the same security holdings. The post-trade allocation is found in Table 13-5.

TABLE 13-5 Post-Trade Allocation	
$t = 0$	
Agent 1	$4 - (1\frac{1}{2})q_x + \frac{1}{2}q_w = 4 - \dfrac{3}{2}\left(\dfrac{10}{4}\right) + \dfrac{1}{2}\left(\dfrac{10}{4}\right) = 4 - \dfrac{10}{4} = 1\frac{1}{2}$
Agent 2	$4 + \frac{1}{2}q_x - \frac{3}{2}q_w = 4 + \dfrac{1}{2}\left(\dfrac{10}{4}\right) - \dfrac{3}{2}\left(\dfrac{10}{4}\right) = 4 - \dfrac{10}{4} = 1\frac{1}{2}$
$t = 1$	
Agent 1	$(1, 5) + 1\frac{1}{2}(2, 0) - \frac{1}{2}(0, 2) = (4, 4)$
Agent 2	$(5, 1) + (-\frac{1}{2})(2, 0) + 1\frac{1}{2}(0, 2) = (4, 4)$

This, unsurprisingly, constitutes a Pareto optimum.[3]

We have thus reached an important result that we summarize in Propositions 13.1 and 13.2.

Proposition 13.1:
When markets are incomplete, the Modigliani-Miller theorem fails to hold and the financial structure of the firm may affect its valuation by the market.

Proposition 13.2:
When markets are incomplete, it may not be in the interest of a value-maximizing manager to issue the socially optimal set of securities.

In our example the issuing of the *right* set of securities by the firm leads to completing the market and making a Pareto-optimal allocation attainable. The impact of the financial decision of the firm on the set of markets available to individuals in the economy places us outside the realm of the MM theorem and, indeed, the value of the firm is not left unaffected by the choice of financing. Moreover, it appears that it is not, in this situation, in the private interest of the firm's owner to issue the socially optimal set of securities. Our example thus suggests that there is no reason to necessarily expect that value-maximizing firms will issue the set of securities society would find preferable.[4]

---

[3]Note that our example also illustrates the fact that the addition of new securities in a financial market does not necessarily improve the welfare of *all* participants. Indeed, the firm owner is made worse off by the transition from F_1 to F_2.

[4]The reader may object that our example is just that, an example. Because it helps us reach results of a negative nature, this example is, however, a fully general counterexample, ruling out the proposition that the MM theorem continues to hold and that firms' financial structure decisions will always accord with the social interest.

13.3   ARROW-DEBREU AND MODIGLIANI-MILLER

In order to understand why V_F declines when the firm issues the richer set of securities, it is useful to draw on our work on Arrow-Debreu pricing (Chapter 7). Think of our economy under financial structure F_2. This is a complete Arrow-Debreu structure in which we can use the information on equilibrium endowments to recompute the pure Arrow-Debreu prices as per Equation (7.1),

$$q_\theta = \frac{\delta\pi_\theta \dfrac{\partial U^k}{\partial c_\theta^k}}{\dfrac{\partial U_0^k}{\partial c_0^k}}, \theta = 1, 2, \qquad (7.1)$$

which, in our example, given the equilibrium allocation (four units of commodity in each state for both agent) reduces to

$$q_\theta = \frac{1 \; \frac{1}{2} \; \frac{1}{4}}{.1} = \frac{5}{4}, \theta = 1, 2,$$

which corresponds, of course, to

$$q_X = q_W = \frac{10}{4},$$

and to $V_F = 5$.

This Arrow-Debreu complete markets equilibrium is unique: This is generically the case in an economy such as ours, implying there are no other allocations satisfying the required conditions and no other possible prices for the Arrow-Debreu securities. This implies the Modigliani-Miller proposition as the following reasoning illustrates. In our example, the firm is a mechanism to produce two units of output in period 2, both in state 1 and in state 2. Given that the date 0 price of one unit of the good in state 1 at date 1 is $\frac{5}{4}$ and the price of one unit of the good in state 2 at date 1 is $\frac{5}{4}$ as well, it must of necessity be that the price (value) of the firm is 4 times $\frac{5}{4}$, that is, 5. In other words, absent any romantic love for this firm, no one will pay more than five units of the current consumption good (which is the numeraire) for the title of ownership to this production mechanism knowing that the same bundle of goods can be obtained for five units of the numeraire by purchasing two units of each Arrow-Debreu security. A converse reasoning guarantees that the firm will not sell for less either. The value of the firm is thus given by its fundamentals and is independent of the specific set of securities the entrepreneur chooses to issue: This is the Modigliani-Miller theorem!

Now let us try to understand how this reasoning is affected when markets are incomplete and why, in particular, the value of the firm is higher in that context. The intuition is as follows. In the incomplete market environment of financial structure F_1, security $\{(2, 2)\}$ is desirable for two reasons: to transfer income across time *and* to reduce period 2 consumption risk. In this terminology, the firm in the incomplete market environment is more than a mechanism to produce two units of output in either states of nature in date 1. The security issued by the entrepreneur is also the only available vehicle to reduce second period consumption risk. Individual consumers are willing to pay something, that is, to sacrifice current consumption, to achieve such risk reduction. To see that trading of security $\{(2, 2)\}$ provides some risk reduction in the former environ-

TABLE 13-6 Agent 1 State Utilities Under F_1		
	Before Trade	*{(2, 2)}; $z^1 = 0.5$ (Equilibrium Allocation)*
State 1	$U^1(c_1^1) = \ln 1 = 0$	$U^1(c_1^1) = \ln 2 = 0.693$
State 2	$U^1(c_2^1) = \ln 5 = 1.609$	$U^1(c_2^1) = \ln 6 = 1.792$
	Difference = 1.609	Difference = 1.099

ment, we need only compare the range of period 2 utilities across states after trade and before trade for agent 1 (agent 2 is symmetric). See Table 13-6.

The premium paid for the equity security, over and above the value of the firm in complete markets, thus originates in the dual role it plays as a mechanism for consumption risk smoothing and as a title to two units of output in each future state. A question remains: Given that the entrepreneur, by his activity and security issuance, plays this dual role, why can't he reap the corresponding rewards independently of the security structure he chooses to issue? In other words, why is it that his incentives are distorted away from the socially optimal financial structure? To understand this, notice that if any amount of Arrow-Debreu-like securities, such as in $F_2 = \{(2, 0),(0, 2)\}$ is issued, no matter how small, the market for such securities has effectively been created. With no further trading restrictions, the agents can themselves supply additional amounts of these securities to one another. This has the effect of empowering them to trade, entirely independently of the magnitude of the firm's security issuance, to the endowment allocation portrayed in Table 13-7.

TABLE 13-7	Allocation When the Two Agents Trade Arrow-Debreu Securities Among Themselves		
	$t = 0$	$t = 1$	
		θ_1	θ_2
Agent 1	4	3	3
Agent 2	4	3	3

In effect, investors can eliminate all *second-period* endowment uncertainty *themselves*. Once this has been accomplished and markets are effectively completed (because there is no further demand for across-state income redistribution, it is irrelevant to the investor whether the firm issues $\{(2, 2)\}$ or $\{(2, 0),(0, 2)\}$, since either package is equally appropriate for transferring income *across time periods*. Were $\{(2, 0),(0, 2)\}$ to be the package of securities issued, the agents would each buy equal amounts of $(2, 0)$, and $(0, 2)$, effectively repackaging them as $(2, 2)$. To do otherwise would be to reintroduce period 2 endowment uncertainty. Thus the relative value of the firm under either financial structure, $\{(2, 2)\}$ or $\{(2, 0), (0, 2)\}$, is determined solely by whether the security $(2, 2)$ is worth more to the investors in the environment of period 2 endowment uncertainty or when all risk has been eliminated as in the environment noted previously.

Said otherwise, once the markets have been completed, the value of the firm is fixed at 5 as we have seen before, and there is nothing the entrepreneur can do to appropriate the extra insurance premium. If investors can eliminate all the risk themselves (via short selling) there is no premium to be paid to the firm, in terms of value enhancement, for doing so. This is confirmed if we examine the value of the firm when security $\{(2, 2)\}$ is issued *after* the agents have traded among themselves to equal second-period allocation $(3, 3)$. In this case $V_F = 5$ also.

There is another lesson to be gleaned from this example and that leads us back to the CAPM. One of the implications of the CAPM was that securities could not be priced in isolation: Their prices and rates of return depended on their interactions with other securities as measured by the covariance. This example follows in that tradition by confirming that the value of the securities issued by the firm is not independent of the other securities available on the market or which the investors can themselves create.

13.4   ON THE ROLE OF SHORT SELLING

From another perspective (as noted in Allen and Gale, 1994), short selling expands the supply of securities and provides additional opportunities for risk sharing, but in such a way that the benefits are not internalized by the innovating firm. When deciding what securities to issue, however, the firm only takes into account the impact of the security issuance on its own value; in other words, it only considers those benefits it can internalize. Thus, in an incomplete market setting, the firm may not issue the socially optimal package of securities.

It is interesting to consider the consequence of forbidding or making it impossible for investors to increase the supply of securities $(2, 0)$ and $(0, 2)$ via short selling. Accordingly, let us impose a no-short-selling condition (by requiring that all holdings of all securities by all agents are positive). Agent 1 wants to short sell $(0, 2)$; agent 2 wants to short sell $(2, 0)$. So, we know that the constrained optimum will have (simply setting $z = 0$ wherever the unconstrained optimum had a negative z and anticipating the market clearing condition):

$$z_X^2 = 0 \qquad z_W^1 = 0$$
$$z_X^1 = 1 \qquad z_W^2 = 1$$
$$\tfrac{1}{10}q_x = MU_1 = \tfrac{1}{2}\left(\frac{1}{1 + 2(1)}\right)2 = \tfrac{1}{3}$$
$$\tfrac{1}{10}q_w = MU_2 = \tfrac{1}{2}\left(\frac{1}{1 + 2(1)}\right)2 = \tfrac{1}{3}$$
$$q_x = \tfrac{10}{3}, q_w = \tfrac{10}{3}$$
$$V_F = \tfrac{20}{3} = 6\tfrac{2}{3},$$

which is as it was when the security $(2, 2)$ was issued.

The fact that V_F rises when short sales are prohibited is not surprising as it reduces the supply of securities $(2, 0)$ and $(0, 2)$. With demand unchanged, both q_X and q_W increase, and with it, V_F. In some sense, now the firm has a monopoly in the issuance of $(2, 0)$ and $(0, 2)$, and that monopoly position has value. All this is in keeping with the general reasoning developed previously. While it is, therefore, not surprising that the value of the firm has risen with the imposition of the short sales constraint, the fact that its value has returned precisely to what it was when it issued $\{(2, 2)\}$ is striking and possibly somewhat of a coincidence. Is the ruling out of short selling realistic? In practice, short selling on the U.S. stock exchanges is costly, and only a very limited amount of it occurs. The reason for this is that the short seller must deposit as collateral with the lending institution, as much as 100 percent of the value of the securities he borrows to short sell. Under current practice in the United States, the interest on this deposit is less than the T-bill rate even for the largest participants, and for small investors it is near zero. There are other exchange-imposed restrictions on short selling. On the NYSE, for example, investors are forbidden to short sell on a down-tick in the stock's price.[5]

13.5 FINANCING AND GROWTH

Now we must consider our second set of issues, which we may somewhat more generally characterize as follows: How does the degree of completeness in the securities markets affect the level of capital accumulation? This is a large topic, touched upon in our introductory chapter, for which there is little existing theory. Once again we pursue our discussion in the context of examples.

Example 13.1:

Our first example serves to illustrate the fact that while a more complete set of markets is unambiguously good for welfare, it is not necessarily so for growth. Consider the following setup. Agents own firms (have access to a productive technology) while also being able to trade state-contingent claims with one another (net supply is zero). We retain the two-agent, two-period setting. Agents have state-contingent consumption endowments in the second period. They also have access to a productive technology which, for every k units of period 1 consumption foregone, produces $\sqrt{k}$ in period 2 in either state of nature[6] (see Table 13-8).

TABLE 13-8 The Return from Investing k Units	
$t = 2$	
θ_1	θ_2
$\sqrt{k}$	$\sqrt{k}$

The agent endowments are given in Table 13-9.

TABLE 13-9 Agent Endowments	$t = 1$	$t = 2$	
		θ_1	θ_2
Agent 1	3	5	1
Agent 2	3	1	5

$\text{Prob}(\theta_1) = \text{Prob}(\theta_2) = \frac{1}{2}$

and the agent preference orderings are now (identically) given by

$$EU(c_0, c_\theta) = \ln(c_0) + \tfrac{1}{2}\ln(c_1) + \tfrac{1}{2}\ln(c_2).$$

In this context, we compute the agents' optimal savings levels under two alternative financial structures. In one case, there is a complete set of contingent claims; in the other, the productive technology is the only possibility for redistributing purchasing power across states (as well as across time) among the two agents.

13.5.1 NO CONTINGENT CLAIMS MARKETS

Each agent acts autonomously and solves:

$$\max_k \ln(3 - k) + \tfrac{1}{2}\ln(5 + \sqrt{k}) + \tfrac{1}{2}\ln(1 + \sqrt{k}).$$

Assuming an interior solution, the optimal level of savings k^* solves:

$$-\frac{1}{3 - k^*} + \left\{\frac{1}{2}\left(\frac{1}{5 + \sqrt{k^*}}\right)\frac{1}{2}(k^*)^{-1/2} + \frac{1}{2}\left(\frac{1}{1 + \sqrt{k^*}}\right)\frac{1}{2}(k^*)^{-1/2}\right\} = 0$$

which, after several simplifications, yields

$$3(k^*)^{3/2} + 15k^* + 7\sqrt{k^*} - 9 = 0.$$

The solution to this equation is $k^* = 0.31$. With two agents in the economy, *economy-wide savings* are 0.62. Let us now compare this result with the case in which the agents also have access to contingent claims markets.

13.5.2 CONTINGENT CLAIMS TRADING

Let q_1 be the price of a security that pays one unit of consumption if state 1 occurs, and let q_2 be the price of a security that pays one unit of consumption if state 2 occurs. Similarly, let $z_1^1, z_2^1, z_1^2, z_2^2$ denote, respectively, the quantities of these securities demanded by agents 1 and 2, who continue to have simultaneous access to the technology.
Agent 1 solves:

$$\max_{k_1, z_1^1, z_2^1} \ln(3 - k_1 - q_1 z_1^1 - q_2 z_2^1) + \tfrac{1}{2}\ln(5 + \sqrt{k_1} + z_1^1) + \tfrac{1}{2}\ln(1 + \sqrt{k_1} + z_2^1).$$

Agent 2's problem is essentially the same:

$$\max_{k_1, z_1^2, z_2^2} \ln(3 - k_2 - q_1 z_1^2 - q_2 z_2^2) + \tfrac{1}{2}\ln(5 + \sqrt{k_2} + z_1^2) + \tfrac{1}{2}\ln(1 + \sqrt{k_2} + z_2^2).$$

By symmetry, in equilibrium

$$k_1 = k_2; q_1 = q_2;$$
$$z_1^1 = z_2^2 = -z_1^2, z_2^1 = z_1^2 = -z_2^2.$$

Using these facts and the FOCs (see the Appendix), it can be directly shown that

$$-2 = z_1^1.$$

It then follows that $k_1 = 0.16$. Thus, *total savings* $= k_1 + k_2 = 2k_1 = 0.32$.
Savings have thus been substantially reduced. This result also generalizes to situations of more general preference orderings, and to the case where the uncertainty in the

states is in the form of uncertainty in the production technology rather than in the investor endowments. The explanation for this phenomenon is relatively straightforward and it parallels the mechanism at work in the previous sections. With the opening of contingent claims markets, the agents can eliminate all second-period risk. In the absence of such markets, it is real investment that alone must provide for any risk reduction as well as for income transference across time periods—a dual role. In a situation of greater uncertainty, resulting from the absence of contingent claims markets, more is saved and the extra savings take, necessarily, the form of productive capital: There is a precautionary demand for capital. Jappelli and Pagano (1994) find traces of a similar behavior in Italy prior to recent measures of financial deregulation.

Example 13.2
This result also suggests that if firms want to raise capital in order to invest for period 2 output, it may not be value maximizing to issue a more complete set of securities, an intuition we confirm in our second example.
Consider a firm with access to a technology with the output pattern found in Table 13-10.

TABLE 13-10	The Firm's Technology	
$t = 1$	$t = 2$	
	θ_1	θ_2
$-k$	$\sqrt{k}$	$\sqrt{k}$

Investor endowments are given in Table 13-11.

TABLE 13-11	Investor Endowments		
	$t = 1$	$t = 2$	
		θ_1	θ_2
Agent 1	12	½	10
Agent 2	12	10	½

Agent preference orderings are both of the form:
$$EU(c_0, c_\theta) = \tfrac{1}{12}c_0 + \tfrac{1}{2}\ln(c_1) + \tfrac{1}{2}\ln(c_2).$$

13.5.3   INCOMPLETE MARKETS

Suppose a security of the form $(1, 1)$ is issued, at a price p; agents 1 and 2 demand, respectively, z_1 and z_2. The agent maximization problems that define their demand are as follows:

Agent 1:
$$\max \tfrac{1}{12}(12 - pz_1) + \tfrac{1}{2}\ln(\tfrac{1}{2} + z_1) + \tfrac{1}{2}\ln(10 + z_1)$$
$$pz_1 \leq 12$$

Agent 2:
$$\max \tfrac{1}{12}(12 - pz_2) + \tfrac{1}{2}\ln(10 + z_2) + \tfrac{1}{2}\ln(\tfrac{1}{2} + z_2)$$
$$pz_2 \leq 12$$

It is obvious that $z_1 = z_2$ at equilibrium. The first order conditions are (again assuming an interior solution):

$$\text{Agent 1:} \quad \frac{p}{12} = \frac{1}{2} \frac{1}{(\frac{1}{2} + z_1)} + \frac{1}{2} \frac{1}{(10 + z_1)}$$

$$\text{Agent 2:} \quad \frac{p}{12} = \frac{1}{2} \frac{1}{(10 + z_2)} + \frac{1}{2} \frac{1}{(\frac{1}{2} + z_2)}$$

In order for the technological constraint to be satisfied, it must also be that

$$[p(z_1 + z_2)]^{1/2} = z_1 + z_2, \text{ or}$$
$$p = z_1 + z_2 = 2z_1 \text{ as noted earlier.}$$

Substituting for p in the first agent's FOC gives:

$$\frac{2z_1}{12} = \frac{1}{2} \frac{1}{(\frac{1}{2} + z_1)} + \frac{1}{2} \frac{1}{(10 + z_1)}, \text{ or}$$
$$z_1^3 + 10.5z_1^2 - z_1 - 31.5 = 0.$$

Trial and error gives $z_1 = 1.65$. Thus $p = 3.3$ and total investment is $p(z_1 + z_2) = 3.3(3.3) = 10.89 = V_F$; period 2 output in each state is thus $\sqrt{10.89} = 3.3$.

13.5.4   COMPLETE CONTINGENT CLAIMS

Now suppose securities $R = (1, 0)$ and $S = (0, 1)$ are issued at prices q_R and q_S and denote quantities demanded respectively as z_R^1, z_R^2, z_S^1, z_S^2. The no short sales assumption is retained. With this assumption, agent 1 buys only R while agent 2 buys only security S. Each agent thus prepares himself for his worst possibility.

$$\text{Agent 1:} \quad \begin{array}{l} \max \frac{1}{12}(12 - q_R z_R^1) + \frac{1}{2}\ln(\frac{1}{2} + z_R^1) + \frac{1}{2}\ln(10) \\ 0 \leq q_R z_R^1 \end{array}$$

$$\text{Agent 2:} \quad \begin{array}{l} \max \frac{1}{12}(12 - q_S z_S^2) + \frac{1}{2}\ln(10) + \frac{1}{2}\ln(\frac{1}{2} + z_S^2) \\ 0 \leq q_S z_S^2 \end{array}$$

The FOCs are thus:

$$\text{Agent 1:} \quad \frac{q_R}{12} = \frac{1}{2} \frac{1}{(\frac{1}{2} + z_R^1)}$$

$$\text{Agent 2:} \quad \frac{q_S}{12} = \frac{1}{2} \frac{1}{(\frac{1}{2} + z_S^2)}.$$

Clearly $q_R = q_S$ by symmetry, and $z_R^1 = z_S^2$; by the technological constraints:

$$(q_R z_R^1 + q_S z_S^2)^{1/2} = \left(\frac{z_R^1 + z_S^2}{2} \right), \text{ or}$$

$$q_R = \frac{z_R^1}{2}.$$

Solving for z_R^1:

$$\frac{q_R}{12} = \frac{z_R^1}{24} = \frac{1}{2}\frac{1}{(\frac{1}{2} + z_R^1)} = \frac{1}{1 + 2z_R^1}$$

$$z_R^1(1 + 2z_R^1) = 24$$

$$z_R^1 = \frac{-1 \pm \sqrt{1 - 4(2)(-24)}}{4} = \frac{-1 \pm \sqrt{1 + 192}}{4} = \frac{-1 \pm 13.892}{4}$$

(taking positive root)

$$z_R^1 = 3.223$$
$$z_S^2 = 3.223$$
$$q_R = 1.61, \text{ and}$$
$$q_R(z_R^1 + z_S^2) = 1.61(6.446) = 10.378 = V_F.$$

As suspected, this is less than what the firm could raise issuing only $(1, 1)$.

Much in the spirit of our previous discussion, this example illustrates the fact that, for a firm wishing to maximize the amount of capital levied from the market, it may not be a good strategy to propose contracts leading to a (more) complete set of markets. This is another example of the failure of the Modigliani-Miller theorem in a situation of incomplete markets and the reasoning is the same as before: In incomplete markets, the firm's value is not necessarily equal to the value, computed at Arrow-Debreu prices, of the portfolio of goods it delivers in future date-states. This is because the security it issues may, in addition, be valued by market participants for its unintended role as an insurance mechanism, a role that disappears if markets are complete. In the growth context of our last examples, this may mean that more savings will be forthcoming when markets are incomplete, a fact that may lead a firm wishing to raise capital from the markets to refrain from issuing the optimal set of securities.

13.6   CONCLUSIONS

We have reached a number of conclusions in this chapter.

1. In an incomplete market context, it may not be value maximizing for firms to offer the socially optimal (complete) set of securities. This is because, in a production setting, securities can be used not only for risk reduction but also to transfer income across dates. The value of a security will depend upon its usefulness in accomplishing these alternative tasks.
2. The value of securities issued by the firm is not independent of the supply of similar securities issued by other market participants. To the extent that others can increase the supply of a security initially issued by the firm (via short selling), its value will be reduced.
3. Finally, welfare is, but growth may not be, promoted by the issuance of a more complete set of markets.[7] As a result, it may not be in the best interest of a firm

---

[7]The statement regarding welfare is strictly true only when financial innovation achieves full market completeness. Hart (1975) shows that it is possible that everyone is made worse off when the markets become more complete but not fully complete (say, going from 9 to 10 linearly independent securities when 15 would be needed to make the markets complete).

aiming at maximizing the amount of capital it wants to raise, to issue the most socially desirable set of securities.

All these results illustrate the fact that if markets are incomplete, the link between private interests and social optimality is considerably weakened. Herein lies the intellectual foundation for financial market regulation and supervision.

References

Allen, F., and D. Gale, *Financial Innovation and Risk Sharing*, Cambridge, Mass.: MIT Press, 1994.

Hart, O., "On the Optimality of Equilibrium When Market Structure Is Incomplete," *Journal of Economic Theory*, 11 (1975): 418–443.

Jappelli, T., and M. Pagano, "Savings, Growth and Liquidity Constraints," *Quarterly Journal of Economics*, 109 (1994): 83–109.

Modigliani, F., and M. Miller, "The Cost of Capital, Corporation Finance, and the Theory of Investment," *American Economic Review*, 48 (1958): 261–297.

A P P E N D I X

Details of the Solution of the Contingent Claims Trade Case of Section 13.5

Agent 1 solves:

$$\max_{k_1, z_1^1, z_2^1} \ln(3 - k_1 - q_1 z_1^1 - q_2 z_2^1)$$
$$+ \tfrac{1}{2} \ln(5 + \sqrt{k_1} + z_1^1)$$
$$+ \tfrac{1}{2} \ln(1 + \sqrt{k_1} + z_2^1)$$

k_1:
$$\frac{-1}{3 - k_1 - q_1 z_1^1 - q_2 z_2^1}$$
$$+ \frac{1}{2}\left(\frac{1}{5 + \sqrt{k_1} + z_1^1}\right)\tfrac{1}{2}k_1^{-1/2}$$
$$+ \frac{1}{2}\left(\frac{1}{1 + \sqrt{k_1} + z_2^1}\right)\tfrac{1}{2}k_1^{-1/2} = 0 \quad \textbf{(A13.1)}$$

z_1^1:
$$\frac{-q_1}{3 - k_1 - q_1 z_1^1 - q_2 z_2^1}$$
$$+ \frac{1}{2}\left(\frac{1}{5 + \sqrt{k_1} + z_1^1}\right) = 0 \quad \textbf{(A13.2)}$$

z_2^1:
$$\frac{-q_2}{3 - k_1 - q_1 z_1^1 - q_2 z_2^1}$$
$$+ \frac{1}{2}\left(\frac{1}{1 + \sqrt{k_1} + z_2^1}\right) = 0. \quad \textbf{(A13.3)}$$

Agent 2's problem and FOC are essentially the same:

$$\max_{k_1, z_1^2, z_2^2} \ln(3 - k_2 - q_1 z_1^2 - q_2 z_2^2)$$
$$+ \tfrac{1}{2} \ln(5 + \sqrt{k_2} + z_1^2)$$
$$+ \tfrac{1}{2} \ln(1 + \sqrt{k_2} + z_2^2)$$

k_2:
$$\frac{-1}{3 - k_2 - q_1 z_1^2 - q_2 z_2^2}$$
$$+ \frac{1}{2}\left(\frac{1}{5 + \sqrt{k_2} + z_1^2}\right)\tfrac{1}{2}k_2^{-1/2}$$
$$+ \frac{1}{2}\left(\frac{1}{1 + \sqrt{k_2} + z_2^2}\right)\tfrac{1}{2}k_2^{-1/2} = 0 \quad \textbf{(A13.4)}$$

z_1^2:
$$\frac{-q_1}{3 - k_2 - q_1 z_1^2 - q_2 z_2^2}$$
$$+ \frac{1}{2}\left(\frac{1}{1 + \sqrt{k_2} + z_1^2}\right) = 0. \quad \textbf{(A13.5)}$$

z_2^2:
$$\frac{-q_2}{3 - k_2 - q_1 z_1^2 - q_2 z_2^2}$$
$$+ \frac{1}{2}\left(\frac{1}{5 + \sqrt{k_2} + z_2^2}\right) = 0 \quad \textbf{(A13.6)}$$

By symmetry, in equilibrium

$$k_1 = k_2; q_1 = q_2;$$
$$z_1^1 = z_2^2 = -z_1^2, z_2^1 = z_1^2 = -z_2^2$$

By Equations (A13.2) and (A13.5), using the fact that $z_1^1 + z_2^1 = z_2^2 + z_1^2$:

$$\frac{1}{5 + \sqrt{k_1} + z_1^1} = \frac{1}{1 + \sqrt{k_2} + z_1^2}$$

Equations (A13.3) and (A13.6) imply:

$$\frac{1}{1 + \sqrt{k_1} + z_2^1} = \frac{1}{5 + \sqrt{k_2} + z_2^2}$$

The equations defining k_1 and z_1^1 are thus reduced to

k_1:
$$\frac{1}{3 - k_1 - q_1 z_1^1 - q_2 z_2^1}$$
$$+ \frac{1}{4}\frac{1}{\sqrt{k_1}}\left(\frac{1}{5 + \sqrt{k_1} + z_1^1}\right)$$
$$+ \frac{1}{4}\frac{1}{\sqrt{k_1}}\left(\frac{1}{1 + \sqrt{k_1} - z_1^1}\right) = 0 \quad \textbf{(A13.7)}$$

z_1^1:
$$\frac{1}{5 + \sqrt{k_1} + z_1^1} = \frac{1}{1 + \sqrt{k_1} - z_1^1}. \quad \textbf{(A13.8)}$$

Solving for k_1, z_1^1, yields from Equation (A13.8):

$$1 + \sqrt{k_1} - z_1^1 = 5 + \sqrt{k_1} + z_1^1$$
$$-4 = 2z_1^1$$
$$-2 = z_1^1.$$

Substituting this value into Equation (A13.7) gives

$$\frac{1}{3 - k_1} = +\frac{1}{4}\frac{1}{\sqrt{k_1}}$$
$$\times \left\{\frac{1}{5 + \sqrt{k_1} - 2} + \frac{1}{1 + \sqrt{k_1} + 2}\right\}$$

$$\frac{1}{3 - k_1} = + \frac{1}{4} \frac{1}{\sqrt{k_1}} \left\{ \frac{2}{3 + \sqrt{k_1}} \right\}$$

$$4\sqrt{k_1}\{3 + \sqrt{k_1}\} = 2(3 - k_1),$$

or, simplifying,

$$-6 + 12\sqrt{k_1} + 6k_1 = 0$$

$$-1 + 2\sqrt{k_1} + k_1 = 0.$$

Let $X = \sqrt{k_1}$

$$X = \frac{-2 \pm \sqrt{4 - 4(1)(-1)}}{2} = \frac{-2 \pm \sqrt{8}}{2}$$

$$X = -1 + \sqrt{2} = -1 + 1.4$$

$$X = 0.4$$

$$k_1 = 0.16 \text{ and,}$$

$$\text{total savings} = k_1 + k_2$$
$$= 2k_1 = 0.32.$$

CHAPTER 14

FINANCIAL EQUILIBRIUM WITH DIFFERENTIAL INFORMATION

14.1 INTRODUCTION

The fact that investors often disagree about expected future returns or the evaluation of the risks associated with specific investments is probably the foremost determinant of financial trading in the sense of explaining the larger fraction of trading volume. Yet we have said very little so far about the possibility of such disagreements and, more generally, of differences in investors' information. In fact, two of the equilibrium models we have reviewed explicitly assumed investors have identical information sets. In the case of the CAPM, it is assumed that all investors' expectations are summarized by the same vector of expected returns and the same variance-covariance matrix. It is this assumption that gives relevance to the single efficient frontier. Similarly, the assumption of a single representative decision maker in the CCAPM is akin to assuming the existence of a large number of investors endowed with identical preferences and information sets.[1] The Rational Expectations hypothesis, which is part of the CCAPM, necessarily implies that, at equilibrium, all investors share the same objective views about future returns.

Both the APT and the Martingale pricing models are nonstructural models which, by construction, are agnostic about the background information (or preferences) of the investors. In a sense they go beyond the homogenous information assumption, but without being explicit as to the specific implications of such an extension. The Arrow-Debreu model is a structural model equipped to deal, at least implicitly, with heterogeneously informed agents. This is because the Arrow-Debreu model can accommodate general utility representations defined on state-contingent commodities where, in effect, the assumed state probabilities are embedded in the specific form taken by the individual's utility function.[2] Thus, while agents must agree on the relevant states of the world,

---

[1] Box 10-1 discussed the extent to which this interpretation can be relaxed as far as utility functions are concerned.

[2] Such preference structures are, strictly speaking, not expected utility.

they could disagree on their probabilities. We did not exploit this degree of generality, however, and typically made our arguments on the basis of time-additive- and state-additive utility functions with explicit and investor-homogenous state probabilities.

In this chapter we relax the assumption that all agents in the economy have the same subjective probabilities about states of nature or the same expectations about returns, or that they know the objective probability distributions. In so doing we open a huge and fascinating, yet incomplete, chapter in financial economics. We will be very selective in the topics we choose to address under this heading and will concentrate on the issue of market equilibrium with differentially informed traders. This is in keeping with the spirit of this book and enables us to revisit the last important pillar of traditional financial theory left untouched thus far: the efficient market hypothesis.

But the import of differential information for understanding financial markets, institutions, and contracts goes much beyond market efficiency. Since Akerlof (1970), asymmetric information—a situation where agents are differentially informed with, moreover, one or a subgroup having *superior* information—is known potentially to lead to the failure of a market to exist. This *lemon* problem is a relevant one in financial markets: One may be suspicious of purchasing a stock from a better informed intermediary, or, a fortiori, from the primary issuer of a security who may be presumed to have the best information about the exact value of the underlying assets. This is so because one may suspect that he would be unwilling to sell at a price lower than the fundamental value of the asset. What is called the *winner's curse* is applicable here: If the transaction is concluded, that is, if the better-informed owner has agreed to sell, is it not likely that the buyer will have paid too much for the asset? This reasoning might go some way toward explaining the fact that capital raised by firms in equity markets is such a small proportion of total firm financing [on this, see Greenwald and Stiglitz (1993)].

Asymmetric information may also explain the phenomenon of credit rationing. The idea here is that it may not be to the advantage of a lender, confronted with a demand for funds larger than he can accommodate, to increase the interest rate he charges as would be required to balance supply and demand. This is because in doing so the lender may alter the pool of applicants in an unfavorable way. Specifically, this possibility depends on the plausible hypothesis that the lender does not know the degree of riskiness of the projects for which borrowers need funds and that, in the context of a debt contract, a higher hurdle rate may eliminate the less profitable, but consequently, also the less risky, projects. It is easy to construct cases where the creditor is worse off lending his funds at a higher rate because at the high rate the pool of borrowers becomes riskier [Stiglitz and Weiss (1981)].

Asymmetric information has also been used to explain the prevalence of debt contracts relative to contingent claims. We have used the argument before (Chapter 7): states of nature are often costly to ascertain and verify for one of the parties in a contract. When two parties enter into a contract, it may be more efficient, as a result, to stipulate noncontingent payments most of the time, thus economizing on verification costs. Only states leading to bankruptcy or default are recognized as resulting in different rights and obligations for the parties involved [Townsend (1979)].

These are only a few of the important issues that can be addressed with the asymmetric information assumption. A full review would deserve a whole book in itself. One reason for the need to be selective is that there is a lack of a unifying framework in this literature. It has often proceeded with a set of specific examples rather than more encompassing models. We refer interested readers to Hirshleifer and Riley (1992) for a broader review of this fascinating and important topic in financial economics.

14.2   ON THE POSSIBILITY OF AN UPWARD SLOPING DEMAND CURVE

There are plenty of reasons to believe that differences in information and beliefs constitute an important motivation for trading in financial markets. It is extremely difficult to rationalize observed trading volumes in a world of homogeneously informed agents. The main reason for having neglected what is without doubt an obvious fact is that our equilibrium concept, borrowed from traditional supply and demand analysis (the standard notion of Walrasian equilibrium), must be thoroughly updated once we allow for heterogeneous information.

The intuition is as follows: The Walrasian equilibrium price is necessarily some function of the orders placed by traders. Suppose traders are heterogeneously informed and that their private information set is a relevant determinant of their orders. The equilibrium price will, therefore, reflect and, in that sense, transmit at least a fraction of the privately held information. In this case, the equilibrium price is not only a signal of relative scarcity as in a Walrasian world, it also reflects the agents' information. In this context, the price quoted for a commodity or a security may be high because the demand for it is objectively high and/or supply is low. But it may also be high because a group of investors has private information suggestive that the commodity or security in question will be expensive tomorrow. Of course, this information about the future value of the item is of interest to all. Presumably, except for liquidity reasons, no one will want to sell something at a low price that will likely be of much higher value tomorrow. This means that when the price quoted on the market is high (in the fiction of standard microeconomics, when the *Walrasian auctioneer* announces a high price), a number of market participants will realize that they have sent in their orders on the basis of information that is probably not shared by the *rest of the market*. Depending on the confidence they place in their own information, they may then want to revise their orders, and to do so in a paradoxical way: Because the announced price is higher than they thought it would be, they want to buy more! Fundamentally, this means that what was thought to be the equilibrium price is not, in fact, an equilibrium.

This is a new situation and it requires a departure from the Walrasian equilibrium concept. In this chapter we will develop these ideas with the help of an example. We first illustrate the notion of a Rational Expectations Equilibrium (REE), a concept we have used more informally in preceding chapters (e.g., Chapter 10), in a context where all participants share the same information. We then extend it to encompass situations where agents are heterogeneously informed. We provide an example of a fully revealing rational expectations equilibrium which may be deemed to be the formal representation of the notion of an *informationally efficient market*. We conclude by discussing some weaknesses of this equilibrium concept and possible extensions.

14.3 AN ILLUSTRATION OF THE CONCEPT OF REE: HOMOGENEOUS INFORMATION[3]

Let us consider the joint equilibrium of a spot market for a given commodity and its associated futures market. The context is the familiar now and then, two-date economy. The single commodity is traded at date 1. Viewed from date 0, the date at which producers must make their production decisions, the demand for this commodity, emanating from final users, is stochastic. It can be represented by a linear demand curve shocked by a random term as in

$$D(p, \tilde{\eta}) = a - cp + \tilde{\eta}$$

where $D(.)$ represents the quantity demanded, p is the (spot) price for the commodity in question, a and c are positive constants, and $\tilde{\eta}$ is a stochastic demand-shifting element.[4] This latter quantity is centered at (has mean value) zero, at which point the demand curve assumes its average position, and it is normally distributed with variance σ_η^2; in other words, $\eta(\tilde{\eta}) = N(0; \sigma_\eta^2)$ where $h(\ )$ is the probability density function on $\tilde{\eta}$. See Figure 14-1 for an illustration. At date 0, the N producers decide on their input level x—the input price is normalized at 1—knowing that $g(x)$ units of output will then be available after a one-period production lag, that is, at date 1. The production process is thus non-stochastic and the only uncertainty originates from the demand side. Because of the latter, the future sale price $\tilde{p}$ is unknown at the time of the input decision.

We shall assume the existence of a futures or forward market[5] that our producers may use for hedging or speculative purposes. Specifically, let $f > 0$ (< 0) be the short (long) futures position taken by the representative producer, that is, the quantity of output sold (bought) for future delivery at the future (or forward) price p^f.

Here we shall assume that the good traded in the futures market (i.e., specified as acceptable for delivery in the futures contract), is the same as the commodity exchanged on the spot market. For this reason, arbitrageurs will ensure that, at date 1, the futures and the spot price will be exactly identical: In the language of futures markets, the *basis* is constantly equal to zero and there is thus no *basis risk*.

Under these conditions, the typical producer's cash flow $\tilde{y}$ is

$$\tilde{y} = \tilde{p}g(x) - x + (p^f - \tilde{p})f$$

which can also be written as

$$\tilde{y} = \tilde{p}(g(x) - f) - x + p^f f.$$

[3]The rest of this chapter closely follows Danthine (1978).
[4]Looking forward, the demand for heating oil next winter, for example, is stochastic because the severity of the winter is impossible to predict in advance.
[5]The term *futures market* is normally reserved for a market for future delivery taking place in the context of an organized exchange. A *forward market* refers to private exchanges of similar contracts calling for the future delivery of a commodity or financial instrument. While knowledge of the credit worthiness and honesty of the counter-party is of essence in the case of forward contracts, a futures market is anonymous. The exchange is the relevant counter-party for the two sides in a contract. It protects itself and ensures that both parties' engagements will be fulfilled by demanding initial guarantee deposits as well as issuing daily *margin calls* to the party against whose position the price has moved. In a two-date setting, in the absence of interim price changes, the notion of margin calls is not relevant and it is not possible to distinguish futures from forward.

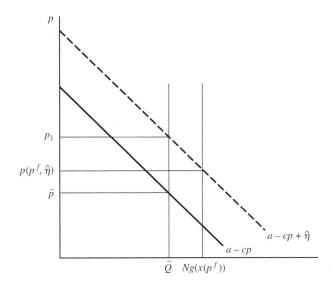

FIGURE 14-1   Market Equilibrium with a Stochastic Demand Curve

It is seen that by setting $f = g(x)$, that is, by selling forward the totality of his production, the producers can eliminate all his risks. Although this need not be his optimal futures position, the feasibility of shedding all risks explains the separation result that follows (much in the spirit of the CAPM: diversifiable risk is not priced).

Let us assume that producers maximize the expected utility of their future cash flow where $U'(\ ) > 0$ and $U''(\ ) < 0$:

$$\max_{x \geq 0, f} EU(\tilde{y}).$$

Differentiating with respect to x and f successively, and assuming an interior solution, we obtain the following two FOCs:

$$x: \quad E[U_1(\tilde{y})\tilde{p}] = \frac{1}{g_1(x)} EU_1(\tilde{y}) \tag{14.1}$$

$$f: \quad E[U_1(\tilde{y})\tilde{p}] = p^f EU_1(\tilde{y}) \tag{14.2}$$

which together imply:

$$p^f = \frac{1}{g_1(x)}. \tag{14.3}$$

Equation (14.3) is remarkable because it says that the optimal input level should be such that the marginal cost of production is set equal to the (known) futures price p^f, the latter replacing the expected spot price as the appropriate production signal. The futures price equals marginal cost condition is also worth noticing because it implies that, despite the uncertain context in which they operate, producers should not factor in a risk premium when computing their optimal production decision.

For us, a key implication of this result is that, since the supply level will directly depend on the futures price quoted at date 0, the equilibrium spot price at date 1 will be a function of the futures price realized one period earlier. Indeed writing $x = x(p^f)$ and

$g(x) = g(x(p^f))$, the implications of Equation (14.3) for input and output levels respectively, the supply-equals-demand condition for the date 1 spot market reads

$$Ng(x(p^f)) = a - cp + \tilde{\eta}$$

which implicitly defines the equilibrium (date 1) spot price as a function of the date 0 value taken by the futures price, or

$$\tilde{p} = p(p^f, \tilde{\eta}). \tag{14.4}$$

It is clear from Equation (14.4) that the structure of our problem is such that the probability distribution on $\tilde{p}$ cannot be spelled out independently of the value taken by p^f. Consequently, it would not be meaningful to assume expectations for $\tilde{p}$, on the part of producers or futures market speculators, which would not take account of this fundamental link between the two prices. This observation, which is a first step toward the definition of a rational expectation equilibrium, can be further developed by focusing now on the futures market.

Let us assume that, in addition to the N producers, n speculators take positions on the futures market. We define speculators by their exclusive involvement in the futures markets; in particular they have no position in the underlying commodity. Accordingly, their cash flows are simply:

$$\tilde{z}_i = (p^f - \tilde{p})b_i$$

where b_i is the futures position ($>0=$ short; $<0=$ long) taken by speculator i. Suppose for simplicity that their preferences are represented by a linear mean-variance utility function of their cash flows:

$$W(\tilde{z}_i) = E(\tilde{z}_i) - \frac{\chi}{2} \text{var}(\tilde{z}_i)$$

where χ represents the (Arrow-Pratt) Absolute Risk Aversion index ($R_A(z)$) of the representative speculator. We shall similarly specialize the utility function of producers. The assumption of a linear mean-variance utility representation is, in fact, equivalent to hypothesizing an exponential (CARA) utility function such as

$$W(\tilde{z}) = -\exp\left\{-\frac{\chi}{2}\tilde{z}\right\}$$

if the context is such that the argument of the function, $\tilde{z}$, is normally distributed. This hypothesis will be verified at the equilibrium of our model.

Under these hypotheses, it is easy to verify that the optimal futures position of speculator i is

$$b_i = \frac{p^f - E(\tilde{p}|p^f)}{\chi \, \text{var}(\tilde{p}|p^f)} \tag{14.5}$$

where the conditioning in the expectation and variance operators is made necessary by Equation (14.4). The form of Equation (14.5) is not surprising. It implies that the optimal futures position selected by a speculator will have the same sign as the expected difference between the futures price and the expected spot price, that is, a speculator will be long ($b > 0$) if and only if the futures price at which he sells is larger than the spot price at which he expects to be able to unload his position tomorrow. As to the size of his position, it will be proportional to the expected difference between the two prices, which is indicative of the size of the expected return, and inversely related to the perceived riskiness of the speculation, measured by the product of the variance of the spot price with the Arrow-Pratt coefficient of risk aversion. More risk-averse speculators will assume smaller positions, everything else being the same.

Under a linear mean-variance specification of preferences, the producer's objective function becomes

$$\max_{x \geq 0, f} E(\tilde{p}|p^f)(g(x) - f) + p^f f - \frac{\xi}{2}(g(x) - f)^2 \operatorname{var}(\tilde{p}|p^f)$$

where $\xi = R_A(y)$ is the absolute risk aversion measure for producers.

With this specification of the objective function, Equation (14.2), the FOC with respect to f, becomes

$$f = g(x(p^f)) + \frac{p^f - E(\tilde{p}|p^f)}{\xi \operatorname{var}(\tilde{p}|p^f)} \equiv f(p^f) \tag{14.6}$$

which is the second part of the separation result alluded to previously. The optimal futures position of the representative producer consists in selling forward the totality of his production ($g(x)$) and then readjusting by a component that is simply the futures position taken by a speculator with the same degree of risk aversion. To see this, compare the last term in Equation (14.6) with Equation (14.5). A producer's actual futures position can be viewed as the sum of these two terms. He may under-hedge, that is, sell less than his future output at the futures price. This is so if he anticipates paying an insurance premium in the form of a sale price (p^f) lower than the spot price he expects to prevail tomorrow. But he could as well over-hedge and sell forward more than his total future output. That is, if he considers the current futures price to be a high enough price, he may be willing to speculate on it, selling high at the futures price what he hopes to buy low tomorrow on the spot market.

Putting together speculators' and producers' positions, the futures market clearing condition becomes:

$$\sum_{i=1}^{n} b_i + Nf = 0, \text{ or}$$

$$n\left\{\frac{p^f - E(\tilde{p}|p^f)}{\chi \operatorname{var}(\tilde{p}|p^f)}\right\} + N\left\{\frac{p^f - E(\tilde{p}|p^f)}{\xi \operatorname{var}(\tilde{p}|p^f)}\right\} + Ng(x(p^f)) = 0, \tag{14.7}$$

which must be solved for the equilibrium futures price p^f. Equation (14.7) makes clear that the equilibrium futures price p^f is dependent on the expectations held on the future spot price $\tilde{p}$; we had previously emphasized the dependence on p^f of expectations about $\tilde{p}$. This apparently circular reasoning can be resolved under the rational expectations hypothesis, which consists of assuming that individuals have learned to understand the relationship summarized in Equation (14.4), that is,

$$E(\tilde{p}|p^f) = E[p(p^f, \tilde{\eta})|p^f], \operatorname{var}(\tilde{p}|p^f) = \operatorname{var}[p(p^f, \tilde{\eta})|p^f]. \tag{14.8}$$

> **Definition 14.1:**
> In the context of this section, a Rational Expectations Equilibrium (REE) is
> 1. a futures price p^f solving Equation (14.7) given Equation (14.8), and the distributional assumption made on $\tilde{\eta}$, and
> 2. a spot price p solving Equation (14.4) given p^f and the realization of $\tilde{\eta}$.

The first part of the definition indicates that the futures price equilibrates the futures market at date 0 when agents rationally anticipate the effective condition under which the spot market will clear tomorrow and make use of the objective probability distribution on the stochastic parameter $\tilde{\eta}$. Given the supply of the commodity available tomorrow (itself a function of the equilibrium futures price quoted today), and given the particular value taken by $\tilde{\eta}$ (i.e., the final position of the demand curve), the second part specifies that the spot price clears the date 1 spot market.

14.4 FULLY REVEALING REE: AN EXAMPLE

Let us pursue this example one step further and assume that speculators have access to privileged information in the following sense: Before the futures exchange opens, speculator i ($i = 1, \ldots, n$) observes some unbiased approximation v_i to the future realization of the variable $\tilde{\eta}$. The signal v_i can be viewed as the future η itself plus an error of observation ω_i. The latter is specific to speculator i, but all speculators are similarly imprecise in the information they manage to gather. Thus,

$$v_i = \eta + \omega_i \quad \text{where the } \tilde{\omega}_i\text{'s are i.i.d. } N(0; \sigma_\omega^2)$$

across agents and across time periods.

This relationship can be interpreted as follows: η is a summary measure of the mood of consumers or of other conditions affecting demand. Speculators can obtain advanced information as to the particular value of this realization for the relevant period through, for instance, a survey of consumer's intentions or a detailed weather forecast (assuming the latter influences demand). These observations are not without errors, but (regarding these two periods as only one occasion of a multiperiod process where learning has been taking place), speculators are assumed to be sufficiently skilled to avoid systematic biases in their evaluations. In this model, this advance information is freely available to them.

Under these conditions, Equation (14.5) becomes

$$b_i = \frac{p^f - E(\tilde{p}|p^f; v_i)}{\chi \operatorname{var}(\tilde{p}|p^f; v_i)} \equiv b(p^f; v_i),$$

where we make it explicit that both the expected value and the variance of the spot price are affected by the advance piece of information obtained by speculator i. The Appendix details how these expectations can actually be computed, but this need not occupy us for the moment.

Formally, Equation (14.6) is unchanged, so that the futures market clearing condition can be written

$$Nf(p^f) + \sum_i^n b(p^f; v_i) = 0;$$

It is clear from this equation that the equilibrium futures price will be affected by the "elements" of information gathered by speculators. In fact, under appropriate regularity conditions, the market-clearing equation implicitly defines a function

$$p^f = l(v_1, v_2, \ldots, v_n) \tag{14.9}$$

that formalizes this link and thus the information content of the equilibrium futures price.

All this implies that there is more than meets the eye in the conditioning on p^f of $E(\tilde{p}|p^f)$ and $\text{var}(\tilde{p}|p^f)$. So far the reasoning for this conditioning was given by Equation (14.4): A higher p^f stimulates supply from $g(x(p^f))$ and thus affects the equilibrium spot price. Now a higher p^f also indicates high v_i's on average, thus transmitting information about the future realization of $\tilde{\eta}$. The real implications of this link can be suggested by reference to Figure 14.1. In the absence of advance information, supply will be geared to the average demand conditions. $\overline{Q}$ represents this average supply level, leading to a spot price $\bar{p}$ under conditions of average demand ($\eta = 0$). If suppliers receive no advance warning of an abnormally high demand level, an above-average realization $\hat{\eta}$ requires a high price p_1 to balance supply and demand. If, on the other hand, speculators' advance information is transmitted to producers via the futures price, supply increases in anticipation of the high demand level and the price increase is mitigated.

We are now in a position to provide a precise answer to the question that has preoccupied us since Section 14.2: How much information is transmitted by the equilibrium price p^f? It will not be a fully general answer: Our model has the nature of an example because it presumes specific functional forms. The result we will obtain certainly stands at one extreme on the spectrum of possible answers, but it can be considered as a useful benchmark. In what follows, we will construct, under the additional simplification $g(x) = \alpha x^{\frac{1}{2}}$, a consistent equilibrium in which the futures price is itself a summary of *all the information* there is to obtain, a summary which, in an operational sense, is fully equivalent to the complete list of signals obtained by all speculators. More precisely, we will show that the equilibrium futures price is an invertible (linear) function of Σv_j and that, indeed, it clears the futures market given that everyone realizes this property and bases his orders on the information he can thus extract. This result is important because Σv_j is a sufficient statistic for the entire vector $(v_1, v_2, \ldots, v_n)$. This formal expression means that the sum contains as much relevant information for the problem at hand, as the entire vector in the sense that knowing the sum leads to placing the same market orders as knowing the whole vector. Ours is thus a context where the answer to our question is: *All* the relevant information is aggregated in the equilibrium price and is revealed freely to market participants. The REE is thus *fully revealing!*

Let us proceed and make these precise assertions. Under the assumed technology, $g(x) = \alpha x^{1/2}$, Equations (14.3), (14.4), and (14.8) become, respectively,

$$g(x(p^f)) = \frac{\alpha^2}{2} p^f$$

$$p(p^f, \tilde{\eta}) = A - B p^f + \frac{1}{c} \tilde{\eta}$$

$$\text{with } A = \frac{a}{c}, B = \frac{N}{c} \frac{\alpha^2}{2}$$

$$E(\tilde{p}|p^f) = A - Bp^f + \frac{1}{c}E(\tilde{\eta}|p^f)$$

$$\text{var}(\tilde{p}|p^f) = \frac{1}{c^2}\text{var}(\tilde{\eta}|p^f)$$

The informational structure is as follows. Considering the market as a whole, an experiment has been performed consisting of observing the values taken by n independent drawings of some random variable $\tilde{v}$, where $\tilde{v} = \eta + \tilde{\omega}$ and $\tilde{\omega}$ is $N(0, \sigma_\omega^2)$. The results are summarized in the vector $v = (\tilde{v}_1, v_2, \dots, v_n)$ or, as we shall demonstrate, in the sum of the v_j's, Σv_j, which is a *sufficient statistic* for $v = (v_1, v_2, \dots, v_n)$. The latter expression means that conditioning expectations on Σv_j or on Σv_j *and* the whole vector of v yields the same posterior distribution for $\tilde{\eta}$. In other words, the entire vector does not contain any information that is not already present in the sum. Formally, we have Definition 14.2.

Definition 14.2:
$(1/n)\Sigma v_j$ is a sufficient statistic for $v = (v_1, v_2, \dots, v_n)$ relative to the distribution $h(\eta)$ if and only if $h(\tilde{\eta}|\Sigma v_j, v) = h(\tilde{\eta}|\Sigma v_j)$.

Being a function of the observations [see Equation (14.9)], p^f is itself a statistic used by traders in calibrating their probabilities. The question is: How good a statistic can it be? How well can the futures price summarize the information available to the market? As promised, we now display an equilibrium where the price p^f is a sufficient statistic for the information available to the market; that is, it is invertible for the sufficient statistic Σv_j. In that case, knowledge of p^f is equivalent to the knowledge of Σv_j and farmers' and speculators' expectations coincide. If the futures price has this revealing property, expectations held at equilibrium by all agents must be (see the Appendix for details):

$$E(\tilde{\eta}|p^f) = E(\tilde{\eta}|v_j, p^f) = E(\tilde{\eta}|\Sigma v_j) = \frac{\sigma_\eta^2}{n\sigma_\eta^2 + \sigma_\omega^2}\Sigma v_j \qquad (14.10)$$

$$\text{var}(\tilde{\eta}|p^f) = \text{var}(\tilde{\eta}|v_j, p^f) = \frac{\sigma_\omega^2 \sigma_\eta^2}{n\sigma_\eta^2 + \sigma_\omega^2}. \qquad (14.11)$$

Equations (14.10) and (14.11) make clear that conditioning on the futures price would, under our hypothesis, is equivalent to conditioning on Σv_j, the latter being, of course, superior information relative to the single piece of individual information, v_i, initially obtained by speculator i. Using these expressions for the expectations in Equation (14.7), one can show after a few tedious manipulations that, as announced, the market-clearing futures price has the form

$$p^f = F + L\Sigma v_j, \qquad (14.12)$$

where

$$F = \frac{(N\chi + n\xi)A}{(N\chi + n\xi)(B + 1) + N\alpha^2\xi\chi\frac{1}{c^2}\frac{\sigma_\omega^2\sigma_\eta^2}{n\sigma_\eta^2\sigma_\omega^2}} \quad \text{and}$$

$$L = \frac{1}{c} \frac{\sigma_\omega^2 \sigma_\eta^2}{n\sigma_\eta^2 + \sigma_\omega^2} \frac{F}{A}.$$

Equation (14.12) shows the equilibrium price p^f to be proportional to Σv_j and thus a sufficient statistic as postulated. It satisfies our definition of an equilibrium. It is a market-clearing price, the result of speculators' and farmers' maximizing behavior, and it corresponds to an equilibrium state of expectations. That is, when Equation (14.12) is the hypothesized functional relationship between p^f and v, this relationship is indeed realized given that each agent then appropriately extracts the information Σv_j from the announcement of the equilibrium price.

14.5 THE EFFICIENT MARKET HYPOTHESIS

The result obtained in Section 14.4 is without doubt extreme. It is interesting, however, as it stands as the paragon of the concept of market efficiency. Here is a formal and precise context in which the valuable pieces of information held by heterogeneously informed market participants are aggregated and freely transmitted to all via the trading process. This outcome is reminiscent of the statements made earlier in the century by the famous liberal economist F. von Hayek who celebrated the virtues of the market as an information aggregator [Hayek (1945)]. It must also correspond to what Fama (1970) intended when introducing the concept of strong form efficiency, defined as a situation where market prices fully reflect all publicly *and* privately held information.

The reader will recall that Fama (1970) also introduced the notions of *weak form efficiency,* covering situations where market prices fully and instantaneously reflect the information included in historical prices, and of *semi-strong form efficiency* where prices, in addition, reflect all publicly available information (of whatever nature). A securities market equilibrium such as the one described in Chapter 10 under the heading of the CCAPM probably best captures what one can understand as semi-strong efficiency: Agents are rational in the sense of being expected utility maximizers, they are homogeneously informed (so that all information is indeed publicly held), and they efficiently use all the relevant information when defining their asset holdings. In the CCAPM, no agent can systematically beat the market, a largely accepted hallmark of an efficient market equilibrium, provided beating the market is appropriately defined in terms of both risk and return.

The concept of Martingale, also used in Chapters 9 and 11, has long constituted another hallmark of market efficiency. It is useful here to provide a formal definition.

Definition 14.1:
A stochastic process $\tilde{x}_t$ is a Martingale with respect to an information set Φ_t if

$$E(\tilde{x}_{t+1}|\Phi_t) = x_t. \qquad (14.13)$$

It is a short step from this notion of a Martingale to the assertion that one cannot beat the market, which is the case if the current price of a stock is the best predictor of its future price. The latter is likely to be the case if market participants indeed make full use of all available information: In that situation, future price changes can only be unpredictable. An equation like Equation (14.13) cannot be true exactly for stock prices as stock returns would then be zero on average. It is clear that what could be a Martingale under the previous intuitive reasoning would be a price series normalized to take account of dividends and a normal expected return for holding stock. To get an idea of what this would mean, let us refer to the price equilibrium Equation (10.2) of the CCAPM

$$U_1(Y_t)p_t = \delta E_t\{U_1(\tilde{Y}_{t+1})(\tilde{p}_{t+1} + \tilde{Y}_{t+1})\}. \tag{10.2}$$

Making the assumption of risk neutrality, one obtains:

$$p_t = \delta E_t(\tilde{p}_{t+1} + \tilde{Y}_{t+1}). \tag{14.14}$$

If we entertain, for a moment, the possibility of a non-dividend paying stock, $Y_t \equiv 0$, then Equation (14.14) indeed implies that the normalized series $x_t = \delta^t p_t$ satisfies Equation (14.13) and is thus a Martingale. This normalization implies that the expected return on stockholding is constant and equal to the risk-free rate. In the case of a dividend-paying stock, a similar, but slightly more complicated, normalization yields the same result.

The main points of this discussion are (1) that a pure Martingale process requires adjusting the stock price series to take account of dividends and the existence of a positive normal return, and (2) that the Martingale property is a mark of market efficiency only under a strong hypothesis of risk neutrality that includes, as a corollary, the property that expected return to stockholding is constant. The large empirical literature on market efficiency has not always been able to appropriately take account of these qualifications. See Leroy (1989) for an in-depth survey of this issue.

Our model of the previous section is more ambitious, addressing as it does, the concept of strong form efficiency. Its merit is to underline what it takes for this extreme concept to be descriptive of reality, thus also helping to delineate its limits. Two of these limits deserve mentioning. The first one arises once one attempts, plausibly, to get rid of the hypothesis that speculators are able to costlessly obtain their elements of privileged information. If information is free, it is difficult to see why all speculators would not get all the relevant information, thus reverting to a model of homogeneous information. However, the spirit of our example is that resources are needed to collect information and that speculators are those market participants specializing in this costly search process. Yet why should speculator i expand resources to obtain private information v_i when the equilibrium price will freely reveal to him the sufficient statistic Σv_j, which by itself is more informative than the information he could gather at a cost? The very fact that the equilibrium REE price is fully revealing implies that individual speculators have no use for their own piece of information, with the obvious corollary that they will not be prepared to spend a penny to obtain it. On the other hand, if speculators are not endowed with privileged information, there is no way the equilibrium price will be the celebrated information aggregator and transmitter. In turn, if the equilibrium price is not informative, it may well pay for speculators to obtain valuable private information. We are thus trapped in a vicious circle that results in the nonexistence of equilibrium, an outcome Grossman and Stiglitz (1980) have logically dubbed "the impossibility of informationally efficient markets."

Another limitation of the conceptual setup of Section 14.4 resides in the fact that the hypotheses required for the equilibrium price to be fully revealing are numerous and particularly severe. The rational expectations hypothesis includes, as always, the assumption that market participants understand the environment in which they operate.

This segment of the hypothesis is particularly demanding in the context of our model and it is crucial for agents to be able to extract a sufficient statistics from the equilibrium futures price. By that we mean that, for individual agents to be in position to read all the information concealed in the equilibrium price, they need to know exactly the number of uninformed and informed agents and their respective degrees of risk aversion, which must be identical inside each agent class. The information held by the various speculators must have identical precision (i.e., an error term with the same variance), and none of the market participants can be motivated by liquidity considerations. All in all, these requirements are simply too strong to be plausibly met in real-life situations. Although the real-life complications may be partly compensated for by the fact that trading is done on a repeated, almost continuous basis, it is more reasonable to assume that the fully revealing equilibrium is the exception rather than the rule.

The more normal situation is certainly one where some, but not all, information is aggregated and transmitted by the equilibrium price. In such an equilibrium, the incentives to collect information remain, although if the price is too good a transmitter, they may be significantly reduced. The nonexistence-of-equilibrium problem uncovered by Grossman and Stiglitz is then more a curiosity than a real source of worry. Equilibria with partial transmission of information have been described in the literature under the heading *noisy rational expectation equilibrium*. The apparatus is quite a bit messier than in the reference case discussed in Section 14.4 and we will not explore it further (see Hellwig (1980) for a first step in this direction). Suffice it to say that this class of models serves as the basis for the branch of financial economics known as *market microstructure* which strives to explain the specific forms and rules underlying asset trading in a competitive market environment. The reader is referred to O'Hara (1997) for a broad coverage of these topics.

References

Akerlof, G., "The Market for Lemons: Qualitative Uncertainty and the Market Mechanism," *The Quarterly Journal of Economics,* 89 (1970): 488–500.

Danthine, J.-P., "Information, Futures Prices and Stabilizing Speculation," *Journal of Economic Theory*, 17 (1978): 79–98.

Fama, E., "Efficient Capital Markets: A Review of Theory and Empirical Work," *Journal of Finance,* 25 (1970): 383–417.

Greenwald, B., and J. E. Stiglitz, "Financial Market Imperfections and Business Cycles," *The Quarterly Journal of Economics,* 108 (1993): 77–114.

Grossman, S., and J. E. Stiglitz, "On the Impossibility of Informationally Efficient Markets," *American Economic Review,* 70(3), (1980): 393–408.

Hayek, F. H., "The Use of Knowledge in Society," *American Economic Review,* 61 (1945): 519–530.

Hellwig, M. F., "On the Aggregation of Information in Complete Markets," *Journal of Economic Theory,* 26 (1980): 279–312.

Hirshleifer, J., and J. G. Riley, *The Analytics of Uncertainty and Information*, Cambridge: Cambridge University Press, 1992.

LeRoy, S. F., "Efficient Capital Markets and Martingales," *Journal of Economic Literature,* 27 (1989): 1583–1621.

O'Hara, M., *Market Microstructure Theory*, Malden, Mass.: Basil Blackwell, 1997.

Stiglitz, J. E., and A. Weiss, "Credit Rationing in Markets with Imperfect Information," *American Economic Review,* 71 (1981): 393–410.

Townsend, R., "Optimal Contracts and Competitive Markets with Costly State Verification," *Journal of Economic Theory,* 21 (1979): 417–425.

APPENDIX

Bayesian Updating with the Normal Distribution

Theorem A14.1:

If we assume $\tilde{x}$ and $\tilde{y}$ are two normally distributed vectors with $\begin{pmatrix} \tilde{x} \\ \tilde{y} \end{pmatrix} \sim$

$N\left(\begin{pmatrix} \bar{x} \\ \bar{y} \end{pmatrix}, V \right)$, with matrix of variances and covariances $V = \begin{pmatrix} V_{xx} & V_{xy} \\ V_{xy} & V_{yy} \end{pmatrix}$, then

the distribution of $\tilde{x}$ conditional on the observation $\tilde{y} = y^0$ is normal with mean $\bar{x} + \Sigma_{xx}\Sigma_{yy}^{-1}\Sigma_{xx}y^0$ and covariance matrix $\Sigma_{xx} - \Sigma_{xx}\Sigma_{yy}^{-1}\Sigma_{xx}$.

APPLICATIONS

Let $\tilde{v}_i = \tilde{\eta} + \tilde{\omega}_i$. If $\begin{pmatrix} \tilde{\eta} \\ \tilde{v}_i \end{pmatrix} \sim N\left(\begin{pmatrix} \bar{x} \\ \bar{y} \end{pmatrix}, \right.$

$\left. \begin{pmatrix} \sigma_\eta^2 & \sigma_\eta^2 \\ \sigma_\eta^2 & \sigma_\eta^2 + \sigma_\omega^2 \end{pmatrix} \right)$, then

$$E(\tilde{\eta}|v_i) = 0 + \frac{\sigma_\eta^2}{\sigma_\eta^2 + \sigma_\omega^2} v_i$$

$$\text{var}(\tilde{\eta}|v_i) = \sigma_\eta^2 - \frac{\sigma_\eta^4}{\sigma_\eta^2 + \sigma_\omega^2} = \frac{\sigma_\eta^2 \sigma_\omega^2}{\sigma_\eta^2 + \sigma_\omega^2}$$

If $\begin{pmatrix} \tilde{\eta} \\ \Sigma v_i \end{pmatrix} \sim N\left(\begin{pmatrix} \bar{x} \\ \bar{y} \end{pmatrix}, \begin{pmatrix} \sigma_\eta^2 & n\sigma_\eta^2 \\ n\sigma_\eta^2 & n^2\sigma_\eta^2 + n\sigma_\omega^2 \end{pmatrix} \right),$

then

$$E(\tilde{\eta}|\Sigma v_i) = 0 + \frac{n\sigma_\eta^2}{n^2\sigma_\eta^2 + n\sigma_\omega^2}(\Sigma v_i)$$

$$= \frac{\sigma_\eta^2}{n\sigma_\eta^2 + \sigma_\omega^2}\Sigma v_i$$

$$\text{var}(\tilde{\eta}|\Sigma v_i) = \sigma_\eta^2 - n\sigma_\eta^2 \frac{1}{n^2\sigma_\eta^2 + n\sigma_\omega^2}n\sigma_\eta^2$$

$$= \frac{\sigma_\eta^2 \sigma_\omega^2}{n\sigma_\eta^2 + \sigma_\omega^2}$$

<h1 style="text-align: center">EXERCISES</h1>

Chapter 1

1.1 Let $U(.)$ be a well-behaved utility function that represents the preferences of an agent. Let $f(U)$ be a monotone transformation of the original utility function U. Why is an increasing function $g = f(U(\ ))$ also a utility function representing the same preferences as $U(\ )$?

1.2 Assume a well-behaved utility function. The maximizing choice for a consumer is preserved under increasing monotone transformations. Show this using the (first-order) optimality condition (MRS = price ratio) for a typical consumer and give an economic interpretation.

1.3 The MRS (marginal rate of substitution) is not constant in general. Give an economic interpretation. When will the MRS be constant? Give an example (a utility function over two goods) and compute the MRS. Is this of interest for us? Why? What undesirable properties does this particular utility function (and/or the underlying preferences) exhibit? In a two goods/two agents setting, what about the Pareto set when indifference curves are linear for both agents?

1.4 Consider a two goods/two agents pure exchange economy where agents' utility functions are of the form: $U(c_1^j, c_2^j) = (c_1^j)^\alpha \cdot (c_2^j)^{1-\alpha}, j = 1, 2$ with $\alpha = 0.5$. Initial endowments are $e_1^1 = 6, e_2^1 = 4, e_1^2 = 14, e_2^2 = 16$ (superscripts represent agents).
   a. Compute the original utility level for both agents. Compute the original MRS and give the (first-order) optimality conditions. What is your conclusion?
   b. Describe the Pareto set (the set of Pareto optima).
   c. Assume that there exists a competitive market for each good. What is the equilibrium allocation? What are equilibrium prices? Comment. What are the utility levels and MRS after trading? What do you conclude?
   d. Assume that the utility functions are now given by $U(c_1^j, c_2^j) = \ln((c_1^j)^\alpha \cdot (c_2^j)^{1-\alpha}), \alpha \in [0, 1], j = 1, 2$. What is the optimality relation for the typical consumer? How does it compare with that obtained at point a? Compute the original utility levels and MRS. What can you say about them as compared to those obtained in item a?
   e. Same setting as in point d: What is the equilibrium allocation if agents can trade the goods on competitive markets? What are the equilibrium prices? What are the after-trade utility levels and MRS? How do they compare with those obtained under a? What do you conclude?

1.5 Figure 1.1 shows an initial endowment point W, the budget line, and the optimal choices for two agents. In what direction will the budget line move? Why?

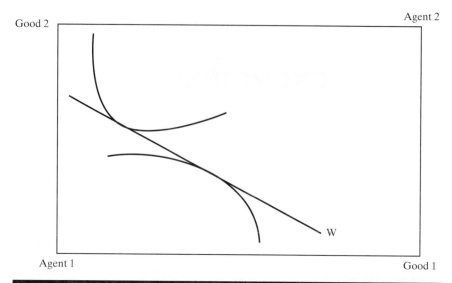

Good 2

Agent 2

Agent 1

Good 1

W

FIGURE E1-1   The Edgeworth-Bowley Box: Initial Endowment *W*

Chapter 2

2.1 Utility function: Under certainty, any increasing monotone transformation of a utility function is also a utility function representing the same preferences. Under uncertainty, we must restrict this statement to linear transformations if we are to keep the same preference representation. Give a mathematical as well as an economic interpretation for this.

Check it with this example. Assume an initial utility function attributes the following values to 3 perspectives:

$$
\begin{array}{ll}
B & u(B) = 100 \\
M & u(M) = 10 \\
P & u(P) = 50
\end{array}
$$

a. Check that with this initial utility function, the lottery $L = (B, M, 0.50) > P$.
b. The proposed transformations are $f(x) = a + bx, a \geq 0, b > 0$, and $g(x) = \ln(x)$. Check that under f, $L > P$, but that under g, $P > L$.

2.2 Lotteries: Discuss the equivalence between (x, z, π) and $(x, y, \pi + (1 - \pi)\tau)$ when $z = (x, y, \tau)$. Can you think of circumstances under which they would not be viewed as equal?

2.3 Inter-temporal consumption: Consider a two-date (one-period) economy and an agent with utility function over consumption:

$$
U(c) = \frac{c^{1-\gamma}}{1 - \gamma}
$$

at each period. Define the inter-temporal utility function as $V(c_1, c_2) = U(c_1) + U(c_2)$. Show (try it mathematically) that the agent will always prefer a smooth consumption stream to a more variable one with the same mean, that is,

$$U(\bar{c}) + U(\bar{c}) > U(c_1) + U(c_2)$$

$$\text{if } \bar{c} = \frac{c_1 + c_2}{2}.$$

Chapter 3

3.1 Risk aversion: Consider the following utility functions (defined over wealth Y):

$$(1)\ U(Y) = -\frac{1}{Y}$$

$$(2)\ U(Y) = \ln Y$$
$$(3)\ U(Y) = -Y^{-\gamma}$$
$$(4)\ U(Y) = -\exp(-\gamma Y)$$
$$(5)\ U(Y) = \frac{Y^\gamma}{\gamma}$$
$$(6)\ U(Y) = \alpha Y - \beta Y^2$$

a. Check that they are well behaved ($U' > 0$, $U'' < 0$) or state restrictions on the parameters so that they are (utility functions (1)–(6)). For utility function (6), take positive α and β, and give the range of wealth over which the utility function is well behaved.
b. Compute the absolute and relative risk aversion coefficients.
c. What is the effect of the parameter γ (when relevant)?
d. Classify the functions as increasing/decreasing risk aversion utility functions (both absolute and relative).

3.2 Certainty equivalent:

$$(1)\ U(Y) = -\frac{1}{Y}$$
$$(2)\ U(Y) = \ln Y$$
$$(3)\ U(Y) = \frac{Y^\gamma}{\gamma}$$

Consider the lottery $L_1 = (50{,}000; 10{,}000; 0.50)$. Determine the lottery $L_2 = (x; 0; 1)$ that makes an agent indifferent to lottery L_1 with utility functions (1), (2), and (3) as defined. For utility function (3), use $\gamma = \{0.25, 0.75\}$. What is the effect of changing the value of γ? Comment on your results using the notions of risk aversion and certainty equivalent.

3.3 Risk premium: A businesswoman runs a firm worth CHF 100,000. She faces some risk of having a fire that would reduce her net worth according to the following three states, $i = 1, 2, 3$, each with probability $\pi(i)$ (Scenario A).

State	Worth	$\pi(i)$
1	1	0.01
2	50,000	0.04
3	100,000	0.95

Of course, in state 3, nothing detrimental happens, and her business retains its value of CHF 100,000.

a. What is the maximum amount she will pay for insurance if she has a logarithmic utility function over final wealth? (Note: The insurance pays CHF 99,999 in the first case; CHF 50,000 in the second; and nothing in the third.)

b. Do the calculations with the following alternative probabilities:

	Scenario B	*Scenario C*
$\pi(1)$	0.01	0.02
$\pi(2)$	0.05	0.04
$\pi(3)$	0.94	0.94

Is the outcome (the comparative change in the premium) a surprise? Why?

3.4 Consider two investments A and B. Suppose that their returns, $\tilde{r}_A$ and $\tilde{r}_B$, are such that $\tilde{r}_A = \tilde{r}_B + \vartheta$, where ϑ is a non-negative random variable. Show that A FSD B.

3.5 Four-part question:

a. Explain intuitively the concept of first-order stochastic dominance.

b. Explain intuitively the concept of second-order stochastic dominance.

c. Explain intuitively the mean variance criterion.

d. You are offered the following two investment opportunities.

Investment A		*Investment B*	
Payoff	*Probability*	*Payoff*	*Probability*
2	0.25	1	0.333
4	0.5	6	0.333
9	0.25	8	0.333

Apply concepts a through d. Illustrate the comparison with a graph.

3.6 An individual (operating in perfect capital markets) with a zero initial wealth, and the utility function $U(Y) = Y^{1/2}$ is confronted with the gamble (16, 4; ½).

a. What is his certainty equivalent for this gamble?

b. If there was an insurance policy that, together with the original gamble, would guarantee him the expected payoff of the gamble, what is the maximum premium he would be willing to pay for it?

c. What is the minimum required increase (the probability premium) in the probability of the high payoff state so that he will not be willing to pay any premium for such an insurance policy? (Note that the insurance policy still pays the expected payoff of the unmodified gamble.)

d. Now assume that he is confronted with the gamble (36, 16; ½). Calculate the certainty equivalent, the insurance premium, and the probability premium for this case as well. Explain what is going on, and why.

3.7 Refer to Table 3.2. Suppose the return data for investment 3 was as follows :

Investment 3	
Payoff	*Probability*
3	0.25
4	0.5
12	0.25

Is it still the case that investment 3 SSD investment 4 ?

3.8 Consider two investments with the following characteristics :

		States		
		θ_1	θ_2	θ_3
	π	$\frac{1}{3}$	$\frac{1}{3}$	$\frac{1}{3}$
Returns	$\tilde{z}$	10	0	10
	$\tilde{y}$	0	10	20

a. Is there state by state dominance between these two investments?
b. Is there FSD between these two investments?

Chapter 4

4.1 Consider the portfolio choice problem of a risk-averse individual with a strictly increasing utility function. There is a single risky asset, and a risk-free asset. Formulate an investor's choice problem and comment on the first-order conditions. What is the minimum risk premium required to induce the individual to invest all his wealth in the risky asset? (Find your answer in terms of his initial wealth, absolute risk aversion coefficient, and other relevant parameters.)

Hint: Take a Taylor series expansion of the utility of next period's random wealth.

4.2 Portfolio choice (with expected utility): An agent has $Y = 1$ to invest. On the market two financial assets exist. The first one is riskless. Its price is 1 and its return is 2. Short selling on this asset is allowed. The second asset is risky. Its price is 1 and its return $\tilde{z}$, where $\tilde{z}$ is a random variable with probability distribution:

$$z = 1 \quad \text{with probability} \quad \pi_1$$
$$z = 2 \quad \text{with probability} \quad \pi_2$$
$$z = 3 \quad \text{with probability} \quad \pi_3$$

No short selling is allowed on this asset.

a. If the agent invests a in the risky asset, what is the probability distribution of the agent's portfolio return $(\tilde{R})$?

b. The agent maximizes a Von Neumann-Morgenstern utility (U). Show that the optimal choice of a is positive if and only if the expectation of $\tilde{z}$ is greater than 2.

Hint: Find the first derivative of U and calculate its value when $a = 0$.

c. Give the first-order condition of the agent's problem.

d. Find a when $U(Y) = 1 - \exp(-bY)$, $b > 0$ and when $U(Y) = (1/1 - \gamma)Y^{1-\gamma}$, $0 < \gamma < 1$. If Y increases, how will the agent react?

e. Find the absolute risk aversion coefficient (R_A) in either case.

4.3 Risk aversion and portfolio choice: Consider an economy with two types of financial assets: one risk-free and one risky asset. The rate of return offered by the risk-free asset is r_f. The rate of return of the risky asset is $\tilde{r}$. Note that the expected rate of return $E(\tilde{r}) > r_f$.

Agents are risk-averse. Let Y_0 be the initial wealth. The purpose of this exercise is to determine the optimal amount a to be invested in the risky asset as a function of the *Absolute Risk Aversion Coefficient* (Theorem 4.4).

The objective of the agents is to maximize the expected utility of terminal wealth:

$$\max_a E(U(Y))$$

where: E is the expectation operator,
$U(.)$ is the utility function with $U' > 0$ and $U'' < 0$,
Y is the wealth at the end of the period,
a is the amount being invested in the risky asset.

a. Determine the final wealth as a function of $a, r_f,$ and $\tilde{r}$.

b. Compute the FOC. Is this a maximum or a minimum?

c. We are interested in determining the sign of da^*/dY_0. Calculate first the total differential of the FOC as a function of a and Y_0. Write the expression for da^*/dY_0. Show that the sign of this expression depends on the sign of its numerator.

d. You know that R_A, the absolute risk aversion coefficient, is equal to $-U''(.)/U'(.)$. What does it mean if $R_A' = (dR_A/dY) < 0$?

e. Assuming $R_A' < 0$, compare $R_A(Y)$ and $R_A(Y_0(1 + r_f))$: Is $R_A(Y) > R_A(Y_0(1 + r_f))$ or vice-versa? Don't forget there are two possible cases: $\begin{cases} \tilde{r} \geq r_f \\ \tilde{r} < r_f \end{cases}$

f. Show that $U''(Y_0(1 + r_f) + a(\tilde{r} - r_f))(\tilde{r} - r_f) > -R_A(Y_0 - r_f) \times U'(Y_0(1 + r_f) + a(\tilde{r} - r_f))(\tilde{r} - r_f)$ for both cases in point e.

g. Finally, compute the expectation of $U''(Y)(\tilde{r} - r_f)$. Using the FOC, determine its sign. What can you conclude about the sign of da^*/dY_0? What was the key assumption for the demonstration?

4.4 Suppose that a risk-averse individual can only invest in two risky securities A and B, whose future returns are described by identical but independent probability distributions. How should he allocate his given initial wealth (normalized to 1 for simplicity) among these two assets so as to maximize the expected utility of next period's wealth?

4.5 An individual with a well-behaved utility function and an initial wealth of \$1 can invest in two assets. Each asset has a price of \$1. The first is a riskless asset that pays \$1. The second pays amounts a and b (where $a < b$) with probabilities of π

and $(1 - \pi)$, respectively. Denote the units demanded of each asset by x_1 and x_2, respectively, with $x_1, x_2 \in [0, 1]$.

a. Give a simple necessary condition (involving a and b only) for the demand for the riskless asset to be strictly positive. Give a simple necessary condition (involving $a, b,$ and π only) so that the demand for the risky asset is strictly positive.

b. Assume now that the conditions in item a are satisfied. Formulate the optimization problem and write down the FOC. Can you intuitively guess the sign of dx_1/da? Verify your guess by assuming that x_1 is a function of a written as $x_1(a)$, and taking the total differential of the FOC with respect to a. Can you also conjecture a sign for $dx_1/d\pi$? Provide an economic interpretation without verifying it as done previously.

Chapter 5

5.1 Comment fully on the following statement: If a portfolio has a high β, then further diversification is possible.

5.2 Consider an equally weighted portfolio of three stocks, each of which is independently distributed of the others (that is, $cov(r_i, r_j) = 0$ for different securities i and j). Assume also that each stock has the same total risk (σ). What fraction of each stock's risk is diversified away by including it in this portfolio?

5.3 What is the difference between the relationship implied by the Capital Market Line (CML) and the Security Market Line (SML)? Consider a particular portfolio P with risk σ_P. Under what circumstances will the CML and the SML give the same $E\tilde{r}_P$?

5.4 Among your numerous assets, you are the owner of a finance company that extends one-year loans to people to buy appliances and other household goods. A young finance whiz that you just hired suggests that since the default risk of your loans is entirely diversifiable, you should charge your customers (those that are borrowing from you) the risk-free rate.

a. What do you think of the suggestion?

b. Assume the risk-free rate is 10%, and that the probability of default is 5% for the next year on a typical loan. In addition, assume that if a borrower defaults, all the principal but no interest is repaid. What rate should your finance company charge for loans over the next year?

c. Suppose the reclaimed appliances have lost 20% of their original value, and that in the event of default no interest is paid. What rate should you set?

5.5 At the moment, all of your assets are invested in asset A with the following return and risk characteristics:

$$E\tilde{r}_A = 10\%$$
$$\sigma_A = 10\%$$

Another asset (call it "B") becomes available; the characteristics of B are as follows: $E\tilde{r}_B = 20\%, \sigma_B = 25\%$. Furthermore, the correlation of A's and B's return patterns is -1.

By reallocating your portfolio to include some of asset B, how much additional return could you expect to receive if you wanted to maintain your portfolio's risk at $\sigma = 10\%$? Hint: Solve for w_B, not for w_A.

5.6 You are a portfolio manager considering whether or not to allocate some of the money with which you are entrusted to the market index of Australian stocks. Your assistant provides you with the following historical return information:

Returns:

	Your Portfolio	*Australian Index*
1992	54%	50%
1993	24%	−10%
1994	−6%	10%
1995	25%	60%
1996	−6%	−20%
1997	54%	80%

a. Show that the addition of the Australian index (AUS) to your portfolio (your) will reduce risk (at no loss in returns) provided

$$\text{corr}(\text{your, AUS}) < \frac{\sigma_{\text{AUS}}}{\sigma_{\text{your}}}$$

(assuming, as is the case, $\sigma_{\text{AUS}} > \sigma_{\text{your}}$)

b. Based on this historical data could you receive higher returns for the same level of risk (standard deviation) by allocating some of your wealth to the Australian index?

c. Based on historical experience, would it be possible to reduce your portfolio's risk below its current level by investing something in the Australian index?

d. What fraction of the variation in Australian stocks can be explained by variation in your portfolio's returns?

e. Is this situation a violation of the CAPM?

Chapter 6

6.1 In the CAPM setting, it is argued that only a fraction of the total risk of a particular asset is priced. Use the CML and SML to prove this assertion.

6.2 Consider two fully isolated economies, economy 1 and economy 2. The same assets are traded in both economies, but the average investor in economy 2 is more risk averse than the average investor in economy 1. Compare the CMLs in both economies.

6.3 Consider two fully isolated economies. Asset returns in economy 2 are, in general, more positively correlated than asset returns in economy 1. Compare the CMLs in both economies.

6.4 Under the CAPM, all investors form portfolios of two assets, a risk-free asset and a risky portfolio M, irrespective of their level of wealth Y. If an investor becomes wealthier, he may want to increase or decrease the proportion of his wealth held in the risky portfolio, and, by the Cass-Stiglitz theorem, unless his preferences have a very specific form, as his wealth changes, he will want to alter the composition of the risky part of his portfolio. The CAPM does not assume such preference restrictions. Yet, the CAPM equilibrium does not seem to permit the desired changes in the composition of the agent's risky portfolio! Is there a contradiction?

6.5 Consider the following 3 assets:

$$e = \begin{pmatrix} \bar{r}_1 \\ \bar{r}_2 \\ \bar{r}_3 \end{pmatrix} = \begin{pmatrix} 1 \\ 2 \\ 3 \end{pmatrix} \text{ and } V = \begin{pmatrix} 1 & -1 & 0 \\ -1 & 4 & -1 \\ 0 & -1 & 9 \end{pmatrix}$$

Compute g and h from our portfolio composition characterization. Identify the MVP. Identify the zero covariance portfolio for asset 3.

$$\text{Note that } V^{-1} = \begin{pmatrix} A & B & C \\ B & B & C \\ C & C & D \end{pmatrix}$$

where $A = 1.346154$
    $B = .346154$
    $C = .384615$
    $D = .115385$

6.6 Consider a two-period economy with I agents, J risky assets, and one risk-free rate asset. You can write the agent's wealth as follows:

$$\tilde{Y}_i = \left(Y_0^i - \sum_j x_j\right)(1 + r_f) + \sum_j x_j(1 + \tilde{r}_j)$$

where Y_0^i = initial wealth of agent i,
    r_f = the risk-free interest rate,
    $\tilde{r}_f$ = the random rate of return on the jth risky asset,
    x_j^i = the amount invested in the jth asset by agent i.

As usual, the individual's choice problem is:

$$\max_{x_j} E[U_i(\tilde{Y}_i)]$$

a. Show that the FOC can be written as follows:

$$E[U_i'(\tilde{Y}_i)(\tilde{r}_j - r_f)] = 0 \tag{1}$$

b. Show that Equation (1) can be written as follows:

$$E[U_i'(\tilde{Y}_i)]E(\tilde{r}_j - r_f) = -\text{Cov}[U_i'(\tilde{Y}_i), \tilde{r}_j] \tag{2}$$

Recall that $\text{Cov}(x, y) = E(xy) - E(x)E(y)$.
c. Using the following property of the covariance $\text{Cov}[g(x), y] = E[g'(x)]\text{Cov}(x, y)$, show that Equation (2) can be rewritten as follows:

$$E[U_i'(\tilde{Y}_i)]E(\tilde{r}_j - r_f) = -E[U_i''(\tilde{Y}_i)]\text{Cov}(\tilde{Y}_i, \tilde{r}_j) \tag{3}$$

d. Aggregating on all individuals (summing on i), show that Equation (3) can be rewritten as follows:

$$E(\tilde{r}_j - r_f) = \frac{Y_{M0}}{\sum_i \dfrac{1}{R_{Ai}}} \text{Cov}(\tilde{r}_M, \tilde{r}_j) \tag{4}$$

where $R_{Ai} = (-E[U_i''(\tilde{Y}_i)])/(E[U_i'(\tilde{Y}_i)])$ is reminiscent of the absolute risk aversion coefficient

$$\text{and } \sum_i \tilde{Y}_i = Y_{M0}(1 + \tilde{r}_M).$$

e. Show that Equation (4) implies:

$$E(\tilde{r}_M - r_f) = \frac{Y_{M0}}{\sum_i \frac{1}{R_{Ai}}} \text{Var}(\tilde{r}_M) \tag{5}$$

f. Derive the traditional CAPM relationship. Hint: Combine Equations (4) and (5).

Chapter 7

7.1 Arrow-Debreu pricing: You are given the following term structure of interest rates for three periods into the future:

$$r_1 = .0989 \qquad r_2 = .1027 \qquad r_3 = .1044$$

a. Construct the Arrow-Debreu prices for these state-dates.
b. Assume that there are three states in each period and that the constant Arrow-Debreu state-matrix is as follows:

$$\begin{pmatrix} .28 & .33 & .30 \\ .27 & .34 & .31 \\ .24 & .28 & .36 \end{pmatrix}$$

Assume we are in state 1. Are these prices consistent with the term structure just given?

7.2 What is the relationship between the price of an Arrow-Debreu security and the corresponding state probability? How is the price of an Arrow-Debreu security affected by a change in the discount factor? What else affects the price of an Arrow-Debreu security?

7.3 Arrow-Debreu pricing: Consider a world with two states of nature. The following matrix provides the one-period Arrow-Debreu prices in all situations

t\t+1	State 1	State 2
State 1	.53	.43
State 2	.45	.52

Describe the term structure of interest rates over three periods.

7.4 You are given the following prices of a set of coupon bonds. Construct the term structure and price of the corresponding date-contingent claim.

	t = 0	1	2	3	4	5
Bond 1	−960	1,000				
Bond 2	−900	100	1,100			
Bond 3	−800	120	120	1,120		
Bond 4	−650	130	130	130	1,130	
Bond 5	−400	150	150	150	150	1,150

7.5 General equilibrium and uncertainty: Consider a two-period exchange economy with two agents. They have identical utility functions:

$$U(c_1, c_2(\theta)) = \ln c_1 + \ln c_2(\theta)$$

where: c_1 is the consumption level at date 1

$c_2(\theta)$ is the consumption level at date 2 if state θ occurs.

Let us assume two possible states of nature at date 2, and the following endowment structure:

	$t = 0$	$t = 1$	
		$\theta = 1$	$\theta = 2$
Agent 1	4	1	3
Agent 2	4	3	1

a. Describe *intuitively* a Pareto-optimal allocation of resources. Is it unique?
b. Suppose only one type of security may be issued. Is it possible to achieve the Pareto-optimal allocation? If so, how?
c. Suppose the commodity in the previously described economy can be *costlessly* stored. No other asset is traded. Describe intuitively how this opportunity will be exploited and why. Is the utility level of the two agents increased?
d. Let us now assume agent 1 is risk neutral and there is aggregate uncertainty, that is, at date 2 the endowment structure is

$\theta = 1$	$\theta = 2$
1	2
3	4

Discuss intuitively what the new Pareto-optimal allocation should look like.
   Assume the existence of Arrow-Debreu securities and characterize the resulting market equilibrium.

7.6 Two-part problem:
a. Think of an economy with two agents with utility functions of the form:

$$U(c) = E(c) - 2 \, \mathrm{var}(c)$$

Their endowments are given by

	$t = 0$	$t = 1$	
		$\theta = 1$	$\theta = 2$
Agent 1	4	1	5
Agent 2	4	5	1

The state probabilities are ¼ for state 1 and ¾ for state 2.
1. Intuitively, what condition should a Pareto-optimal allocation satisfy in this particular setup?
2. Are there several Pareto optima? If so, characterize the set of Pareto optima.

3. Is the following allocation a Pareto optimum? Why?

	$t = 0$	$t = 1$	
		$\theta = 1$	$\theta = 2$
Agent 1	4	2	2
Agent 2	4	4	4

b. Now the agents have a utility function of the form:

$$U(c) = c_1 + E(\ln(c_2))$$

The endowments are:

	$t = 0$	$t = 1$	
		$\theta = 1$	$\theta = 2$
Agent 1	4	1	5
Agent 2	4	5	1

1. Describe the Pareto optimum or the set of Pareto optima for this utility function and compare it with the one under item 7.6.a.1.
2. Two Arrow-Debreu securities denoted by $Q1$ (state 1) and $Q2$ (state 2) are introduced. Both are in zero net supply. Compute the competitive equilibrium allocation. Is it Pareto optimal? Discuss intuitively its characteristics (the determinants of the prices of the two securities and the post-trade allocation).
3. Suppose only one Arrow-Debreu security depending on state 1 is traded. It is in zero net supply. Compute the competitive equilibrium allocation. Is it Pareto optimal?

7.7 Think of a simple exchange economy with two agents that have the following utility functions:

$$U_1(.) = 0.25c_0 + 0.5E[\ln(c_1(\theta))]$$
$$U_2(.) = c_0 + E[\ln(c_1(\theta))]$$

where θ denotes the two equally likely states at date 1. The endowments are

	$t = 0$	$t = 1$	
		$\theta = 1$	$\theta = 2$
Agent 1	2	2	4
Agent 2	4	4	2

a. Describe the Pareto optimum or the set of Pareto optima. Is it unique? Is perfect risk sharing achieved? Why or why not? Answer the same question if the state 2 endowments were 5 for agent 1, and 3 for agent 2.
b. Agents can trade with two Arrow-Debreu securities denoted by Q (with payoffs $(1, 0)$), and R (with payoffs $(0, 1)$). Calculate the competitive equilibrium allocation. Is it Pareto optimal? Discuss intuitively its characteristics (the determinants of the prices the two securities and the post-trade allocation).
c. Suppose that no security can be traded at the beginning and there are no short-selling constraints. A firm has zero cost of introducing one unit of either

security and it wants to maximize its profits. Which security should it introduce? For which agent is this introduction more valuable? Is the outcome Pareto optimal? Why or why not?

Chapter 8

8.1 Two-part question:
  a. To what extent should we care whether the current organization of markets leads to a Pareto-optimal allocation?
  b. Are markets complete? Do we care?
8.2 Options and market completeness: Remember that in certain circumstances, it is not possible to achieve market completeness with call options only (why?). Show that in the following market structure with three assets and four states, introducing a put option on the first asset with exercise price 1 is sufficient to achieve market completeness (i.e., to generate a complete set of Arrow-Debreu securities for those four states.

$$\text{Asset 1: } (0,0,0,1)$$
$$\text{Asset 2: } (1,1,0,1)$$
$$\text{Asset 3: } (0,1,1,1)$$

8.3 Three-part question:
  a. Describe intuitively the idea of an Arrow-Debreu security. Arrow-Debreu securities are not observed in real markets. Is the concept nevertheless useful? What is the link between Arrow-Debreu securities and options?
  b. You observe the following assets with the corresponding state-dependent payoffs:

Securities	A	B	C
	3	7	8
States	1	2	9
	7	16	25

Is this market complete?
  c. Is the following market structure complete?

Assets		A	B	C
	1	1	5	12
States	2	3	6	14
	3	12	7	16
	4	15	8	20

If the market is not complete, introduce a derivative security to complete it. Construct an Arrow-Debreu security by introducing calls or puts on these assets. Can you reproduce the same structure by using only puts?

Chapter 9

9.1 Consider a two-date economy where there are three states of the world at date 1. Consumption per capita at date 1 will be $5, $10, or $15. A security that pays one unit of consumption next period is worth $8 today. The risk-free security pays a gross

return of 1.1. A call option on per capita consumption with an exercise price of $12 costs $1. The probabilities of the three states are 0.3, 0.4, and 0.3, respectively.
a. Are markets complete? If yes, what are the state prices?
b. Price a put option on per capita consumption with an exercise price of $8.
c. Can you derive the risk-neutral probabilities?
d. Suppose that an investor has the following expected utility function: $\ln c_0 + \delta E \ln c_\theta$.

9.2 Arrow-Debreu pricing: Consider a two-period economy similar to the one we are used to, but with the following basic data:

	$t = 0$	$t = 1$	
		$\theta = 1$	$\theta = 2$
Agent 1	10	1	5
Agent 2	5	4	6

The agents have utility functions $U(c_1, c_2(\theta)) = c_1 + E[\ln(c_2(\theta))]$, and the state probabilities are Prob $(\theta_1) = \frac{1}{3} = 1 - \text{Prob}(\theta_2)$.

Construct the risk-neutral probabilities and compute the value today of agent 2's period 2 endowment.

Chapter 10

10.1 CAPM versus Consumption CAPM:
a. Contrast the two models in words.
b. Explain why, in principle, the consumption CAPM is more satisfactory.
c. Can you think of circumstances where the two models are essentially identical?

10.2 Consider an endowment economy identical to the one considered in the discussion of the consumption CAPM. Consider an option that entitles the owner to exercise the right to buy one unit of the asset one period in the future at a fixed price p^*. The price p^* is known at period t, whereas the option to buy is exercised at period $t+1$.

Suppose the representative agent's utility function is $U(c) = \ln(c)$. You are asked to price the option.

Follow these steps:
a. Write the value of the option at expiration as a function of the price of the underlying asset.
b. Write the price of the asset at the later date as a function of the state at that date, θ, the total quantity of good available.
c. Given the chosen utility function, write $q(\theta, c)$, the Arrow-Debreu price.
d. Use the Arrow-Debreu price to price the option.

10.3 Consider the setting described previously with the following modification: The asset in question requires the owner to buy the asset at a price p^* (a forward contract). Price the security.

10.4 Consider the usual representative agent economy. Suppose that the representative agent has log utility, $U(c) = \ln(c)$. Define the wealth portfolio as a claim to all future dividends available for consumption in this economy.

a. Show that the price of this wealth portfolio is proportional to consumption itself.
b. Show that the return on this portfolio is proportional to consumption growth. Hint: Think about the definition of the return on an asset to write down the return on the wealth portfolio.
c. Finally, express the price of a cash flow paying off $100 at each date for the next two periods in terms of the return on the wealth portfolio.

10.5 Begin with the fundamental equation $E[mR_i] = 1$ where R_i is the gross return on asset i, and m is the pricing kernel. Noting that this fundamental equation should hold for the gross returns on the riskless asset and on the market portfolio (R_M) as well, obtain a CAPM-like expression. Define a functional relation between m and R_M so that you will obtain precisely the CAPM expression.

Chapter 11

11.1 Consider an economy where the endowment is given by the following binomial process:

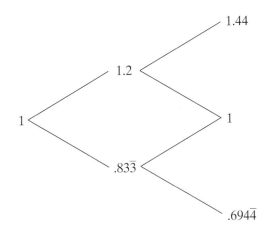

a. Solve for the expected utility of the representative agent. Assume that $\delta = 0.96$.
b. Solve for Arrow-Debreu prices, risk-neutral probabilities, and the pricing kernel.
c. What is the value of the consumption stream at date 0?
d. Price a one- and a two-period bond. Can we observe a term premia? What do you conclude?
e. Price a European call on consumption at date 0. The expiration date is just immediately after the representative agent has received his endowment at date 1 (strike = 1).
f. Let us assume that you are an outsider to this economy and you do not observe the representative agent. Price the call with the binomial method presented in Chapter 11. Note that the consumption stream can be interpreted as dividends and assume that the representative agent announces the price process (!) as well as the interest rate.
g. Do not hesitate to comment on your results (i.e., show the unique relationship between the methods).

Chapter 12

12.1 Suppose the existence of three assets with the following characteristics:

	$E(r_i)$	b_i
A	.07	.5
B	.09	1.0
C	.17	1.5

Assume that the specific risk can be eliminated through diversification and that the return model can be written:

$$r_i = E(r_i) + b_i F_1 + e_i$$

a. Plot the three assets on a $E(r_i) - b_i$ graph.
b. Using assets A and B, construct a portfolio with no systematic risk. Do the same using assets B and C.
c. Construct an arbitrage portfolio and compute its expected return.
d. Comment and describe how prices will adjust as a result of arbitrage opportunity.
e. Suppose now that $E(r_A) = .06$, $E(r_B) = .10$, and $E(r_C) = .14$. Plot the three assets in the graph in item a. Is it still possible to construct an arbitrage portfolio with positive expected return? Comment.

12.2 Assume the following market model:

$$\tilde{r}_j = \alpha_j + \beta_{jM}\tilde{r}_M + \tilde{\varepsilon}_j$$

with $\tilde{r}_j$ = the expected rate of return on asset j
  α_j = a constant
  β_{jM} = the sensitivity of asset j to fluctuations in the market return
  $\tilde{r}_M$ = the expected market return
  ε_j = a stochastic component with $E(\tilde{\varepsilon}_j) = 0$, $Var(\tilde{\varepsilon}_j) = \sigma_{\varepsilon_j}$, and $cov(\tilde{\varepsilon}_i, \tilde{\varepsilon}_j) = 0, \forall i, j$.

a. Prove that $\sigma_j^2 = \beta_j^2 \sigma_M^2 + \sigma_{\varepsilon_j}^2$.
b. Prove that $\sigma_{ij} = \beta_i \beta_j \sigma_M^2$.

12.3 CAPM and APT:
a. Briefly describe these two models: Capital Asset Pricing Model and Arbitrage Pricing Theory. What are their main assumptions?
b. CAPM and APT are so-called valuation models. In fact, they permit us to compute the *expected rate of return* of a security. How can this be used to derive a *current price*?
c. Contrast the two models. Are they compatible? Are they identical under certain conditions?

12.4 Draw the parallels and underline the key differences between the Arbitrage Pricing Theory (APT) and Arrow-Debreu pricing.

12.5 The APT does not assume individuals have homogeneous beliefs concerning the random returns of the assets under consideration. True or false? Comment.

Chapter 13

13.1 General equilibrium and uncertainty: Consider a two-date economy with two agents and one good. Assume two states of nature at the second date with probabilities π and $1 - \pi$. The resources are the following:

	$t = 0$	$t = 1$	
		$\theta = 1$	$\theta = 2$
Agent 1	1	1	1
Agent 2	1	0	2

Agent 1's utility function is: $U_1 = c_0^1 + \delta E(c^1(\theta))$

Agent 2's utility function is: $U_2 = \ln c_0^2 + \delta E(\log c^2(\theta))$

The subjective discount rate is the same for both agents (i.e., δ).

a. Comment on the form of the utility functions.
b. Determine the Pareto optimum.
c. Assuming markets are complete, compute the contingent prices, taking the good at date 1 as the numeraire.
d. Assume there is only one asset (a bond), which gives one unit of good in each state of nature.
   1. Give the price of the bond. Hint: Look at agent 1's program.
   2. Find the competitive equilibrium.
   3. Compute the equilibrium allocation for $\pi = 0.5$ and $\delta = \frac{1}{3}$. Is this allocation Pareto optimal?

13.2 Summarize what we have learned about the Modigliani-Miller theorem in the context of incomplete markets.

13.3 General equilibrium and uncertainty: Consider a two-period, two-agent economy with preferences and endowments as follows:

	$t = 0$	$t = 1$		Preferences
		$\theta = 1$	$\theta = 2$	
Agent 1	20	1	5	$U_1(.) = c_0^1 + \pi(\theta_1)\frac{1}{2}\ln c^1(\theta_1) + \pi(\theta_2)\frac{1}{2}\ln c^1(\theta_2)$
Agent 2	30	15	15	$U_2(.) = c_0^2 + \pi(\theta_1)\frac{1}{2}c^2(\theta_1) + \pi(\theta_2)\frac{1}{2}c^2(\theta_2)$ (risk neutral)

The state probabilities are: $\pi(\theta_1) = \frac{1}{3}$, $\pi(\theta_2) = \frac{2}{3}$.

a. Imagine that in this economy only the asset $Q = (1, 0)$ is traded. Construct the financial equilibrium. Will risk sharing take place? Is the initial allocation already Pareto optimal? How would you answer if the state probabilities were equal?

b. Now we are in the initial setup where trade with $(1, 0)$ is still possible. Assume that asset $R = (0, 1)$ is also traded. What will be the price of this asset? How much of the two assets will be exchanged? What is the post-trade allocation? Is it Pareto-optimal?

13.4 Consider a two-date, two-agent economy, with the following initial endowments:

	$t = 0$	$t = 1$	
		$\theta = 1$	$\theta = 2$
Agent 1	4	6	1
Agent 2	6	3	4

The agents' utility functions are:

$$\text{Agent 1} \quad \tfrac{1}{2} \cdot \ln c_0^1 + E \ln c_\theta^1$$
$$\text{Agent 2} \quad \tfrac{1}{2} \cdot c_0^2 + E \ln c_\theta^2$$

The probability of each state is $\text{Prob}(\theta = 1) = 0.4$ and $\text{Prob}(\theta = 2) = 0.6$.
a. Compute the initial utility of each agent.
b. Suppose now there is a firm that generates an uncertain output at time $t = 1$ of $(2; 3)$. The firm owner is interested in consuming only at date 0 and accordingly he would like to sell his claim of ownership to the output of the firm. He solicits your advice as to the type of security that he should issue. Suppose first that he issues a stock, that is, a claim to two units of good in state $\theta = 1$ and three units in state $\theta = 2$.
  1. What is the price of the security/the stock market value of the firm?
  2. What are the post-trade allocations?
  3. What are the post-trade utilities?
  Discuss intuitively how your results would have differed if the two states had been equally likely.
c. What happens if, instead of a stock claim, the firm owner issues Arrow-Debreu securities? Discuss intuitively (no calculations needed) how your answer to these same questions would need to be modified.
d. Now forget the firm. The situation is different: A foreign government would like to market a risk-free security, specifically a claim promising payment of two units of the good next period, irrespective of the state. How much money will this bond issue generate? What are the post-trade allocation and utilities? Are you surprised?
e. In one line, tell us how the problem would be altered if the bond issuer is not a foreign government but the local government.

13.5 Consider a two-period economy with two agents and one good. Assume two possible states of nature at the second period with same probability. The agents only care about their second-period consumption level. They maximize their expected utility.

$$\text{Agent 1's utility function is:} \quad U_1 = c_1$$
$$\text{Agent 2's utility function is:} \quad U_2 = \log(c_2)$$

a. Agents can trade in a complete contingent security market system. Show, in full generality, that the price of the contingent security is the same for the two states of nature. Show that agent 2's consumption doesn't depend on the state of nature.
b. Assume that, in addition to their endowments, the two agents each possess one-half of a firm. The firm invests two units of input in period 1. The output is available at period 2.
   There are two possible technologies. With the first one, one unit of input produces one unit of good, independently of the state of nature. With the sec-

ond one, one unit of input produces three units of good in the first state of nature and none in the other one.

Let $x \in [0, 1]$ be the part of input used with the second technology. The sale of the goods at the second period is the agents' only resource, so each of them receives $(x + 1)$ in the first state of nature and $(1 - \frac{1}{2}x)$ in the second.
1. Assuming that the markets are complete. Write the agents' budget constraints as a function of the parameter x.
2. Determine the consumption and utility levels as a function of the parameter x. Show that the agents agree about the optimal choice of x. What value will they choose?
c. From now on, suppose there are no markets for contingent security. However, the good can be traded on a spot market during the second period. Compute the equilibrium utility level attained by the agents as a function of x. Determine the preferred investment policy of each agent. Show that they disagree on the optimal level of x.
d. Assume that the agents can trade two securities at period 1: One security pays one unit of good independently of the state of nature, the other one is a share of the firm just described. Show that the markets are complete. What will agent 2 do in such a context? (No formal proof is required.)

Chapter 14

14.1 Assume the following speculator's program:

$$\max_{f} EU[\bar{c} + (p^f - p)f]$$

Is it true that $f* \gtrless 0$ if and only if $p^f \gtrless Ep$?

14.2 Show that it is always better, that is, more profitable, for a producer to speculate on the futures market than on the physical market.
   Assumptions:

- no uncertainty in production
- no basis risk

Definition: To speculate on the physical market means producing because an increase in price is expected, although in terms of the futures price, the production is not profitable (marginal cost is not covered).

14.3 The law of demand states that a price increase leads to a decrease in the quantity demanded. Comment on the applicability of the law of demand when the object being exchanged is a financial asset.

14.4 Provide at least one example where price and volume behavior is significantly different in a market with heterogeneously informed agents than it would be in a market where agents are homogeneously informed.

14.5 Consider a firm facing exchange rate risk for its output commodity: The production decision is made at date t and the output is sold in foreign currency at date $t+1$. Assume that no currency futures market exists, however, a market for a domestic financial asset is available. You can write the profit of the firm as follows:

$$\tilde{\pi} = py\tilde{e} - \frac{1}{2}y^2 + z(q^f - \tilde{q})$$

where p = the known foreign currency price
y = the output
$\frac{1}{2}y^2$ = the cost function
e = the exchange rate
z = the number of shares of the domestic asset sold short at date t
$\tilde{q}$ = the nominal payoff of the domestic financial asset at date $t+1$
q^f = the date t price of the domestic financial asset

It is assumed that $E(\tilde{q}) = q^f$ (i.e., the date t price of the financial asset is an unbiased predictor of the future price).

Suppose the firm maximizes a mean-variance utility function:

$$\max_{z,x} E(\tilde{\pi}) - \frac{\gamma}{2} \operatorname{var}(\tilde{\pi})$$

- Write $E(\tilde{\pi})$ and $\operatorname{var}(\tilde{\pi})$.
- Compute and interpret the FOCs.
- Show that output is greater in the case of certainty than in the case of uncertainty.

INDEX

absolute prudence, 70
absolute risk aversion, 44–46, 62–63
Akerlof, G., 288
Allais paradox, 33–35, 38
arbitrage bounds, 182–184
arbitrage opportunity, 138, 145, 175, 178–179, 184–187
arbitrage pricing models, 261–269, 287
  See also risk-neutral evaluation model (Martingale pricing theory)
arbitrage pricing theory (APT), 262–268
Arrow, K. J., 12, 44, 60, 62, 64, 126
Arrow-Debreu pricing model
  analogous stock and bond economy, 193–194
  vs. APT, 262, 267
  vs. CAPM, 124
  CCAPM setting, 206–209, 225, 227
  competitive equilibrium, 127–129
  forward pricing, 144–145
  general model of, 125–127
  and investors' information, 287–288
  limitations of, 147, 172–173
  linear independence hypothesis, 139–140
  market completeness, 132, 138–140
  in multiperiod setting, 160–164
  no arbitrage condition, 184–186
  and option pricing, 150, 152, 153–160
  pareto optimality, 129–137
  representative agent construction, 197–198
  risk-free investments, 140–144, 163–164
  risk-neutral probability measures, 174–182
  value additivity theorem, 145–147
  verification test, 164
Arrow-Debreu securities (contingent claims)
  definition of, 125–126
  description of, 12–13

issuance of, 136–137, 271–274, 276–278, 280–283, 285–286
Arrow-Pratt measure, 62, 292, 293
asset allocation. *See* portfolio allocation
asymmetric information assumption, 4, 288–289
at the money option, 149
axioms and conventions, expected utility theory, 30–31

banks
  banker role, 4–5
  credit extension, 7, 9
Barro, R. J., 6
Bayesian framework, 300
Becker, G., 67
Bernanke, B., 9
beta coefficient, 106, 113–116, 263
binomial model of equity derivatives valuation
  continuous time setting, 256–257
  dynamic trading strategies, 242–245
  examples of, 233–239
  price evolution using Black-Scholes formula, 240–242
  setting, 231–233
  simulation context, 252–253
  and stock price, 239–240
Black-Scholes option pricing model, 157, 168–171, 240–242, 255–256
bonds, 140–144, 193–194
Brownian motion, 248–250
Burmeister, E., 262
business cycles, 8–9

call options, 150–152, 166–167, 252–256
  See also options
canonical portfolio problem, 59–60
capital asset pricing model (CAPM)
  vs. Arrow-Debreu pricing model, 124
  assumptions, 118–119
  certainty equivalent (CE), 192

description of, 103–107, 172
efficient frontier, 107–112, 116, 122
equilibrium price, 204–205
investors' information, 287
limitations of, 124
Market Model, 262–263
perfectly divisible share, 199–200
proof of, 121
research issues, 119–120
security issuance, 278
standard form, 116–118
zero-beta form, 113–116
capital issues. *See* security issuance
capital market line (CML), 104–105
CARA (constant absolute risk aversion), 63, 66, 198, 292
cardinal utility, 33
Cass, D., 66
Cass-Stiglitz theorem, 81
CCAPM (consumption capital asset pricing model). *See* consumption capital asset pricing model (CCAPM)
certainty equivalent (CE), 47–50, 173, 192
Chen, N. F., 266
choice theory, 25–29
  See also expected utility theory
compensatory precautionary premium, 72
competitive equilibrium, 10–11, 18–20, 127–132, 197–198
complete markets, 13–14, 132, 138–140, 174–184
complex securities, 138–140
Conner, G., 262
constant absolute risk aversion (CARA), 63, 66, 198, 292
constant relative risk aversion (CRRA)
  consumption-savings problem, 73
  multiperiod portfolio choice, 75–76, 77, 78, 79
  representative agent economy, 198
  and risky portfolio allocation, 65–66
  and wealth, 64